RUPTURES IN THE EVERYDAY

SPEKTRUM: Publications of the German Studies Association
Series editor: David S. Luebke, University of Oregon

Published under the auspices of the German Studies Association, *Spektrum* offers current perspectives on culture, society, and political life in the German-speaking lands of central Europe—Austria, Switzerland, and the Federal Republic—from the late Middle Ages to the present day. Its titles and themes reflect the composition of the GSA and the work of its members within and across the disciplines to which they belong—literary criticism, history, cultural studies, political science, and anthropology.

Volume 1
The Holy Roman Empire, Reconsidered
Edited by Jason Philip Coy, Benjamin Marschke, and David Warren Sabean

Volume 2
Weimar Publics/Weimar Subjects
Rethinking the Political Culture of Germany in the 1920s
Edited by Kathleen Canning, Kerstin Barndt, and Kristin McGuire

Volume 3
Conversion and the Politics of Religion in Early Modern Germany
Edited by David M. Luebke, Jared Poley, Daniel C. Ryan, and David Warren Sabean

Volume 4
Walls, Borders, Boundaries
Spatial and Cultural Practices in Europe
Edited by Marc Silberman, Karen E. Till, and Janet Ward

Volume 5
After The History of Sexuality
German Genealogies with and beyond Foucault
Edited by Scott Spector, Helmut Puff, and Dagmar Herzog

Volume 6
Becoming East German
Socialist Structures and Sensibilities after Hitler
Edited by Mary Fulbrook and Andrew I. Port

Volume 7
Beyond Alterity
German Encounters with Modern East Asia
Edited by Qinna Shen and Martin Rosenstock

Volume 8
Mixed Matches
Transgressive Unions in Germany from the Reformation to the Enlightenment
Edited by David M. Luebke and Mary Lindemann

Volume 9
Kinship, Community, and Self
Essays in Honor of David Warren Sabean
Edited by Jason Coy, Benjamin Marschke, Jared Poley, and Claudia Verhoeven

Volume 10
The Emperor's Old Clothes
Constitutional History and the Symbolic Language of the Holy Roman Empire
Barbara Stollberg-Rilinger
Translated by Thomas Dunlap

Volume 11
The Devil's Riches
A Modern History of Greed
Jared Poley

Volume 12
The Total Work of Art
Foundations, Articulations, Inspirations
Edited by David Imhoof, Margaret Eleanor Menninger, and Anthony J. Steinhoff

Volume 13
Migrations in the German Lands, 1500–2000
Edited by Jason Coy, Jared Poley, and Alexander Schunka

Volume 14
Reluctant Skeptic
Siegfried Kracauer and the Crises of Weimar Culture
Harry T. Craver

Volume 15
Ruptures in the Everyday
Views of Modern Germany from the Ground
Andrew Bergerson, Leonard Schmieding, et al.

Ruptures in the Everyday
Views of Modern Germany from the Ground

Edited by

Andrew Stuart Bergerson & Leonard Schmieding

Published in 2017 by
Berghahn Books
www.berghahnbooks.com

© 2017, 2019 Andrew Bergerson and Leonard Schmieding
First paperback edition published in 2019

All rights reserved. Except for the quotation of short passages
for the purposes of criticism and review, no part of this book
may be reproduced in any form or by any means, electronic or
mechanical, including photocopying, recording, or any information
storage and retrieval system now known or to be invented,
without written permission of the publisher.

Library of Congress Cataloging-in-Publication Data
Names: Bergerson, Andrew Stuart, editor. | Schmieding, Leonard, 1978-, editor.
Title: Ruptures in the everyday: views of modern Germany from the ground / Andrew Bergerson (lead co-editor), Leonard Schmieding (lead co-editor).
Description: New York: Berghahn Books, [2017] | Series: Spektrum: Publications of the German Studies Association ; 15 | Includes bibliographical references and index.
Identifiers: LCCN 2017000398 (print) | LCCN 2017001439 (ebook) | ISBN 9781785335327 (hardback : alk. paper) | ISBN 9781785335334 (eBook)
Subjects: LCSH: Germany--Social conditions--1990- | Germany--History—Social aspects--20th century, | Germany--History--Social aspects--21st century. | Social change--Germany--Psychological aspects. | Adjustment (Psychology)--Germany. | Identity (Psychology)--Germany. | Life change events--Germany--Psychological aspects--Case studies. | Microsociology--Case studies. | Germans--Attitudes. | National characteristics, German.
Classification: LCC DD290.26 .R87 2017 (print) | LCC DD290.26 (ebook) | DDC 943.087--dc23
LC record available at https://lccn.loc.gov/2017000398

British Library Cataloguing in Publication Data
A catalogue record for this book is available from the British Library

ISBN 978-1-78533-532-7 hardback
ISBN 978-1-78920-082-9 paperback
ISBN 978-1-78533-533-4 ebook

CONTENTS

List of Illustrations	vi
List of Maps	viii
Acknowledgements	ix
List of Abbreviations	x

1. Wende
   Andrew Stuart Bergerson, Mark E. Blum, Thomas Gurr, Alexandra Oeser, Steve Ostovich, Leonard Schmieding, and Sara Ann Sewell — 1

2. Self
   Leonard Schmieding and Paul Steege — 32

3. Interpersonal Relationships
   Mark E. Blum, Eva Giloi, and Steve Ostovich — 55

4. Families
   Phil Leask, Sara Ann Sewell, and Heléna Tóth — 79

5. Objects
   Jonathan Bach, Cristina Cuevas-Wolf, and Dani Kranz — 113

6. Institutions
   Elissa Mailänder, Alexandra Oeser, Will Rall, and Julia Timpe — 143

7. Anti-Semitism
   Susanne Beer, Johannes Schwartz, and Maximilian Strnad — 168

8. Violent Worlds
   Michaela Christ, Mary Fulbrook, and Wendy Lower — 201

9. Taking Place
   Jason Johnson, Craig Koslofsky, and Josie McLellan — 227

10. Telling Stories
    Andrew Stuart Bergerson, Mark E. Blum, Thomas Gurr, Alexandra Oeser, Steve Ostovich, Leonard Schmieding, and Sara Ann Sewell — 253

References	273
Authors	311
Index	317

ILLUSTRATIONS

Illustration 1.1. Collapsing House, Mecklenburg-Vorpommern, 2010. 14

Illustration 2.1. Ernst Jünger, frontispiece to *In Stahlgewittern*, 1920. 35

Illustration 2.2. TJ Big Blaster Electric Boogie Performing during the Rap Contest, Dresden, ca. 1989. Private Archive Nico Raschick—"Here We Come." 41

Illustration 2.3. B-Boys Posing in the Imaginary Bronx, Dessau, ca. 1987. Private Archive Nico Raschick—"Here We Come". 42

Illustration 2.4. The Performance License of Alexander Morawitz from 1989. Front and back. Private Archive of Alexander Morawitz. 49

Illustration 3.1. Max Scheler in Driving Costume, with Maria Scheler and Dr Rolf Hoffmann. 56

Illustration 4.1. Collecting Donations for Red Aid, Leipzig, 1925. 85

Illustration 4.2. Children in the Young-Spartakus-League Playing Reds versus Whites. 86

Illustration 4.3. Red Women and Girls' League Demonstration, Worms, July 1930. 107

Illustration 5.1. Peter Ghyczy, *Egg Garden Chair*, 1968. White Polyurethane casing and blue upholstery. 114

Illustration 5.2. Display of GDR-Era Telephones, GDR-Geschichtsmuseum, Perleberg, 2010. 124

Illustration 5.3. Display of GDR-Era Kitchen, GDR-Geschichtsmuseum, Perleberg, 2010. 126

Illustration 5.4. Display of GDR-Era Radios, GDR-Geschichtsmuseum, Perleberg, 2010. 127

Illustration 5.5. Peter Holzhauer, *Art Rack in the Wende Museum's Vault*, 2013. Digital photograph, courtesy of photographer Peter Holzhauer. Top, Heinz Drache (1929–1989), *Das Volk sagt 'Ja' zum friedlichen Aufbau* (The People Say "Yes" to Peaceful Construction),

1952; Bottom Left, Lothar Gericke's *Stadtlandschaft mit Liebespaar* (Cityscape with Lovers), 1978; and Bottom Right, a Painting by Lutz Voigtmann (1941–1997), *Düstere Stadt* (Dismal City), 1978.   134

Illustration 5.6. Brigade Karnatz Scrapbook, 1969. Title Page, "Kampf um den Staatstitel, Kollektiv der sozialistischen Arbeit."   136

Illustration 7.1. Erich Bloch, *Bloch/Begall*, 1946. Reprint from Kläre-Bloch-Schule 1992: 9.   168

Illustration 7.2. The Guggenheimer Family, Unknown Location, Mid-1920s. Alfred Sitting in Front, Annemarie to His Right, Their Daughter Ursula Standing behind.   174

Illustration 7.3. Hertha Ließ, Profil, Ravensbrück, 1941. Photo attached to her application forms for the SS-Rasse- und Siedlungs-Hauptamt (RuSHA) in order to marry SS-Unterscharführer Hans-Joachim Ehlert.   179

Illustration 9.1. *Treatment of the Whites.* Illustration in Groeben, *Guineische Reise-Beschreibung*, 1694.   233

Illustration 9.2. *King Peter of Rio Sesder.* Illustration in Groeben, *Guineische Reise-Beschreibung*, 1694.   234

Illustration 9.3. Surveillance Photographs, Area around the Youth Club at Veteranenstrasse, Meeting Place of the Sonntagsclub, Berlin-Mitte, 1986.   243

Illustration 9.4. Lesbians in the Church at the Friedenswerkstatt, Berlin Erlösergemeinde, n.d. (1980s).   250

Illustration 10.1. Abandoned Apartment Building, Mecklenburg-Vorpommern, 2010.   260

~: MAPS :~

Map 1.1. Germany Post-1945   9
Map 1.2. Modern Berlin   10
Map 1.3. Germany in Europe 1648–1945   11
Map 1.4. European Trade Sites in Seventeenth-Century West Africa   12

ACKNOWLEDGMENTS

This project has gestated for six years, and many people helped us realize it. We would like to thank the German Studies Association for promoting integrative scholarship; the Historicum at the Ludwig-Maximilians-Universität in Munich for hosting us in May of 2013; the Fritz Thyssen Stiftung for funding that international interdisciplinary workshop and subsidizing this book; David Lübke and Berghahn Books for publishing this unconventional project; and our families for their enduring support and understanding.

Our project benefitted from the constructive criticism of Monika Black, Douglas Catterall, Alon Confino, Joachim Häberlen, Marion Kaplan, Alf Lüdtke, Larson Powell, Rolf Rieß, Eli Rubin, Edith Sheffer, Jeremy Straughn, and Dennis Sweeney; the Research Network "Welt Aneignen: Alltagsgeschichte in transnationaler Perspektive" funded by the Deutsche Forschungsgemeinschaft; as well as anonymous outside reviewers. Above all, the project leaders would like to thank the other twenty-four members of our team for their hard work, commitment, patience, endurance, and good will. This project demanded much more of these qualities than any of us imagined it would. We are so very appreciative of your professionalism and dedication. It has been a real pleasure to work collaboratively with such a talented group of scholars.

Drew Bergerson and Leo Schmieding
Kansas City, MO and Washington, D.C.
August 2015

ABBREVIATIONS

ADCV	Archiv des Deutschen Caritasverbandes; Archive of the German Caritas Organization
AmtsG	Amtsgericht; Municipal Court
APMM	Archiv der Staatlichen Gedenkstätte Majdanek; Archive of the Majdanek Memorial
ArchGdW	Archiv Gedenkstätte Deutscher Widerstand Berlin; Archive of the German Resistance Memorial Center
BAC	Brandenburger African Company
BArch	Bundesarchiv
BayHStAM	Bayerisches Hauptstaatsarchiv München
BDM	Bund Deutscher Mädel; League of German Girls
BSG	Betriebssportgemeinschaften; Company-Facilitated Sports Activities Club
BStU	Bundesbeauftragte/r für die Unterlagen des Staatssicherheitsdienstes der ehemaligen DDR
DCV	Deutscher Caritasverband; German Caritas Organization
DHM	Deutsches Historisches Museum; German Historical Museum
DLaM	Deutsches Literaturarchiv Marbach
EEC	European Economic Community
EU	European Union
FDJ	Freie Deutsche Jugend; Free German Youth
FRG	Federal Republic of Germany
GDR	German Democratic Republic
Gestapo	Geheime Staatspolizei
GrePo	Grenzpolizei; Border Police
GWIC	Geoctroyeerde Westindische Compagnie
HdG	Haus der Geschichte der Bundesrepublik Deutschland
HH	Freie und Hansestadt Hamburg
HIB	Homosexual Interest Group Berlin
HJ	Hitlerjugend; Hitler Youth
ICOM	International Council of Museums
IKL	Inspektion der Konzentrationslager; Inspection of Concentration Camps
ITS	International Tracing Service

KdF	Kraft durch Freude; Strength through Joy
KBio	Walter Kempowski Biographie Archiv; Walter Kempowski Archive of Biographies
KPD	Kommunistische Partei Deutschlands; Communist Party of Germany
KrLkS	Kreisrat des Landkreises Schleiz; Schleiz District Council
LAB	Landesarchiv Berlin
LaBO	Landesamt für Bürger- und Ordnungsangelegenheiten, Berlin
LaKw	Landesamt für Kommunalwesen
LAPD	Los Angeles Poverty Department
MeWo	Memminger Wohnungsbau e.G. (eingetragene Genossenschaft)
MfS	Ministerium für Staatssicherheit der DDR; Ministry for State Security of the GDR
MfSk	Museum für Sepulkralkultur, Kassel
MGR	Mahn- und Gedenkstätte Ravensbrück; Ravensbrück Memorial
MM	Memmingen
MV	Mecklenburg-Vorpommern
NARA	National Archives and Records Administration, United States
NATO	North Atlantic Treaty Organization
NKVD	Narodnyy Komissariat Vnutrennikh Del; People's Commissariat for Internal Affairs
NLG	Nachlass Guggenheimer; Guggenheimer Papers
NSDAP	Nationalsozialistische Deutsche Arbeiterpartei; National Socialist German Workers' Party
NSV	Nationalsozialistische Volkswohlfahrt; National Socialist People's Welfare
NVA	Nationale Volksarmee; National People's Army
OFD	Oberfinanzdirektion
PdR	Palast der Republik; Palace of the Republic
PMB	Personalmeldebögen
PrBayGrePo	Präsidium der Bayerischen Grenzpolizei
RFB	Roter Frontkämpferbund; Red Front Fighters League
RFMB	Roter Frauen- und Mädchenbund; Red Women and Girls' League
RSHA	Reichssicherheitshauptamt; Reich Main Security Office
RuSHA	Rasse- und Siedlungshauptamt; Race and Settlement Main Office
SAPMO	Stiftung Archiv der Parteien und Massenorganisationen der ehemaligen DDR (in BArch)

SBZ	Sowjetische Besatzungszone; Soviet Zone of Occupation
SED	Sozialistische Einheitspartei Deutschlands; Socialist Unity Party of Germany
SFI	Shoah Foundation Institute for Visual History and Education at the University of Southern California
SPD	Sozialdemokratische Partei Deutschlands; Social Democratic Party of Germany
SpKA	Spruchkammerakten
SR	Sozialistische Republik; Socialist Republic
SS	Schutzstaffel
StadtA	Stadtarchiv
StAM	Staatsarchiv München
StBG	Stiftung Brandenburgische Gedenkstätten
ThHStAW	Thüringisches Hauptstaatsarchiv Weimar
ThStAG	Thüringisches Staatsarchiv Greiz
TNA	The National Archives of England and Wales, Kew/Richmond
U.K.	United Kingdom
U.S.	United States
USSR	Union of Soviet Socialist Republics
WM	The Wende Museum of the Cold War
WO	War Office
WVHA	Wirtschaftsverwaltungshauptamt; SS Main Economic and Administrative Department
ZFL	Zeitgeschichtliches Forum Leipzig

CHAPTER 1

Wende

After that it all began with the Wende ... and after that ... the downsizing; we were the first, see? That we were no longer necessary. Sure we had our profession, but we could no longer practice it: we were no longer useful, see?
—Dieter, Interview, 2010

In 2010, a fifty-eight-year-old man named Dieter talked to one of the authors of this book about losing his job at a shipyard in the early 1990s. It left him without a steady job for more than a decade. The epigraph to this chapter is part of his semiautobiographical narrative: Dieter's attempt, in cooperation with an interviewer, to make sense of his life by telling stories from and about it. It is interesting that Dieter accounted for being fired neither in terms of his job performance nor in terms of a structural crisis in the economy. He framed his personal crisis in terms of a major historical event for German-speaking Central Europe called *the Wende*.

Dieter was born in 1952, so for him, Germany had simply meant the German Democratic Republic (GDR). During the Cold War from 1947 to 1989, Germany was divided into a smaller Communist East and a larger Capitalist West—the Federal Republic of Germany (FRG). These two Germanies, along with a neutral Second Austrian Republic, were ground zero for the Cold War in Europe. The GDR was integrated into the East, led by the Union of Soviet Socialist Republics (USSR), through the Council for Mutual Economic Assistance and the Warsaw Pact. The FRG was integrated into the West, led by the United States, through the Marshall Plan, the North Atlantic Treaty Organization (NATO), and the European Economic Community (EEC). The stakes in Germany were high for the two superpowers, but they were even higher for the Germans themselves, who were recovering from the mass destruction and total defeat of World War II.

Germans helped create this Cold War, including the Berlin Wall that divided East from West Germany from 1961 to 1989. They also challenged it at regular intervals, and they helped ultimately to undermine it (Port 2007; Steege 2007; M.W. Johnson 2008; Major 2009; Klimke 2010; Lemke 2011). In the 1980s, Mikhail Gorbachev, the general secretary from 1985 until 1991 of the Communist Party of the Soviet Union, had signaled his willingness for reform of the communist systems in satellite countries by introducing policies of openness, transparency, and restructuring—called glasnost and perestroika—in the USSR. When the stubborn, gerontocratic politburo of the GDR opposed the Soviet reform models, it isolated the satellite state from its big brother and found itself in a position of weakness by fall 1989.

In Leipzig during a regular series of demonstrations on Mondays, the demands for domestic reform grew to include the opening of the Wall to inter-German traffic. Protests quickly spread across the GDR, further undermining both the legitimacy and the confidence of the Socialist Unity Party (SED). The leaders of the GDR conceded to opening the Wall and to general, democratic elections. Days later, and somewhat in contradiction to these earlier goals, voices of both East and West Germans began demanding the reunification of these two Germanies. With the support of the Western Allies, FRG chancellor Helmut Kohl moved quickly to admit the *Länder*, or federal states, of the East into a so-called reunited Germany (Maier 1997; Pfaff 2006; Richter 2007; Fischer 2014).

Germans on both sides of the Wall were bewildered by the rapid pace of these massive transformations in the economics and geopolitics of East Central Europe (Maier 1997; Herspring 1998; Pfaff 2006). These remarkable events sent shock waves into the village in the GDR where Dieter lived. Looking east, he observed the collapse of the Warsaw Pact along with the Communist regimes throughout East Central Europe and the Soviet Union. Looking west, Dieter watched as his community was absorbed into—some would say annexed by—the larger and richer West Germany. By default, Dieter fell under the protection of NATO and became a citizen of the EEC, soon to be renamed the European Union (EU). Through these national, regional, and global institutions, a Western-style social market economy penetrated into the East, destroying many of the formerly state-owned industries that were no longer competitive.

A Wende means *a turn* or, better, *a pivot*. The *Wende* refers collectively to this series of rapid-fire events that took place between 1989 and 1991 during which Dieter's country, the GDR, collapsed and was absorbed into the FRG. In framing his long-term unemployment in terms of the Wende, Dieter employed his *historical imagination*. He depicted his personal biography as part of a linear, temporal sequence of events driven by causes and consequences. Many people believe that the Wende marked a *turning point* in history: a brief moment in time when a relatively solid and fixed set of structures suddenly became fluid—and changed.

Dieter's way of telling his life story also involved a *sociological imagination* (Mills 1959). He implicitly associated this turning point in his life with a turning point in the lives of a larger *imagined community* (Anderson 1983) of people called *Germans*. Both ways of interpreting his experience arose out of the "general everyday life scheme of expectations" (Schütze 1975: 1005; Berger and Luckmann 1996); and yet Dieter had an agenda. In light of the Wende's detrimental consequences for people like him, Dieter implicitly challenged the legitimacy of its outcome: German reunification. In doing so, he made his personal struggles into a problem for Germans writ large. As he asserted, "It all began with the Wende."

Losers and Winners

Referring to the Wende in the singular may give the false impression that these very different experiences were all part of one coherent story. Dieter is perhaps a typical example of a so-called *Wende-loser*: someone who lost out as a result of the Wende. But we could have just as easily begun this book with a story of a *Wende-winner*: an East German who was able to make the successful transition to capitalist democracy in a reunited Germany. It is hardly surprising, given this diversity of experiences, that there has been little consensus on the meaning of the Wende among Germans.

The imposition of a global system of capitalism left many East Germans like Dieter without a steady job for the long term (Lepsius 2013). Ironically, it was the pillars of the former GDR—the factory, mine, and farmworkers of the so-called *Workers' and Farmers' State*, as the GDR named itself—who faced the most uncertain and precarious future. Two polls were conducted in fall 2014, excerpts of which were published widely on 1 October 2014 in the German media (e.g., Kleditzsch, "25 Jahre nach …"; Berlin Aktuell, "Jeder Zweite …"). One was by the Allensbach Institute (Wertewandel Ost) and commissioned by the newspapers in Eastern Germany in collaboration with the magazine *Super Illu* (Burda Newsroom, "SuperIllu bringt …"); the other by the television station N24 and Emnid (Presse Portal, "N24-Emnid-Umfrage …"). According to both polls, most East Germans are still proud of their Eastern heritage, though they do not all identify primarily as East Germans.

A minority of East Germans, however, still describe themselves as Wende-losers, feeling like second-class citizens. They sometimes express retrospective nostalgia for the East (*Ost*)—a phenomenon known as *Ostalgie*—and believe that German reunification cannot be called a success story. To use literary terms, the plots of their Wende stories are *tragic* (White 1973, 1987): they depict human protagonists overwhelmed by forces beyond their control.

By contrast, Wende-winners believe that they benefitted more than they were disadvantaged by the Wende. It took some time and effort, but they made the transition by adapting their old practices to new circumstances. The plots of their Wende stories are *romantic* (White 1973, 1987): they depict human protagonists overcoming sublime challenges in tales that culminate in happy endings.

Nonetheless, Wende-winners maintain a sense of their difference from Westerners—called the *Wall in their heads* (Schneider 1982; Straughn 2016). As of 3 October 2014, British historian Frederick Taylor, author of a book about the Berlin Wall (2006), concluded (in a radio interview in 2014) that this Wall is getting smaller—particularly as new generations are born who do not remember divided Germany. But it is still there.

Histories are both factual accounts and literary narratives. Understood as rhetorical devices, labels like Wende-winners and -losers connect everyday lives to a larger story of Germany and the world, but in the process, they reduce a very wide range of stories to either success or failure. And there are many other ways to use storytelling to shape the interpretation of events. When people write historically, they make interpretive choices to begin and end their tale at particular points in time. They choose which figures to use as their protagonists and which sources best exemplify the past. As we have seen, they embed the wide and often unruly range of human experience into a plot. These ordinary tools of the storyteller all help make the story more compelling (White 1973, 1987; Schütze 1976, 1995; Rosenthal 1995).

We selected Dieter as the first protagonist for this book in part because his account of the Wende speaks directly to our plot: a story of ruptures in the everyday lives of modern Germans. Still unresolved at the time of the book's publication, the challenges he faces raise the prospect that these ruptures will remain unresolved for modern Germans as well. His story also allows us to raise scholarly questions about the purpose and impact of writing interpretively about the everyday. We have already raised a first concern: that we misrepresent the facts when we reduce the multiple and oft-contradictory experiences of many people to a discrete event (Vann 1998; Magnússon and Szijártó 2013).

Consider Dieter. He has found no happy ending to his Wende story. His story is more of an *existential tragedy* in which the protagonist is fully aware of, but can never escape, the purgatory of his condition. His initial unemployment marked only the first in a series of ongoing personal crises that ended in permanent underemployment, drunkenness, and an array of family problems: "And I wasn't bringing any money home, and no wife could accept that, right? And I had two children, then the divorce came, that came next, then everything took its course, and we were no longer needed." Dieter has been paralyzed by this *cumulative mess* (Strauss 1985; Riemann and Schütze 1991). Underemployment led to disinterest, self-limitation, resignation, and then despair.

And then I jumped from the balcony, because—because I could no longer endure it ... Fourth floor, see? Then things fell apart afterwards just as before. I was away 14 days ... A drainpipe altered my fall [chuckling] and I landed on the grass ... Afterwards one can laugh, but—

Even after his suicide attempt, Dieter's story took another unexpected pivot: he survived. So now he tells his story like a *black comedy*, whose protagonists find only a temporary reprieve through ironic engagement with the very gallows that condition their lives.

Reducing Dieter's experiences to only one story would miss the whole point (Klein 1995). His life kept turning and pivoting, each time abruptly and in unexpected and profoundly disruptive ways. Even for Dieter, there was no single Wende.

Our Trajectory

This book is designed to introduce a generally educated reader to some of the big themes of German studies. The authors of this book want to provide a different point of entry into this interdisciplinary field than the traditional surveys of German culture, economics, politics, and society. Rather than a typical survey of major figures, social groups, broad statistics, geographic regions, or abstract ideas, this book offers views of the everyday lives of modern Germans on the ground. Their stories make for particularly compelling reading because of the repeated tragic and often violent disruptions that they experienced. Indeed, they were so frequent, and so severe, that it makes little sense to treat them as exceptions to the rule. For modern Germans, ruptures were their *normal*.

For scholars, this book offers an alternate approach for how one might study everyday life in Germany or elsewhere. Everyday life is fragmented, multivocal, ambiguous, dynamic, and contradictory. It is the locus of complex interactions between elites and masses, micro and macro, public and private, the ordinary and the extraordinary. It contains a confusing mix of structure and agency, myths and experience, propriety and unruliness. These qualities have made it hard to pin down precisely. To make matters worse, this book addresses a particularly messy layer of human experience that resists smooth incorporation into overarching stories: the ruptures of everyday life. Identifying a relatively coherent approach is no small task, as there are many different doorways through which prior scholars have entered into it. Our response to this challenge, outlined here in this first chapter, is to place the paradoxes of the everyday at the core of our approach.

Gradually over the course of this book, we develop four interrelated concepts for analyzing the everyday. We treat its features as inherently *plastic* in nature in the sense of being potentially fixed or fluid in any given social situation. They acquire this characteristic, we argue, thanks to the way people interact with one another in everyday life—what we call *microsocial interactions*—and the way that people lay claim to the right to shape the features of everyday life as they see fit—what we call *self-authorizations*. Remarkably, people still come to a common, pragmatic, if provisional, kind of *consensus* about its nature in order to get on with the business of living. How modern Germans chose to do so shaped—for better or for worse—not only their own lives but also the lives of many other people around the world.

We fully explore these analytic concepts only in the final chapter because we derive our concepts ethnographically from engagement with the evidence. For similar reasons, we will not introduce you here to the various sources and methods of each individual case study, for there are too many different ones. You will find that information too in the chapters to follow. Instead, we use this first chapter to describe the scope of this study in broad theoretical terms: what we mean by *ruptures in the everyday* and *views of modern Germany from the ground*. Unconventionally, we engage already in this chapter with empirical evidence to derive our theories and methods. As a result, this introduction is longer than usual and reads a lot like a body chapter. These breaks with academic tradition are all appropriate for a book about rupture.

The trajectory of this book is not linear. We move abruptly between fragmentary anecdotes of personal experience from everyday life and various kinds of shared, pragmatic understandings about it. Dieter's struggle to figure out how to frame his experiences illustrates the scope of the challenge: *how can he fit his experiences of rupture into a coherent story of his life? and into a collective story of modern Germans?* It is hard to make sense of everyday life when it has been so repeatedly and fundamentally disrupted. Yet the authors of this book think that it is worth attempting. Here is how we plan to do so.

Modern Germans

The topic of this book, as promised by the title, poses a number of analytic challenges. Take the term *modern* for instance. Colloquially it refers to the present in contrast to the past, but modern also implies a rejection of the old in favor of the new. The repudiation of traditional or sanctified forms often led to chronic instability and an experience of existential alienation. Moreover, that process of replacing the old with the new never took place evenly, all at once, or without conflict. Indeed, the introduction of the new and the destruction of the old is one major source for the disruptions with which this book is centrally concerned. The modern everyday is thus paradoxically conditioned by its own ruptures.

As German scholars, we too use modern as an analytic concept to refer to a period of human history generally characterized by instability, alienation, juxtaposition, unevenness, and rupture (Burckhardt 1860; Harootunian 2000; D. Harvey 2003). German accounts of modernity are particularly useful to scholars for two reasons. Those experiences of instability, alienation, juxtaposition, unevenness, and rupture were particularly evident in the German versions of modernity. And in response, German intellectual and popular culture have made precisely those issues into the subject of critical reflection (e.g., Tönnies 1926; Kracauer 1963; Benjamin 2006 also Chakrabarty 2000; Harootunian 2000; Durst 2004).

Although the scope of the modern is highly debated in the literature, we limit it—solely for the purposes of this book—to the period from 1914 to 2015. We begin our story roughly with the memory of World War I; we pay considerable attention to the Weimar Republic, Nazi Germany, and the GDR; and we end with the memory of the Wende in the FRG. Writing in 1994, and therefore ending his periodization in 1989, British historian Eric Hobsbawm referred to this period as *the short twentieth century*. We end our periodization in the present in terms of the consequences of the Wende, and we include a few outliers from the Second Empire before 1914 and even earlier in Brandenburg-Prussia. These outliers hint at some of the origins of these modern events and remind us that the periodization of modern Germany is fraught with problems.

Politically, the conflicts of the twentieth century were structured by the three-way struggle between capitalist democracy, communism, and fascism for world dominance. Geopolitically, however, those conflicts centered in part on Germany, owing to unresolved conflicts relating to its boundaries, political system, and disproportionate strength vis-à-vis its European neighbors. One way of posing the so-called German question, at least in the modern era, points to the many different proposals for fitting the different Germanies into a united one that is also located within a larger, peaceful, and stable framework for Europe and the world (Habermas 1997).

The Great War, World War II, the Cold War, and other conflicts were fought over these and other fundamental issues. One turning point in these stories, for many historians, was the Great War from 1914 to 1918. It began as an internal European civil war but escalated into a global conflict. It saw the collapse of old European empires in East Central Europe and the emergence of fascism and communism as modern political movements. During the mislabeled *Interwar Period*, these conflicts only shifted strategies and battlefields. In fact, many have continued to the present.

In this account of modern German history, the apparent defeat of fascism in 1945 marked only the midpoint of seventy-five years of conflict. World War II concluded formally with the so-called Two-Plus-Four

Treaty by the Allies and the two German states in 1990. It closely coincided with the crisis of European communism, the fall of the Berlin Wall during the Wende, and the collapse of the Soviet Union. Yet this periodization makes sense only if you accept the story of the Wende as the inevitable, ultimate victory of Western-style capitalist democracy over the forces of totalitarianism at the "end of history" (Fukuyama 1992). Such a rendering of events is quite misleading. As of 2016, communism is still a powerful force in world politics and fascism is once again a growing threat. More to the point, events like the Wende were never the inevitable product of historical forces but the product of the agency of leaders and citizens alike (Mazower 2000).

A static and discrete definition of *Germany* is also an analytic challenge. Germany has always been a compilation of pieces: a multiplicity of political, social, economic, and cultural units on different levels. In the modern period, the region loosely called *Germany* frequently changed its borders, reflecting the fact that Germany has always been a place in the making. Reunification in 1990 only partially resolved this issue. In post-Wende Germany, we see ongoing tensions, for instance, between former East and West Germans, between natives and immigrants, and between member states of the EU about German dominance. The four maps created for this book, seen below, capture only some of this rich diversity and particularism in the wide range of German places.

For a study of everyday life, however, national boundaries are only one feature and perhaps not the most salient. Our maps of Germany would be far more splintered and conflicted if we were to include its many other divisions of politics, society, religion, economy, and culture. It makes even less sense to speak of Germans as a whole when we take into consideration the wide range of experiences of everyday life, for instance within particular social milieus. Furthermore, it would be a mistake to leave out the many Germans who lived outside the borders of the German states or inside them but on the peripheries. Particularly during the twentieth century, Germans crossed boundaries in all sorts of complicated ways, resulting in hybrid senses of self, while changing state borders and fluctuating populations similarly complicated the self-image of the people who stayed put.

We address these issues in two ways. First, we follow modern Germans as they move to, trade with, and conquer other lands and places; as they move within and between various German states and regions; as they construct borders, communities, and worlds; and as they negotiate their sense of self—all transnationally. Second, we devote some attention to places within the nominal boundaries of Germany that are peripheral or outliers in the way we think about modern Germany. In both ways, we define modern Germans not as a fixed identity but a relational one. Accordingly, the four maps we created are not exhaustive; they list only the places that are relevant for the stories we tell in this book. We encourage our readers to refer back to them for reference in this and subsequent chapters.

During the Cold War, the GDR was just such a periphery. In the East, it marked the furthest extent of the Soviet empire in Europe; in the West, it was viewed pejoratively as the other German state.

Map 1.1. Germany Post-1945[1]

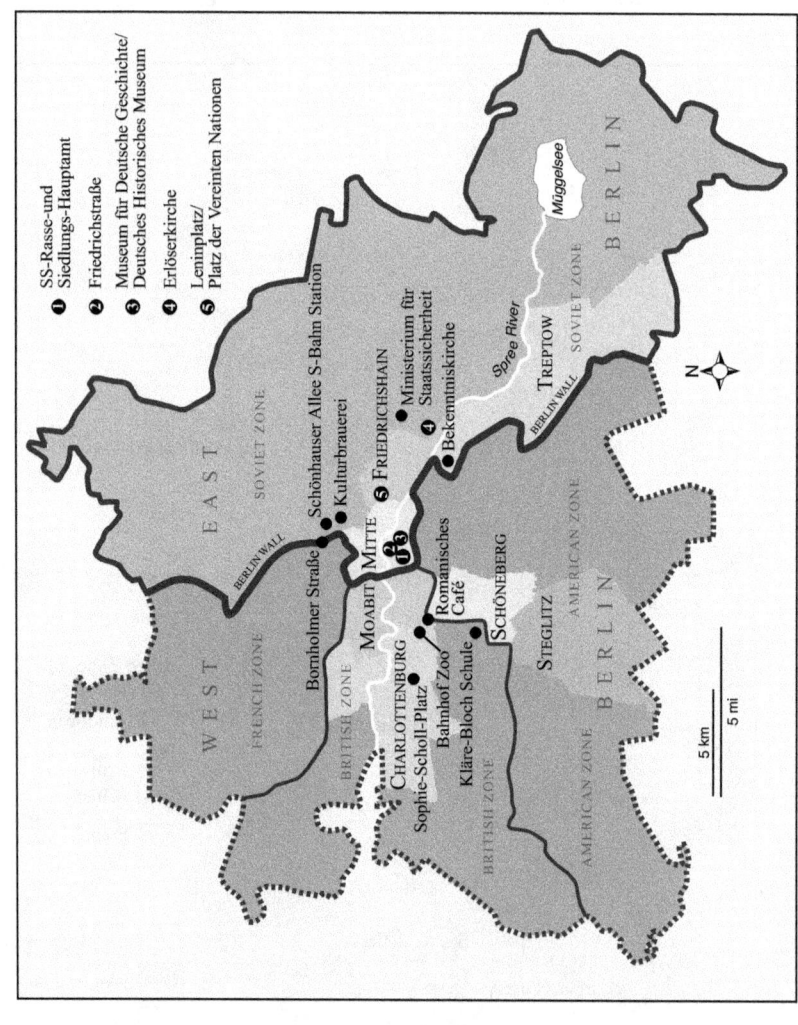

Map 1.2. Modern Berlin[2]

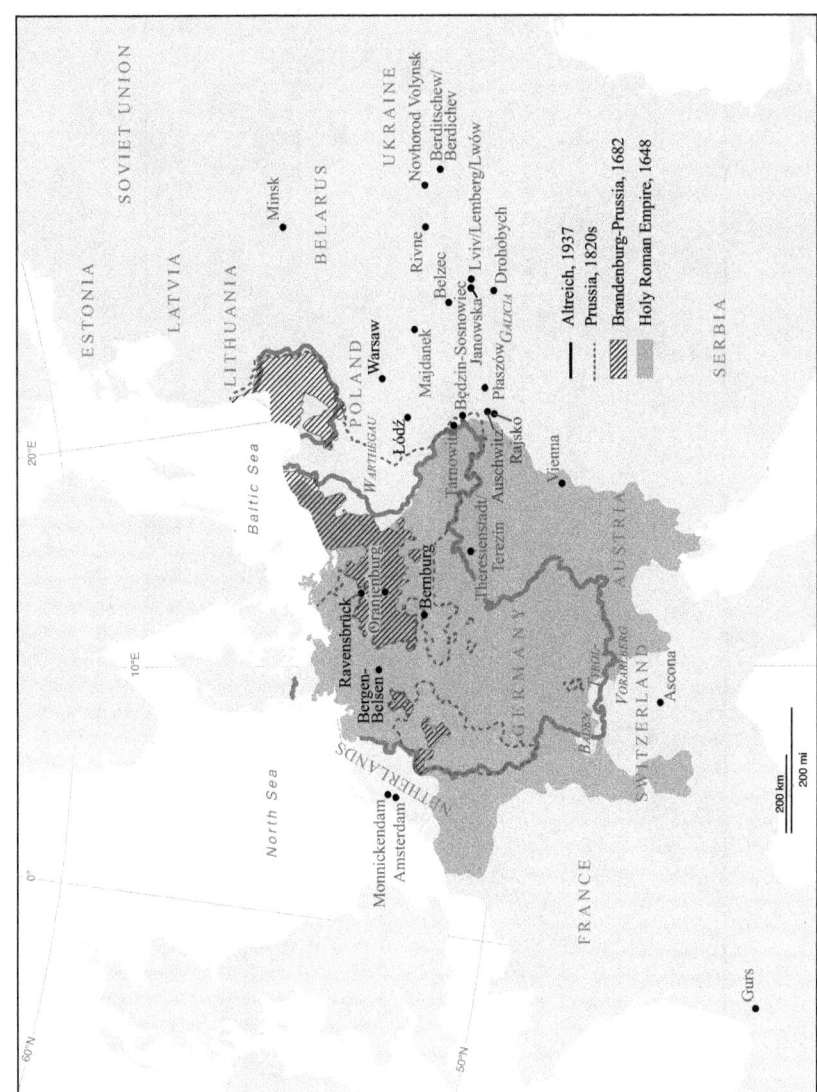

Map 1.3. Germany in Europe 1648–1945[3]

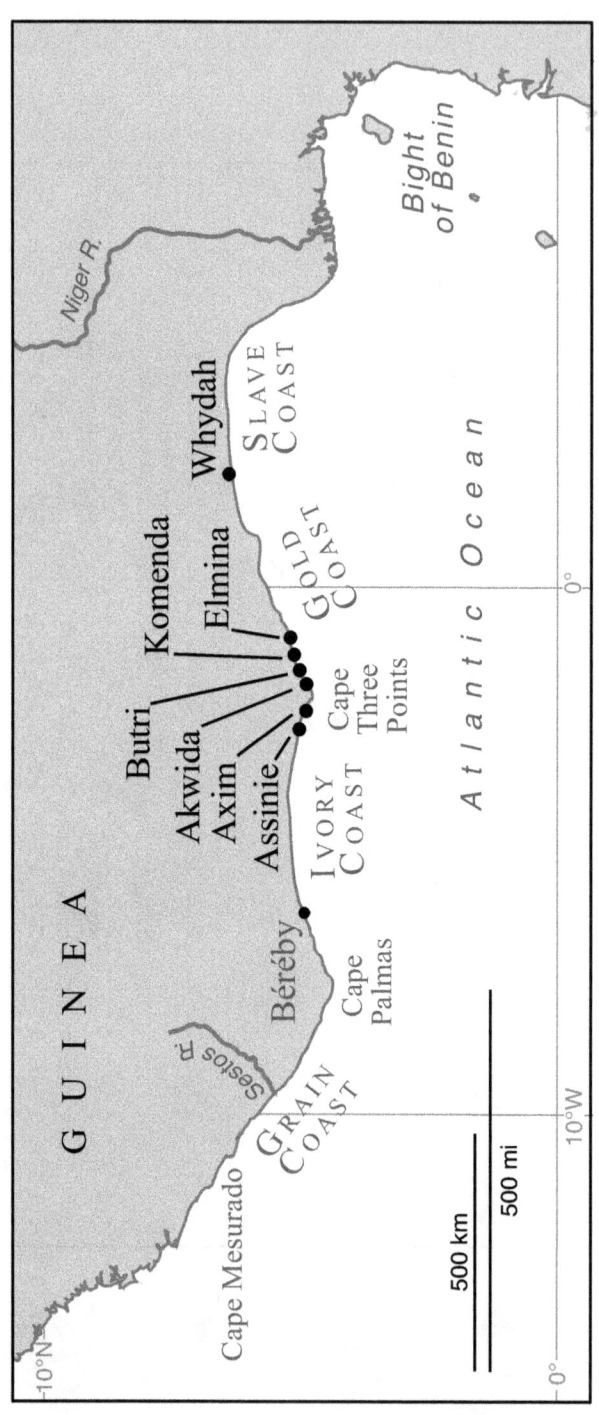

Map 1.4. European Trade Sites in Seventeenth-Century West Africa[4]

Mecklenburg-Vorpommern (MV), the provincial land where Dieter lives, was the periphery of this periphery. Located along the coast of the Baltic Sea, it marks the northern border of German-speaking Central Europe. East Berlin, capital of the GDR, and Berlin, subsequent capital of the reunited FRG, were located just to the south within the Land of Brandenburg. Yet in Berliner dialect, MV is the very definition of *janz weit draussen* meaning *very far away* (also abbreviated *j.w.d.*).

MV is paradoxical in many ways. A largely rural land, it was deeply embedded in industrial production during the GDR only to deindustrialize after the Wende. With the exception of a few cities and tourist centers, commentators have described life there today in depressing terms: empty apartments; poor traffic connections; consolidation and closing of offices, hospitals, post offices, and small businesses; loss of population; declining birthrate; aging population; lower qualification levels; reduced social connections; and a thinning out of social networks. Negative taglines dominate media coverage of these regions, including *suffering, desolation, empty highways, depopulated space, pensionopolis, return of the wolves,* and *call of the barren*. As these labels suggest, this German region has been not only physically but also *symbolically degraded*, to borrow a phrase from French sociologist Pierre Bourdieu (1993: 166). MV does not fit comfortably in the success story of reunified Germany.

But that is precisely why it belongs in a book about ruptures: outliers like this one refuse to sit comfortably with normative assumptions about everyday life. As scholars of the everyday have long argued (Niethammer 1989; Ginzburg and Poni 1991; Medick 1994, 1996; Prakash 2000; Magnússon and Szijártó 2013), the life stories of marginal individuals shed light on the structures and norms of everyday life by their very *alterity*. The differences in their conditions, attitudes, and action are part and parcel of the juxtapositions, unevenness, alienation, and disruptions of modernity. Outliers are thus not really outside at all.

One way of summarizing the problem with the category of modern Germans is to note its inherent *discontinuities*. What it means to be German in the modern period depends on one's class, ethnicity, gender, generation, race, region, sexuality, state, and so on. Yet these definitions change over time. Considered natural in one situation, they can suddenly be questioned and perhaps reinvented in the next (Scott 1988; Butler 1990; Foucault 1994; Connell 1995; Connell and Messerschmidt 2005).

The danger of broad generalizations about modern Germany thus lies in their tendency to erase all of this messiness. Thinking about ruptures requires careful attention to contradictions, crises, details, discontinuities, fragments, outliers, and particularities. Hence our preference is to speak of modern Germans. It seems to capture most clearly the cacophony of voices insisting on sharing their own unique stories of everyday life.

Collapsed Houses

The Wende began long before 1989, and its impact was still felt long after (Wowtscherk 2014). Illustration 1.1, a photograph of a house in MV taken by one of our authors in 2010, is an example. The worn-out exterior of the house on the right side of the image—draped in sepia, the ubiquitous color of Eastern Europe before the Wende—seems to stand in sharp contrast to the newly painted white exterior of the house in the center—probably repainted after the Wende. This juxtaposition seems to imply that the problems in MV can be traced back to the communist system of the GDR. By contrast, the collapsed roof, the dirt road, the graffiti, and the trash bins all seem to suggest that the social decay is more a matter of the capitalist system of reunified Germany. Taken together, though, they suggest longer-term processes of change in everyday life that transcend the political divisions of East and West.

When struggling to comprehend how these changes took place, scholars tend to organize their thinking in terms of either *structures* or *agency*. Agency refers to the actions of intentional individuals, which then shape the conditions of the possible for other people. Structures refer to the patterns of power, markets, relationships, and meanings that also both constrain and enable that

Illustration 1.1. Collapsing House, Mecklenburg-Vorpommern, 2010. Photo: T. Gurr.

action. It has been quite some time since scholars called for *poststructuralist* approaches that move beyond this rather unhelpful distinction (e.g., Bourdieu 1974; Lloyd 1991; Sewell 2005). Understanding everyday life requires this kind of synthetic approach. Dieter's experiences in MV can once again help us to illustrate ours.

MV is not urban, but it is also not strictly rural. During the GDR, many agricultural workers there were employed in various forms of collaborative and cooperative farms. They were not farmers in the traditional sense but trained workers specializing in particular tasks within or in support of these agricultural enterprises. These enterprises structured everyday life, providing early childhood education, sporting facilities, cafeterias, and sometimes also local public transportation. The long-term structural decline of agriculture was therefore more sudden and shocking in the East. Whereas only 3 percent of all workers in the FRG were employed in the agricultural sector at the time of the Wende, it had been 10 percent in the GDR (Lutz and Grünert 1996: 101–20).

The Wende almost completely destroyed those structures. Within two years of the fall of the Wall, the number of people employed in agriculture shrank from around 850,000 to 250,000, which included 150,000 in short-term or part-time jobs (Meyer and Uttitz 1993: 221–47). When local agricultural production cooperatives in MV failed, so too did the sociability that was based on the services they provided. An equally dramatic set of structural adjustments took place in the industrial branches, which is where Dieter had been working. Seventy percent of the people employed in industry lost their jobs as a result of reunification. To be sure, some industrial concerns, like the shipyards of MV, were kept alive through privatization but only through massive reductions in employees. Their former workers lived in a continual state of crisis characterized by high unemployment, declining work skills, and dependence on welfare (Hauss, Land, and Willisch 2006: 34; also Merkl 2012).

Drawing attention to these structures is essential for understanding everyday life. In both sectors, it was the working classes rather than the white-collar workers who were let go and who then lacked other viable alternatives for employment. Both also lost the high status that they had enjoyed as workers and farmers in the Workers' and Farmers' State. Although they both lived in rural settings, neither could turn back to traditional agricultural practices or ways of life to substitute for this collapse, as those traditions had long disappeared. To be sure, similar processes of deindustrialization and privatization have taken place in many other regions around the modern world; the situation in the GDR differed in that its citizens faced both at the same time and in both industry and agriculture.

The GDR was partially to blame: they failed to reinvest sufficiently in industry in the years before the Wende. Yet the reunited German government proved similarly unwilling to commit resources necessary to modernize these concerns thereafter. Unable to compete globally, the only other choice seemed to be liquidation and closure. The celebrations of the twenty-fifth anniversary of reunification praised the successful transition of a few of these firms but with only a fraction of the original employees; and the stories of those who lost out from these structural changes entered into the media stories mostly in terms of *Ostalgie*.

The benefit of a structural analysis is that it can demonstrate the impact of changing conditions on the people experiencing them. The people interviewed for this study had all completed their training as skilled workers in the former GDR, but despite the high value placed on such training, they were all dismissed from work after 1989. The thing that most disappointed them about the Wende was their feeling of being dispensable. They were industrial workers in deindustrialized and postindustrial areas. They quickly lost the sense of belonging—not just to the GDR but also to Germany, the working classes, their village, their families. They became outcasts. German scholars called them *decoupled, surplus, superfluous*. These labels tell stories (Klein 1995: 292).

Dieter's long-term unemployment is certainly evidence of a larger structural problem in the economy. Yet the fact that Dieter framed his personal struggles in terms of the Wende illustrates a more complex phenomenon. People respond to their circumstances with actions, interactions, and stories of those experiences. These responses lie at the heart of this study of the everyday precisely because of the way that they incorporate both structure and agency. It is in everyday life that human beings put structure into action. They do so through various processes of implementation, negotiation, adoption, and adaptation; and they make sense of those dynamics through storytelling.

The point is a fine but important one about the human condition. Most people cannot predetermine their circumstances before they act; they must make do with the circumstances available to them. But more often than not, those circumstances were created for them by their fellow human beings. That is to say, all structures are also the products of agency, just as all agency is made possible by structures. To capture this particular paradox of human experience, scholars of everyday life often quote Karl Marx's *The Eighteenth Brumaire of Louis Napoleon* (1852; Ginzburg 1985: 48; Niethammer 1988: 11; Lüdtke 1991a: 110; Röhr and Berlekamp 1995: 330; Wierling 2002: 9; see also Rosa Luxemburg 1913). In our loose translation: "People make their own history, but they do not make it as they please; they do not make it under circumstances of their own choosing but under circumstances already existing—given and transmitted from the past."

The photo in Illustration 1.1, *Collapsing House*, documents at least two examples of people making their own history even if not under circumstances of their own choosing. One of the first repairs that East German families undertook after the Wende was to replace roofs as housing materials became more readily available. Evidenced by the newly tiled roof on the white house, someone clearly believed that the Wende would bring an improvement to the local economy. Yet the roof collapsed—a fact that suggests that the structural changes anticipated in a reunited Germany, like the home improvements themselves, were not well constructed.

No doubt, this house also contained a family. In the early years after the Wende, they were probably still embedded in a network of social relationships in the village, land, and GDR more broadly. Yet the collapsed roof implies that they chose to abandon their home and those relationships in search of better prospects. In response to the multifaceted structural crisis of the former GDR, some 3.7 million people chose similarly to emigrate out of the former East Germany between 1989 and 2007 (Wolf 2010). Home construction and emigration reflect both structures and agency at the same time. To understand the everyday lives of modern Germans, we need to analyze them in poststructuralist terms as both the objects and the subjects of history.

Life out There

The first step to do so is to view everyday life from the perspective of the modern Germans themselves, that is, through the stories of their own experiences. Those anecdotes are often fragmentary and contradictory. Dieter can help us once again to find some ways to think through the challenges of working with this kind of material.

Given the personal hardships that Dieter faced as a result of reunification, we were rather surprised by his appreciation for the West. In spite of his long-term unemployment, Dieter admitted to finding some aspects of his new life in the FRG agreeable. At the same time, he did not wish to become a burden on anyone else. Dieter remained largely isolated socially and physically from "life out there," as he called it, and he implied that this isolation was generally a good thing.

More than anything else, this phrase reflects Dieter's efforts to reorganize his everyday life in a way that removed the pressure for him to make any decisions whatsoever. Still, this phrase hints at subtle shifts in the nature of Dieter's village as a periphery—a redefinition of Dieter's relationship to these various modern Germanies that in turn redefined his relationship to Germanness. For the residents of rural MV, "life out there" prior to the Wende had referred to the pulsing life of the big cities in East Germany like East Berlin and Leipzig. But the GDR was their Germany, and most residents of MV, Dieter included, still felt a sense of belonging to it.

After the Wende, this phrase still evoked his experience of living on a rural periphery, but "life out there" now referred primarily to Western cities like Hamburg, Munich, and the reconstructed capital of Berlin. Moreover, "life out there" now conveyed a sense of alienation from a reunited Germany. Dieter's choice to remain in his small and isolated village allowed him to maintain an insular existence even as the village crumbled around him; dismissing "life out there" seemed to legitimize the choice to stay put. At the same time, this phrase evoked layers of memory that contradicted and undermined that conviction.

Dieter's case study derives from ethnographic fieldwork conducted in 2010 by one of our authors, a sociologist by training, with twelve former East Germans between the ages of fifty-three and fifty-nine years old. All of them experienced long-term unemployment since the Wende, though interrupted by some very short periods of temporary work. Applying an *action-oriented grounded theory* approach (Strauss and Corbin 1990) to this series of autobiographical interviews provided this researcher with insight into the everyday lives of this cohort, their memories of the past, and their expectations for the future.

Like many others marginalized by the modern capitalist economy, this cohort tended to inhabit a world that was not only relatively restricted but also isolated. Personal contacts could not be taken for granted, and these individuals even tended to avoid family members out of a feeling of not wanting to be a burden. Lacking social contact and relational security, they experienced a persistent sense of doubt about their situation and decisions. The Wende, broadly defined, thus robbed them of not only a sense of belonging to reunited Germany but also the support of community relationships to confirm a sense of self.

A rather confusing array of concepts can be found among different schools of thought as to how to refer to that world of experience, and scholars often use them in different ways. To make matters worse, these debates are rather political because Germans have often deployed these terms for political purposes. So for instance, some scholars consider the concept of a *life world* to be discredited because of its connotations of *rootedness* in a particular *Heimat*, or homeland. Associated with the philosopher Martin Heidegger, the concept of rootedness was politicized as part of the Nazi ideology of *blood and soil* (Wolin 1992; Heidegger 2014). Among other scholars, however, it is an accepted term, referring to the reality we construct for ourselves through our actions and interactions with people and objects (Schütz 1971; Husserl 1973: 41–46 para. 10; Schütz and Luckmann 1973; Luckmann 1979; Berger and Luckmann 1996; Honer and Hitzler 2011: 11–26).

The basic premise here is that human beings determine their reality in terms of the way they apprehend it. By *apprehension* we mean the use of all senses and the brain to collect and make sense of phenomena in the world. Along with *make sense of*, we use *comprehend, evaluate,* and *interpret* as shorthand for this phenomenological process of apprehension. Some scholars say that the dimensions of our life world are determined by the so-called horizon of relevance. That external boundary of the life world is inscribed, they argue, by directing attention to the things within it and away from other things (Schütz 1971; Husserl 1973: 41–46 para. 10; Schütz and Luckmann 1973; Luckmann 1979; Berger and Luckmann 1996; Honer and Hitzler 2011: 11–26). So when Dieter referred disparagingly to "life out there," he was not only making a geographic and political distinction. His actions also drew a boundary between the inside and outside of his life world.

Some of us would go further. Even within the horizon of relevance, the life world is also determined by how people interpret its features. There are no human actions without meanings associated with them, so it follows that the life world is shaped by what people do in, to, and with the things in it. But these interpretive acts can generate confusion or even conflict. There might be considerable dissonance between the life worlds of different people, or *particular life worlds*. Here we are not referring just to the *partial life worlds* of distinct social milieus (Honer and Hitzler 2011: 11–26) but to differences in subjective experience for individuals. If every person makes sense of the world to some degree in their own way, then each of us inhabits slightly different particular life worlds.

Each of these twelve informants inhabited their own world in relative physical, social, and psychological isolation. Some filled their everyday lives with simple tasks, like cleaning, that created a sense of order in their household. These new rituals provided solace, intimacy, and stability. Many cherished finding functional, long-lasting, bargain-priced household items. They also used furniture and clothing to insulate themselves from a disheartening outside world. They devoted considerable time and effort to the construction of this new normalcy.

To be sure, we should not draw too broad a generalization from this small sample. Other people have responded to long-term unemployment by improving their economic activities or redirecting them, for instance, into the black market or artistic pursuits (Schnapper 1981). The extreme kind of isolation described here is far more typical of the kind of "upheaval" unemployment we have seen with the Wende (Vogel 1999). In all cases, however, their life worlds have been shaped by both structure and agency; and even people living seemingly similar everyday lives can inhabit life worlds that are radically particular.

On the Ground

Life worlds are dynamic phenomena, for they are the byproducts of our actions, interactions, and experiences in everyday life. Paying close attention to the way that people tell their life stories is one way that researchers can access and reconstruct this process. Yet we do not wish to imply that life worlds somehow take place within this framework or container called everyday life (cf. Honer and Hitzler 2011: 12). Everyday life has particular qualities of its own. We understand the temptation to seek more analytic stability in the concept of everyday life, given the dynamic and idiosyncratic nature of life worlds. But everyday life as a concept is no more reliably fixed than the life world. It, too, is a product of the things we do in it and with others *on the ground* (Mailänder Koslov in Bergerson et al. 2009: 571).

The German term for everyday life is *Alltag*, and it has been the subject of much scholarly attention in many fields (e.g., J. Douglas 1971; Lefebvre 1974; Elias 1978; Hammerich and Klein 1978; Thurn 1980; Alheit 1983). Generations of cultural critics, philosophers, political scientists, and sociologists have employed this term, for instance, in their effort to understand urban modernity. Within the framework of critical theory inherited from Marxism, *Alltag* emerged along with the concept of *ways of life* to bridge the theoretical gap between the two layers of the Marxian dialectic: the infrastructure and the superstructure. Marxists argue that society is shaped essentially by the mode of production, which in turn shapes consciousness, culture, politics, and agency. For some theorists, it made sense to talk about everyday life as the place where these mediations took place, particularly if one wished to understand and influence those outcomes (Katznelson and Zolberg 1986; Lüdtke 1991b, 1991c, 1993).

German historians refer to the study of the history of everyday life as *Alltagsgeschichte*. This approach emerged in the 1960s out of an interest in the experience, actions, and compliance of the working classes, women, and other supposedly concrete and ordinary Germans at key points in modern German history. For many historians of everyday life, the *Alltag* served as the place where one could observe, and connect on a variety of scales, the dynamic interactions of politics, economics, society, and culture (Niethammer 1982; Borscheid 1986; Eley 1989; Lüdtke 1995, 2003; Steege et al. 2008; Lindenberger 2014; cf. Wehler 1988). All of the authors of this book are familiar with this school of scholarship, and some of us were trained in it specifically.

In both colloquial German and English, *Alltag* and everyday are often used to refer to something that happens frequently or in a repetitive, consistent, or ritualized fashion. As a concept, everyday life seems to some to be particularly well suited to describing the modern, rationalized, mechanized, industrial world of mass production and consumption. Others, by contrast, theorize the everyday in more paradoxical ways, arguing that it already includes disruptions and discontinuities (Lüdtke 1991b: 110). In colloquial speech, the everyday can also refer to what is *normal* in the sense of what the common people do; but it can just as readily refer to what is *normative* in the sense of referring to what one is supposed to do. We begin to see how the everyday creates its own myths, if disruptions are disguised by rationalization and the normative is being treated as normal.

Also in colloquial speech, the everyday is often defined by what it is not. It seems to refer to the realm of the profane rather than the sacred, the familiar and homey rather than the uncanny and foreign. It can be used to refer to what is not political. The elites who have power and status seem far from the so-called ordinary people who inhabit everyday life. This insularity of the everyday can be expressed geographically in the sense of a political core and its dependent peripheries, hierarchically in terms of authorities and their subordinates, or spatially in terms of inside and outside.

But these dichotomies often disguise as much as they explain. If we were to believe the myths of everyday life, the calamities of disease and death, the violence of conflict and war, indeed history itself—when reduced to a classical story of policies and politics—all seem to penetrate and disrupt everyday life from the outside. The outbreak of the Great War or the Allied bombardments of German cities are examples of historical ruptures that sometimes appear, from the perspective of ordinary people, as interruptions of their everyday lives. Many East Germans experienced the Wende similarly as a series of extraordinary events that happened to them. Such distinctions between history writ large and the everyday lives of ordinary people may very well be tropes for how we tell these kinds of stories. Yet those dualities become structural features of our everyday lives when we speak in those terms, experience them as real, and act accordingly (Bergerson 2008, 2010).

It would be more accurate to say that experiences of the ordinary or the extraordinary are embedded in one another, constituting each other dynamically in dynamic circumstances. For Wende-losers like Dieter, it was the loss of a job that remained the biggest source of dissatisfaction and the biggest stumbling block on the path to a new normal. Like the vacant and decrepit factories around them, the unemployed felt superannuated: their skills were no longer required in the labor market of reunited Germany.

During the interviews, their comments suggested that they remained deeply committed to a healthy work ethic, in which personal worth and status is tied to making a living through hard work, but they were also distraught that that opportunity was not afforded to them. Some found it unbearable to be receiving welfare, as this status conflicted with their self-image. They responded to this contradictory situation by trying to avoid thinking about it. They submerged into their new daily routines based on reduced circumstances and possibilities. Here, even the ordinary and the extraordinary become tools for the construction of reconfigured life worlds. This cohort ironically used routines to banish the extraordinary, as if another rupture would only call into question their newly and provisionally constructed ordinary lives.

Clearly, the everyday is not just a synthetic but also a dynamic category. Its structures shape what people can do, and what they imagine they can do, just as those structures often also derive from the kinds of practices people use to act in it. Indeed, most of the categories you will find in this book—from the self to the state—are often redefined in use. It is the question of how people construct, negotiate, and express these categories in everyday life that concerns us here.

In order to study this dynamic process, we adopt a perspective *from the ground*. We try to avoid dividing our subjects into elite and ordinary Germans, respectively, shaping events *from the top down* or *from the bottom up*. Viewing the German *Alltag* on the ground seeks to wed these perspectives—though maintaining an astute sensitivity to the differences of power and status that empower different kinds of actions and interactions. With our focus on the ground, our lens can capture particular life worlds as they are shaped and experienced in practice.

Following from the way ethnographers engage in fieldwork, this approach strives to simultaneously and self-critically maintain the informant's *emic* perspective from within their life world and the scholar's *etic* perspective from outside it (Headland, Pike, and Harris 1990), for that is also an everyday interaction. The meaning of everyday life thus depends on the movement of meaning between figure and ground akin to the way artists represent the world and art viewers appreciate the work of art (Mitchell 1994). Viewing everyday life on the ground means that we pay close attention to the interplay of meaningful practices that both constitute and rupture everyday life.

Rupture

So the everyday is neither fixed nor stable. As people act and interact within it, they also act on it. Reproducing and transforming its features, these manifold actions can often interrupt or even disrupt the flow of daily life in terms of its established authorities, norms, patterns, relationships, and practices. Rather than seeing ruptures as an extraordinary break in the ordinary, the inherent dynamism of everyday life implies that they are part and parcel of it. We use the term *ruptures* to refer to these disruptions and interruptions, some of which were also quite destructive and violent (Mailänder 2010: 32; Gudehus and Christ 2013: 1–15). Ruptures refuse to be fixed or contained within discrete frameworks of time, space, experience, or memory. Because of their centrality to the experience of modern Germans, they are the overarching theme of this book.

From the evidence already provided about the Wende in MV, we could identify at least five layers on which ruptures take place. We could point first to the *physical* destruction of the living environment like houses, roads, or factories, often leaving only object remnants behind.

Second, we could add the way that ruptures can undermine or destabilize *topographic* features such as roofs, walls, highways, and borders together with the economies and polities they support. Note that these topographic ruptures can be subtractive or additive: a collapsed roof, building a wall, or painting graffiti on it.

Third, we could identify the collapse of the *institutional* structures like families, governments, or organizations. These are, in a sense, more important than asphalt and concrete because of their integrative functions in society.

Fourth, we would like to emphasize the undermining of *interpretive* frameworks that inform those physical and institutional structures. These frameworks are particularly significant for the problem of rupture, as they have a dual role to play. Not only are they important in themselves, but they also provide the structures of meaning that allow people to engage with their physical, topographical, and institutional environment. The loss of these frameworks hinders people's ability to make sense of events both as they are taking place and then again in retrospect.

And fifth, we would also like to emphasize the disruptions to the *self*—individual understandings of gender, class, ethnicity, and so on—that make it even harder to locate the self in the new situation. The Wende undermined or destroyed many of these features of everyday life in the GDR, making it hard not only to adjust to the profound changes but also to come to terms with those events.

Consider Dieter again as an example. It is hard to know for sure the degree of Dieter's integration into the former GDR. His memories have been influenced no doubt by the overwhelming impact of the Wende, perhaps also by *Ostalgie*. But there is probably some basis for that nostalgia in his experience. Though unwilling to change the system, the GDR leadership had been able to elicit integration, participation, and even identification from its citizens by meeting some of their needs and responding to some of their demands with compromise. GDR citizens responded with a familiar mix of cooperation and independence (Lüdtke 1994a, 1994b; Lindenberger 1999, 2007, 2014; Fulbrook 2005; Madarász 2006; Port 2007; Schmieding 2014).

The Wende then forced Dieter to reframe his self in terms of the reunified German nation–state. His experiences of it have made that into a many faceted and complicated maneuver. Moreover, he now relates his new self to these various incarnations of Germany across temporal and spatial ruptures—to both the existing FRG and the former GDR. Dieter's personal sense of Germanness transgresses historical periods and topographic boundaries, ironically even while he stayed put in his provincial home. Notice, then, that staying put does not mean that Dieter stayed the same.

The Wende was hardly the first such rupture that modern Germans have faced. Let us imagine the biography of Dieter's grandparents. If they had been born in 1900 in MV, they would have participated in the creation and destruction of multiple German nations and empires. They would have lived through no fewer than seven political systems: the Wilhelmine Empire, the Weimar Republic, the Third Reich, the Soviet Occupation, the GDR, the FRG, and a reunified Germany within the EU. They also would have been part and parcel of long-term structural changes in capitalism and socialism, modernization and globalization. Examples here include the hyperinflation after World War I, the economic transformations after World War II, and of course the Wende. They would have experienced multiple revolutions in the political, economic, social, and cultural order ranging from the fall of the monarchy to the systematic extermination of the Jews of Europe to postwar revolutions in consumption and sexuality (Herzog 2005; McLellan 2011; Steinbacher 2011).

These many different ruptures were distinctly German in at least three senses: they took place in German-speaking Central Europe; Germans played a significant role in implementing them; and in many cases, Germans were directly responsible for them. Yet they were not limited to Germany. They often sent massive shock waves around the world, and many were hardly unique to Germany. The challenge for modern Germans lies in the sheer number, scale, and frequency of the ruptures. For many modern Germans, it was not only the seismic nature of these changes but also the dizzying pace of them that made them so hard to handle.

Dangerous Memories

Some of these systematic changes were peaceful, like the much contested and far from consensual effort in the postwar Germanies to deal with the Nazi past—referring to the period of rule in Germany and Europe by the National Socialist German Workers' Party (NSDAP). Yet many were exceptionally violent, like the Nazi war of annihilation launched for so-called living space. This genocidal project led to an unprecedented destruction of human lives as well as their living environments, social institutions, political geographies, cultural frameworks, and senses of self. German thought on the issue of rupture derives in large part from the struggle to deal with this past, and the six main authors of this chapter developed their understanding of this concept in this context. Dieter did not directly mention these events in the interviews, but because he was born in 1952, they necessarily shaped his self. Like the Wende, these events created dangerous memories that, with their demands on the present, disrupt the normative linearity of history.

Notice how difficult it is even to name this rupture. At the time, it was framed as the *Final Solution to the Jewish Question* by anti-Semites, while bureaucratic killers used terms like *special treatment* to refer to mass murder euphemistically. Today it is called the *Shoah* in Hebrew, meaning *calamity*. In English, it is called the *Holocaust*, which is a Greek translation of the ancient Israelite practice of offering a burnt offering in the temple in Jerusalem: an *olah*. Insofar as this liturgical act was originally designed to sanctify the children of Israel, it seems inappropriate as a term for a system of industrial mass murder designed particularly for killing Jews along with many others. The difficulty in naming these events typifies the challenge of understanding ruptures.

Scholars also debate which part of these mass atrocities stands at the core of the Shoah: ghettos, camps, mass shootings, trains, gas chambers, or crematoria. The German political theologian Johann Baptist Metz prefers *Auschwitz*, the name of one of the most notorious networks of industrial mass murder, as a more specific metonym for genocide (Metz 1981, 1998). Yet emphasizing Auschwitz prioritizes the last of the great killing centers, perhaps falsely because Western scholars had more access to the historical records of this camp while the bulk of the murder took place farther east.

An emphasis on trains and gas chambers seems to support an interpretation of these events as industrial genocide or an incarnation of modernity in its most terrible form. By contrast, an emphasis on the unremitting mass shootings throughout Eastern Europe seems to underscore both the personal roots of anti-Semitism and the personal experience of the genocide in which the killers confronted their victims face to face (Hilberg 1961; Bauman 1989; Browning 1992; Goldhagen 1996; Megargee 2007; Gigliotti 2009; Snyder 2010).

Different perspectives arise from different experiences. Compare the Jews of Central Europe who successfully left Germany before 1939 to the Jews of Eastern Europe. The rupture of the Shoah took place for the former when they lost citizenship, jobs, and property and were forced to leave Germany; for the latter it came with the invasion of the Germans and the murders to follow. Meanwhile, the primary rupture for non-Jewish Germans—at least the way they often tell the story—was the bombardment of German cities by the Allies (Thiessen 2007; Arnold 2011; Fuchs 2012; also Swett 2013) followed in close succession by the experiences of forced migration, rape, and occupation (Liebman 1995; Naimark 1995; Moeller 2001; Niven 2006; Grossmann 2007, 2011; Demshuk 2012; Douglas 2013; Greiner 2014). It is hard to put together into a single story (Klein 1995) such a wide variety of horrific actions and experiences, including the many ways of dying and killing. Choosing one story over the other only seems to validate one group's suffering at the expense of another.

Still, the sixty-five million inhabitants of Germany, all in one way or another, had to adjust to the new order established by the Nazi regime. Some less and some more, they abandoned civility and democracy for the fascist and racist community envisioned by the Nazis as a *Volksgemeinschaft* (Diner 1988; Bergerson 2004; Bajohr and Wildt 2009; Wildt 2012a, 2012b, 2013). The vast majority of non-Jewish Germans also contributed to the Nazi conquest of a European empire through waging a war of extermination, benefitted from it, or both. By fault or default, they became so-called *Aryans*—the Nazi term for the Germanic race. Only in the wake of this complicity and as a consequence of it did they experience strategic bombing, resettlement, rape, and occupation. Whether or not acknowledged as such, those subsequent ruptures were always experienced in relation to the previous ones (Lüdtke 1989: 11; Bergerson 2004).

These memories of suffering and death thus disrupt the sense of mastery over the past that we typically assume when telling the stories of nations. When one considers the physical destruction of the lived environment, the collapse of institutional structures, the devastation of the political landscape, the undermining of interpretive frameworks, and, most of all, the tremendous loss of life and fundamental challenge to our humanity, the Shoah remained present as the absence at the heart of German everyday life long after 1945. Even after the war, modern Germans necessarily reconstructed the self as postwar—always defined in relation to those earlier ruptures.

Debates about the legitimacy of remembering or forgetting the Nazi past, or of identifying with the perpetrators or victims, miss the point; ruptures break with simple categories of identification and the simple linearity of history. These *shattered pasts* prove hard to fit into overarching stories of Germans as a whole (Jarausch and Geyer 2004), which in turn make a German identity hard to pin down precisely. Many Germans and the scholars who study them have concluded that the process of making sense of these experiences is, and should remain, ongoing, which ties German identities to that process of memory work (Krondorfer 1995; Habermas 1997; Sider and Smith 1997; Neumann 2000; Confino and Fritzsche 2002; Moses 2007; Berger and Nevin 2014). But even that laudable strategy in no way simplifies the challenge of dealing with the ruptures in the everyday lives of modern Germans.

Take Metz, for example. Because he is a theologian, the context for his reflection is religious tradition, in his case Roman Catholic Christianity, although it was nurtured by, rather than rejecting, its Jewish roots. As a specifically *political* theologian, though, he has resisted turning Christianity into a privatized faith in service of the spiritual longings of individuals. For him, ruptures are more than private traumas: they have a political dimension and effectiveness. Moreover, he worries that explaining genocides, as scholars are wont to do, could ironically serve to close off critical engagement with them. Instead, Metz reads the central story of Christianity—the suffering, death, and resurrection of Jesus of Nazareth—as embodying a debt that cannot be repaid and a wound that cannot be closed. It keeps the door open to human suffering and its critical import (Metz 1998, 2006; Ostovich 2002).

To explain this debt, Metz turns to the concept of *dangerous memory*, adopting and adapting the ideas of Walter Benjamin, the Jewish German philosopher of modernity who developed this notion in the 1930s (Ostovich 2002). Metz, following Benjamin, labels the kind of triumphant historical interpretation that characterized German reunification a "victor's history" (2007: 60–84, 114–27). He argues that there are memories that "break through the [historical] canon of all that is taken as self-evident" and "subvert our structures of plausibility."

Such dangerous memories "illuminate for a few moments and with a harsh steady light the questionable nature of things we have apparently come to terms with" (Metz 1972: 15, also 2007: 89). Here Metz is showing how dangerous memories question the normative notions of time and the official histories built on them to forge links of solidarity between past and present. To forge those links, he calls for a kind of *anamnestic reason*. He means a historically and politically situated form of thinking that operates in "solidarity backwards" with the victims of history (Metz 1992; Ostovich 2006, 2010).

Ruptures break with normative trajectories of historical time. French anthropologist Alban Bensa and sociologist Eric Fassin (2002) insist that "events" constitute "ruptures of intelligibility" in the sense that they not only separate the past from the future but force us to rethink and reorder past, present, and future. Ruptures place demands on the present, compelling us to rethink the past and identify backward with the victims. Dieter's memories of the Wende fit this model of refusing to stay put temporally. Although not horrifically violent like the Shoah, the Wende represents a rupture nonetheless (e.g., Lahusen 2013). Many West Germans might have initially accepted the official version of reunification as a triumph of freedom; but it is clear that, just as the topography of MV has been physically and symbolically degraded, many East Germans' material, mental, and psychological suffering continued long after reunification. Those stories underscore the persistent struggle in everyday life to deal with the past when Germany as a whole appears to have moved on.

The point we are making here is that the wars, revolutions, and genocides in modern German history did not end when the violence stopped or the turning point turned. They continue to disrupt the present: not only with the destruction of physical resources or conceptual frameworks (Wagner-Kyora 2014), or even with the psychological impact of trauma (Brunner and Zajde 2011), but also with memories of the ethical debt owed to the victims. To understand Dieter's everyday life today, we must "brush history against the grain" (Benjamin 2003: 396).

Our Stories

In bringing our first chapter to a close, we should admit that this book represents an experiment in our scholarly everyday (Lüdtke and Prass 2008). It is an attempt at large-scale coauthorship.

The project was conceived, organized, and led by Andrew Stuart Bergerson and Leonard Schmieding. Our coauthors were Jonathan Bach, Susanne Beer, Mark E. Blum, Michaela Christ, Cristina Cuevas-Wolf, Mary Fulbrook, Eva Giloi, Thomas Gurr, Jason Johnson, Craig Koslofsky, Dani Kranz, Phil Leask, Wendy Lower, Elissa Mailänder, Josie McLellan, Alexandra Oeser, Steve Ostovich, Will Rall, Johannes Schwartz, Sara Ann Sewell, Paul Steege, Maximillian Strnad, Julia Timpe, and Heléna Tóth.

For the purposes of this book, we refer to ourselves collectively as *ATG26*, shorthand for our *AllTag* Group of *twenty-six* people. We come from a wide range of countries, social backgrounds, and positions in our academic careers. We bring experience working in anthropology, art history, history, literary criticism, museum studies, philosophy, political science, sociology, and theology among other disciplines.

This book is historical in that most of our stories take place in the past, and yet it is not a history in any strict disciplinary sense. The experiences we seek to understand disrupt the normative flow of time in simple chronological sequences. We move rather suddenly between case studies of very different times and places. We frequently shift the tenor of our interpretations from one discipline to the next. And we embed ourselves in the story of the German *Alltag* that we seek to understand. These choices seem appropriate for a study of everyday life that resists disciplining. So we ask the reader to be prepared for a somewhat rocky ride.

Throughout the book, we will strive to identify to whom precisely this *we* refers at that moment. Each chapter was written by a team of two to five scholars but with lots of inspiration and input from other authors. The first and last chapters, serving somewhat as an introduction and conclusion, derived from the middle ones and were written last. The whole book was revised many times in response to considerable internal and external peer review. The names listed at the end of each chapter correspond to the scholars who feel primarily responsible for that chapter—and who may or may not wish to take responsibility for other parts of the book. Not all of the authors of this book wish to take responsibility for this introduction, for instance. Yet no part of this book could have existed without the significant input of many members of ATG26, this chapter not least. In the end, our book has become much more than an edited collection. It is a collaborative monograph—hardly a new genre but one that deserves more serious use.

Like the people we study, we wrote this book based on the preexisting circumstances of our—scholarly—everyday. We gathered this particular set of cases through an electronic call for papers in 2010. In a sense, the topics represent the research interests of our authors and a self-selecting sample of scholarship at that point in time. Placing these anomalous stories together in one book made for hard work. We worked with the plastic evidence given to us in everyday life, shaping it into interpretations while also adapting those interpretations in response to its resistance. Grounded in microsocial interactions, self-authorizations, and consensus building, the writing process represented an effort to develop scholarly practices that more closely correspond to the everyday we seek to understand.

No doubt the reader might find many frustrating gaps in our sample: for instance, there is a certain lack of stories from the Federal Republic, almost no mention of Austria, and an overemphasis on mass dictatorships. Yet one could make the case that our sample is closer to empirical reality precisely because our evidence was not handpicked by the authors in advance in order to create a sense that we have covered the topic completely. Any attempt to do so is necessarily artificial and inevitably erases the outliers. We also gain a certain representativeness through the multiple, interdisciplinary lenses that we bring as twenty-six different authors to the material. In this way, we make connections that are far broader than the standard kind of scholarly work whose interpretations are dictated by a solo author.

This eclectic array of life stories also allows us to make connections between cases that cross ethical, political, and spatial divides. In the book, you will read about elites and masses; communists and Nazis; East and West; homosexuals and heterosexuals; capital cities and provinces; Jews, Slavs, and Aryans; Europe, the United States, and Africa; and so on. In juxtaposing these unfamiliar bedfellows, the authors are not trying to normalize criminal behavior or regimes. We do not wish to give the impression that the suffering or the circumstances of these different situations are comparable. We have no desire to diminish the ethical, political, or geographical differences between, for instance, perpetrators, bystanders, resistance fighters, and victims. Moreover, there are many good reasons for distinguishing between political systems. It makes an enormous difference to the people involved if they lived in a constitutional monarchy, a republic, or a fascist or a communist dictatorship; if their society was focused on mass consumption or mass destruction; if children were raised in the shadow of prosperity and security or rubble and trauma; or if neighborly interactions were based on civility or racism. And these were just a few of the many varied contexts at work in modern German history.

Yet this book begins elsewhere. We accept the inevitably fragmentary nature of any representation of ruptures in the everyday lives of modern

Germans. In seeking to understand them, we look for those dynamics that tend to go unnoticed by laypeople and scholars alike. Intertwining these seemingly incongruent stories will enable us to think differently about the political multiplicities of the twentieth century. Studying them from the same perspective on the ground affords a much more finely tuned picture of how these different political systems functioned. It also allows for a better understanding of how everyday actions and interactions produce dynamics of their own—relatively independent of the political or ethical systems in which they are embedded.

In the chapters to follow, we invite you to enter the interdisciplinary study of modern Germany through this different doorway—not of leading figures, collective groups, ideal types, or abstract forces but of the Germans themselves. The extraordinary and the ordinary are embedded in their same stories. If we have an overarching interpretation in this book, it is that ruptures were part and parcel of the everyday lives of modern Germans. We tell those stories to draw attention to how Germans created, experienced, and responded to those ruptures in common.

We begin in the next chapter with the self. From there we move through ever larger forms of social complexity: interpersonal relations, families, objects, memories, institutions, policies, and violence. We finish along multidimensional borders, where we try to think about how everyday practices play out on different scales at the same time. Overall, the trajectory of this book is to move us from fragmentary experiences in everyday life to some kind of shared, pragmatic understanding of it.

What then are the contributions of this book? In terms of general theory, it tries to move the already very fruitful debates about everyday life onto new ground. We offer microsocial interactions, plasticity, self-authorization, and consensus as ways to think about the everyday practically, synthetically, and integratively. In terms of research design, we propose a collaborative method of coauthorship grounded in these same everyday practices. The book works on the premise that, if we adapt our scholarly *Alltag* to correspond more closely to the everyday lives we seek to understand, then we may discover new and different insights. In terms of interdisciplinary German studies, our insights center on the ruptures in the everyday lives of modern Germans. But we will not provide any more of a preview of that story up front, the way most academic books do. We insist on keeping the everyday experiences themselves at the center of attention.

We invite you to listen closely to all of the different voices speaking in these stories of the German *Alltag*: hundreds of different informants, twenty-six authors, and many other scholars, reviewers, audience members, and editors. We encourage you to add your own views on the matter as well. Because of its multivocality, this book should be read as less orderly than it seems. The messy experiences of everyday life, particularly in the case of modern Germans, can never quite fit comfortably into a single story.

Andrew Stuart Bergerson, Mark E. Blum, Thomas Gurr, Alexandra Oeser, Steve Ostovich, Leonard Schmieding, and Sara Ann Sewell

Notes

1. Cartography by Mark Livengood, November 2016. The base geographic data for this map was downloaded from Natural Earth (www.naturalearthdata.com), except for the German states, which were downloaded from www.gadm.org, an open-source geospatial database of "global administrative areas." The map uses the Albers Equal Area Conic projection and the European 1950 geographic coordinate system. The scale is 1:4,500,00. Cities were located using Google Maps and the zones of Allied occupation are based on by the map "Deutschland nach dem Zweiten Weltkrieg 1.9.1945" published on the website IEG-MAPS, Server für digitale historische Karten (www.ieg.maps.uni-mainz.de). Additional locations were provided by the authors.
2. Cartography by Mark Livengood, November 2016. The base geographic data for this map was downloaded from Open Street Map (http://download.geofabrik.de/europe/germany/berlin.html). The map uses the Albers Equal Area Conic project and the European 1950 geographic coordinate system. The scale is 1:1,000,000. Sites were located using Google Maps and zones of occupation were determined by the map "Deutschland nach dem Zweiten Weltkrieg 1.9.1945" published on the website IEG-MAPS, Server für digitale historische Karten (www.ieg.maps.uni-mainz.de) and other sources.
3. Cartography by Mark Livengood, November 2016. The base geographic data for this map was downloaded from Natural Earth. The map uses the Albers Equal Area Conic projection and the European 1950 geographic coordinate system. The scale is 1:10,500,000. German boundaries are based on three maps published on the website IEG-MAPS, Server für digitale historische Karten: "Deutschland 1648"; "Der Deutsche Bund nach dem Frankfurter Territorialrezess um 1820"; and "Das nationalsozialistische Deutschland 1937."
4. Cartography by Mark Livengood, November 2016. The base geographic data for this map was downloaded from Natural Earth. The map uses the Albers Equal Area Conic projection and the WGS 1984 geographic coordinate system. The scale is 1:18,000,000. Map locations are based on a map of the voyage of Groeben 1682–83 published in Adam Jones, *Brandenburg Sources for West African History, 1680–1700*, Stuttgart: F. Steiner Verlag, 1985, fig. 1, and other locations provided by the authors.

CHAPTER 2

Self

take the chance to be the one you really are ... you have to be ready to do the things you want to do, work until you're perfect for yourself ... don't imitate.
—TJ Big Blaster Electric Boogie, "Time to Fite," 1988

In the summer of 2014, the authors of this chapter were struck by something they saw on television, a practice that stands at the core of the self in the new millennium. Each year during the Tour de France, the cyclists climb through several high mountain passes. Usually the victor of this sporting event emerges during these decisive stages in the competition. The cyclists snake the narrow streets up Mont Ventoux, known as *king of the mountains* in Provence. The higher they get, the more spectators line the streets. They form a crucial part of the event, having come to cheer on the cyclists as they race up the steep slopes—the most challenging part of the competition.

At points near the top, the event coordinators install fences to try to keep spectators off the road; but every once in a while, a spectator steps out onto the asphalt. As the cyclists race up the mountain road, they turn around and stretch out their arm in order to take a photograph. They intend, certainly, to capture one or more cyclists in the frame, but the focus of this self-portrait is themselves—the spectator. Even to the extent that they capture their efforts to support the riders with costumes, makeup, banners, and enthusiasm, they nonetheless make themselves into the momentary center of attention, going so far as to step out onto the stage of the main event.

Often they create a dangerous situation because they do not pay attention to the riders and are apt to cause accidents. The television cameras in turn capture this moment—taking pictures of people taking pictures of themselves—and the program directors broadcast it for global viewing. These self-portraits interrupt the flow of the race to document practices of spectatorship. Officials complain about these disruptions, and other spectators sometimes try to prevent them, but neither effort at formal or informal policing prevents spectators from shooting these self-portraits.

In colloquial language, the name for this kind of self-portrait is a *selfie*. It is made possible by all sorts of technologies—like smartphones and tablets with cameras, selfie sticks, and internet connections—which support the almost instantaneous taking and broadcasting of personal experience. In the second decade of the twenty-first century, the selfie has become one of the most explicit ways that people attempt to locate themselves, visually, in time and place. This self-contextualization also symbolically lays claim to a self (Frank 2014: 22), in this case, that of the enthusiastic Tour de France spectator. Yet this act of locating oneself in the midst of an event, or in the midst of everyday life more generally, necessarily demands that one look away from the experience in order to register a self-image as a digital record of it. Individuals thus simultaneously perform their presence in, and distance themselves from, that experience. While framing themselves within the event, they literally turn their backs on it.

Selfies represent an attempt to lay claim to experience, to bind an individual's everyday life to the passing sweep of history, for which the Tour de France serves as a particularly apt example. But these attempts sometimes fail. Sometimes the selfie taker aims poorly and cuts off their head or fails to capture the scene in focus. Even when they fail, however, selfies capture the process of self-fashioning (Greenblatt 1980)—for selfie takers take many such selfies, select the ones that seem to best represent their self-image, edit them accordingly, and post the best ones to any range of social media along with a caption that embeds the image in their life story. Wittingly or unwittingly, these people thus document how their practices of self are embedded in social relations and power structures. They offer us a point of entry into efforts to weave personal stories out of a complex of images, names, and locations.

Ironically, the selfie seems to fix the self; and yet the process of staging, selecting, editing, and posting this ongoing series of selfies belies that stability. We take the position that the self emerges from, and is tied to, practices of self-fashioning. There is no end product, no self per se, independent of or abstracted from those practices. Our method follows from this argument: we find the evidence we need for understanding the self in people's practical attempts to author that self. This self is never stable: it is situational, adjusting to differences in time and space. It is also relational: it changes depending on dynamic human interactions and cultural contexts. And it is phenomenal in that people's ability to notice the self is inextricable from the practices that seek to realize it.

In this chapter, we undertake a critical analysis of some unrealized, and unrealizable, attempts at self-fashioning in the German *Alltag*. We explore three particular ways of practicing self: naming, locating, and sharing. To do so, we turn to two seemingly unrelated individuals whose lives bracket the chronological sweep of this book from World War I to the end of the Cold War. The German author Ernst Jünger was born in 1895 and is perhaps familiar to some readers for his memoir of World War I, *Storm of Steel*. The East German hip-hop artist known in the 1980s as TJ Big Blaster Electric Boogie was born in Dresden in 1964 as Alexander Morawitz, and he is no doubt less familiar to readers. Comparing these two very different individuals, from such very different times and places, may seem jarring, but it illustrates our approach. We use the contradictory fragments of different life stories to make sense of everyday life. What we discover in both of these cases is a common effort to craft a narrative of self amid the ruptures in their everyday lives.

These efforts at self-fashioning left traces in a diverse set of sources: published and performed literary and musical works, diary and memoir accounts, letters, interviews, and state records. On their own, these figures hardly constitute a representative sample. Obviously, but worth mentioning, both were men, a fact of which the two male historians who drafted this chapter remain quite aware. Contested versions of masculinity and class register in all their performances of self—whether as rapper, soldier, or writer. Over the course of this book, we will extend this analysis of self-practices to informants of many other sorts, including those we might identify as women, Jews, workers, lesbians and gay men, communists and national socialists, and East and West Germans. We ask the reader to remain sensitive to how Germans practice the self as they read the other chapters of this book. We use Jünger and TJ Big Blaster Electric Boogie just to begin that observation.

What can such an analysis of the self tell us about the German Alltag? We focus on the self because individuals must make sense of everyday life in terms of their experiences. The self emerges from these practices of making sense, and those practices involve interactions between mind, body, and world (Hunt 2014: 1582). At once individual and collective, the many practices of self are facilitated by and embedded in complex and often contradictory spatial and temporal contexts. In the end there is nothing uniquely German about this interplay between self and *Alltag*, even if it is only in the particular geographic and historical contexts that any self-practicing can be discerned. Our case studies for this chapter take place in Dresden during the GDR and in interwar Berlin, but they involve imagining other places and looking back and forward in time. It is in these interactive processes where we will search for the fragmentary evidence of the self.

Self-Images

The first of our individuals, Ernst Jünger, has produced a well-known and heavily researched literary oeuvre. Most scholars see Jünger as a celebrity eyewitness to the German twentieth century. We, however, turn to his *Alltag*. We look for his life on the ground in order to study how he produced, and sought to control, his representations of self. Obviously, Jünger did not produce selfies, but there were other technologies available in the 1920s for self-fashioning.

We therefore start our discussion of this author and decorated World War I soldier with an image, in fact, a photograph.

Published as the frontispiece to the first edition of his famous World War I memoir *In Stahlgewittern* (*Storm of Steel*, 1920), the photograph in Illustration 2.1 shows Jünger in army uniform, a fur-lined greatcoat carefully opened to reveal his decorations, including the *Pour le Mérite* medal at his

Illustration 2.1. Ernst Jünger, Frontispiece to *In Stahlgewittern*, 1920. Courtesy of Deutsches Literaturarchiv Marbach.

throat. Jünger's head is bare, his cap and gloves held casually in his left hand. Much more than just an author photograph, Jünger the writer uses this image to claim a status that also authorizes his right to produce a memoir—that of the *soldier–hero*. Our decision to use an image to launch our analysis helps us to challenge the common misunderstanding that a self-image is the product of an autonomous individual who is also a coherent self. By examining the content and context of the visual image, we can begin to make sense of the contested discourses—between individuals and even within the self—that are in play in any attempt at self-fashioning (Greenblatt 1980).

The figure of the front soldier remained deeply contested in the politically divided Weimar Republic. For instance, the painter and World War I machine gunner Otto Dix graphically illustrated those injured in battle in his famous painting from 1920: *War Cripples*. These shattered bodies were mirrored in the photographs of mutilated veterans that the radical pacifist Ernst Friedrich included in his 1924 antiwar polemic *War against War* (2014: 194–217). As early as 1915, Ernst Ludwig Kirchner had painted *Self-Portrait as Soldier*. The German title, *Selbstbildnis als Soldat*, gestures even more explicitly to the idea of a self-image: he imagined his right arm ending in a bloody stump, effectively putting into doubt his ability to function as either soldier or artist.

By contrast, Jünger used his frontispiece intentionally to embed his own story in a normative category of heroic masculinity and German nationalism. He attached himself to this particular photographic image in an effort to assert the authenticity of his war account. After all, his version of World War I had earned him the medals that decorated his uniform. At least in part he sought to translate his wartime experiences into an authorial voice that might legitimately comment on war, violence, and the nature of modern life. That authorial voice depended on a claim to a coherent self—of being a soldier who, despite his numerous wounds, emerged from the war whole. This choice of photograph rendered that self visible for a reading public.

Any such claim to coherence and ready decipherability, however, depends on a viewer's presumptive ability to solidify the malleability and multiplicity that remained just beneath the surface of the image. Staging the scene for the photo and producing the image of a soldierly self required serious efforts on Jünger's part. The greatcoat opulently frames the decorations marking Jünger's heroic status; yet it seems to derive from a carefully planned wartime envisioning of his postwar needs. In a letter dated 16 August 1918 to his brother Friedrich Georg (DLaM Bestand: Jünger), he asks that he purchase for him "a peacetime uniform with a light gray greatcoat, a blue jacket, and the necessary accessories; also a pair of corduroy riding breeches." This letter suggests the pragmatic preparations for an officer anticipating his continued military service after the end of the war. This future was almost undone by Jünger's nearly fatal wounding later that summer, but his plan nonetheless laid the foundation for an ongoing effort to craft a particular kind of heroic–soldierly self.

Readers can also find a literary realization of this heroic–soldierly self in the revisions of his wartime notebooks that served as the basis for much of his postwar publishing. Investigating this history allows us to see Jünger's self-authorization: how he imagined this particular self-image and then carefully constructed it. The multiple, dramatically altered versions of his *Storm of Steel* underscore how malleable that narrative proved, even in the 1920s and 1930s. *Does this mean that Jünger's image of a soldierly self was inauthentic, perhaps even a fantasy and fake?* We would argue otherwise. Authenticity is itself culturally constructed (Bendix 1997). By consciously creating this sort of self-image, Jünger demonstrated how the imagined self emerges in and out of the material and social practices of everyday life.

Jünger was not alone in this effort. His wife Gretha, among others, participated in creating and maintaining this image. In her account of the founding moment of their relationship, she retrospectively enlivened this static photographic image. In a 1955 memoir, she recalled the first sight of her future husband in 1922, when she was only sixteen years old. She describes how Jünger "appeared in the distance: a swirling military greatcoat, an army cap, a trailing saber. At his open collar, shining from afar, a blue star" (Jeinsen 1955: 167–69). Luminescent with charisma, this celebrity encounter transcended the ordinary act of walking down the streets of Hannover, where Jünger had grown up and to which he returned after the war. With the authority of the eyewitness, Gretha validated Jünger's claim not only that he was a soldier–hero—he was bemedaled after all—but that this identity remained stable over time.

This autobiographical narrative also marked her collaboration in identifying the man she would name in private but also in her memoirs as her "sovereign" (*Gebieter*). This occasionally ironic reference to her place within the household simultaneously emphasized conservative gender, perhaps also sexual, roles and hinted at how she shaped their practice. At her husband's suggestion, however, she concealed her participation in the work of coauthoring her husband's veneer of the heroic soldier by publishing her memoir under her maiden name: von Jeinsen. She also narrated her autobiography by occasionally using opaque pseudonyms for the figures in the story. These choices helped her, in the public realm, to distance herself from Jünger, who remained politically suspect in postwar West Germany. They reflected at least in part his and the publisher's economic calculus; but for the purposes of this chapter, they also reflect the uneven, multifaceted roles played by multiple authors in producing narratives of any self in practice.

Telling stories, and not only about the past, plays a vital role in this sort of effort to fashion a self—a point that we will revisit throughout this book.

Storytelling about or from the perspective of the self involves acts of ventriloquism. We put words about the self in the mouths of others, in our own mouths, and even in the mouths of objects. Behind Jünger's self-portrait, we can catch a glimpse of the lips moving in the background, telling stories about him as a way to imagine that self as he wanted it to be. Our point here is that these versions of self arise historically and in common. Thus any "moment of apparently autonomous self-fashioning" reflects less a freely chosen identity and more a "cultural artifact" that exposes traces of the structures of power and authority within and against which any self-fashioning necessarily operates (Greenblatt 1980: 256). When considering the work of the self on the self, Foucault—in philosopher Paul Veyne's explanation (1993: 7)—compared it to

> one of those pagan temple columns that one occasionally sees reutilized in more recent structures. We can guess at what might emerge from this diagnosis: the self, taking itself as a work to be accomplished, could sustain an ethics that is no longer supported by either tradition or reason; as an artist of itself, the self would enjoy that autonomy that modernity can no longer do without.

In imagining the self as "a new strategic possibility" (idem), Foucault thus rejects any obligation for a self to mediate between society and some sort of morality, however that may be defined. Instead, he implies that the very attempt to realize some version of self contains its own revolutionary potential. This understanding of self-fashioning as a kind of aesthetic project, as "an artist of itself," hints at the ways that such efforts operate within artificial boundaries to demarcate a field of play that nonetheless remains part of the world around it. For this reason, we analyze how the cultural artifact of the self—not as product but as a process that involves a variety of practices—operates within particular historical contexts. The first step in trying to delineate that process is, quite simply, to give it a name.

Naming the Self

What is in a name? For Alexander Morawitz, everything. He was born in Dresden in 1964 and raised by his mother, who supported his early interest in music by paying for piano lessons. Talented enough to be accepted by the world famous Dresden Kreuzchor, at age eleven he entered the Kreuzschule, its boarding school for boys, which sponsored the renowned choir. The school and its choir became his musical and spiritual home, and his experience of its community of teachers and students influenced his coming-of-age and understanding of self. In a 2008 interview, he remembered that the common prayers, meals, and choir rehearsals in the Kreuzschule cultivated a feeling of security and created a safe haven in which to grow up beyond the SED's intrusive reach.

In 1979 as a result of his refusal to fulfill his service in the National People's Army (Nationale Volksarmee, NVA) after graduation, he was expelled from the school and had to return to the polytechnic high school he had previously attended. Deprived of his formal musical instruction, he broke completely with classical music and took his education into his own hands by turning to modern pop and rock music from the United Kingdom and the United States. In December 1987, he renamed himself TJ Big Blaster Electric Boogie and started performing as a hip-hop DJ and rapper in Dresden's youth clubs (Morawitz 2008).

In the context of living in the GDR, Morawitz tried to translate the hypermasculine boasts of an American rap culture into German, but he stumbled at first due to the clumsiness of his English phrase making. Naming himself the *High Emperor of Sound Mystery Key* in a letter to Lutz Schramm in 1989 (Private Collection) did not craft a coherent self or even a comprehensible title. Rather, his invented moniker makes evident the process by which he sought to navigate between German and English and thus between the social and political cultures of Dresden and the Bronx. In choosing this nom de guerre, Morawitz not only declared himself a hip-hop artist but also implicitly modeled how he believed hip-hop artists acted out the promises and pronouncements of their names.

He followed his American role models, whose choice of new names served to "highlight certain characteristics of their bearers." Morawitz explained his logic in a 1988 interview. "JUST-ICE for example attests himself a cool, superior discipline. Hence his name. Or think of AFRICAA BAMBAATAA's Funk Zulu Nation, or of SUN RA's myth of the sun" (Gürtler 1988: 13). For these rappers, their new names do not matter as names per se; rather they use those names to underscore a self that is simultaneously imagined and performed.

Two-thirds of a century after Jünger, but in an act comparable to that author's visual self-presentation, Morawitz sought carefully to author and authorize his self. Like the soldier turned writer, he produced a self-image, but unlike Jünger, he did not use a photograph published as part of his memoir. Rather he employed highly symbolic language to describe what his new self could do.

By calling himself TJ Big Blaster Electric Boogie, Morawitz laid claim to a particular set of abilities. *Electric Boogie* referred to specific breakdancing techniques and thus indicated that he provided the music for this style. *Big Blaster* made clear, in a boasting manner, that he had the necessary equipment for this undertaking. And calling himself *TJ* rather than *DJ* pointed to the well-known fact that he did not have the discs—the vinyl records—at his disposal to cut and mix hip-hop music. He used tapes instead and thus called himself a *tape jockey* (Schmieding 2008).

Morawitz used his name to highlight his skill set as a rap artist and a TJ. "I think all these names are a way of coming closer to oneself," he explained

(Gürtler 1988: 13). In spelling out this belief, Morawitz articulated his understanding of a self to which he, and arguably other hip-hop artists, aspired. This self did not exist in the abstract realm of language but in practical skills that demonstrated talent.

By claiming this new name, Morawitz began to craft the story of TJ Big Blaster Electric Boogie. As we analyze this practice of the self, we can challenge his claims to authenticity, to a coherent story, and, consequently, to a stable self. On the one hand, it makes sense to us, in his case, to use definite articles to refer to *the* self or *this particular* self because he stakes a claim to something that seems fixed; he aspires to something resembling an essentialized type of artistic self. On the other hand, his act of renaming suggests something else, something that only really even functioned on the level of practice. Morawitz effectively admitted that his self was malleable and fluid; after all, he crafted and claimed a new name. Once he had become TJ Big Blaster Electric Boogie, however, he edited his own autobiography to imagine a self out of time, detached from his past.

He went so far as to prohibit people from using his old, given name, which might only be interesting for "the historian." Even though our interest seems to prove him right, we, in our effort to take his *Alltag* seriously, argue that his acts of renaming mattered at the time and not just in retrospect. So we push back against his decision to declare off limits his musical past in the Dresden Kreuzchor or even as a teenage drummer in the rock band Dekadance. It has "nothing to do with my current work," he claimed in 1988—the work by which he sought to define his self (Gürtler 1988: 13). Morawitz cultivated a self by drawing attention away from its historicity. We should not be disturbed by the latter operation: this kind of self-deception is in fact quite common (Bergerson et al. 2011). For Morawitz, the work of distancing himself from the past helped him to imagine and then fashion this new self.

In this naming process, Morawitz also distanced himself from the musical cultures he encountered in the 1980s. He contrasted his work as a hip-hop musician with both traditional German folk music and contemporary rock music in the GDR, both of which he found alien.

> German folk music does not relate to the present, whether rhythmically, textually, or in any other way [... and] rock music made in the DDR [GDR] produces only bad copies of other musical fashions ... I can't identify with the musical culture of this country; with hip-hop, however, I do identify deeply; since December 1987 I have worked with hip-hop as with no other music before. (Gürtler 1988: 12–13)

For Morawitz, identifying with hip-hop meant that he had found a cultural repertoire that empowered him to achieve something new and allowed him to move away from the socialist state in which he lived.

Jump-starting this new biography required that he operate within a larger, transatlantic context. On the one hand, he had to accommodate himself to the socialist rules and regulations that prescribed how he could practice hip-hop culture as a DJ and rapper in the GDR. On the other hand, he strove to break out of the very system that imposed these rules, but he could only do so on an imaginary level and only by simultaneously conforming to the socialist state's regulations. Since Morawitz did not and could not see a place for himself within the GDR's cultural landscape, he responded to this predicament by playing by the rules in order to play with them. He imaginatively relocated himself to a musical facsimile of the Bronx that he deployed in both the official and unofficial performance venues in Saxony and Berlin.

As TJ Big Blaster Electric Boogie, he emulated what he perceived to be hip-hop culture in the Bronx and organized parties, rap workshops, and rap contests. He drew inspiration from the American film *Beat Street*, which the GDR had imported for official release in 1985 (Schmieding 2012). Its account of Bronx teenagers pursuing their hip-hop dreams modeled the transformative possibilities inherent to that cultural practice in ways that he believed might translate to the GDR. Illustration 2.2 suggests the dilemma inherent to this effort. Dressed as he imagined an early 1980s American rapper would and

Illustration 2.2. TJ Big Blaster Electric Boogie Performing during the Rap Contest, Dresden, ca. 1989. Private Archive Nico Raschick—"Here We Come." Courtesy of Nico Raschick.

accompanied by two b-boys in the midst of their breakdance routines, this staging used clothing and lyrics in an effort to mimic New York City even though the performers and audience could have no illusions about the physical limitations of the East German socialist youth club that served as the venue for his parties, contests, and workshops.

As TJ Big Blaster Electric Boogie, Morawitz rapped in English to demonstrate his claim to belong to a cultural community located somewhere beyond the Iron Curtain. By referencing his American role models and thus paying respect to the pioneers of hip-hop, he used lyrical gestures to create an imaginary hip-hop universe. He and his fellow East German hip-hop aficionados declared his style as authentic because it thus related his performance practices to the Bronx—the birthplace of hip-hop. His claim to the status of an authentic hip-hop artist fit into a global practice in which rappers modeled their performances on their Bronx idols in order to authenticate their practice of hip-hop (Klein and Friedrich 2003: 8–11). Nonetheless the location within which he enacted this self remained distinctive: he carved out an alternate space within the *Alltag* of the GDR, simultaneously with and against its political, social, and cultural idiosyncrasies, in order to perform whom he wished to be.

As Illustration 2.3 shows, Morawitz acted out his new name in an imaginary space—somewhere between the GDR and New York City—that he created along with a community of East German hip-hoppers. This

Illustration 2.3. B-Boys Posing in the Imaginary Bronx, Dessau, ca. 1987. Private Archive Nico Raschick—"Here We Come".

experience put him in a position to narrate his life in Dresden in terms of Bronx hip-hop culture and to use its vocabulary to voice his grievances with East German socialism. At the same time, these performances present us with the opportunity to explore Morawitz's pursuit of self in terms of a process moving through a time and place that must be both imagined and named.

"The self is a perspective," historian Lynn Hunt argues, "and depends on continuous reactivation of memories of the past and memories of plans and projects for the possible future—in other words, a historical or narrative sense" (2014: 1581). Although Morawitz could declare himself TJ Big Blaster Electric Boogie and imagine himself in the Bronx, he remained in Dresden and in the GDR. His experiences effectively capture the tension described by Hunt in which a "sense of self emerges from the mind's interpretation of the body's interaction in the world." Even if this way of imagining an "embodied self" proves unstable (ibid.: 1582), its narrative claims open for reinterpretation, it nonetheless offers up something more than mere language. Even liminal spaces are located somewhere.

Locating the Self

Jünger moved his family to Berlin in June 1927 at least in part to play the role of revolutionary, that is, in an attempt to transform the world into an imagined alternative. He hoped to rally a circle of followers to a vision of national renewal that might be realized by the joint efforts of an invigorated German youth and the returning generation of front soldiers. Of course, Jünger imagined himself to be that generation's authentic representative and authoritative voice. As early as the first edition of his war memoir, he claimed this status by introducing the image of the soldier returned from war, whole and decorated. To the extent that scholars have paid much attention to Jünger's six years in the German capital (1927–1933), it has been as part of a focus on his writing during the Weimar Republic.

At least since German–Jewish critic Walter Benjamin denounced a 1930 book edited by Jünger as articulating "theories of German fascism" (1979), debates about Jünger's character have concentrated on assessing the nature of his prose. But obsessing over the modernist, postmodernist, or fascist character of Jünger's literary style risks extracting Jünger from the historical settings in which he placed himself, reducing debates about Jünger's cultural and political significance to a textual realm unconnected to any particular place. Taking a closer look at these locations allows us to revisit the processes of self-authorization with which he, like Morawitz in the GDR, sought to navigate his interactions with the world.

In June 1927, Jünger moved from Leipzig to Berlin along with his wife Gretha and his young son Ernst, junior, or Ernstel. Over the course of more than six years, the family moved back and forth across the German capital from Schöneberg to Friedrichshain, Moabit to Steglitz. In these four apartments, they experienced many of the urban flavors that comprised the German capital, from gritty working-class neighborhood in the city's eastern industrial areas to tree-lined sanctums of the suburban bourgeoisie. Jünger was part of this multifaceted Berlin; and while it may be comforting to exclude Jünger from a city better known for its left-wing politics and avant-garde culture, locating Jünger in Weimar Berlin allows us to highlight his self-formulation as a process, regardless of what identity we attempt to assign him.

As Jünger later recounted, the 1920s remained a period in which he was still working through his World War I traumas. He used this fact to explain their intense presence in almost all of his writing at the time, even when that writing ostensibly addressed other subjects. Despite the street violence that marked the interwar period in the city and a rhetoric that imagined it as a political battleground, Berlin was never a war front like that he had experienced in France and Belgium. Nonetheless, his World War I experiences comprised important elements of the process with which he explained his exploration of the city, that is, how he located himself in Berlin. This act of locating also involved constructing a narrative, of his wartime past certainly but also as an articulation of a point of view within his present.

His first return to the site of his wartime heroics occurred at a distance, from the air. In the spring of 1927, in other words, just before he moved to Berlin, Jünger flew to Paris.

> For the first time and with mixed feelings, I saw the front again. For a moment, the searing residue of the explosion that drifts up just before an attack seemed to be passing by, but all of this is too close to use, too confusing and the more anonymous indifference of myth is still too far away. (1979: 9.117–18)

He goes on to explain his lack of real interest in returning to those wartime sites by suggesting that, like the Roman Forum, they are being preserved for American tourists. The tour guides will then reduce these particular places "where we lived more decisively than just in time and space" to the formulaic "here you can see ..." (in English in the original). In a similar vein, Jünger explains his hatred of all war photographs, which seek to give "an unseemly currency" to the events of that time. Instead, he suggests that he would prefer that the ruins of the battlefield vanish into lonely forests and, like the tales of the Nibelungen, live on only in distant sagas of "eternal fruitfulness" (idem). As we read earlier, Foucault offers an alternative take on this sort of iconic ruin, celebrating the work of repurposing them into "modern" structures. In that context, the past and present are bound not by an idea or a moral declaration but by the work of self-fashioning, which we might also imagine as self-locating in both time and place.

Of course, Jünger's war and the war more generally never retreated comfortably into the mythology he claimed to have desired. Within two years, he edited a volume of war photographs and contributed an essay, "War and Photography," that celebrated photographs for preserving "the image of those ravaged landscapes which the world of peace has long since reappropriated" (Jünger 1993: 24–26). While at least some portion of his motivation to publish this volume may have been to tap into the money-making opportunities in the war picture book genre, this book, along with the collection of essays he edited that same year, *War and the Warrior* (1930), reflected the extent to which Jünger's wartime past remained part of how he navigated his urban present.

As he wandered about the city of Berlin, he necessarily encountered, but seems not to have reflected on, the visible and very human remains of that war in the midst of the city and its culture. By attempting to call to mind the veterans whose bodies publicly bore the scars of wartime violence, we can recognize how Jünger located his war stories elsewhere and, most importantly, how it did not depend on interacting with those figures and their explicit marks of the past war.

The best source to trace Jünger's process of staking out a place in the city is his 1929 book *The Adventurous Heart* (1979). This book is at once an imaginative work that moves between an occasionally nightmarish dreamscape and a narrative recounting of Jünger's acts of urban exploration. His walks around the city—which he subsequently frames in terms of a relationship between day and night, waking and dreaming—anchor many of the twenty-five text sequences in his book. He then tries to integrate these experiences of the urban *Alltag* into a fantasy of war—the arena that still served as the foundational source of his authorial power, even when he extracted it from its particular 1914 to the 1918 context. "But what held in the fiery dream landscapes of war," he insists, "is not dead in the alertness [*Wachheit*] of modern life" (1979: 9.67, 148).

Strolling through the streets of Berlin, he reimagined the city as an apocalyptic landscape. He described this feeling like opening the throttle of an airplane straining to leave the ground or riding an express train through an industrial landscape punctuated by "caps of fire" that "tear the darkness." This "very modern feeling" encapsulated, he claimed, production and destruction simultaneously: "O, you steel snake of knowledge—you, whom we must enchant if you are not to strangle us" (1979: 9.154; Bullock 1992: 133–34). By rejecting reason and appealing for the return of enchantment, he thus reinterprets the modern urban setting as a site for individual experience and feeling.

In the next section of *Adventurous Heart*, he moves from the metaphoric landscape of apocalypse to a more mundane postwar setting in which veterans exchange war stories. He describes how, over the past couple of years, he has been spending a great deal of time with pilots. For him, they represent a particularly positive "intensified worker- and soldierliness, stamped into a good metal." They also enthrall him with their discussions of dogfights during the last years of World War I. In their detailed images and war stories, Jünger comes to realize that a battle in and for civilization does not depend on "nerves of steel" but a "high degree of sensitivity" (1979: 9.154–5).

He is in effect talking about himself through these encounters, but it is now his sensitivity to the industrial resonance encountered on his nighttime stroll around Berlin that offers a path to connect to the forms and images of imagined air sorties, past and future. Here Jünger was expanding the list of masculine qualities that authorize soldierliness and authorship; and like many other contemporaries, he was exploring new ways to integrate the extraordinary into the ordinary of the urban *Alltag*. More generally, this blurring of past, present, and future parallels Morawitz's imaginative effort to place himself somewhere between Dresden and the Bronx. As such, it also reflects Hunt's understanding of how individuals articulate their self in the interplay of mind and body in relation to the world.

Jünger's narrative move not only breaks the spatial logic of the war, fought on a front many miles from Berlin but also disrupts any straightforward chronology of his life, as he retroactively used those same war experiences to justify and legitimate his authority in the present. No matter that this self-presentation depends on a new formula: here he claims an alternative war fantasy as the foundation for his authorship instead of the heroic soldier presented in the 1920 frontispiece. Rather than imagining himself as a soldier engaged in a battle, this multilayered narrative retrospectively stakes out for Jünger the status of *detached observer* on the edge of the century's cataclysms.

In his metropolitan *Alltag*, Jünger found opportunities to adopt and adapt his soldierly self-image to his changing needs, whether as would-be revolutionary, connoisseur of nighttime Berlin, or detached observer of urban life. The defining characteristics of Jünger's self lay ultimately in its fluid, unstable, and multiple nature—a plastic expression constantly reworked in relation to an equally dynamic ground—and its interplay with a constantly changing set of observers.

Sharing the Self

Following the publication of his *Storm of Steel* in 1920, Jünger never lacked for an audience. On one level, not surprisingly for an author, it consisted of tens of thousands of readers. His books never sold on the scale of Erich Maria Remarque's runaway 1929 bestseller, *All Quiet on the Western Front*—the famous antiwar novel that was also made into an acclaimed film. But Jünger's books resonated with a broad public that included prominent figures as diverse as Remarque himself, who reviewed *Storm of Steel*, and Adolf Hitler, who wrote Jünger a laudatory letter in 1926. Jünger also addressed an audience more intimately familiar with his experiences and his practices, not just as witnesses or even coauthors to his rhetorical and literary performances but as coparticipants. Here Jünger was doing something quite similar to Morawitz: formulating a self by staging it. Jünger needed the help of his multiple audiences to make it convincing, just as Morawitz needed the help of his rap audiences to authenticate his hybrid performance of GDR hip-hop culture.

A more explicit but also more public staging of Jünger as imagined front soldier underscores the extent to which that self-presentation needed validation from collaborative participants. Edmund Schultz was one of the young men who entered into Jünger's circle in Berlin. Schultz had read Jünger's books and introduced himself after recognizing the author in the subway.

Schultz utilized his chance encounter with the celebrity Jünger to initiate a relationship that subsequently unfolded in both private and public. In a letter dated 19 April 1929 (DLaM Bestand: Jünger), Schultz described a night that began at a public lecture on Remarque's book but ended with a public proclamation of Jünger's alternative narrative of World War I. Schultz, Jünger's brother Friedrich Georg, and the jurist and writer Friedrich Hielscher had gone to hear the lecture and discussion, and the opening presentations left them despairing. Suddenly, an unidentified man rushed the stage and "sounded [Jünger's] name. The opposition awoke as if hit by a bolt of electricity. Thunderous applause. What his speech lacked in depth was made up for in fire and force. And that's something more, in the end."

The man identified himself as an *altes Frontschwein*: literally an *old front pig*, referring to himself in a self-ironizing way as a veteran of the Great War. For Jünger's friends, this front soldier gave voice to Jünger's image as he might have imagined it in literary terms. This image quite literally reached the stage as a counterargument to Remarque's version of the war, which had been the subject of the evening's educational discussion. As in the case of Morawitz, we see how the self can be validated through public performance, but at least Morawitz was present at the performance in order to take the leading role. Jünger was in Italy during this incident. Individuals can be both the subjects and the objects of such performances; the audience can choose how, and whether, to interact with them regardless of whether they are present or absent. As the unruly *Frontschwein* showed, an author's public image remains open to alternative performances and potentially divergent interpretations, all of which operate beyond the author's control.

Far from posing a threat to the self, this implicit loss of control proves necessary for people like Jünger and Morawitz as they manage the constant unraveling and reweaving of self. For these members of Jünger's circle, the battle over Jünger's asserted self took place both in his absence and in the midst of a lengthy evening of drinking. This loss of control fit comfortably into the kind of ecstatic experience that accompanies dance parties, celebrity sightings, and self-performances of all sorts. Yet it seems to us that this loss of self-control—whether through excessive alcohol consumption or in the course of modern experiences in general—paralleled Jünger's own loss of control over his self. For his self-image was now being publicly invoked in his absence and seemed to have taken on a life of its own. As we listen in with Jünger's circle, the speaking of his name in public underscores the reality that that self cannot but slip away. Any attempt at self-authorization must remain a collaborative and therefore a contested undertaking and, in the end, a transitory phenomenon.

Such transitory experiences manifest themselves particularly in ritual practices, which constitute a vital undercurrent to everyday life (Steege et al. 2008). Although rituals may be imagined as transformative performances, their significance lies not just as a transitory passage to something new but also as something "betwixt and between" (Turner 1969, 1986) that matters in its own right. This interstitial location sustains the paradoxical character of the self that needs stability and at the same time calls for constant revision. Such a liminal state accounts for a process that disrupts and yet is also part of the phenomenal flow of everyday life. It is the ritual performance of the self that captures this duality of being at once embedded within the ordinary and yet simultaneously part of or marked as something quite extraordinary. In all senses of ritual performance—from religious initiations to cultural events and from quotidian acts to symbolic gestures—what emerges is the constantly changing experience of the modern *Alltag*.

In the case of Morawitz, the entanglement of collaborating, contesting, and being contested helps explain his striving for authenticity in the course of both authoring and authorizing the self. He felt that he could only express his real self as the hip-hop artist TJ Big Blaster Electric Boogie—hence the new name and the effort to conjure up the Bronx. But in his interactions with both of his audiences, the socialist cultural authorities as well as the hip-hop scene, the kind of authenticity that he was looking for remained constantly under threat.

While he had to collaborate with representatives of the regime in order to have a stage from which to voice his grievances with that state, it was in his collaboration with the hip-hop scene that he looked for validation of that criticism. Although he sought to educate his hip-hop collaborators in the terms and even the language with which he hoped they would evaluate his critiques of the GDR regime, that audience often approached his performance with very different expectations: as a good party and not a protest, for example.

Thus, in every performance, he was caught between these two audiences and his understanding of how best to speak to them.

In his communication with the cultural functionaries of the GDR, Morawitz retained his old name. In fact, despite his public criticism of socialist popular culture, he conformed to the rules and regulations imposed on the practice of hip-hop. Accepting the fact that he needed to collaborate in order to perform, he filed for a license, reproduced in Illustration 2.4, and underwent an official rating as an *Unterhaltungskünstler*, or artist of light entertainment. For the socialist cultural authorities, this license served as a measure to control artists and their practices.

Introduced in the early 1970s under the new and—at least toward the outside—more liberal head of state Erich Honecker, this license was part of a

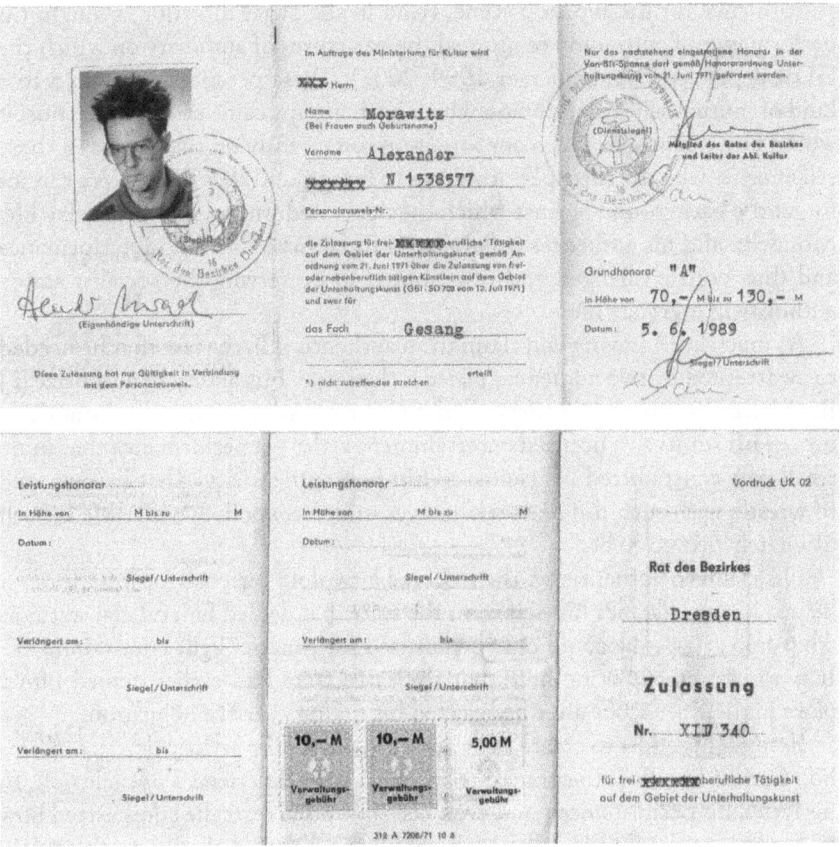

Illustration 2.4. The Performance License of Alexander Morawitz from 1989. Front and back. Private Archive of Alexander Morawitz. Photo: Leonard Schmieding.

hegemonic strategy to secure artists' loyalty by rewarding them not only with the official permit to perform but also with material incentives (Ohse 2003: 347–56). Morawitz saw through this "repressive tolerance" (Ohse 2003: 304), however, and used it against the state and its claims to authority. Since he did not "fit neatly into any existing artistic category," he agreed to the category of "voice," a designation that remained open to his interpretation. While it proved difficult for him and his peers to obtain licenses in hip-hop, their tactic of filing for a license as a "folk art collective" (Gürtler 1988: 12–13) gave them the unique opportunity to express their loyalty on paper and practice hip-hop as they wanted.

It was on the basis of this permit that Morawitz organized all of his hip-hop parties as TJ Big Blaster Electric Boogie. In an almost classic example of what historian Alf Lüdtke termed *Eigensinn*, his conformist performance for the audience of cultural functionaries facilitated his rather nonconformist performance for the hip-hop scene. Read in the other direction, though, his performance of autonomy reinforced the structures of authority on which the GDR depended (Lindenberger 1999, 2007). These practices amounted to a kind of mutual self-deception on which both groups came to depend. Thus, it would be a mistake to focus our attention too intently on the figures in these self-images, who use their performances to foreground themselves. We cannot forget the background against which they operated. In the same everyday life, Morawitz and his audiences collaborated to fabricate his self in performance and thus both challenged and contributed to preserving the socialist state's authority in everyday life.

As much as Morawitz laid claim to an authentic self, the fact that he needed to be accepted by two audiences posed a challenge. His ability to authorize TJ Big Blaster Electric Boogie depended on his success in convincing the authorities of his status as a licensed entertainment artist—a performance that in no small part contradicted his claims to hip-hop authenticity. That he managed to wrestle with such different self-images underscores how malleable his self ultimately proved to be.

His claim to authenticity, then, served a twofold purpose for him. First, it helped him to distance himself from the state that denied him official status as a hip-hop artist—he could only be licensed for generic "light entertainment." It is worth remembering here that the same state had earlier denied him a place in the Kreuzchor after he rejected his military service obligation.

Second, his effort to create a community around the artistic practice of hip-hop framed his effort to come to terms with both experiences of exclusion. In his lyrics, his performances, and even his conceptual texts, he emphasized how important he deemed it to be authentic—and he used that term to explain his desire to be validated by an audience that not only appreciated but also practiced this self-promoted authenticity: the hip-hop scene.

As an aspiring hip-hop artist, Morawitz devoted time and training to compose his lyrics and music. Through his connections in the underground culture of Dresden-Neustadt, he was able to receive a handful of vinyl records by American rap artists, which he copied onto tape. Having preserved these rare material artifacts, he could work with the copies to make his own mixes without damaging the originals, even though that decision meant he could only aspire to be a TJ and not an authentic DJ. He intensely studied the English-language lyrics on the records' covers to learn what his idols had to say in their critiques of American society; he then transposed their topics, motives, and expressions into his own criticism of socialism.

He was concerned about the authenticity of his English lyrics, so he had them checked by two native Britons who worked as English teachers for the Technical University of Dresden. Of course, his self-styled experts were themselves far removed from the urban American idiom and culture he hoped to channel. He rapped in English because German was, in his opinion, "disgusting" and "stupid" and at the same time "too soft" to convey his message (Gürtler 1988: 12–13)—even as he remained constrained by his German location.

Since most of his peers in the GDR did not know English well enough to write their own texts, many of them just copied lines from American rappers they admired. Morawitz critiqued this practice vigorously. In a call for entries for a rap workshop in January 1989, he had his coorganizer Peter Figas provide the following advice to participants: "All lyrics have to be written yourself. Please write down all texts, so we can work on them during the workshop; important are content and its presentation—the music has to be original, if possible (you may use playback, but only in parts)" (Private Collection Sandro Bartels: no pagination). In a similar way, he advised rapper SBJ from Arnstadt in Thuringia to produce original texts in order to become what he imagined to be an authentic artist. In a letter concerning the production of a rap album, he wrote in 1989:

> With regard to your plans to write texts, I strongly advise against using clichés and thus taking the easy way out. Nothing is worse than stealing other people's lines. It is better to make grammatical mistakes, better to use only a limited vocabulary, as long as you have texts that you wrote yourself. (Idem)

Here we see how he used his interaction with the hip-hop scene in the GDR to communicate his understanding of the social and political context in which he worked. He challenged the mere copying of lyrics and encouraged his fellow rappers to be original, to find their own voice. Offering workshops and contests, he reached out to them to collaborate with him in the community of hip-hop.

Morawitz used his performances to deliver the same message—and more, as he combined his call for authenticity with his criticism of the socialist state.

His 1988 rap "Time to Fite" (Private Collection Lutz Schramm) features his observations of everyday life, the problems that emerge there between himself and others, and his solution for them as a mastermind of hip-hop. He begins by listing the reasons his fellow GDR citizens fail to comprehend his performance as DJ and rapper. "People are astonished about the things we do/ because it doesn't fit their fashion scheme." He boasts that "our new culture which we call rap" is "the new soulmusic: don't talk any shit!" You "had better belong to my posse" (idem).

This statement serves as a warning and an invitation at the same time. Musicians who play like "craftsmen" and "dead musician-computers" as well as people who believe in Goethe and the "nonsense of cultural heritage" have excluded themselves from his group, since they are not only old but also follow the rules and regulations of the socialist regime. Morawitz locates his community in opposition to the "old farts and bureaucrats of the music scene" (idem).

In his performance as TJ Big Blaster Electric Boogie, Morawitz also invites the people of his generation to stay and join the group at the same time as their shared experience of the performance itself constitutes that group. He wants to "overcome the old structures" because, as he raps, "we don't believe in them." Here he has posited a *we* for the audience that unites them with him in an affective relationship mediated by musical performance. "On the stage," he declares, "no prison! We are free." So "do it in your life; do it like we do" (idem). In this style of music, the public performance of the self is central to the experience of community. Morawitz reiterated the advice he had given to his fellow rappers earlier. In order to become free, he rapped, one had to be authentic:

> Take the chance to be the one you really are …
> You have to be ready to do the things you want to do,
> Work until you're perfect for yourself …
> Don't imitate. (Idem)

The role Morawitz devised for TJ Big Blaster Electric Boogie was to function as the organizer and mentor of Dresden's hip-hop community—the charismatic, visionary leader who called for rebellion in connection with good beats and authentic lyrics. In this ongoing exchange, Morawitz collaborated with a wide range of participants who he involved in authoring and authorizing what he imagined would be an authentic self. But whatever success he achieved in realizing any version of self came only in the course of interactive processes within which he remained but one participant.

In an act that underscored the dubious nature of any assertion of authenticity, Jünger did more than just allow a late Weimar expression of self to slip away. He consciously erased its traces. At some point following a police search of his Steglitz apartment in May 1933—perhaps in 1934—Jünger destroyed his diaries from the fourteen years before. He remained relatively confident in the inoculating power of his World War I record, exemplified by the *Pour le Mérite* he received in September 1918. Still, he remained nervous about the personal danger posed by the Nazi seizure of power. In 1970, Jünger expressed regret at the loss of his Weimar era journals as a primary source for his own experience: "It is not the facts I lack; it is the first version of the impression. After all, in the facts we only have the seashell—not the protoplasmatic movement of the grey being that constructs it far from all beauty and logic" (1978: 11.121–22).

Like Morawitz, Jünger fantasized about laying claim to some sort of fundamentally authentic experience. He longed to recapture this ego document as a way to tap into the imaginings, the practices, and the performances that facilitated his self-expression and self-fashioning. While this longing reflects at least in part a desire to have more material to revise into a published form, it also illustrates how any claim to authenticity confronts the spatial and temporal ruptures that comprise the everyday. All claims to an authentic self thus prove illusory.

Conclusion

In this chapter we have tried to draw out the implications of the stories that two artist–activists told about their place in the world. Jünger and Morawitz attempted to author and authorize a self but faced a series of ruptures in their own life stories: gaps in the narrative, holes in the image, breakdowns of coherence. Some were violent and destructive, like trench warfare; all were personal and disruptive.

They were not dissimilar to the challenges faced by Dieter—the protagonist of our first chapter—in terms of the Wende; but they also share commonalities with many other modern Germans in a wide range of situations over the course of the twentieth century. So it makes sense to use the stories of ruptures as a point of analytic entry into the modern German *Alltag*. Indeed, modern Germans played a significant role in thinking about the everyday in terms of its ruptures—a topic we will explore in more detail in the next chapter. Beginning with the self helps us to cultivate a language that we can also apply in these seemingly larger analytical cases. But even at this smallest and most interior scale, the ruptures and incoherence are apparent, and our recognition of when and how these accounts break down push us to theorize the everyday as a way to address the gaps that are produced in its midst. The self remains an attempt that can never be fully realized.

The self emerges in the course of efforts to make sense of those experiences, a process which takes place not on one's own but among others. Everyday lives are all constituted socially. And given the dynamic nature of microsocial interactions, those meanings change continuously, not least to the degree that others contest them. It will thus not come as a surprise to discover in the subsequent chapters—as we pursue the practices of self in other situations—how elusive self proved for modern Germans, whether they sought it among celebrities in a modern city, negotiated its claims as a member of a family in the Weimar Republic, or navigated the passage from past to present as a visitor to a museum.

The effort to decipher our relationship to a German *Alltag*, as readers and scholars, thus demands that we account for the limits to any one individual's understanding and underscore the need for collaboration in the process of making sense of our world. Here we are reminded of the selfie stick: a telescoping device that allows people to take selfies on their own from a distance, without needing to ask a passerby to help them take the shot, and seemingly more completely under their individual control. For, even this self-image—taken in social situations, using socially produced goods, transmitted in social media, and embedded in social norms—is never the autonomous work of a sole author.

Leonard Schmieding and Paul Steege

CHAPTER 3

Interpersonal Relationships

> *One only experiences his fellowman as he does the other objects of his environment—in a character of "sameness." He sees the movements of his fellowman as he sees the movement of the stars; he hears his fellowman speak just as he hears the roll of thunder. And others know as little of his own movements and thought ... as they know anything substantial of the sun or the clouds.*
> —Friedrich Adler, "Friedrich Engels and Natural Science," 1906–07

Born in 1874 to a Lutheran father and Jewish mother, Max Scheler was a German thinker who could have appeared in the previous chapter alongside Ernst Jünger and TJ Big Blaster Electric Boogie as an example of the performative aspect of the self. Scheler liked playing roles, as is evident in Illustration 3.1, a photo of Scheler dressed up for motoring. He had a magnetic personality and has been described as a flamboyant showman who could move a crowd like Girolamo Savonarola (Staude 1967: 25, 27), the charismatic and unruly Dominican friar of Renaissance Italy.

Scheler's role-playing was sometimes scandalous and included sexual escapades, extramarital affairs, and publicly contested divorces. By his own admission, "I seem to myself like a naughty child who runs again and again to a precipice and whom God, in his infinite mercy, brings back each time just before he falls into the abyss" (Staude 1967: 140). This behavior often caused Scheler problems in the universities where he sought to make a career, and his professional life was chaotic.

In his intellectual work, Scheler explored, among other things, the nature of interpersonal relationships. He thought of himself as searching for an "essence" of human thinking but realized this essence had to be anchored historically and sociologically in experience (Scheler 1963: 15). Our interest for now is not in the essence he found—we will return to it at the end of the chapter—but in how and where Scheler worked: he did most of his research, thinking, and writing while seated in busy cafes and restaurants.

In part, this choice was a matter of expedience during those times that he found himself excluded from university posts. For example, in 1911, when his soon-to-be first ex-wife took her case to the newspapers and Scheler lost his position in Munich, he moved in with a friend in Göttingen; since Scheler

56 :~ *Ruptures in the Everyday*

Illustration 3.1. Max Scheler in Driving Costume, with Maria Scheler and Dr Rolf Hoffmann. Courtesy of Bayerische Staatsbibliothek München, München/Ana 315.F.I.2.h.

had no official place at the university there, the friend rented a hall in a café, where Scheler gave private lectures. But this was also Scheler's preferred environment in which to work. As John Raphael Staude points out, "Restless in the quiet of a library or study, he preferred the bustle of chattering people and the clink of glasses, even for his most serious writing" (1967: 27). Scheler chose the semipublic spaces of urban modernity, with its conflicts and complexities, rather than withdrawing from it into the world of abstraction in the interests of clarity and control.

For several reasons, this chapter reads a little differently from the last. We want to draw the reader's attention to the microsocial interactions between the self and others; but to do so, we need more precise concepts that can better describe the nature and consequences of these interpersonal relationships. This kind of theorizing is necessary for a book about ruptures in the everyday: people often internalize everyday categories, making them seem as if they were a natural part of modern existence, because they make the course of our social lives smoother. We tacitly adopt, and also adapt, rules and procedures designed to manage masses precisely because those are the conditions of our modern existence. Moreover, we do not usually look critically at these norms or the underlying dynamics they disguise, which leaves much about everyday life implicit. Yet that also leaves much of everyday life relatively unexamined.

As the contemporary German thinker Hans-Georg Soeffner describes it, "in a world where everything is self-evident" (2004: 25), one moves about in a sphere of unproven possibilities. For Soeffner, the given *Alltagswelt*, or everyday world, was a frame for experience in which contexts of meaning are both restricted and marked by a specific cognitive style. In that way of thinking, doubts, novelty, and the unusual are reduced to what already is familiar. It is this act of comprehending disruptive experiences in terms of customary practices and an existing stock of knowledge—that is, applying those experiences to so-called common sense—that renders them ordinary. Note however that, in this situation, what we accept as self-evidently normal in the everyday is not just given but constructed: it is the product of a particular way of apprehending the world. Indeed, the everyday construction of the ordinary is reinforced through repetition of accepted patterns and rituals for interaction that obviate the need for decisions.

By contrast, we try to approach the everyday lives of modern Germans more critically by making explicit the acts of perception and interpretation, the role of the investigator, and the practices of the investigative community. We turn to a set of German thinkers from the late nineteenth and early twentieth centuries, which is to say to the period in which Germans were first coming to terms with the modern *Alltag* itself. This intellectual tradition for the concept of *Alltag* is less familiar to some German scholars who work in cultural studies and the history of everyday life; it is based on the work of philosophers, political scientists, and sociologists rather than historians. Moreover, it would be a mistake to explore their ideas solely through theoretical abstraction when it is the experiences of everyday life—and particularly its ruptures—that stand at the heart of this book.

This chapter can therefore be read as an intellectual history of interpersonal relationships as well as an everyday study of intellectuals—like Scheler—whose experience of urban modernity presented both the challenge and the inspiration for their concepts. This integrative approach will follow that of the thinkers we are studying. It is *phenomenological* in that our reflecting begins with experience itself. Like the figures we study, we try to think from within the everyday first rather than trying immediately to get outside it. We try to rely on critical intuition before coming to concepts and abstract methods. At the same time, this chapter is explicitly *sociological*. We widen the focus of our attention from practices of self-fashioning to include the interactions between self and others.

As we discussed in the first chapter, the everyday in colloquial terms evokes all that is routine, normal, unremarkable, mundane, *ordinary*. In contrast to the ordinary, the *extraordinary* implies what is unusual, exciting, strongly felt, remarkable. The sociologist Max Weber, writing in early twentieth-century Heidelberg, captured the distinction in his native German language. He contrasted the words *alltäglich* and *ausseralltäglich*, which we translate as *everyday* and *outside the everyday*. Such distinctions allow us to communicate clearly by including certain meanings and excluding others; and this kind of clarity is useful for both everyday and scholarly communication. Yet we are nervous about defining the everyday in terms of a dichotomy, as it does not reflect accurately what happens on the ground, for the precise borders and relationship between these categories change with each situation. And in many of the uses we uncovered, the ordinary and the extraordinary were not mutually exclusive after all.

We prefer to define the everyday in terms of the plasticity we experience in the everyday, whereby its forms and categories resist anchoring in any firm definitions. Such an approach asks us to pay attention to the terrain that these figures navigated, the people they encountered, and how those moments can become sites for the extra/ordinary. To derive our concepts, we investigate two particular kinds of situations: people traversing the streets of a metropolis and people sitting in a darkened cinema. We will observe how German thinkers experienced and interpreted these encounters, mapping the extra/ordinary onto human experience.

In the German language, the word *experience* itself illustrates the difficulties of negotiating modern everyday life. As with the extra/ordinary, German thinkers have distinguished between two kinds of experiences that constitute the German *Alltag*: they use *Erfahrung* to refer to an experience that shapes and fits into the everyday flow of events and *Erlebnis* to refer to an experience of a rupture in that flow. It would be a mistake to treat these categories in isolation. For many of our informants, the challenge, and the shock, lay in integrating these two forms of experience. Here then is a subtle yet powerful form of rupture understood as an underlying element of everyday lives—something that is so common to modern experience, and so normalized over the course of the twentieth century, that its existential character can be easily overlooked.

We will still pay attention to other words and what they can reveal to us. The word *ordinary*, for instance, derives from the Latin *ordinarius* meaning *in the usual order*. It refers to the order of ordinal numbers, like first, second, third, and so on. This mathematical quality of ordering makes itself known in interpersonal encounters situated among the objects and beings in space and in events situated in the flow of time. We make sense of the everyday through microsocial interactions, in terms of experiences embedded in time and space, and in terms of stories with their own temporalities. To be sure, meaning and significance also arise through disruptions of this flow when something extraordinary occurs, is noted, and is remembered, just as one kind of interpersonal relationship can draw our attention to other kinds that it is not. We make sense of the everyday not only in terms of what fits into that flow of apperception and storytelling but also in terms of what disrupts it.

Investigating the everyday therefore demands both establishing the order of the ordinary and looking for its disruption in the extraordinary. It involves paying close attention to experience, but experience understood richly as both *Erfahrung* and *Erlebnis*. This empirical reality is a challenge. The everyday appears to us as text and context, fixed and dynamic; and it responds to our efforts to apprehend it. We respond to that complexity in much the same way that modern Germans did. We survey the everyday in order to act on it and interact in it.

The Social Question

Change can reveal the presence of the extra/ordinary in the everyday, and a major transformation marks the beginning of awareness and attention to the everyday among modern German scholars. During the nineteenth century, German-speaking Central Europe, along with other regions, rapidly and radically urbanized. Urbanity became one of the defining features of the *Alltag* in modern Germany. Note how different this situation is to that of Dieter in the first chapter, who was living in the rural margin of contemporary Germany. This variability presents one of the challenges for working through the *Alltag* critically.

The *Alltag* was urban for most Germans by the turn of the twentieth century. In 1800, 85 percent of the German population lived in small towns and villages. By 1900, only 40 percent still lived in rural areas. Berlin stood at the pinnacle of this rapid urbanization: by the 1880s, Berlin's population had reached the million mark; by 1910, the city and its suburbs housed three million people (König 2000: 208; Levinger 2000: 21). Although a colossus, Berlin was not unique: forty-eight cities in Germany at the time had a population of over 100,000—the number that defined a *Großstadt*, or metropolis, to contemporaries—and housed 21 percent of the German population (Hübner and Moegelin 1910: iv; König 2000: 208; Ross 2008: 13). This fundamental shift in the social organization of space marked a major rupture in the German *Alltag*.

As the urban world increased in its demographic and technological complexity, the *Alltag* became a conscious problem for German scholars, intellectuals, and artists from across the humanities and social sciences (*Geisteswissenschaften*), who all began to explore the problem of this new urban human condition. Wilhelm Dilthey formulated the phenomenological aspect of the term *Erlebnis* in 1883 (1959: 94, 159, 345 n.19) as that immediacy of personal experience in which intentions are known directly with and among others. Phenomenological philosophers like Franz Brentano (1973: 88–94) and Edmund Husserl (1970: 552–56) examined lived experience with an eye for comprehending how the humane and the inhumane become normed within the new societal structure.

Modern poets, writers, and filmmakers studied *Erlebnis* in terms of gesture, verbal expression, and even silence within an interpersonal encounter in the hopes of building a society that could be more truly a community of cooperating individuals. Many of the great German writers of the day—Theodor Fontane, Thomas Mann, and Franz Kafka—captured with phenomenological acuity the alienation of modern society as well as moments of community (Blum 2011). They all tried to make sense of what this new urban spatial organization meant for interpersonal relationships. Old patterns of association no longer worked in the new contexts; and while some people responded to this new urbanity with a sense of liberation from traditional constraints, others responded with feelings of increased isolation and even alienation.

One of the first, and still one of the most influential, efforts to make sense of the rupture of urbanization was made by Ferdinand Tönnies with his book, *Gemeinschaft und Gesellschaft*, translated into English as *Community and Society*. Born into a farming family in Schleswig in the far north of Germany, he was living in Hamburg by the time he published this book in 1887. In this landmark study (1926: 247–52), he raised one of the central issues about everyday life in modern Germany: *how can one find community within society?* Generally known to Germans in the pre–World War I era as the *social question*, scholars and intellectuals of many varieties were concerned with the causes and amelioration of social alienation.

Prior to Tönnies, *Gemeinschaft* and *Gesellschaft* were used interchangeably, but he gave the terms more precise meanings. Tönnies defined the first term, *community*, as an association based on mutual concerns and values along with relationships that afforded sympathetic cooperation. He assumed that rural communities have stronger, more organic, and empathic interpersonal connections than a modern society. By contrast, he used the second, *society*, to refer to the public world: impersonal in its laws and normative in its modes of interpersonal association (1926: 247–48).

In a factory, for instance, workers operate under standardized conditions: their wages are set regardless of their personalities, there are fixed rules of when and how long to work, and the quality of their work is judged by people who do not know them personally. Tönnies implied that, as the population moved from small towns and villages to the urban areas of employment, communal relationships had become increasingly impoverished. In urban society in particular, people have little prior or ongoing association, and without a thick web of social bonds, ordinary Germans experienced alienation. To find community within society required establishing new relationships that might approximate those mutual concerns and sympathy.

Tönnies also was looking for a concept to refer to *the essence of human beings*, which he understood not as an abstract concept but rather as a concrete embodiment or *konkreten Inbegriff* of that humankind. He argued that the essence of being human can only be known by examining immediate acts among persons. He called this way of being collectively the "most general and essential" aspect of human nature—in German, *das Allgemeinst-Wirkliche*, which we translate as "that real that is *incommon*." We use the term *incommon* throughout this book.

Tönnies was suggesting that this most essential nature of human beings has something to do with both collectives and individuals but cannot be reduced to either. "It is all the more completely explained," he wrote metaphorically, "the more that these ever more narrow spirals create bridges between them" (1926: 171). These connections between individuals and collectives are hard to recognize, for they are never stable and always provisional. One common response is to imagine these essences in terms of ideal types, particularly if one wishes to keep the differences between them clear. But rigid distinctions will not work for our purposes because we see these distinctions only as the products of those connections at one particular here and now. In the next situation, the everyday will appear differently.

Another response is to theorize these essences; yet metaempirical representations are also a dead end for a study of the everyday. Tönnies insists that you can feel the full spirit and power of such a collective only in life— "only through the natural congress of the bodies actually living at that time in their totality," or for our readers of German, "*jedesmal lebenden wirklichen Leiber in ihrer Gesamtheit*" (1926: 172). To be sure, the incommon is not a product of our work per se: it exists already as that which we share as humans. Yet discovering it is hard—as it has been hard for the twenty-six authors of this book—given the impersonality of societal norms. The incommon becomes, in our everyday context, something quite extraordinary.

Charisma

Tönnies paid special attention to spaces; he recognized how the modern everyperson seemed to be everywhere on the crowded pavements of the new megacities. Take Berlin in 1900: not only did its population number in the millions but 60 percent of so-called Berliners had not been born there (Koshar 2000: 51). Pedestrians here were strangers, physically close but emotionally unknowable. Theodor Heuss, a political journalist, liberal parliamentarian, and later the first president of the FRG after World War II, described this experience as "a heaping together of individuals, not a solid social structure, as in the village, in the small town" (Hübner and Moegelin 1910: v–vii).

Navigating between these strangers required a new form of walking based on "civil inattention" (Urry 2007: 76, 172) or polite nonengagement: looking at people only fleetingly, closing oneself off from others, wandering "As if in a dream/Tacking blindly along" (Leis 1926: 1139). Yet it was also in these impersonal city streets that the extraordinary emerged within the ordinary. Paradoxically, anonymous urban walking attuned pedestrians to expect a highly personalized, metaphysical exaltation in daily life. Max Weber captured this phenomenon in his concept of *charisma*.

Like Tönnies, Weber was interested in how communities organize power and how influence and hegemony functioned. *What made people voluntarily follow their leader's commands without the overt threat of force?* In answering this question, Weber distinguished three basic types of authority. The first was *traditional authority*, in which notables, such as the aristocracy, drew on inherited structures of family name, legal status, wealth, or social breeding to ensure deference from subordinates. This type of authority was most clearly at home in Tönnies's *Gemeinschaft*. In smaller communities, kinship networks, inherited land ownership, symbiotic farming systems, and local village lore bolstered the status of bloodline elites. Weber's second type of authority—*bureaucratic authority*—was more common to Tönnies's *Gesellschaft*. In modern societies with large industrial cities, leaders relied on professional qualifications, expertise, and elected offices to press their claims to dominance. Here, technical credentials, not family status or local lore, determined an individual's status.

Weber is best known for his third category of authority: he used *charisma* to refer to a force of personality residing in a visionary leader who seemed "endowed with supernatural, superhuman, or at least specifically exceptional powers or qualities" (1968: 1.241). Charisma was based on the follower's desire to commune intensely with a remarkable individual, one who was, in Weber's terms, *ausseralltäglich*: literally *outside the everyday*. This outsider status was key to Weber's understanding of how charisma functioned.

While Weber acknowledged that personal magnetism was a political asset to any leader, he also noted that traditional and bureaucratic elites did not depend solely on their force of personality to keep them in office. The local baron could be a complete ninny, but that did not cost him his inherited title or the respect it incurred from the surrounding countryfolk. Not so for the ideal-type charismatic, the pied piper who—unmoored from the scaffolding of institutional support—drew followers purely by his sense of mission, his vision of how things should be, and his promises of future power. Looking back into history, Weber perceived pure charisma in Christ's apostles, Joan of Arc, and Oliver Cromwell: religious visionaries who led political and social revolutions (Weber 1968: 1.216, 3.1114).

In his own age, which he regarded as heavily marked by bureaucratization and rationalization, potential charismatics were muzzled by the mundane workings of party politics. Certain political figures exuded a force of vision akin to charisma. Weber thought in particular of U.S. president Theodore Roosevelt and British prime minister William Gladstone. Yet ultimately they lost the battle against the system, as the orderly functioning of the political machine disciplined the firebrands within its midst lest they upset party routine (1968: 3.1130–33).

Germany was no different—perhaps even worse, in Weber's view—in its tendency toward soulless, impersonal administration in the state, political parties, the army, and even the established churches (1968: 3.1400–1401). At his death in 1920, Weber had only witnessed the predawn of the age of political demagoguery so soon to be mastered by Benito Mussolini and Adolf Hitler. Yet Weber had a different type of charismatic leader in mind when he pinpointed three contemporaries as examples of this charismatic propensity.

The first was the Mormon prophet Joseph Smith. A second was Kurt Eisner, the littérateur who became minister president of the Bavarian Republic in 1918. The third was the poet Stefan George, whom Weber knew personally and who practiced a particular brand of mysticism among his disciples in his circle called the *George-Kreis* (1968: 1.242, 245). Here it is worth mentioning that charisma is not the same thing as fame and celebrity (Berenson and Giloi 2010). In all three cases, Weber was interested in what he called "modern charismatic movements of artistic origin" and their correlate, the "extraordinary psychic, particularly religious state" of mind (1968: 3.1114, 1121, 1393).

To Weber, the capacity of art to be charismatic lay in its ability to move people to radical action. Weber shared this conviction with the German *Bildungsbürgertum* or educated bourgeoisie. Before World War I, many members of the middle classes were drawn to the artistic charisma that flourished in the so-called *Lebensreform*, a loosely affiliated set of reform movements and alternative communities that tackled existential questions of human nature and how to live a meaningful life (Buchholz 2001).

For *Lebensreform* adherents, these issues took on a quasireligious nature as they sought communion with the sublime in nature and culture. Through an analogy between the natural world and the natural state of man, *Lebensreform* promised to free mankind from the repressive bonds of civilization through natural remedies, vegetarianism, uncorseted clothing, free love, nudism, sun worship, and a spiritually symbolic form of dance called *eurhythmics*. Reformers also pursued authentic humanity through cultural ecstasy embodied by the artist as cultural hero. They agreed with the playwright Gerhard Hauptmann (1924: 5, 8) that art is "the ultimate metaphysical activity." In it, the artist "sinks [his being] into the eternal." Steeped in these assumptions, they emulated cultural celebrities as life models, sometimes in dramatic variance to established customs.

Nowhere was the confluence of personal transformation, nature, art, and cultural celebrity as evident as in the resort town of Ascona, Switzerland, which

Weber visited in 1913 and 1914 to revive his shattered nerves (Marianne Weber 2009). High on the edge of town sat Monte Verità—the so-called Hill of Truth. This hotel was a *Naturheilstätte* or natural sanatorium, popular in *Lebensreform* circles for promoting health through natural remedies, alternative medicines, and vegetarianism.

The spa also promised to reveal the truth about human nature through *life experiments*—many of them utopian, anarchistic, and Dionysian in nature—from free love to psychoanalysis to experimentation with mind-altering drugs (Buchholz 2001). Nudism and modern dance, in particular, were practiced on the hotel's Parsifal Lawn as a direct homage to Richard Wagner. Inspired by Wagner's vegetarianism as much as his notion of the Gesamtkunstwerk, or *total work of art*, the spa's founders, like other Wagner acolytes, were moved by the composer's pronouncements on life conduct, which they practiced as dogma and proselytized as revelation (Conrad 1886: 244–47).

Ascona was one of several places in which Weber found cultural charisma at work among the *Bildungsbürgertum*. The desire for mystic communion also pervaded Stefan George's cult of personality, which Weber observed firsthand, as well as the German Youth Movement, of which Weber was a mentor. This personal context informed Weber's theoretical analysis of charismatic authority; like us, his definitions of the everyday emerged out of his social experiences.

But Weber never explained why his contemporaries turned to artists—rather than to their priest or lord, as they had in the past—for solutions to life's mysteries. *Why did they regard charisma, and especially the charisma of cultural celebrities, as a plausible form of authority in the first place?* One answer lies in the new megacities and their urban *Alltag*. Despite their reverence for nature, the *Lebensreform* movements all originated as urban phenomena, with their epicenter in Berlin (Jefferies 2003: 91–106). The new metropolises provided fewer opportunities for tight-knit communities than Tönnies's small-town *Gemeinschaften*, but they did offer something else: the opportunity to commune with the cultural sublime through startling, emotionally charged, street-based interactions with cultural celebrities, or what one might call *urban celebrity sightings*.

It is worth revisiting the urban experience itself. Not only was Berlin, as we have seen, filled with strangers and immigrants whose foreignness obscured the proper order of traditional social relations, but the city itself had grown to such a sprawl that it could not be grasped in its entirety. People living in the city forged personal connections to individual places—their local neighborhood (*Kiez*), place of work, favorite pub, or regular marketplaces. All of these points had social meanings attached as loci of kinship, friendship, and business relations. But they were also usually isolated from each other.

Rarely did an urban dweller live next to their place of work. And even if the favorite pub was nearby, they often traveled far to go to privileged shopping areas or special entertainments. To travel between these discrete, disconnected islands of social significance, walkers had to move through *nonplaces*: the anonymous, impersonal spaces in between, to which narrative meanings had not, or not yet, been ascribed (Augé 1995). For the individual walker, these impersonal, interstitial spaces were peopled with anonymous *everypersons*, the strangers with whom one engaged in a dance of polite nonengagement: never looking directly to avoid being rude, but looking just enough to avoid collision. Only once the walker reached the intended destination—that place of personal engagement and belonging—did established hierarchies and social practices reassert their control.

Readers in German studies may be more familiar with the analysis of the *flaneur* described by the French poet Charles Baudelaire and introduced into critical theory by the German philosopher Walter Benjamin. They used the term to refer to the gentleman stroller who entered into the street life of the city while observing it with detachment. We will return to this figure and its theorists in a moment; first, we want to draw your attention to a different dynamic also at work in urban everyday life: intentionally not noticing. Walking through the spaces of nonmeaning encouraged walkers to engage in intentional nonnoticing.

We turn to a more recent French scholar to help us think through this phenomenon. In his famous essay "Walking in the City," Michel de Certeau draws on the linguistic term *asyndeton* to explain such urban walking. As a speech act, *asyndeton* means omitting linking elements like conjunctions such as the missing *et* in the Latin phrase *veni, vidi, vici*; as a "pedestrian speech act," Certeau uses it to refer to ignoring the spaces of nonmeaning as one walks from place to place (1984: 101). Just as walkers practiced polite nonengagement with other pedestrians, they also blocked out the sharp contours of the interstitial space. In the act of commuting, walkers found the intervening travel space either too dull for full recognition or too full of messy but insignificant details to be absorbed in a meaningful way. Either way, walkers redirected their attention inward to their subjective thoughts and consigned the external, conjunctive spaces to the edges of awareness.

It is here, in the asyndetic act of walking the city, that the cultural sublime interrupted the everyday through unexpected encounters with cultural celebrities. Spontaneous celebrity sightings created a kind of double take moment when the recognition of a familiar but exceptional face broke like a lightning flash into the mundane routine of everyday life. These sightings were shocking precisely in the interstitial regions of the city because the walkers did not anticipate meaning in these nonplaces. If walking from point A to point B created a nowhere to be traveled through, seeing cultural celebrities in those nonplaces brought back a sense of meaningful location by calling to mind the imagined community of the nation and the values of the educated classes.

Serendipitous celebrity sightings were a new phenomenon of the megacities. The new urban sightings were different from seeing elites in the orderly setting of the smaller community. When, say, the king or another authority figure passed through a small town—and rumor preceded the visit—such an anticipated event could be attended with foresight and in the proper mood, and thus absorbed according to preestablished hierarchies (e.g., Bernus 1984: 21). In the large city itself, the sudden celebrity sighting was also qualitatively different from the older practice of *celebrity tourism*. Tourists and fans had stalked Goethe, Schiller, Schubert, and Wagner, but these encounters were only a surprise to the celebrities, not to the pursuers who deliberately planned and executed them (e.g., Fallersleben 1868: 2.50–52; Alexis 1905: 282–95).

Instead, in the urban celebrity sighting, pedestrians experienced a shock of sudden recognition for which they were not prepared. The effect of surprise was further heightened when the encounters took place in the asyndetic space of nonmeaning, those travel spaces that were usually relegated to the edge of awareness. Here, cultural significance was suddenly present in the most unexpected, banal space; and this unruly tear in the fabric of the ignored, interstitial space suggested that the sublime could reach out at any moment. The experience was emotionally profound—but not always pleasant. Fans felt anxious or even annoyed when they saw celebrities acting as regular citizens: it was "disconcerting" to see the lyrical poet Rainer Maria Rilke at an academic lecture on finance, for instance (Roth 1972: 62, 73–74). When sighted spontaneously, cultural heroes were meant to bring the exceptional into the ordinary, not to be ordinary within the ordinary.

How did city dwellers respond to this new rupture in everyday life? For the urban walker, the question became how to respond to this moment of being "drawn up" by the celebrity sighting. In his analysis of pedestrian speech acts, Certeau (1984: 99) further notes the *phatic* function of certain styles of walking, that is, actions intended to "initiate, maintain, or interrupt contact" with fellow walkers. Phatic walking used body language to say, "Hello, how are you?" "Can't talk now!" or "See you later." In the urban celebrity sighting, the fan's phatic response to the cultural hero was ambivalent. While some fans responded eagerly, even aggressively, when seeing their idols, most expressed a certain reticence.

For the German educated elite at the turn of the century, *active* engagement came in celebrity tourism: in expected encounters that one intentionally sought out and for which one could prepare emotionally and intellectually (Kroll 1967: 56–57). The "startled awe" of the spontaneous sighting, by contrast, could too easily rob one of the ability to speak so that it felt safer and more pleasurable to remain on the plane of voyeurism (Seidel 1935: 157–58). The celebrity sighting remained a virtual encounter, external to the oblivious celebrity, and made manifest purely in the fan's physical, bodily response:

the furtive glances with which one tried to catch Friedrich Huch's eye as he strolled past, the "little jolt" one felt in the back of the knees when seeing the poet George arm in arm with a disciple, the spectral experience of hearing Paul Klee play the violin on the other side of a garden gate (ibid.: 157–58, 161; Kaschnitz 1986: 15; also Casey 1987: 196).

Finally, seeing the celebrity by chance—a vision unadulterated by the realities of social interaction—allowed the fan, in their mind's eye, to "muse on the apparition long afterwards" (Seidel 1935: 157–58; also Thompson 1995: esp. 219–20). The physically restrained, internalized nature of such voyeurism made it feel covert, hidden, like the secret initiation into an elect circle, exempt from the routinization of everyday life. Thus Theodor Heuss, as a university student and aspiring author in 1905, felt closer to literature simply by seeing famous writers walk down Munich's Ludwigstraße, even if he was too shy to approach them directly (1963: 86). The bodily nature of the fan's phatic response gave those sightings a physical immediacy and lent phenomenological credibility to the feeling that the sublime could appear in the everyday.

In the celebrity sighting, we have the key qualities of Weber's charisma: the feeling of transcendence and heightened meaning; the intense, tingling, emotional–physical response to the vision of the hero; the private revelation; the sense of inner initiation into a secret; the feeling of being singled out for discipleship; the heightened emphasis on the celebrity's individual personality as the symbolic representative of the nation's hidden, artistic soul. In fin de siècle Germany, the *habitus* (Bourdieu 1977) of city life led urbanites to expect the unexpected: metaphysics in the *Alltag*. Weber was living in an age when charisma itself was *ausseralltäglich*, but its integration into a new urban normalcy was fostered by a particular phenomenology. Through it, future disciples were primed to believe that charisma was a plausible form of leadership, on equal footing with traditional or legal authority.

Weber, like Tönnies, not only was concerned with the nature of the extra/ordinary but also possessed an astute sensitivity to the challenge of integrating the fragmentary experiences of a modern life. Terms like *ordinary* and *extraordinary* are thus a moving target. Their meanings shift in changing circumstances. Those meanings also depend on the phenomenal act itself: apprehending and making sense of a fleeting impression or intentionally not noticing only to be shocked by it after all. Their only constant nature is their dynamism: they serve as a persistent locus for coherence and disruption. As such, these encounters are potential foundations for new forms of authority.

Cinema

In fin de siècle Berlin, cultural charisma worked best for the educated middle classes. They were able to experience artistic epiphany in the streets because they knew not only the works of contemporary artists and poets but also what these cultural heroes looked like. That corpus of relevant knowledge (Honer and Hitzler 2011: 13f.) was a necessary condition for asyndetic walking to be interrupted by a charismatic encounter. But for the working classes, who were unfamiliar with the cultural hero's face, seeing an artistic celebrity could hardly create a shock of recognition. *How could the broader urban population fill the gaps in everyday experience to create coherence out of fragments?* One modern institution that offered a way to address that need was cinema.

One of the great creative minds to take up the problems attached to the social question was Walter Benjamin, who reflected on the effects of the relatively new technology of cinema on everyday life. We read him in terms of the problems outlined by Tönnies and Weber: *how can ordinary people integrate the multiple experiences, contradictory wills, and fleeting encounters of a modern society into coherent stories of an urban* Alltag? Benjamin was not insensitive to the question of power: he wrote many of the works we look at here while he was in exile from his native Germany in Paris as a Jew escaping the Nazis.

Benjamin's famous essay from this period, "The Work of Art in the Age of Mechanical Reproduction" (1998), theorized some of the threats and opportunities of this new medium for mass mobilization. He was another one of these modern German thinkers who engaged in a close phenomenological reading of everyday practices. In this period, Benjamin engaged in two carefully focused studies—his book on Charles Baudelaire (2006b) and the *Arcades Project* (2002)—both of which concerned lived experience in urban societies in the middle decades of the nineteenth century. Somewhat more optimistic than Tönnies and Weber, Benjamin did not rule out a positive cultural outcome— or at least he still held out hope for realizing community within society.

Benjamin found in Baudelaire a poet who anticipated many of the challenges of living in the modern *Alltag*, specifically of integrating the intention to be communal with the intention to be social. Baudelaire tried to capture in his writing the sensibilities of the new urban *Alltag* that fascinated him. In his famous essay "The Painter of Modern Life" published in *Le Figaro* in 1863, Baudelaire was the first to define modernity in terms of these fleeting ephemeral encounters typical of the modern metropolis. "By 'modernity,'" Baudelaire wrote, "I mean the transitory, the fugitive, the contingent which make up one half of art, the other being the eternal and the immutable" (1995: 13). Baudelaire knew the demands of urban life in Paris in part because he walked its streets, just as Benjamin did a century later (2003: 25); but neither walked with the determination of the walkers described above, who had a destination in view; instead, they moved as *flaneurs*, wandering aimlessly and noticing life on the street. In his poem "To a Passerby" (quoted from Benjamin 2003: 25), Baudelaire described this experience:

> The street around me roared, deafening.
> Tall, slender, in deep mourning, majestic in her grief,
> A woman passed—with imposing hand
> Gathering up a scalloped hem—
> Agile and noble, her leg like a statue's.

Like Benjamin, Baudelaire interrogated the immediacy of his own lived experience.

> And as for me, twitching like one possessed, I drank
> From her eyes—livid sky brewing a storm—
> The sweetness that fascinates and the pleasure that kills.

But also like Benjamin, Baudelaire treated those people he encountered on the urban sidewalk as passing objects.

> A lightning flash ... then night!—Fugitive beauty,
> Whose gaze has suddenly given me new life,
> Will I see you again before the close of eternity?

Benjamin saw in these fleeting encounters an anticipation of the new medium of film. Like the way film editors juxtapose images, Baudelaire's poetry had an almost cinematic quality akin to montage. Baudelaire seemed to splice fragments of different scenes into a moving picture.

> Elsewhere, very far from here! Too late! Perhaps never!
> For where you're off to I'll never know, nor do you know where I'm going—
> O you whom I could have loved, O you who knew it too!

Notice the duality of this experience. Benjamin read Baudelaire as a moving picture with both isolation and encounters, even if the latter only takes the form of love at last sight. This woman has more *magnetism* than charisma or celebrity (Berenson and Giloi 2010). Still, experiences like these constitute the new normal in a modern city. These *Erlebnisse* were ordinary in the sense that they were embedded within modernity, but they were also extraordinary in terms of how they disrupted expectations and refused to fit comfortably into established narratives. As with celebrity sightings, Baudelaire's fleeting encounter with this object of desire is both integrated into and disruptive of the *Alltag*.

Here is where Benjamin can help us to better understand the everyday. He pushes the question beyond Tönnies and Weber not only in that he noticed how the extraordinary emerges from the ordinary: he also suggested that it was *the noticing itself* that makes these *Erlebnisse* extraordinary. In terms of celebrity sightings, one could say that seeing the celebrity would hardly be disruptive if the people did not identify the celebrities as such. In the case of cinema, Benjamin went even further in this direction. He drew attention to the fact that it was the new film audience, together with the filmmakers, who were noticing the images and making sense out of them. He was also suggesting that it was the act of noticing the extraordinary in the ordinary that offered the hope of finding a more balanced integration between the communal and societal in the urban everyday.

To Benjamin, cinema offered a new possibility for shared experience in modern society. In fin de siècle Berlin, people passed each other by on the street; they hardly knew one another when they walked into the theater. Yet the film helped them to see and inhabit a common world. They saw the common vision of a world on-screen, and they shared a common experience of watching the film. Benjamin understood that the darkness of the theater still engendered a sense of separateness, but he also believed that cinema culture had begun to shape experience of the wider world. For instance, it expanded the opportunities for celebrity culture and charisma described in the previous section to the working classes. A mass culture, film provided an imagistic grammar for common experience.

Then there is Benjamin's own prose, best described as *paratactic*. In language, *parataxis* refers to a grammatical expression—verbal or nonverbal—that lacks conjunctions. Like asyndeton, it lacks the connecting terms that create a smooth continuum of meaning from the individual elements of language. In his writing, Benjamin juxtaposes images in order to evoke associations in the reader's mind that stimulated a broader comprehension of connections between them. For example, Benjamin wrote about his own *Berlin Childhood around 1900*:

> Not far from the swimming pool was the municipal reading room. With its iron gallery, it was not too high for me and not too chilly. I could scent my proper domain. For its smell preceded it. It was waiting—as if under a thin bed that concealed it—beneath the damp, cold smell that welcomed me in the stairwell. I pushed the iron door timidly. But no sooner had I entered the room than the peace and quiet went to work on my powers. (2006a: 94)

The sensuous images that succeed each other are a product of Benjamin's shifting awareness as he moved through the spaces of his urban world.

> In the swimming pool it was the noise of voices, merging with the roar of water in the piping, that most repelled me. It rang out even in the vestibule, where everyone had to purchase a token of admission made of bone. To step across the threshold was to take leave of the upper world. (2006a: 95)

His writing style approximated the way editors construct a story from film stock. Isolated images are edited together in montage sequences such that the story, the film, is moved forward image by image.

Parataxis was Benjamin's literary response to ruptures in the German *Alltag*. It fuses together the broken juxtaposition of moments in ways that jar the changes of perspective—the lightning flash of Baudelaire's poem. Yet a story emerges nonetheless. To be sure, in film we do not engage with the figures on the screen directly but observe them from a distance. Parataxis can be viewed as a grammatical expression of the impersonal, objective relations of society. Yet, it can be as primary and direct in its sensuous presence as the images we have ourselves experienced. Cinematic imagery—in terms of its paratactic splicing of human gesture, sound, and partial life worlds—can be a learning experience for the viewer, a school for the incommon shared by the audience as well as by our on-screen instructors.

What Benjamin realized is that the parataxis of film guided the eye more compellingly than prose. Reading generated a bombardment of verbal cognition, much like any page of a newspaper in its juxtaposed columns. By contrast, observing parataxis in film came closer to how we physically see: our eyes are used to fusing multiple images into a smooth visual experience. Benjamin's contemporaries criticized cinema as a "spectacle which requires no concentration and presupposes no intelligence" (1998: 18, 2003: 267).

Yet Benjamin turned this criticism on its head when he suggested that film offered another form of intelligence, where "the distracted masses absorb the work of art into themselves" (1998: 18, 2003: 268). It was not just a parallel to the asyndetic act of walking in the modern city; it was a kind of replacement for it. Where the urban walker experienced disconnected gestures and fleeting encounters, the film screen served as a kind of prosthesis for making sense out of the modern *Alltag*. It enabled the viewer to discern or imagine the narrative connections that could serve as a new ground for the human intentions of everyday life (cf. Buck-Morss 1989: 267–70, 2000; Stiegler 1998).

This complicated point is worth explaining in more detail because it strikes at the heart of the methodological problem of this book: how people create a coherent sense of the everyday out of a series of fragmentary experiences. Benjamin is making an argument for cinema as a mechanical tool for enhanced personal cognition—one that could possibly help humans to cope with, indeed benefit from, the chaotic, dismembering experience of both modern society and mass culture.

> With the close up, space expands; with slow motion, movement is extended. And just as enlargement not merely clarifies what we see indistinctly … but brings to light entirely new structures of matter, slow motion not only reveals familiar aspects of movements, but discloses quite unknown aspects within them. (2003: 265–66)

The problem with film is what might be called the *apperceptive distraction* by which the filmgoers absorb knowledge. Insofar as the camera seems to shift its attention randomly from one object to the next, the camera mimics the disinterested kind of encounters of urban society that had so troubled German thinkers like Tönnies and Weber. And yet film operates in the opposite way as well. In so copying this now familiar quality of everyday life, the filmgoers find their own experiences, and even their unappreciated intentions, reflected in the film. In this ironic way, film has the potential of generating an empathic connection with others in the very everyday situations where face-to-face, focused, mutual understanding are undermined by the pace and technologies of modern life (Benjamin 1998: 14, 2003: 265).

Benjamin suggests that, through cinema, modern Germans were potentially capable of creating an integrated narrative of their everyday experiences that did not sacrifice the fragmented nature of those experiences. For Benjamin, cinema was a form that met "the desire of the present-day masses to 'get closer' to things spatially and humanly" (1998: 5, 2003: 255). Cinema offered a tactile aesthetic that became productive through what might be called a *haptic* intelligence, the kind of thinking that privileges the sense of touch and perception through sensation.

By observing the bodies of others on the screen, audience members appropriated instructive images of gesture and movement and taught their own bodies to adopt similar strategies through *mimesis*, or mirroring. These physical moments carried their attendant feelings into the viewer's own habits of relating to others performatively in terms of bodily gesture and movement as well as knowing oneself in this habit of bodily, facial, and interactional proximity (Benjamin 1998: 18, 2003: 268–69). In Benjamin, cognitive styles are intimately related embodied practices. He believed that we could even come to know strangers more deeply through our awareness of gesture, movement, and facial expression because actions are indications of states of mind. Through the mass culture of film, then, we find our long way back from society to some kind of partial or temporary community (Honer and Hitzler 2011: 22f.).

Through our mimesis—guided by and in conjunction with the cinematic image—community is a possible outcome within alienated society. Cinema addressed the modern problem of interpersonal relationships that Benjamin saw Baudelaire as also having raised:

> Before the development of buses, railroads, and trams in the nineteenth century, people had never been in situations where they had to look at one another for long minutes or even hours without speaking to one another … [One's] gaze [is] stunted or turned inward. It arises in a social situation, conditioned by technology, in which humans in public spaces cannot return the gaze of others. (2006b: 23)

Benjamin likened the artistic practice of cinema to a surgeon's exposure and treatment of bodily tissues. He also compared this operation to the deeper revelations of the everyday interaction offered by Sigmund Freud's *Psychopathology of Everyday Life* (Freud 1938: 150; Benjamin 1998: 12–13, 14–15; 2003: 263, 265). Benjamin artfully applied cinema as a kind of *homeopathy*, or home remedy, for urban alienation. Community in society after Benjamin could be realized by appreciating both the challenges and opportunities of mass culture and humane encounters. Rather than reducing community to face-to-face relations, affective relations could also be mediated through mass culture. And all of it could be accomplished technologically.

Multiple Intentionalities

Benjamin's insights into the possibilities for finding meaning in the life of the modern *Alltag* return us to the question of *who* is having these experiences and *how* the social question challenges our understanding of what it means to be a person. As we have seen above, Tönnies shared this concern. To study social bonds within the new urban context, Tönnies focused on human intention and behavior, that is, he framed this social question in terms of agency and will. *What kind of intention motivates your interaction with others?*

His interpretive choice established the conceptual bases for the sociological studies of Max Weber and Georg Simmel as well as those of Werner Sombart before World War I and Max Scheler in the years during and immediately thereafter. These scholars all focused upon the direction of willed acts toward another person or persons as well as the conscious, yet often prereflective intentions that initiated those acts. Just as Tönnies had distinguished between society and community, he also distinguished between two kinds of intentionalities: *societal will* and *communal will*. These terms imply that society and community do not exist as such: one has to create them. And the choice between them depends on how one approaches incommon encounters.

Tönnies referred to the will to be social as *Kürwille*, drawing on the word *Kür*, which connotes both rational choice, *Kür*, and arbitrariness, *Willkür*. He argued that the will to be social establishes impersonal relationships. This kind of intentionality seeks to live by generally accepted rules, many of them freshly minted for the emergent urban society. This desire to be normal or to live by socially acceptable norms fosters values that diminish what might be exceptional in oneself or someone else. It imagines an abstract *Jedermann* or everyperson as the beginning and the end of public interaction. The societal will fosters a new kind of common existence in everyday life, for it allows integration into an incommon through predictive behavior—what this imagined everyone does.

But society comes at a price. The societal will sees others primarily within the context of public associations, be it the workplace or the many public facilities of social, administrative, and legal urban existence. The intention to be social reduces interpersonal empathy for others experienced as individuals. In an article titled "Friedrich Engels and Natural Science" for *Die Neue Zeit* in 1906–7 (629; also Blum 2015), Friedrich Adler, the Austrian Social Democrat, wrote insightfully about these kinds of encounters in the public world of his day:

> One only experiences his fellowman as he does the other objects of his environment—in a character of "sameness." He sees the movements of his fellowman as he sees the movement of the stars; he hears his fellowman speak just as he hears the roll of thunder. And others know as little of his own movements and thought, of his worldview, as they know anything substantial of the sun or the clouds. Yet, he presumes they do, and he presumes it with the highest degree of probability, because the movements and the expressions of his fellowman in their reality are so extraordinarily similar to his movements and expressions.

Adler so beautifully described this crucial aspect of his *Alltag* that we used his take on microsocial interactions as the epigraph for this chapter. In the context of modern society where the societal will became the dominant way in which people interacted with each other, it was an active sympathy with others that became extraordinary.

By contrast, Tönnies defined the communal or, as he also understood it, the *natural* will in terms of those impulses for love, hate, and association associated with the instincts of *homo sapiens*. He saw the human being as Aristotle did: as a *communal being*, or *Zoon politikon*. Yet, these communal associations were a shifting potential that could assume different societal forms. At the heart of all collectivities was the natural will to cooperate and live within an incommon agreement. Yet every collective also required rules. Those rules became that community's societal will—taking on various degrees of impersonality in their normative expectations or in the form of coded laws. In the context of the impersonal will of society, the intent to be communal—with emotional depth toward others—seemed extraordinary.

Still, Tönnies believed that the will for a community of cooperating individuals existed in the modern Germany of his day, even if the urban *Alltag* made a natural, cooperative, empathic mutuality difficult to realize. Human beings have a natural inclination to affective directness. The communal will (*Wesenswille*) is that natural, emotional, even caring outreach of persons to persons that seeks empathic comprehension of the other (1926: 85ff.). By labeling it *essential* (*wesentlich*), he was claiming that there could be communities with others that went beyond the contractual limits of normed behavior. In such a community, which Tönnies felt had been the norm in nonurban settlements, mutual association had expectations. Still Tönnies believed that these were more easily tempered or changed than in an incommon strictly governed by the impersonal expectations of written laws or customary practices.

Tönnies believed the communal will was inherent to human nature and had a certain primacy over normativity and the behaviors associated with the societal will. Weber, in *The Protestant Ethic and the Spirit of Capitalism* (1958: 181–82), described those networks of norms and rules pejoratively as the *iron cage* of society. Weber used this metaphor to suggest that the norms and rules of modern society confine human nature. The more that norms and regulations channeled actions in the societal will, the harder it became to assume a direct, affective relation with other people.

Weber is hardly the only German thinker in this period seeking some kind of response to the ruptures in the *Alltag*. Tönnies, too, troubled over this question of how ordinary people might find healthy ways to integrate these various dimensions of being human into a community. *How can we integrate the intention to adjust our behavior to informal norms and formal rules (the* Kürwille) *with the intention to engage with others in terms of sympathy, empathy, and cooperation (the* Wesenswille)? Quite a challenge—and yet, only this integration could make the collective life of the *Zoon politikon* fully effective as well as humane.

To further explore this problem, Tönnies distinguished between primary, secondary, and tertiary kinds of relationships, each increasingly impersonal. Where our natural intention succeeds in creating affective directness, it creates primary relations of love, hate, and the like. Yet the will to be social tends to replace primary relations with secondary and tertiary ones. Secondary relations occur in places like the workplace, where cooperative praxis among one's coworkers or known societal officials thrives. Tertiary ones might be understood, in the context of small-scale nonurban communities, in terms of strangers. In the large-scale urban world, they refer to those unfamiliar individuals who are solely the objects of ends and means, like the people we pass on the street, the clerk in the shop, or the streetcar driver. While Tönnies knew that the new urban *Alltag* required lots of secondary and tertiary relations for its smooth operation, he wondered whether an infusion of the natural will in its empathic potential could create more primary relations and therefore lead to a more balanced life.

It was no small challenge to strike this pragmatic balance between these various contradictory wills or to negotiate social networks that included both personal and impersonal relations. In the novellas, poetry, and dramas of the period, characters are either able to integrate these contradictory wills effectively in a new normalcy or they find themselves at cross-purposes. Playwright Herman Bahr, for example, in his 1914 play, *Der Querulant* (The Quarrelsome Person), tells the story of an older person struggling to comprehend and adjust to the new normalcy. The protagonist lives in a small, provincial community that is being drawn into an expanding world of modernity, urbanity, and nationality. He becomes quarrelsome in that context because he insists on continuing to use old-fashioned, informal affections as the basis for incommon interactions. Bahr's stage directions for this four-act comedy provide thorough instructions for the actors on how to articulate the impersonal and the personal. The very speech patterns of the characters reflect either the societal or the natural will.

The protagonist's extraordinariness emerges from his ordinary yet increasingly unusual, eventually abnormal, habits. The characters in this play engage each other with different sets of expectations for the nature of those interactions, and the encounter changes their sense of which kinds of interpersonal behaviors are normative. It is the shock of this particular experience that transforms the protagonist from an experienced person into a disagreeable one. The characters in this small provincial town each act and speak from their *Erfahrung*; their communal wills enable the smooth apprehension of and response to a phenomenal world. Yet their normative interactions begin to rupture because newer societal norms were transforming how authority impinged upon their daily lives. These crosscurrents of old and new generated *Erlebnisse*. This complex amalgam of multiple intentionalities at cross-purposes hindered an integrated apprehension and response to the phenomenal world.

A Collective Person

In conclusion, we return to the social question in the form it assumes in this context—*how do we become familiar with everyday life in ways that allow us as subjects to live in common with others*—and to the work of Max Scheler. Scheler also was concerned with the problem of community within society. Building on Tönnies's study of the societal and the communal wills, Scheler argued that each of us is in fact a *collective person* consisting of a multiplicity of intentions. That *Gesamtperson* cannot be reduced to only one form of intentionality. The person depends on that variety of wills—such as primary, secondary, and tertiary—in order to navigate the many different kinds of relationships in everyday life.

In his work, Scheler identified a variety of differently toned intentions in both social interactions and social contexts. The nature of our intentions, he insisted, can be both complex and multiple. He was more interested in the range of audiences—an impersonal other or someone providing care to a familiar person—than the diverse material goals toward which these intentions were exercised among others.

But above all he argued that what constituted community depended not on the objects of our actions but on our intent. "For," he wrote in his 1913–16 work *Formalism in Ethics and Non-Formal Ethics of Values* (1973: 521): "It is by virtue of their intentional *essence,* and not on the basis of their contingent *objects* or what they empirically have in common, that these acts are factual acts, that is, *social* acts, acts that find their fulfillment only in a possible community." For instance, Scheler argued that even a person alone on a desert island would still need to have a cooperative intention to be fully human. "An imaginary Robinson Crusoe endowed with cognitive–theoretical faculties would also coexperience his being a member of a social unity in his experiencing the lack of fulfillment of acts or act types constituting a person in general" (idem).

Similarly, one could imagine a person writing a diary with no intention to share it with anyone, and yet the diarist necessarily experiences that lack of fulfillment as a form of cooperative intent in noticing the absence of the other as audience. In Scheler's estimation, the problem was to identify those inherently social acts hidden in their intentional objects. "Each social unit in its intentional object—the logic by which the phenomenon is structured—harbored differing manners of coexisting, cooperation, and coresponsibility" (1973: 525). To be sure, modern society often undervalues these connections given the emphasis on autonomous individuality. The individual often imagines the self not as embedded in relations with others but independent from them and even sovereign over them. But here we find another modern German scholar trying to help ordinary people to rediscover themselves as collective persons.

Understanding the person as inherently collective means we cannot know our self abstracted out of sociality. "We must designate as *collective persons,*" Scheler wrote, "the various centers of *experiencing*" (using the term *Erlebens;* 1973: 520). Scheler meant that *Erlebnis* as a whole contains multiple intentionalities and objects, but our apperception foregrounds certain ones. We discover ourselves as a self against this background of a totality of interconnected yet fragmentary experiences in which we are also participants.

Scheler is not clear about how precisely this myriad collection of fragmentary experiences becomes concentrated into coherent forms. We refer to this coherence diachronically as *history* and synchronically as *society* or, in his terms, *social unity.* As the locus for navigating extra/ordinary experiences, we might better call it *everyday life.* Narrating coherence from the ruptures in everyday life is thus not a problem just for the authors of this book but for the figures we are studying. Dieter struggled to do so in terms of the Wende in MV, Jünger in terms of the front experience in Berlin, and TJ Big Blaster Electric Boogie in terms of the Bronx in Dresden. In Scheler's terms, we discover ourselves as a "person *acting with others*" or a "man with others" (1973: 520). Not only does this self exist only in relation to others—the ones among and through whom we made this self-discovery—but this *Gesamtperson* is also "coresponsible" for everything morally relevant in that totality (1973: 520, 525).

In the *Gesamtperson,* Scheler establishes a set of relations inherent to the categories themselves that collapses the dichotomy between individual and collective. There is a wide variety of collectives that help form our self and in which the self is embedded, including families, classes, genders, races, sexualities, markets, parties, institutions, states, nations, empires, and so forth. For example, the act of spotting the celebrity allows spotters to give evidence of their membership in the educated middle classes.

What we learn from thinkers like Scheler is that these seemingly solid collectives are the byproducts of sociological and phenomenological microdynamics embedded in everyday life. The fact that they can be valued both positively and negatively is significant too. We encounter repeated situations in the other chapters of this book in which actions directed in contradictory political directions for instrumental purposes served to validate the same principles. Arguably it is this instrumental agreement on fundamentals, sometimes even at the expense of other intentionalities, that gives the everyday the quality of being self-evident.

At the same time, Scheler's concept of the *Gesamtperson* insists on an irreducibly complex self. He is not simply reminding us to consider the subjectivity of the investigator in the act of investigation. He is insisting that there is no single, stable self in which to ground our knowing, being, or doing; we are learning the same lesson here that we learned about the everyday self in the previous chapter. We cannot bring the everyday subject under control by reducing it to a fixed class, gender, or political position, despite our need to provide that contextualization for it; nor would further abstraction allow us to capture the complex condition of the *Alltag* subject, despite our temptation to develop ever more comprehensive theories as tools for understanding.

In place of these false alternatives, Scheler offers the possibility of multiple, simultaneous objectivities following from the multiple wills available to us as subjects. Ruptures were part and parcel of urban modernity. The complexity of experience calls us to employ multiple approaches and varied case studies in the search for understanding. Each fragment of lived experience disrupts the smooth flow of our narrative. Those fragments are, we would argue, signs that we are approaching an ever more adequate understanding of everyday life, but we should not imagine narrating that understanding as a single, coherent story.

A danger in following the trajectory of this chapter is that we may overestimate our capability to reintegrate traumatic *Erlebnisse* into the new normalcy of modernity. The examples found in this book so far—of Dieter, Jünger, Morawitz, Weber, Benjamin, and Scheler—disabuse us of any such notions. No matter how we try to fix it once and for all, the everyday disrupts that stability. The solution here is a familiar one: to think through differences in search of common expressions and experiences.

Mark E. Blum, Eva Giloi, and Steve Ostovich

CHAPTER 4

Families

Through my sons, everything has become clear to me, and I know that only through a united fight in the Red Class Front can the emancipation of the proletariat be realized
—"Wie ich zur Roten Front kam" *Frauenwacht*, 1928.

In the GDR, Peter Erdmann (a pseudonym) worked as a waiter. He had carried out his army service and was a well-respected volunteer with the Volkspolizei, the People's Police. He was twice divorced but continued to share a flat with his second ex-wife, Ingeborg. Both he and Ingeborg were on friendly terms with a Lieutenant P. of the Volkspolizei, one of Erdmann's colleagues. On 26 November 1976, Ingeborg ran into Lieutenant P. in the street. They chatted.

In their conversation, Ingeborg told P. that her ex-husband was the one who was responsible for the handwritten notices that had appeared around the town saying simply, "Solidarity with Biermann." The so-called Biermann affair involved the cancelling of the citizenship of the popular singer and songwriter Wolf Biermann, a critic of the ruling communist party (SED), while he was performing in West Germany. Ingeborg wanted her ex-husband's actions to end because she did not want him to get into serious trouble, as she said in the formal statement to the police that followed this conversation. She explained that she had no interest in the Biermann affair.

Erdmann was arrested by agents of the Ministry for State Security (MfS) known colloquially as the Stasi; he was then tried and sentenced to a year in prison for agitation against the state. Upon his release, he returned home and continued to live with his ex-wife, not knowing that it was she who had caused him to be arrested. He only discovered this fact sixteen years later, after the end of the GDR, when he read his Stasi file.

Erdmann's case highlights some of the tensions that can arise within families as well as between families and outside institutions. The previous chapters explored the dynamism of self and its relations with others. Its own inherent plasticity as well as the variety of intentions through which the self relates to others should not be interpreted as full autonomy. While individuals do author and authorize their everyday lives, they still must face and respond to the pressures of power, politics, and even violence.

This chapter examines these dynamics of self and society within the institution of the family. We treat the family as the site of affective relationships between spouses, children, and other relatives. The family is also intimately connected to friends, comrades, neighbors, and colleagues. We see the family as a primary locus of interactions between individuals and various levels of social organization, including state institutions. We are interested in exploring both sets of relationships: interpersonal relations within the family and intersection points between the family and external institutions. With regard to families, the political is personal.

The family represents many things. On the one hand, families contain individuals who aspire to privacy: the family is one site where they expect to see this aspiration realized. To be sure, the concept of privacy within the family is a relatively recent historical phenomenon in Western culture and was not a reality for working-class families who lived in overcrowded housing. By the nineteenth century, which marks the start of our story of the modern *Alltag*, Germans increasingly expected that, within the family, they would experience freedom of thought, action, conscience, and emotional expression. They also hoped that, within this realm, they would be granted freedom from intrusion by external institutions.

On the other hand, the family is itself an institution of culture, economics, society, and politics; and it experiences internal tensions along with formal and informal pressures from the outside. The family seeks to protect and advance its own members while simultaneously shaping them as any institution shapes its members; at the same time, the family as an institution serves as a mediator between individual family members and outside institutions.

Given the family's ideological and practical place at the core of society, its operations affect other institutions just as they are affected by them. Not only is the family a site for cultivating affective relationships, fashioning self, and aspiring to personal goals, it is also a site of social control that attempts to compel normative behavior, preferably through naturalized forms of power or by force if necessary. Further, the family is a theme for and locus of strategic maneuvers by political movements, parties, and states. The conflicts that result from the intersection of these multiple intentions are inherently political. We are interested in all of these various microsocial interactions and their implications for everyday life. This multiplicity of operations taking place in the everyday lives of families creates a mutual embeddedness between families and external entities, resulting in a dynamism that neither side can fully control.

Such dynamic interactions are historically specific. In this chapter, we consider families who were members or sympathizers of the German Communist Party (KPD) during the Weimar Republic, when communists stood on the margins of German society, as well as families living in East Germany after World War II, when communists ruled the GDR. The choice to use communist examples for the everyday lives of families is, again, an atypical one; yet this choice yields useful insights into the history of the everyday, revealing the particular ways in which the personal and the political intersected. Our examples demonstrate the multifaceted tensions that resulted from conflict both within the family unit, when individual emotions and desires clashed, and with outside institutions and representatives of the Communist Party or state. We thus expand the scope of our study of self and social relations into the realms of affect, force, power, and politics.

Accessing the everyday experiences of communist families is not as hard as it may sound. While the private sphere is generally less documented than public life, there is a plethora of documentation about families during the GDR. And even communist working classes during the Weimar Republic produced a large amount of material on daily life. Still, the normative assumptions and propagandistic messages relating to the family mean that, when examining family sources, it is often challenging to distinguish fact from fiction. One way to get over this hurdle is to use a variety of sources. Another way is to recognize the multiple and often conflicting intentions inherent in everyday acts and representations of such acts. We follow our subjects through the lives of their actual families as well as their acts of representing that family life in political or in what they intended to be nonpolitical ways.

The ruptures faced by families in everyday life come not only from politics. Families endured the challenges of poverty and unemployment, problems with neighbors and housing, efforts to fashion new selves, conflict between genders and generations, and the advent of divorce and death. As institutions, families can sometimes address and overcome such disruptions in their daily lives, but sometimes not. We are interested in this chapter in how these ruptures interact with political movements, state institutions, and historical events. In a sense, we are trying to be more explicit about the connections between the micro and the macro. Dieter, as we saw in the first chapter, made this connection: he treated the politics of reunification as personal for his family. Erdmann made this same connection after the Wende, only to discover that the ruptures in his family life began long before 1989. One way of thinking about ruptures could be in terms of the circumstances under which these small-scale events take on large-scale meaning.

The historical circumstances themselves were rather disruptive. The Weimar Republic came into being in 1919 in the aftermath of World War I after Emperor Wilhelm II abdicated and a wave of revolution swept through Germany. As a democracy, the new political arrangement oversaw some historic breakthroughs, including women's suffrage and state labor arbitration. But the Weimar Republic's existence was fragile from its inception. Saddled with the Versailles Treaty, which resulted in significant territorial losses and wartime reparations, politicians sought to challenge the treaty overtly in 1923; their decisions plunged Germany into severe economic dislocation, known as *hyperinflation*.

By the end of 1924, Germany's economy had stabilized, but economic dislocation persisted. By 1930 a new wave of severe economic turmoil commenced as the Great Depression spread to Germany. Germany's economic troubles profoundly affected families, who became radicalized, rallying to revolutionary politics, including Nazism. Discontented with a system that left them in a precarious economic condition, a significant minority of working-class families turned to the communist movement.

After Nazi Germany was defeated in 1945, Germany was divided into occupation zones, with a large area of Eastern Germany becoming the Soviet Zone of Occupation (SBZ). Soviet authorities facilitated the coming to power of the SED through a forced merger of the old KPD and the SPD (Social Democratic Party of Germany), the two workers' parties that had been enemies in the Weimar years. The communists soon took control of the SED, turning it into a Marxist–Leninist party based on the Soviet model. Other parties were forced to accept the leadership and then the total domination of the SED. As the Western Allies moved toward turning their zones into the Federal Republic of Germany in 1949, the Soviet Union and the SED worked together to form the German Democratic Republic that same year.

East Germany was transformed into an industrialized state under the dictatorship of the SED. The party's aims were to force the disappearance of the "bourgeoisie" and to develop a workers' and peasants' state in which socialism would be built, laying the foundation for the eventual establishment of a communist society. The GDR thus represented the fulfillment of the dreams of the communists who had been politically active in the Weimar Republic.

Both communist families in the Weimar Republic and families living in the GDR illustrate the complexity and contradictions in communist thinking on the family. Since the middle of the nineteenth century, socialists had widely denounced many conventions associated with the patriarchal nuclear family. Karl Marx and Friedrich Engels had theorized in *The Communist Manifesto* (1972: 478–79) that a radical social transformation would include fundamental changes to family life. Despite such radical pronouncements, German socialists during the late nineteenth century subordinated the needs of the family, especially those of working-class women, to the imperative of class struggle. To this extent, they built upon a long-standing tradition of conceding to the patriarchal tendencies that were at work in society at large.

With the 1917 Bolshevik Revolution in Russia, such patriarchal views of sexual and family relations, both within society at large and in the communist movement, came under fire. Alexandra Kollontai, a prominent Bolshevik and director of the party's women's sections, promoted a new socialist morality and form of love in which sexual relations would be based on both class and gender equality, with comradely solidarity between men and women. Under Kollontai's leadership, the Bolsheviks radically rewrote family law, providing wives and mothers with many more rights than they previously had enjoyed.

However, this experiment in familial relations led to the perception by the Soviet leadership of an "epidemic of sexual depravity" and to subsequent demands by the leadership for greater moral vigilance. As a result, by the 1930s new laws based on a repressive, puritanical view of the family were issued in the Soviet Union and subsequently taken up by European communist parties, strongly influencing the everyday lives of families in postwar Eastern Europe (Miller 1998: 95).

Taking their ideological cues from the Soviet communists, German communist leaders in both Weimar Germany and the GDR viewed the family, specifically its internal structure, in fundamentally conservative terms. Relying upon the nuclear family as the kernel of political and social organization, they promoted a traditional, self-contained, and stable nuclear family. Party organization, they reasoned, required familial stability, which was best served by the nuclear family (Hoffrogge 2011: 90–98). To this extent, communist leaders were not concerned with private life within the family as such; rather, they saw the family mainly as a political partner that would both carry forward specific policies and act as a vehicle for inculcating values they saw as desirable. Internal emotional tensions and conflicts within the family, in their view, were of little relevance to the family's political and social functions.

A particular set of tensions thus emerged between the family and communist institutions. The first tension concerned the incongruity between communist rhetoric and practice. Despite pronouncements advocating a fundamental restructuring of family life that would parallel radical social transformation, the ways that communist leaders thought about the family in practice were fundamentally conservative. The second tension concerned unfulfilled expectations. While families hoped that the KPD in the Weimar period and then later the SED in the GDR would support them, party leaders expected that families would serve communist politics and social organization.

This chapter looks at examples of how families adapted communist policies and practices during the Weimar period—reshaping rather than reflecting such policies and practices—and how, in the GDR, they ignored or doggedly resisted attempts to use families to reinforce socialist culture, including taking advantage of state policies for their own personal benefit. Both sides were often disappointed. Families realized that communist leaders and organizations presented them with unrealistic expectations or abandoned them altogether, especially at their most vulnerable moments. Communist leaders came to recognize that families were not reliable partners that carried out the duties the party assigned to them. This chapter emphasizes the uneasy partnership between families and communist institutions.

Families in Opposition

The German labor movement began to idealize the working-class family as a stable, predictable institution in the late nineteenth century. Operating in a historical context in which the patriarchal structure was considered the norm, the SPD generally assumed that the nuclear family stabilized relations within the family as well as between families and external institutions. This belief was reinforced by the social and political conditions in Imperial Germany. From 1878 to 1890, the SPD faced state persecution. Banning socialist organizations, meetings, and printed materials, though still permitting socialist representation in parliament, the Anti-Socialist Law of 1878 led to the development of extensive socialist underground activities.

Persecuted and separated from mainstream society, socialists built an organization that provided an "alternative culture" to meet all of the needs of its members. Within this working-class milieu, the nuclear family became a tool of socialist organization (Lidtke 1985; Goyens 2007). For example, the SPD routinely disguised political activities as family events, such as family picnics in the countryside and workers' choral societies (Halder 2006: 65). Meanwhile, the SPD committed itself to providing for the families of exiled or underground activists. In the context of persecution, the socialist family had to be a reliable political partner, and that required familial stability, which socialists believed the traditional nuclear family ensured.

By 1890, when the Anti-Socialist Law lapsed, the SPD was the largest party by vote in Germany. By the turn of the twentieth century, the SPD had become largely a reformist party that renounced Marxist revolutionary rhetoric and praxis (Schorske 1983). It was wedded to many socially conservative tenets, including focusing on organizing working-class men to the exclusion of women and promoting the ideal of a stable nuclear family. As Franz Walter (2009: 20–21) notes, the SPD's ambitious and successful attempts at internal organization, training, and education along with the development of party cultural activities had a powerful emancipatory effect on supporters. At the same time, these developments encouraged party members to become inward looking, increasingly content to enjoy private life within the confines of the family.

The prewar SPD's cultivation of the nuclear family as a mainstay for its political culture left a powerful imprint on working-class political organization during the Weimar Republic. Founded in the final hours of 1918 in the midst of the German Revolution, the KPD was dedicated to revolutionary struggle, modeling itself on the Bolsheviks in the Soviet Union in an effort to make a clean break with the reformist traditions of the SPD. Like the prewar SPD, however, the KPD saw the nuclear family as a central pillar for party organization, and this conservative view was only reinforced by the increasing skepticism about radical family law in the Soviet Union. As the KPD worked to politicize the nuclear family, it continued to prioritize organizing men in heavy industry. But by the mid-1920s, it also began to see the family as a political unit that could be mobilized for political action. Concurrently, the KPD founded an array of social organizations, such as youth and women's organizations, to court each member of the working-class family separately.

The KPD saw the family as the central vehicle for mobilizing the working classes in proletarian boroughs. Reasoning that families were ideally positioned to recruit their neighbors, the KPD charged families with various political activities, including membership recruitment, electioneering, and newspaper sales. Illustration 4.1 is a photograph of a father, mother, and son collecting funds for Rote Hilfe, or Red Aid, a KPD organization that provided support

Illustration 4.1. Collecting Donations for Red Aid, Leipzig, 1925. SAPMO Bild Y 1-103/88. Courtesy of BArch.

for political prisoners. While it is not clear if this photo represents an actual experience or merely a political representation staged by the KPD, it does seem likely that the family volunteered for the work and even agreed to the picture.

The photograph depicts the family as a stable nuclear one—precisely the kind that KPD leaders sought. It also suggests that the family functioned as a single political entity, with each member fulfilling an active and collective role. It further implies that familial relations underpinned the political activity of ordinary communists, at least in part, and that political allegiances, handed down from one generation to the next, were derived primarily from socialization within the family. Nevertheless, this family had propagandistic value for the KPD, and they used it strategically for political mobilization. This image sent the message that the KPD relied upon working-class families and was organized around the nuclear family.

The KPD's mobilization of working-class families focused not only on families per se but also on the spaces that families occupied in their daily lives. Overtly politicizing daily life, the KPD sought to transform ordinary spaces in proletarian neighborhoods into highly charged political forums. As evidence of the politicization of working-class districts, consider Illustration 4.2: a photograph of a KPD youth group playing a game of Reds versus Whites.

Illustration 4.2. Children in the Young-Spartakus-League Playing Reds versus Whites. Berlin, ca. 1930. SAPMO Bild Y 1-646-88. Courtesy of BArch.

Brandishing red flags and toy rifles, these children play radical politics. Their transformation of one of interwar Europe's epic political battles into play demonstrated the ways that the KPD influenced families' everyday activities and shaped children's political consciousness. This photograph further sheds light on how communist politics refashioned neighborhood spaces, infusing them with radical politics that made revolution seem ordinary—a mere neighborhood game.

Because the KPD frequently operated outside the law and was often barred from public spaces, it used the private spaces of families for political purposes, such as concealing weapons, hiding police suspects, and distributing banned literature from their homes. The KPD also encouraged families to display party symbols from their windows to disseminate communist politics. During the Weimar Republic, the KPD promoted a set of radical symbolic practices, such as flying red flags and singing revolutionary songs, to politicize the everyday overtly (Korff 1986: 86–107; Bodek 1997; Weitz 1997: esp. ch. 7). Communist families, along with supporters of both the SPD and the Nazi Party, peppered private and public spaces in working-class districts with political emblems. Particularly during election seasons, working-class districts overflowed with flags, placards, and banners. They made public the political sympathies of those who resided in the decorated apartments (Bergerson 2004). These symbols converted families' intimate spaces into militant political forums.

The display of communist symbols routinely catalyzed conflict in proletarian boroughs. Indeed, working-class neighborhoods were rocked by both symbolic and physical battles that drew families into an overtly political fray. This change was especially evident after May 1929, when violent encounters in Berlin between state police and communist-led May Day demonstrators resulted in the deaths of thirty-three people and the subsequent banning of the KPD's paramilitary organization, the Red Front Fighters League or Roter Frontkämpferbund (RFB), along with its symbols (Bowlby 1986: 137–58; Kurz 1988).

Escalating political tensions were further evident during the November 1932 election season for the German federal parliament, the Reichstag: police reportedly stormed a Cologne neighborhood and destroyed the communist propaganda displayed by families. We have an account of these events, "Police Hunt for [KPD] Flags and Banners," thanks to one of many anonymous Arbeiterkorrespondenten, that is, worker correspondents who wrote articles about everyday life for communist newspapers. In this one, published in the local KPD organ, the *Sozialistische Republik* (*SR*), on 10 November 1932, one resident recounted: "The police were upset especially with the flags and banners that were hanging from nearly every worker's apartment. They advanced with a leader and took … the housewives' brooms from the apartments and tore down these 'state-threatening' advertisements." This report illustrates that families' display of KPD symbols decidedly raised the political stakes in working-class neighborhoods.

But it was not only the police who were alarmed by the display of KPD symbols. Political enemies, especially Nazis, routinely confronted communists in working-class neighborhoods over the exhibition of communist symbols, especially red flags (Schumann 2012: 215–71). In one case, reported by a worker correspondent in the *SR* on 11 September 1932, Nazi storm troopers attacked "a young worker." In this incident, these "hoodlums" reportedly beat and stabbed a young man as a warning that Mülheim, in Cologne, "is now going to be cleared out. You won't be hanging any more red flags outside!" Both as propaganda about everyday life and reporting on the German *Alltag*, these interventions were designed to encourage identification with the victims, to increase working-class activism, and to build support for communist politics among and within individual families.

This particular mode of practicing the self echoes the arguments of previous chapters that the self is inherently unstable and influenced by both the performative situation and human interactions. Located in the context of violent street politics, the young man was attacked for his assumed allegiance to communism. Whether or not he actually identified as communist is not clear, but the Nazis transformed him into an archetypical representation of communism. Whether he also experienced this violence as a rupture in his everyday life also remains unclear. Other individuals, however, did practice a communist self with some degree of intentionality. By opting to march in KPD demonstrations, sing communist songs in public, and hang red flags, they chose to represent themselves as communists. And many understood the risks associated with doing so boldly in public.

As these examples illustrate, working-class families' political activities provided a way of making everyday life intelligible as a site of political struggle. For the KPD, families' political activism was an indispensable political asset that promoted the communist movement. Concurrently, families' political actions transformed everyday life, fashioning a new normalcy. Above all, families embedded political acts in their daily lives, whereby flying a militant flag became commonplace. Families thus made their political beliefs into matters of public scrutiny, with the potential for antagonizing foes and igniting a political firestorm.

Families and the Building of Socialism

The struggle between National Socialism and communism intensified during World War II; what had been local conflicts for families at the level of the neighborhood became a clash of ideologies and a struggle for power on a global scale. In turn, the Allied victory over Nazi Germany in 1945 brought with it the Soviet conquest of Eastern Europe and the creation of two German states: a Western-oriented capitalist FRG and an Eastern-oriented communist GDR. These two Germanies embodied the central ideological divide that came to frame the history of the second half of the twentieth century. Most East German leaders had been active in the KPD during the Weimar Republic. They were virtually all men who had lived in exile in Moscow and survived both Nazi and Stalinist persecution. Under the wing of the Red Army, yesterday's communists in revolutionary opposition became today's communists in power in the GDR.

The recent past deeply informed the attitudes of GDR leaders. Specifically, they continued to think of the family as an essential partner in effecting a fundamental social transformation. The struggles of communist families prior to 1945 became important points of reference and identification thereafter. In an effort to create founding myths for the new GDR, the SED disseminated stories of the antifascist work of families during the Weimar Republic and the Third Reich (Nothnagle 1999).

The SED oversaw the publication of scores of pamphlets that narrated stories showing the active support of families for the Soviet Union and against Nazi rule (*Deutsch-sowjetische Freundschaft* 1975). In addition to canonizing antifascist families, the GDR developed a body of fiction to reinforce this founding national myth (Feinstein 2002). Novels by Anna Seghers (1946), Hans Fallada (1988), Bodo Uhse (1955), and Willi Bredel (1981) took up the issue of resistance to Nazi rule with families as a central point of reference (also Nothnagle 1999: 10; Leask 2012: 55–67). The SED strenuously promoted all of these novels.

With the founding of the German socialist state, moreover, communists were for the first time in a position to determine the way that the German family would be structured and how it would function in the GDR. The GDR did not operate in a historical vacuum, however. The Third Reich had enacted a series of policies that promoted the traditional nuclear family, such as pushing women out of employment, until they were needed again during the war. Meanwhile, the Nazi regime also viewed family life as an extension of the political realm, thus largely denying the existence of a private sphere. As Paul Betts explains, the Third Reich "effectively 'deprivatized' marriage by subordinating an autonomous contract between two people to the ideals and dictates of the 'racial state'" (2010: 96). The GDR leadership had to take into account the long and complicated traditions of family life in German society, including the legacy of the immediate past, as it began to build a new socialist state.

In contrast to the Nazis' approach to the family, the SED had no interest in revolutionizing the family as an institution. Particularly given the pressing concerns of the postwar era, the party harked back to the family of the Weimar period. For the socially conservative leaders of the SED, the traditional nuclear family, as they imagined it to have been during the Weimar Republic, was essential for creating the social stability necessary to transform East Germany. In the late 1950s and early 1960s, the GDR declared the family to be a vital social unit with marriage as its foundation.

This period is notable for two events. First, Walter Ulbricht, general secretary of the Central Committee of the SED—and as such, the effective leader of the GDR—issued his "Ten Commandments of Socialist Morality" in 1958. Second, the SED at its Sixth Party Congress in 1964 declared that the party and the state would improve the opportunities open to women in employment. They would also give women more advice on how to bring up their children along with direct assistance through the provision of nurseries and kindergartens and longer school hours. These policies were designed to help them, not their husbands, to better manage the joint claims of family and employment and to ensure that they and their children would become more committed to the socialist cause (*Neues Deutschland*, 25 January 1963).

These measures followed early historic changes, such as the promulgation in 1949 of a constitution that guaranteed equality between men and women (H. Weber 1986: 158). Yet the SED leaders did not radically alter their views on the family from the Weimar years. As historian Donna Harsch explains, "Although jurists touted the proletarian family, they actually envisioned a tightly knit nuclear family, except that the SED version would have an employed wife" (2007: 199). Primarily, the leaders of the GDR were concerned with entrenching their own power and building the industrial and economic foundations of socialism. In this context, the family could in principle be a private entity, but it also was expected to cooperate actively in building socialism.

The SED adhered to the KPD's views on the role of the family in political organization and social transformation. East German leaders continued to see the family as a critical institution for expressing the state's core values. According to Betts (2010: 96), "The family was to assume its place alongside the workplace as the primary site of socialist personality formation." Nonetheless, East German leaders permitted a degree of personal autonomy within the family unit, marking a clear break with everyday life during the Third Reich. Betts notes that the family was neither an extension of the regime nor a real locus of privacy, but something in the middle. The state cultivated the family as the "primary location of love, intimacy, and private emotions"—an approach it saw "as distinctive of socialism" (2010: 90).

In an effort to mobilize citizens for socialism, the GDR cultivated a set of social models that exemplified the "modern, socialist" way of life. Socialist models for the family attempted to ensure that the family, as an institution, as well as individual family members adopted and committed themselves to socialism through their attitudes and behaviors. This process was especially evident in lifecycle events and highly emotional events such as death and divorce, when affective relationships within families were forged or broken. Such moments of familial interaction were not generally consistent with communist leaders' understanding of and expectations for the family. Indeed, while the SED leadership viewed families as partners that would promote a socialist moral order, there was never a sense or even a pretense that the family would be an equal partner. Instead, it was the SED's worldview, with its specific value system and moral order, that was to be promoted at these critical family moments.

At its 1958 Fifth Party Congress, the SED developed new rites of passage designed to be tools of collective socialist education and to demonstrate the organic connection between the individual and society, a connection that would, in principle, reduce any sense of autonomy for the family and its individual members. East German cultural institutions popularized these new rites through a series of manuals, such as the one issued by the Zentralhaus für Kulturarbeit in Leipzig and written by Gustav Freidank (1975: 6–7). It was significant for the collective whether a child would be baptized or have a socialist name-giving ceremony, whether a couple would be married in a church or at the civil registry office, and whether a deceased family member would be buried with a priest or a socialist orator in attendance.

One of the most emblematic East German rites of passage was the *Jugendweihe*, the socialist equivalent of the Christian confirmation ritual. *Jugendweihe*, introduced in 1954, had an impeccable antifascist pedigree dating back to the nineteenth-century *Freidenker*, or Free Thinker movement. Moreover, because the Nazi regime had effectively banned *Jugendweihe*, it was an ideal means to reeducate the population in the socialist tradition. Throughout the GDR's history, the state invested heavily in it and integrated it into the education system, where it was celebrated as part of the academic year. In addition, the state established its own "*Jugendweihe* commission" within the propaganda department (*Gesellschaft für Deutsch-sowjetische Freundschaft* 1975: 180).

The GDR provided models for other rites of passage as well, including ones not necessarily connected to public institutions (Black 2010: 220). From the early 1950s, various ministries took part in the development of socialist funeral rituals. Even painful moments of rupture, such as the death of a family member, were to be used to promote the building of socialism. SED leaders drew upon the KPD's funerary culture, which had sought to invoke dead comrades in order to persuade mourners to recommit themselves to socialism (S. Sewell 2009). The funerals of political figures, such as Wilhelm Pieck, the

GDR's first president, were particularly important. His 1960 funeral was a key moment in both the history of the GDR and the history of East German funerary practices.

Seeking to mobilize the entire population, this funeral suggested that individuals' lives were important building blocks in the development of socialism. Citizens in every locale participated by performing symbolic funerary practices that paralleled the main ceremony in Berlin. Organizers were especially keen on ensuring that children participated in ways that corresponded with the new socialist culture. For example, teachers talked about Pieck to their classes and observed the national minute of silence (Redlin 2009: 85–97). The Pieck funeral marked the coming together of the country as a community of mourners to honor the deceased with an array of emotionally charged rituals that disseminated socialist values.

The state's efforts to thrust funerals onto the political stage went beyond the last rites for political and intellectual elites, beyond an official cult of the dead (Rader 2003). SED leaders also attempted to "move [people] from the 'I' to the 'We'"—that is, to use funerals to inculcate communal values (Happe 2001). To do so, the GDR reformed burial practices for ordinary citizens, with a new model that was designed to demonstrate publicly that mourners were committed to socialism. Indeed, GDR leaders expected families to downplay the emotional impact on the family of the death of a loved one and to choose the socialist funeral model. In doing so, the state sought to make the family outward looking and self-sacrificial, accepting the death as an opportunity to promote socialism.

Essential to the East German funeral was the inculcation of secular traditions. Similar to those of other Eastern Bloc states, the East German constitution guaranteed freedom of religion, which in theory meant that political loyalty and religious beliefs were compatible. As families made decisions regarding funerals, however, they quickly faced a series of questions that placed them squarely in the so-called ideological battle between worldviews. One decision that families faced was whether to choose cremation. Administrative procedures favored a secular funeral and cremation, which had ties to German labor traditions (Fischer 2010: 66–78). Families opting for burial and a religious ceremony had to make separate arrangements and pass a series of administrative hurdles.

The state did not apply direct pressure to choose cremation over burial or a socialist over a religious funeral. However, handbooks on secular funerals emphasized that "the socialist society partakes in the fate and development of the citizens, in the happiness and suffering of the individuals and in particular of the families." It made clear that, while secular funerals were based on the principles of scientific materialism and therefore on the principle on which the modern, socialist society was supposedly founded, religious funerals were relics of the past (Freidank 1975: 4–5). Similarly, cremation was presented in this literature as a modern, progressive, socialist practice, while inhumation was presented as an antiquated form of disposing of dead bodies.

By following the secular model, families were seen as cooperative partners in the building of socialist culture. This connection between the individual and the collective was reinforced by the eulogy, in which individual biographies were linked to the past, present, and future of socialism. According to handbooks on rites of passage, the eulogy should explain how the deceased had contributed to building socialism. For example, after the death of Konstanze Haderk, a young leader of a pioneer group, the funeral orator structured the eulogy to stress her personal characteristics as assets that enhanced her work in the East German youth organization. Emphasizing her diligence, trustworthiness, and personal ambition, the orator declared her work to be vital to the building of socialism (Freidank 1975: 19).

The emphasis on her political biography meant that Haderk's good relationship with her parents was important because "her education in the family home helped Konstanze to become an exemplary student." The orator declared, "They always stood by you as you were carrying out your great and beautiful tasks." Similarly, the orator emphasized that Haderk's marriage had contributed to building socialism: "Your life together was, for both of you, a constant inspiration to improve yourself politically and professionally" (Freidank 1975: 21). As this eulogy demonstrated, the socialist funeral functioned as a political stage upon which the biographies of ordinary people were framed to support the socialist moral order, regardless of how the families themselves might have wanted to interpret such biographies or express their sorrow in a more inward looking and personal manner.

For state authorities, eulogies were particularly important, for they were to both reaffirm socialist aims and offer inspiring examples to mourners. While the biography of the deceased demonstrated the importance of building socialism, the tales of inspiration were to offer solace without referring to transcendental values. Many families did in fact opt for a secular socialist funeral. When doing so, their motivations ranged from genuine support for socialism to mere opportunism. However, even such opportunism implicated them politically, for no matter how apolitical they thought they were being, families that participated in socialist funerary rituals projected the image of society and its desired future that the SED propagated.

GDR administrators tried to ensure that families made correct funeral choices—a process they considered a "task in educating taste" or *geschmacksbildende Aufgabe* (Institut für Kommunalwirtschaft 1979). The funeral offered a stage for orators to integrate the deceased's biography into the state's master narrative of the universal relevance of socialism, even when such views were not necessarily consistent with the family's beliefs.

Additionally, by conducting the ceremony in a dignified way, the orator demonstrated socialist culture at work. A well-conducted secular funeral was proof that religion was not necessary to face emotionally challenging situations. As Freidank pointed out in his 1975 handbook for funerals, "Only such persons should be engaged as funerary orators who are examples in a political–moral sense and at the same time who are able to live up to the rhetorical task; in other words, only those who are true orators" (9). Adapting a verse of the poet laureate of the GDR, Louis Fürnberg, Freidank's manual was appropriately titled *Alles hat am Ende sich gelohnt*—it was all worth it in the end.

In practice, tensions between families and the state mounted, especially in relation to the eulogy. From the regime's perspective, the biography of the deceased was the raw material for showing how socialist society functioned, but it was also a potentially dangerous resource that had to be managed because biographies were rarely linear or primarily political. Funeral orators dissuaded families from including too many details of the deceased's private life, not only for stylistic reasons but also to shift the emphasis away from inconvenient biographical details, such as bad marriages, divorces, and children from multiple relationships.

Funeral handbooks recommended euphemisms to help the orator navigate around the messy aspects of personal life. They encouraged the orator to talk generally about children in the case of several marriages and to draw attention to the uncomplicated aspects of the biography (Redlin 2009: 180–81). By focusing on the deceased's professional life and relationship to the SED rather than his or her private life, the eulogist inserted the deceased's life into the socialist vision.

Lifecycle rituals like funerals are designed to provide support for families confronted with ruptures in everyday life. But by downplaying the unpredictable and often chaotic nature of private life and by ignoring the feelings of grieving families, official funeral practices demonstrated the SED's general failure to understand human emotions. Funeral manuals, like the one published by the Institut für Kommunalwirtschaft, *Weltliche Bestattungsfeiern*, emphasized that familial conduct should help to set an "atmosphere expressing dignity and contemplation." If strong emotions were expressed, orators were instructed "to handle them effectively and in a way that is fitting to the situation" (1979: 10–11). As such instructions illustrated, party leaders believed that in the alleged unity of thinking and feeling, thinking always predominated. Therefore, they developed a set of policies and practices that generally overlooked the private struggles and emotions, particularly at critical moments of personal rupture such as the death of a family member.

An Inconsistent Partner

Communists were ill prepared to deal with the full range of divergent interests among the working classes because they believed that divergent interests existed only in a capitalist world. In the political realm, multiple parties representing multiple interests were needed only so long as there were multiple classes. By contrast, in a socialist society, as in the workers' movement, there was no need to recognize or attempt to resolve conflicting interests since theoretically these would disappear as the former dominant class was eliminated. Yet just as families who supported communism in the Weimar Republic had many different interests, so too did families continue to have aspirations that diverged from the state's in the GDR.

Moreover, while families were the focus of party and state efforts to mobilize the masses in support of the KPD and later the SED regime, these same families were also engaged in struggles within the family over their personal or familial aspirations. As a result, microsocial interactions for families in both eras were subject to many conflicting crosscurrents that made it less likely that the family would be a reliable partner in the building of socialism. Indeed, families engaged with state or party institutions in ways that did not always conform to communist leaders' expectations. Rather than executing party directives, families' actions were informed primarily by the events of everyday life and how these events affected them either as familial units or as individuals. Most importantly, the conflicting emotional or political interests within the family itself shaped interactions both within the family and between the family and communist institutions, making them inconsistent political partners.

This dynamic was already at work among communist families in the interwar years, when the communists were a small minority party on the far left of the political spectrum. Family happenings, from making ends meet to dealing with noisy neighbors, politicized families; and many turned to communist politics to address their everyday problems. These families were political partners with the KPD, but partners who frequently prioritized family matters over party strategy, adapting communist politics accordingly. Even becoming a communist could be a complex endeavor, with family relations often trumping both party politics and social conditions as the primary motivator of an individual's politicization. In "How I Came to the Red Front" in the *Frauenwacht* in 1928, one woman testified:

> My husband fell in battle. After the war, my son [Karl] came home one evening and said, "Mother, we are social democrats, but only up until now: The leaders have betrayed us. Today it all became much clearer to me after a discussion at a [KPD] oppositional union meeting. Everything is getting worse and worse

for us ... From now on, I belong to the [KPD] Opposition and I'm going to listen to what the KPD [has to say]. In any case, I'm going to quit the SPD." Then I said, "From now on, you don't need to come back home anymore." A few days later, my youngest son came in and said, "Mother, I'm also joining the communists. Karl was right. He explained everything to me!" I said, "I will kill you both!"

This story demonstrates how becoming a communist could be fraught with familial conflict, particularly during a critical moment of rupture in the family. With a dead father and the threat of violence between the mother and sons, this family was not the stable family that KPD leaders had envisioned as one of the kernels of party organization.

Still, the family was an incubator for political identity. Indeed, both of the sons and the mother herself in the end joined the communist movement. As she explained, "Through my sons, everything has become clear to me, and I know that only through a united fight in the Red Class Front can the emancipation of the proletariat be realized." At first glance, the mother's political conversion functions as a morality tale, laden with propagandistic overtones. Her story is most interesting, however, for what it illustrates about how family politics intersected with public politics; for it was primarily the familial bond that drew the mother and younger brother into the communist movement. This story could and probably did end differently in many other cases, for unpredictability characterized the complex political partnership between the communist movement and the families who supported it. Nevertheless, this narrative underscores the ways that familial relations helped to forge political bonds.

While the KPD certainly instrumentalized families to serve the party, families conversely used the KPD to address challenges in their everyday lives. For most proletarian families in Weimar Germany, daily life itself was a series of economic struggles, especially once the Great Depression took hold after 1929. These challenges politicized families, and many turned to the communist movement for help. Families' everyday political struggles were acutely evident at the welfare office, where they battled with representatives of an inadequate system (Crew 1998: 114). Disputes with welfare officials, in turn, further radicalized families. However, when families joined the KPD to challenge welfare policies, they adapted party strategies to their needs in everyday life, reshaping communist politics at the local level.

Proletarian families criticized welfare in terms of three central grievances. First, they complained about the inadequacy of assistance. In the article titled "There Is Only Clothing for the Fourth Child" appearing on 23 June 1930 in *For the Proletarian Woman*, one mother recounted how a welfare administrator had refused to provide clothing for her new baby. "In this warm weather," the officer allegedly said, "a child can lie quietly naked in the cradle." Second, families objected to welfare officials' attempts to impose middle-class standards of mothering on them (Hagemann 1990: 213). Another woman reported in the same paper on 12 May 1930 about the requirement that unemployed housewives attend homemaking classes. "It is pure mockery," she rejoined. "As if the worker's wife can't do this. She learned long ago how to cook lunch out of nothing and how to sew her children's clothes from patches and rags."

Third, families perceived that welfare officials manipulated assistance to probe into their private lives. In an article titled "A Female Welfare Snooper," written by a worker correspondent and published in the SR on 5 July 1932, a woman described an interrogation by an administrator:

> The welfare officer asked me ... if I went to bed on Sunday evening at an appropriate time since I looked "so exhausted." As if a mother of four small children and an infant on her breast would have the time and the money to lead a dissolute life. Hopefully, this welfare officer goes to bed as early as I. Is it not a shame that you must let such ladies, who have no idea about [your] life and receive a decent salary, poke their noses into your business and bully you? And then these men wonder when somebody loses all of their patience at the [welfare] office!

Reading and reporting such stories offered working-class women the chance to identify with the critics of the welfare system, and the KPD press provided the medium to share those familiar experiences.

Angered by their bad experiences, families frequently turned to communist politics. The KPD, for its part, consistently challenged welfare policies by opposing cuts at city council meetings and organizing protests. Families, by contrast, lashed out at welfare bureaucrats, both personalizing and politicizing disputes at the local welfare office. One common method of resistance was to denounce welfare officials in the party press. Female officials especially came under fierce attack by rank-and-file communists who characterized them as callously relishing their power over clients.

One KPD member wrote a scathing article for the SR on 19 April 1929 titled "The Lot of Families with Many Children." Denouncing a certain Sister Sophie who ran a residential facility, he claimed that she "swings her whip and tyrannizes the occupants to the marrow. She sticks her nose in every pot to see if there is too much fat in the food as a way to reduce welfare support." Such denunciations demonstrated that communist politics unfolded differently on the ground than at the highest echelons of the party. While party leaders primarily challenged welfare laws, families targeted administrators. In their opinion, the main problem was not the law but unsympathetic bureaucrats.

That family politics on the ground diverged from KPD directives was also evident in the ways that families responded to their neighborhood foes. With the rise of the Nazi Party in the early 1930s, Communists and National

Socialists battled for control over neighborhoods by engaging in daily acts of violence. Since Eve Rosenhaft's landmark study on the subject (1983: esp. 207), a number of scholars have demonstrated that the rules of political engagement fundamentally changed when neighborhoods with the involvement of families displaced factories as the epicenters of working-class agitation (Mallmann 1996: 373–80; McElligott 1998: 163–97; Swett 2004).

In proletarian districts, new forms of mobilization emerged, measured most patently by violence between the political adversaries. Rank-and-file communists testified to this escalating violence, but communists also maintained that conflict was more pervasive than historians once asserted. It often erupted in response to the banal disputes of everyday life. The politicization of the ordinary was one of the defining features of the political sphere in the late Weimar as families were frequently drawn into political conflict in their backyards.

In September 1930, after the Nazi Party became the largest party in the Reichstag, the KPD founded the Fighting League against Fascism, or Kampfbund gegen den Faschismus. Hermann Weber (1969: 364–65) places membership in the Fighting League at approximately 100,000 in 1931. Organized in working-class neighborhoods, the Fighting League sought to challenge the Nazis primarily through public protest (Friederici and Welckerling 1975). Families also took part in this battle, but their struggles often resulted more from personal conflict with Nazi neighbors than party directives.

One worker correspondent addressed these issues of personal conflict among neighbors in an article for the *SR* on 14 August 1931 titled "We Are Marching on the Renter Front." The writer described how one woman, upset that her upstairs neighbor stomped on his floor as if he were "marching in a Nazi parade," attended a KPD-sponsored tenant meeting to complain. Noise—a common source of dispute in apartment housing—provided the catalyst for this woman's politicization. Expressing herself strategically in the name of the family, she employed KPD institutions to challenge her Nazi neighbor. Yet this woman's response was not entirely consistent with KPD tactics. This incident, in which one resident accused another of making characteristically Nazi noises, showed how the label *Nazi* could be used indiscriminately as an epithet to defame quarrelsome neighbors.

Rank-and-file communists deployed similar tactics to denounce others in the neighborhood. As narrated in an article titled "A Foretaste of the Third Reich," probably written again by a worker correspondent and published in the 6–7 August 1932 edition of the *SR*, a homemaker reported that Nazis had ordered her to relinquish her streetcar seat to a middle-class woman wearing a swastika. After refusing, she claimed, "One of the brown heroes rushed toward me and threatened me with a raised fist." He allegedly shouted, "I will hit you right in the trap." A report by the neighborhood KPD cell in Mittweida on 14

August 1931 for the *Rote Fahne*, another communist newspaper, stated that a Nazi had dumped the contents of a chamber pot on a working-class family because its members were not wearing swastikas as they strolled by his house. Immediately after, the man's servants attacked the victimized family, allegedly striking the eight-month pregnant mother.

The implication of many such articles is that these kinds of class-based tensions and recriminations were remarkably common. Viewed more broadly, these stories suggest that everyday life during the Weimar Republic was infused not simply with power and force but also with politics in the traditional sense of public pronouncements, activism, mobilization, and even violence in the service of parties. As these examples illustrate, families became partners with communism in protest when their private lives were disrupted by neighborly conflicts; but their intentions and tactics often differed from those of the KPD leadership, making them awkward political partners.

State Objectives in the GDR

The problematic partnership between families and the Communist Party was similarly evident in East Germany but within a different historical framework. In theory, the main sources of conflict that characterized the everyday life of families during the Weimar Republic were addressed in the GDR, giving the state the opportunity to improve the quality of life of ordinary people within a socialist framework. In practice, however, the state focused more on mobilizing families for building socialism than on responding to their everyday concerns. Indeed, GDR family policy showed little regard for personal circumstances or desires. The lives of East German families, communists and noncommunists alike, rarely conformed to official rhetoric; for private life was often shaped more by personal interests, concerns, and desires and by the internal dynamics of the family than by socialist theory. Though they were influenced by state policy, family members' decisions neither completely defied nor consistently corresponded to leaders' expectations.

At the core of the incongruence between state policy and families' lives was the fact that the private sphere included an array of personal choices. As Josie McLellan shows in her work on sexuality in the GDR (2011: 13), socialist culture was a work in progress that created space for private choice. Nevertheless, the regime made clear that some choices suited socialism better than others. It was precisely at these points of intersection between private choices and state objectives that families acted unpredictably, making them unreliable partners in the building of socialism. With this in mind, we consider two moments of rupture in a family's life: death and divorce.

Funerary practices demonstrated how families' interests and the state's could diverge in unexpected ways. An example is the collective urn ceremony. In conjunction with reforming funeral culture in the 1960s, the GDR offered families the option of burial in collective urns. During the ceremony, the ashes of the deceased were buried with dozens of others in an unmarked field (Happe 2001). The propagation of this rite had both an ideological and a practical rationale, as it was much cheaper to organize collective funerals than a series of individual ones. This example confirms McLellan's proposition (2011: 12–13) that GDR moral rhetoric often had a solidly pragmatic basis. This rite was also motivated by ideology, for no other funeral ritual so clearly reflected the primacy of the collective as the collective urn ceremony; socialist values were not only embedded in the experience of the bereaved but also embodied in what was done to the corpse itself.

Nonetheless, the collective urn funeral never became the most popular form of burial in the GDR. Even when families were willing to situate the biography of their loved ones within a broader socialist narrative, they generally shied away from allowing the representation of the deceased's life and the symbolic act of his or her burial to be completely shaped according to the needs or demands of the socialist collective. In fact, by the middle of the 1980s, only 15 to 18 percent of funerals were collective urn ceremonies. There were also strong regional differences in the distribution of collective funerals, with cemeteries in Zwickau and Karl-Marx-Stadt (Chemnitz) producing the highest rates: 85 and 83 percent, respectively. Yet the popularity of collective funerals in these cities was not necessarily due to citizens' commitment to secular sepulchral culture. It appears more likely that it was a result of the bonus that cemetery administrators received for each collective funeral they organized (Redlin 2009: 237).

The uneven support for collective urn ceremonies arose from and contributed to the many tensions between family desires and state objectives. Families often adopted some socialist funerary practices, such as allowing the orator to play the main role in the ceremony, but they also sought to retain some creative input. For example, families had the right to suggest quotations for inclusion in the ceremony and to choose the corresponding music. However, the state remained cautious about families' wishes, fearing that their choices might be politically unsound.

Consequently, the state directed funeral officials to limit families' input and to ensure that families consented to socialist funerary practices. As a handbook on secular funerals by the Dresden Institute for Municipal Economy noted, families' recommendations regarding musical selections had to match the state's vision. "Requests regarding music, based on the so-called 'last will' of the deceased, should be considered binding but only inasmuch as they harmonize with the rest of the ceremony" (Institut für Kommunalwirtschaft

1979: 11). This conversation between the funeral orator and the family about the ceremony was cast as communication between equals; but in practice, the state sought to use this discussion to reshape families' attitudes.

A divergence of interests also sometimes surfaced over the eulogy. Although families could provide specific details for the eulogy, orators often softened or recast the content, particularly in regard to politically sensitive issues. When Titus T. organized his sister's funeral, for example, his version of the eulogy would have suggested that the division of Germany had made it difficult for his sister to visit her siblings in West Germany: "The contact with her family members was good, but it was painfully interrupted through the political and spatial division, which made [contact] … hardly possible." This direct reference to the Cold War division of Germany was unacceptable.

Although families were allowed to provide specific details for the eulogy, orators often softened or recast the content, particularly in regard to politically sensitive issues like this one. In response to this delicate situation, the orator subtly revised the description of the deceased's life to assume a more neutral stance: "Living apart from her siblings was difficult for her" (Redlin 2009: 181). Orators thus subordinated the family's desires for the funeral to the socialist vision by obscuring biographical details that did not fit neatly into the socialist narrative. Families could grumble about the eulogy after the ceremony, but the eulogy was literally the last official word on the life of the deceased.

Sometimes families rejected certain funerary practices altogether, especially when funeral employees did not properly consult them. In a complaint to state authorities, a woman from Dresden described her family's experience at her mother's funeral: "The coffin stood undecorated in front of a dirty tiled wall. Visible numbers had been scrawled in chalk on the coffin. At that time—five minutes before the ceremony—a *Herr* appeared, and tried to explain to my father that he was the speaker." He had not consulted with the family about the deceased. "How can such a speaker," she complained, "understand the deep pain of the bereaved and in his speech pay the deceased last respects? … We declined his speech" (Schulz 2008: 125).

Rejecting the orator's eulogy represented an exceptional example of self-authorization in the face of the power of the state. In the sense of both authorship and authority, this woman claimed the right of the family to determine the meaning of her mother's life. It marks a claim that the deceased self was unique and that memorialization should be personal and individual, not abstract and oriented toward the collective. Yet funeral officials did often reduce families' private moments to mere formulas. Due to the shortage of funeral labor, cemetery officials routinely glossed over families' grief, thereby contributing to families' mounting dissatisfaction with GDR funerary practices (MfSk, Thomas, unpublished: 4).

While the state hoped that families would be silent, compliant executors of its policies, families often behaved with the autonomy that they theoretically enjoyed as partners in the national effort to build socialism. Asserting their own wishes, which were generally tied to the emotional challenges of mourning, brought families into conflict with funeral officials. A constant point of contention was the question of flowers. Flowers were not welcomed at the cemetery because administrators interpreted the act of leaving flowers on a grave as a celebration of death, which was contrary to socialist values.

In addition, the removal of dead flowers created extra work. Consequently, cemetery employees sometimes confiscated families' flowers immediately upon their arrival, which enraged grieving families. As a petitioner from Dresden complained: "For the farewell we were led into a room; there the flowers were taken from me, against my will. I wanted to throw them on the coffin—that was not possible!" (Schulz 2008: 125) Yet families found ways to leave flowers. As exasperated officials noted, families left flowers on graves in "old glasses and cans … on which one can still see the labels." As far as the officials were concerned, these informal memorial practices undermined the dignity of the cemetery (Kramer 1974: 35).

Thus, even when opting for socialist funerals, families still failed to conform completely to the state's social and political norms. Families countered official arguments by asserting that cemetery personnel failed to tend the graves. Felix Robin Schulz (2008: 126) quotes a letter writer from Dresden who complained that the cemetery "resembles a dump yard for rubble! Yesterday we once again observed that the last burial site [of the collective urn] from May is covered in weeds, and it is intended for people who dedicated all of their energy to the construction of our Republic!"

While cemetery officials and families agreed that the cathartic elements of the funeral were subverted, they each placed the blame on the other. From the families' point of view, the problem was the funeral's formulaic rituals; from the administrators' perspective, the problem was families' stubbornness. Both testify to the fact that practices and experiences of actual families did not fit easily into the SED's ideal models for them.

Attempting to shape and constrain expressions of suffering was one of the many methods the state used to influence family practices and to embed the family in the state. Through funeral rites, the SED sought to make the body of the deceased function as a central prop in a performance that would strengthen socialist commitment. East German leaders similarly attempted to shape family relations to instill socialist values. Beginning with the 1950 Law for the Protection of Mother and Child and the Rights of Women, the state worked actively to ensure that families contributed to the building of socialism by following policies that promoted marriage and childbearing. In the context of a population decline caused largely by emigration, the law provided various incentives to marry and have children. These included paid maternity leave, payments for the birth of each child, and extra payments if the mother was employed (Zimmerman 1993: 192–240; Harsch 2007: 134–35).

In parallel, the state initially made divorce relatively difficult. During the 1950s, the GDR regime adopted a censorious, moralistic approach to the breakdown of marriages (Betts 2010: 96). Even in the 1960s, the state saw marriage problems as a general concern for all of society, and it believed that such problems could ideally be solved by collective discussion, preferably without ending in divorce (Harsch 2007: 286–87). In the late 1960s, however, political leaders adjusted family policy in response to declining fertility rates by extending maternity leave, increasing financial benefits for families, and providing substantially more childcare. In an effort to offer more support for both married and unmarried mothers and children, the regime also assumed a more relaxed attitude toward divorce in line with undeniable social changes (Betts 2010: 108, 113).

In the eyes of SED leaders, divorce prioritized individuals' personal needs and emotions over society's interests. Therefore, the state sought to manage the process of breaking up so that something could be salvaged that would serve the building of socialism and be compatible with official family policies. Divorced people could, in principle, get on with their new lives, as long as they continued to bring up their children responsibly and remained economically active. In theory, divorce involved two parties who could separate, remarry, and have more children unencumbered by the past. The SED usually assumed that the mother would have custody and that, as a full-time worker with extensive physical and financial state support, she would not be financially dependent on her former husband (Klose 1996: 257–61; Mertens 1998: 78–80). As with funerals, however, the failure of the state to consider families' private feelings was evident in the case of divorce policy, which created difficult situations that deeply alienated families.

One practical problem that made divorce messy was the failure of the state to fulfill its promise of adequate housing. Because the GDR did not invest sufficiently in housing, shortages led to social problems that directly affected families (Harsch 2007: 175–77). By the 1960s, many families limited their sizes because of poor and overcrowded housing. Erich Honecker, when he took over the position of general secretary of the SED from Ulbricht in 1971, promised substantial new investment in housing. At that time, 92 percent of houses and apartments had no central heating, 60 percent had no bathroom, and 29 percent had no running water (Harsch 2007: 277).

By the late 1970s, as Mark Allinson notes (2009: 261), popular discontent arose out of the SED's unfulfilled promises that had increased citizens' expectations of improvements. Continuing housing shortages meant that newly divorced couples were often forced to return to the home they had shared together, where they now had to try to build emotionally separate lives. According to the SED's logic, social conflict was based on class conflict, and emotions were determined more by one's class position than by interpersonal differences. Accordingly, for the SED, the only problems that might arise from this situation were those caused by the lack of physical, as opposed to emotional, space in the apartment.

Personal examples of divorce demonstrated that family life with its high emotions was not as uncomplicated as East German legislators presumed. Above all, the shortage of housing, when coupled with divorce, contributed to emotional complications, the impossibility of having a private life, and sometimes even personal danger. Generally all of these experiences were overlooked by the state. The life of Michael Mandelbaum (a pseudonym) is a case in point. Mandelbaum recounted his story in his unpublished memoir from 2001 (KBio 6588). It illustrates how state policy contributed to persistent family conflict and personal turmoil.

The title of this memoir is *Wie ein Mensch wird, was er ist, oder Wir sind die Sklaven unseres Verstandes, oder Studie eines Lebens*, meaning "How Someone Becomes Who He Is, or, We Are Slaves to Our Senses, or, the Study of a Life." The title itself suggests that this memoir was an intentional practice of the self. Yet memoirs are ambiguous documents that narrate only selected events. In the case of Mandelbaum, his memoir simply recalled a series of events in his life with little reflection on the wider context outside his family life.

He portrays himself, quite consciously, as someone with no interest in the political and sees his problems as arising from a combination of being sexually driven but unable to sustain relationships. In the context of this chapter, Mandelbaum's memoir is useful because of the things he did not set out to convey: insight into the everyday life of an adult in the GDR in the 1970s and 1980s who was living in an apparently politically disconnected way, in a society in which politics was intended to permeate so many aspects of everyday life. Unlike Alexander Morawitz, whom we met in chapter two, Mandelbaum almost never seriously considered how the state impinged on him. He took what happened to him in relation to the authorities as a given, something to shrug off or to endure if necessary. But the state did impinge on Mandelbaum, with its decisions contributing significantly to his private turmoil.

Born in Leipzig in 1957, Mandelbaum was clearly a fragile person: he made several suicide attempts. Most of his personal struggles seemed to stem from the failure of his many families, the one he was born into and the ones he subsequently formed. All of these families were chaotic, inward looking, and too concerned with the search for personal pleasure—particularly sexual satisfaction—to be consciously involved in the building of socialism. In his memoir, Mandelbaum presents himself as an unloved child from a marriage devoid of affection. His father, who was violent toward his mother and at times toward him, divorced and went to live with another woman. When that relationship failed, he returned to reside with his former wife, a pattern repeated by his son. The torments of the son's childhood, which included coming home to discover that his father had hanged himself, left Mandelbaum anxious, prone to bed-wetting, desperate to be loved, and unable to establish stable relationships.

In the context of the GDR's severe housing shortage, divorce led to many personal problems, including uncertainty, emotional confusion, ambiguity in private relations, and the ongoing financial interdependence of divorced spouses. In the mid-1970s, Mandelbaum, already married and divorced, was living with his mother in her apartment as well as with his new girlfriend, Anngret, and his former wife. In 1978, he married Anngret and had a child with her. The new family then moved into an apartment that he renovated to make habitable.

In 1984, he divorced Anngret but continued to live with her; that is to say, as Mandelbaum had nowhere else to go, he was again in the unenviable position of having to live with a former wife. This situation contributed to sexual tension and conflict over money between the former spouses. It was further exacerbated by Anngret's numerous relationships with men, who often reacted aggressively to Mandelbaum's presence. Driven by the need to be loved and by sexual desire, Mandelbaum started a fraught relationship with a third woman, Kirsten, who lived with her mother in the apartment below and who also had a daughter. This relationship also ended and restarted a number of times.

In the course of his three marriages and three divorces, Mandelbaum's principal point of connection with the state was through the housing office, whose decisions contributed to the difficulties of Mandelbaum's families. In 1987, the state allocated an apartment in need of repair to Mandelbaum for his new family on the condition that he undertook all renovations. This presented real challenges due to the need to use barter and even theft to acquire the necessary building materials. He and Kirsten moved in and eventually got married, but when the relationship collapsed, the court—his next point of contact with the institutions of the state—gave the apartment to Kirsten and her daughter in the divorce settlement. Once again, Mandelbaum lived with Anngret and his daughter before finally returning to his mother's home.

As Mandelbaum's personal history illustrates, state policies regarding family law and housing contributed markedly to his personal disarray. In particular, ex-spouses who were forced to reside in the same apartment experienced sexual tension, for they were often still attracted to each other; yet they could hardly overcome this problem because they could not separate themselves physically. Their lack of separation and privacy, which was a major hindrance to moving on after a divorce, resulted primarily from the failure of the state's housing policies. While the state did not set out to cause personal turmoil, its inability to remedy the severe housing shortage contributed to family crises.

Additionally, while the state sought to develop a socialist personality in its citizens, Mandelbaum's chaotic lifestyle and living conditions meant it was unlikely that he would develop a clear sense of self or identity. His self was not something he felt he could control or construct; it was fragmented, pulled in many directions at once, unable to be consistently performed or used as a basis for looking outward and involving himself in the life of the collective.

Families' private struggles were also a result of the persistent failure of the SED to take into account the distress of divorced families. Bound by a class-based ideology, SED officials believed that emotions arose out of class relations and that the primary source of personal identity and feelings was work. If people were unhappy in marriage, there were objective problems that could be solved with the application of reason. If a marriage had to end, there allegedly would be no continuing emotional entanglements or sexual tension between the divorced spouses because the objective conditions that once gave rise to such conflicts under capitalism had been eliminated in a classless society.

In reality, however, emotional entanglements rarely ended with divorce. Mandelbaum and Anngret continued to be torn by desire for each other and by jealousy over new lovers, something that led to outbursts of rage and even violence. This lack of concern on the part of party leaders for how their policies added to the private turmoil of families was the underside of the GDR's informal social contract between the state and families; the degree of privacy that citizens were allowed also meant that they were left alone with their personal problems. In sum, East Germany failed to produce the desired family that internalized socialist values and committed itself to building socialism because some state policies undermined other efforts by the state to fashion families into reliable political partners.

The Politics of the Everyday

For both communist families during the Weimar Republic and East German families under communism, private life was replete with conflict, some of it intensely personal, some of it arising out of disputes with outside authorities. As an oppositional party during the Weimar Republic, the KPD led the charge to confront government policies. Many proletarian families readily followed the party's lead; but families often altered the KPD's agenda and tactics to meet the needs of everyday life, thus conducting communist politics in unexpected ways. In the GDR, similar attempts to impose the SED's ideology upon private matters were frequently met with stubborn resistance by families who managed funerals or sought to cope with divorce. Citizens quietly, or sometimes not so quietly, resisted the state's efforts to control their private lives.

The same could be said of individuals within families. Let us look at another example from the Weimar Republic when communism was on the margins, rather than at the center, of state power. Although communist families often actively promoted KPD platforms, family members limited the extent to which they allowed the party to shape their private lives. The complex relationship between the party and its members was particularly evident in the KPD's efforts to mobilize women through the Roter Frauen- und Mädchenbund (RFMB), an organization for communist women and girls founded in late 1925.

KPD leaders envisioned the RFMB as a vital tool to recruit women who were reluctant to join the party itself (S. Sewell 2012). In their official guidelines as well as conference materials from 1926, the KPD leaders instructed the RFMB to target housewives by engaging with them in their everyday spaces such as grocery stores and their homes (BArch SAPMO RY1/I 4/3/1). In the report of the RFMB on 7 May 1926 (BArch SAPMO RY1/I 4/3/2), RFMB leaders instructed members to bring women into the KPD by politicizing issues that they faced in their daily lives, including the prices of goods, welfare, and reproductive rights.

The following photograph is instructive. Illustration 4.3 depicts a 1930 RFMB demonstration under the banner "Without Women There Can

Illustration 4.3. Red Women and Girls' League Demonstration, Worms, July 1930. SAPMO, Bild Y 1-69/71. Courtesy of BArch.

Be No Proletarian Revolution." Marching in the center were women who sported the RFMB uniform, a blue knee-length skirt, a white or grey blouse, a tunic without a belt, and simple shoes. That they covered their bodies with communist attire attested to their willingness to serve as political partners with the KPD.

But not all of these women were so disciplined. The most striking figure in this photograph is the woman standing in the center of it, who seemingly posed for the camera. Refusing to conform to the communist feminine ideal, she sported many of the popular fashion trends that RFMB and KPD leaders denounced: hat over her ears, curls popping out of her hat, a fashionable dress, a clutched purse, and stylish high-heeled shoes. She clearly sympathized with communist politics, for she participated in the demonstration; but she also marked the limits of the KPD's capacity to transform the private lives of its members. Putting self-authorization ahead of ideology, she resisted the call to mold her body to conform to the communist feminine aesthetic. To this extent, she indicated a limit to her reliability as a political partner of the KPD.

Two decades later, families in the GDR proved themselves to be similarly unreliable. Despite the different historical contexts, there were clear continuities between the ways communist families in Weimar Germany and East German families engaged with or were involved in activities that were political in their everyday lives, for neither set of families ever fully subscribed to communist politics. As the GDR worked to steer family behavior in moments of peace as well as crisis, such as divorce and funerals, families cooperated, but only to the extent that the state's policies met their needs or when they had no choice. Only rarely did the SED's expectation that ideological commitment should be the basis of everyday choices turn into reality.

Even when East German families did conduct themselves in accordance with the SED's expectations, they often had different motivations and priorities from those of the state. The constant complaints of many families showed that the negotiations between families and state officials were anything but harmonious. Families, in other words, were often political liabilities in the building of socialism.

The case of Peter Erdmann (a pseudonym), who was introduced at the beginning of this chapter, provides a compelling example of political conflict at a moment of personal crisis. Erdmann's Stasi file with his accompanying impassioned letter about his treatment (2001 KBio 6232) provides a clear picture of how the state's actions and blindness to human emotions contributed to the private turmoil of ordinary families. In particular, the pervasiveness of the state apparatus encouraged individuals to compromise their own integrity, if only for self-protection. In this way, the GDR state undermined affective relations within the family.

Born in 1947, Erdmann was working in a restaurant in Meiningen in Thuringia in the mid-1970s and living with his second wife, Ingeborg, from whom he was divorced. In 1976, Erdmann was one of many ordinary citizens who protested alongside prominent intellectuals when the GDR authorities deprived the singer Wolf Biermann of his citizenship. According to the police report dated 19 November 1976 in his Stasi file, Erdmann handwrote and distributed about fifty small placards expressing solidarity with Biermann. According to the court report in the file (3 March 1977, 072, p. 7) Stasi officials arrested and interrogated Erdmann some days later; and in 1977, he was sentenced to fifteen months imprisonment "for incitement against the state."

While he was in prison, Ingeborg pursued another relationship and had a child. Upon his release from prison, Erdmann went back to live with her. Ingeborg, under pressure from her father, subsequently moved to an agricultural cooperative, but she later invited Erdmann to join her there. In total, they lived together for three years after his release, until further pressure from her father made him leave for good.

As noted earlier, it was only after the collapse of the GDR that Erdmann learned that the Stasi's source of information about his actions was Ingeborg. The documents from his Stasi file (292, 302) show that Ingeborg was aware of the seriousness of her actions. In fact, she asked for and was given a promise that her statement would not be shown to her ex-husband. Though it is impossible to discern whether Ingeborg was being malicious or simply naïve, self-deception was clearly at play here, for informing on Erdmann was not going to make things better for her ex-husband. Yet, to protect herself from feeling overwhelmed by her betrayal and collaboration with the state, she asserted that her actions were in his best interest.

By offering up information about her family life to a representative of the state, the supposedly nonpolitical Ingeborg compromised her integrity to protect herself. As Gabriele Taylor theorizes (1985: 121–22, 29; also Bergerson et al. 2011: 35–92), external factors such as the deliberate politicization of private life can cause ethical confusion, ambiguity, and self-deception. In the GDR, such self-deception was a widespread feature of daily life, for it was tempting to take advantage of the opportunities the intrusive state offered to inflict pain on former partners.

Thus the state's involvement in family relations often destroyed real intimacy and trust. This undermining of the family was both a subversion of the SED's ostensible aim of promoting the family as the "primary location of love, intimacy and private emotions" (Betts 2010: 90) and a demonstration of the extent to which the state had inserted itself into the private space of the family. The net result was to radically undermine trust in others or in society more widely. This dynamic of state and society introduced a fundamental rupture in the everyday lives of East German citizens long before the fall of the Wall.

What is striking about the examples here is that they suggest that much of everyday life was lived not only as if previous customs and traditions still applied but also as if life were fundamentally chaotic, driven by personal desires and emotions. The GDR could not accept that previous customs and traditions might be relevant in an ostensibly Marxist–Leninist society. Nor could it, with its mechanistic approach to the unfolding of history and therefore the development of society, cope with the complexity and unpredictability of personal lives. Its attempts to inculcate socialist ways of being involved a denial of the way people actually were and how they behaved. Administrative measures had at best a limited impact on behavior. At worst, they encouraged a culture not of socialist cooperation but of denunciation, whereby individual family members used the state and its processes to pursue their own interests, ahead of loyalty to others in the family.

A Failed Partnership

For communists, the family was both a political asset and a liability. The family served as a locus of political mobilization for the KPD and the SED. It was the party's ability to help families manage everyday life that served as the yardstick against which families measured the viability of the socialist undertaking. Yet it was often at the intersection between families and political institutions that individuals acted unpredictably and seemingly irrationally. Driven more by emotions than by calculation or ideological purpose, their actions had consequences that were not foreseen by either families or party members.

Communist leaders considered the family to be a vehicle for political mobilization and the potential embodiment of socialist values; but the family was also a social unit complicated by affective relations and one in which individual members expected to be able to lead autonomous, private lives. Families campaigned for the KPD, participated in its underground operations during the Nazi rule, and were, in some cases, willing partners in the building of socialism in the GDR. Families' political loyalties were often tied to their perception of the degree to which the Communist Party helped them to advance their personal agendas. When families felt let down by the party as they encountered the challenges of everyday life, the bonds of loyalty between families and communist organizations frayed.

As the Communist Party moved from being in opposition to being in power after World War II, its ability to determine the framework of everyday life changed significantly. Effectively in control of public discourse, political culture, and public space, East German leaders conceded a degree of autonomy to families in an implicit social contract between the state and its citizens. Yet the evidence suggests that the terms of this contract were imprecise, and this imprecision had two consequences.

The first was that families found ways to realize their personal desires, as a collective or as individuals within this collective, even as the state tried to deny them this possibility. Families were more autonomous, more self-authorizing, and more shaped by emotions than the state had anticipated. The pursuit of personal fulfillment could result not only in greater freedom to live a life based on individual inclination but also in a loss of personal integrity in everyday dealings with others as the state found ways to invade private life.

The second derived from the fact that the East German state formulated models for a socialist way of life. Families found themselves unable or unwilling to follow such models unconditionally. The resulting contradictions undermined families' participation in the SED's plans to build socialism.

The creators of socialist culture hoped that, within a couple of generations, the population would be sufficiently educated to make ideologically correct choices. Instead, the state's efforts to educate by allowing choice resulted in the emergence of parallel structures that compromised the building of socialism. The socialist, secular funeral never completely replaced the religious funeral ceremony, and the family never became truly socialist, largely because of the incongruence between the understanding of the family as a united social unit and the consequences of policies relating, for instance, to housing and divorce. As a result, several models of cohabitation and family relations emerged that defied categorization according to ideological criteria. In an effort to create a uniform socialist society, East German leaders unintentionally generated diversity, which undermined their efforts to advance models of socialist conduct for families and family members.

This nexus of private desires and state objectives is reminiscent of the stories of the Wende-losers we met in the first chapter. We certainly understand why many tend to romanticize everyday life in the former GDR, where employment was relatively secure. Yet this chapter on the everyday lives of families suggests that this kind of *Ostalgie*, or nostalgia for former East Germany, overlooks crucial parts of their earlier experiences. Family life in the GDR was replete with private struggle, as it is everywhere.

Death and divorce disrupted family life in ways that destroyed intimate bonds. Ignoring the emotional impact of lifecycle events, the SED sought to whitewash families' private turmoil with eulogies that affirmed socialist values or living arrangements that denied personal turmoil. We can now pick up this story of ruptures in the post-Wende *Alltag* of German families and trace it backward to the GDR itself. If the Wende created an even greater diversity of winners and losers among the families of the former GDR, that crisis, as extreme as it was, should be understood in terms of the longer histories of families in everyday life.

This chapter has looked at situations associated with the supposed ordinariness of everyday life: children's play, squabbles with neighbors, marriages, divorces, and funerals. Yet it was precisely here on the ground that certain kinds of politics took place. They involved a wide range of people, including welfare recipients, funeral orators, worker journalists, and memoir writers as well as families and family members of all kinds. The people we have looked at engaged in a wide range of practices such as fighting, enlisting, protesting, grieving, cremating, mating, reproducing, divorcing. Parties and states sought to determine the rituals and the meanings associated with families and to give them specifically political meanings, but the party never fully succeeded. It was these microsocial interactions—at once practices of family and politics, self and society—that gave the family its weight in private and public life.

In sum, our exploration of families and communist politics uncovered a dynamic relationship. The public and private spheres never operated in isolation or even distinctly; there were constant microsocial interactions both internally in the family and between members of the family and representatives of state power. These interactions made life complex and contradictory for all involved and in ways that saw power and influence shifting back and forth in unpredictable ways. Both in opposition and in power, communists sought to make use of the political potential of the family, but with variable results.

In turn, the family or individual members of it tried to use the state to achieve personal ends. Self-authorization led, perhaps, to small victories in the search for some kind of personal autonomy. It also perhaps contributed to a sense of loss, disorientation, and a lack of belonging either within the family or within the wider society. And finally, self-authorization perhaps led to betrayal: of oneself and those to whom one should, in principle, have remained loyal. Whether or not families saw themselves operating according to the terms set out by those holding or purporting to hold power, in all cases the personal was political, the political was most certainly personal, and the self was constantly pulled in many different, conflicting directions.

Phil Leask, Sara Ann Sewell, and Heléna Tóth

CHAPTER 5

Objects

Why is the GDR "Rondo" coffee brand similar to a neutron bomb?
The person dies, the cup remains.
—a widespread joke from the GDR

On the front cover of this book, we adapted an object of material culture from the GDR—the now popular, seemingly innocuous, plastic eggcup—into a representation of German *Alltag*. Found in abundance at such places as flea markets and eBay, it once graced the breakfast table as part of the morning ritual. By contrast, consider the vintage design of the egg garden chair from the GDR, pictured in Illustration 5.1. It was conceived in West Germany by the Hungarian designer Peter Ghyczy for the West German company Elastogan. Because its manufacture was outsourced to East Germany, which continued to manufacture the chair after Elastogan went bankrupt, it is considered a GDR design object. Adults and children enjoyed sitting in the garden in its pod-shaped seat on a summer's day. Today we see both objects as historical references for understanding the role of plastics and modernist aesthetics in fashioning East German everyday material culture. They visualize the technological utopianism of the postwar period in both East and West.

This chapter begins in contemporary Germany, where the task of representing everyday life in the GDR remains a highly politicized endeavor. It continues the story of self-fashioning in that remembering the socialist everyday involves imagining, naming, locating, and performing a self. It also takes up the story of the nature of the everyday itself—a product of how we make sense of the world in common. Finally it follows closely on the heels of our chapter on family because the political dynamics discovered there continued even after the GDR had collapsed.

That socialist everyday persists in Germany today in myriad ways—not only as ruptures that place demands on the present but also quite literally in the form of material remnants that evoke memories of those everyday lives. The media has long reported on the psychology of the so-called *wall in the head* between East and West as well as corresponding attitudes and practices carried into the home and workplace. If Dieter's story reminded us of the people

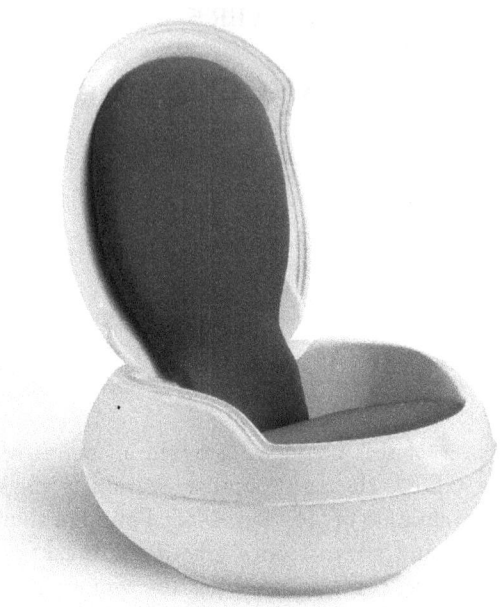

Illustration 5.1. Peter Ghyczy, *Egg Garden Chair*, 1968. White Polyurethane casing and blue upholstery, 2008.245.001. Courtesy of the Wende Museum of the Cold War, Culver City, California.

---

who lost out from the Wende, this chapter looks at a different kind of remainder of the everyday: the objects left behind, as it were, after reunification. East German objects are particularly interesting because of how they function as both the source for and challenge to memory in contemporary Germany.

In this chapter, we are interested in how these objects became the subject of memory. *What social processes make these ordinary things extraordinary in terms of their claim to be representative of everyday life in the GDR?* To address this question, we examine how surviving remnants from the GDR came to be located in museums and how they became the focal point of heated political debates about whether, and how, to represent the East German *Alltag*.

Although we begin with the state-funded national institutions of German memory, we focus on those that emerged outside this system during the first twenty-five years of united Germany, when the memories of the past coincided with the lived experiences of many people. Our investigations go beyond the walls of the traditional museum to connect more broadly to the larger scholarly and popular debate about the scope and content of German memory in particular and collective memory and material culture in general.

While the case we examine is German, we see a broader significance to the ruptures in memory and the dynamic operations by which the former East German everyday is represented. It is a useful case for understanding how institutions—in this case, museums—seek to manage dangerous memories from the recent past.

We have already seen that one dilemma for Wende-losers following reunification was their economic obsolescence. But dealing with obsolescence of their culture—their everyday attitudes, habits, and things—was a more general problem faced by most if not all former GDR citizens. The collapse of the GDR in 1989–90 and its swift integration into the political and economic structures of the FRG forced them to struggle with new practices from workplace to education to shopping at the grocery store. Literally and metaphorically, a space had to be cleared immediately for a new everyday; and this challenge meant that the old everyday had to disappear, one way or another.

In the everyday, however, habits are formed both by and in response to dominant discourses. Even as former East Germans were forced to adapt, as quickly as possible, to new circumstances, the old everyday remained *under erasure*. We borrow this term from the French philosopher Jacques Derrida, who in turn derived it from a correspondence between Heidegger and Jünger (Derrida 1997: xiv–xv; Taylor and Winquist 2000: 164). This term refers to the act of crossing out a word in a text because it does not fully capture the intended meaning; but because there is no better word, the deletion itself remains, keeping the original word and the act of deletion visible. We use it here to evoke the complex dynamics of rupture: the way that the practices of erasing and preserving the memory of the past are embedded in one another and require constant doing. In this sense the East German *Alltag* persists.

A resulting dilemma concerned both East and West: *what role should the everyday in particular play in the united German memory of the GDR?* The *Alltag* had been conspicuously lacking in the German government's highest profile attempt to come to terms with the GDR past—in German, *Aufarbeitung*. In 1993 the German Bundestag initiated an Enquete Commission to help shape the official history of the GDR and to provide guidelines for federally supported cultural institutions. A subsequent effort in 2004 to develop official guidelines for the implementation of GDR history through cultural institutions made this lack explicit. Known as the Sabrow Commission after its director, historian Martin Sabrow, the Commission found that everyday life and the areas of negotiation between state and society, loyalty and resistance were largely missing from both the historical dialogue and the cultural institutions that dealt with the GDR (Boyer 2005; Sabrow 2007; Beattie 2011).

Yet it was precisely the Sabrow Commission's recommendations concerning the everyday that were largely left unfunded and unimplemented. The everyday, it seemed, was too susceptible to misunderstanding and manipulation as a form of nostalgia for good old days to be easily incorporated into the memory landscape of united Germany. The mundane experiences of so-called ordinary Germans, with their romantic memories of small pleasures, seemed to pull against the overarching narrative of the GDR as an unjust, totalitarian system. The unreliable subjectivity of the eyewitness is said colloquially to be the enemy of the contemporary historian, who wants to work with facts rather than memories; similarly, the everyday—especially in the hands of nonspecialists—brings with it fears of trivializing a dictatorship or, worse, of using memory as an apology for dictatorship.

These fears have been part of a heated ongoing debate about how to characterize the GDR's form of government. It was a state where the communist party held a monopoly on power and where the Stasi brutally enforced laws intended to squelch dissent and keep citizens from traveling to the West. It shot its own people trying to cross the border without permission, killing at least 137 people along the Berlin Wall alone (Hertle and Nooke 2011). It was a form of dictatorship, and at the same time, the word *dictatorship* in Germany also conjures images of the Nazi regime. Yet founded on socialist principles, the GDR sought a degree of legitimacy in its opposition to National Socialism; and most citizens, at least on the outside, participated in efforts at both antifascism and building socialism.

Konrad Jarausch (1999: 60) coined the term *welfare dictatorship* to try to express both the emancipatory rhetoric and repressive reality. Similarly, Mary Fulbrook writes that the dictatorship was

> sustained by the actions and interactions of a vast majority of the population. This was a system that was more like a honeycomb full of crisscrossing little cells than a simple homogenous pot of "the people" with a repressive lid, the "regime" clamped down on it to keep the contents from boiling over. (2005: 292)

Following unification, politicians, publicists, and the media sought to instrumentalize the question of the nature of this dictatorship and reduce a complex phenomenon to simple judgments in order to stake out positions across the political spectrum. One of the main battlefields over how to interpret the East German regime concerns precisely the question of whether its everyday was so implicated in its ideology that it must be treated as an extension of the repressive apparatus or whether, without ignoring the larger context, it constitutes a field of experience that can be engaged on its own terms.

Historical memory is imbued with force, naturalized as power, and thoroughly political. "To claim the right to memory is," Pierre Nora (2011: 441) writes, "to call for justice." Who, and what, is entitled to be remembered are key elements that shape any society. For a society like the former GDR in reunited Germany that just experienced the rupture of the Wende, the question goes to the heart of identity and the sense of belonging in the new united German incommon. Historians share their role as interpreters of that past with judges, eyewitnesses, media, and politicians as well as the ordinary citizen, most recently enabled by the internet, to lay claim to the right to memory in new ways. We face today a situation in which private citizens, politicians, academics, museum amateurs, and museum professionals interact and debate the memory landscape (Bach 2005; Kalela 2012).

Museums are where objects go not only to die, as the saying goes, but also to be pressed into service for master narratives. In the case of ancient archaeology or medieval history, the representation of everyday objects in the museum is often the work of experts who painstakingly seek to reconstruct societies about which little is known and to which there are no living links. In the case of contemporary history, however, there are plenty of people who remember these events; so the creation of narratives about its past is a living, contested, and open-ended process.

Everyday objects often function in that process as carriers of authenticity and authentication—symbols of the real and arguments for a particular kind of historical interpretation. These objects become loci where communicative and cultural memories converge and are negotiated. Managing these memories thus often involves the ability to compel particular interpretations of these objects and the power to naturalize them as self-evident truths.

In the case of the former GDR, we see this political process not only in the traditional museums funded by the German state but most actively on the margins of the German museum landscape. This chapter looks at two kinds of institutions that emerged outside the plans of the mainstream institutions: privately funded collectors' museums located within Germany and a grant-funded nonprofit museum located outside of it. We argue that, in the *Alltag* of these contemporary museums, quotidian objects start to appear as relics. They function to highlight the *auratic* quality of personal memory: as resources that focus on the exhibition value of historical narration and as material culture that encapsulates both in relation to contemporary issues. How these objects are deployed helps define the place of the GDR in the process of dealing with the recent German past.

For our first example, we look at museums run primarily by amateur collectors, with no state support and often outside the standards and nomenclature associated with professional museums. Their very existence depends on the effort of private citizens who take responsibility for collecting and displaying objects in their personal or rented spaces, most always located in the former territory of the GDR. These exhibitions exemplify a wish to remember their past on their own terms, unencumbered and in some ways in opposition to the museum and archival regulations of united Germany. Like the East German families discussed in the previous chapter, these museums fail to conform comfortably to the normative museum landscape of the FRG.

We then turn to an in-depth look at the Wende Museum of the Cold War (WM) in Los Angeles, California, an art museum, archive, and educational institute run by historians and art historians. It is informed explicitly by Lüdtke's notions of *Eigensinn* as well as the history of everyday life (1994b). This fact reminds us that scholars both within the ivory tower and in the museums and archives participate in shaping the very everyday we seek to study. Combining an ethnographic interest in the everyday with a scholarly and educational motivation, the WM locates its concern for the preservation of East German culture and history within the larger task of creating a Cold War era Eastern European and Soviet memory culture based on everyday objects.

Its wide audience incorporates the immigrant community of Los Angeles. This transnational German context reminds us of the degree to which the German *Alltag* informs a global politics debate about memory. It also makes plain that a museum in Los Angeles can contribute to this debate, introducing new perspectives rather than ultimate solutions.

We find a compelling parallel between how the WM operates, the approach of this book, and everyday life itself. Just as the WM is grounded in microsocial interactions between museum staff, visitors, and objects, the people who are embedded within institutions of memory claim the authority to author meaningful stories for themselves in common with others. This chapter will show how multiple intentions and practices in and around museums and their artifacts intersect to remake and unmake existing narratives. Here we track one trajectory in a widespread—and we think fundamentally social democratic—process of questioning normative conventions about how the museums represent the recent past.

Situating the GDR

During the four decades of the GDR's existence, material culture played a major role in forging both the lived reality under socialism and forms of opposition. People's daily interactions at both home and work were shaped by state efforts to produce a limited number of products that carried socialist messages of functionality and equality. Interactions were equally shaped by the attempts of ordinary people to acquire Western products, to assemble their own goods out of available materials, and to find innovative ways of acquiring and preserving goods. High-quality goods were all too often scarce, and many goods were of low quality due to persistent problems in production and distribution (Fulbrook 1995). The lives of these objects were intimately intertwined with work and leisure activities, childhood, entertainment, and other areas of ordinary life.

The fall of the Berlin Wall in November 1989 and the subsequent integration of the GDR into the former West German Federal Republic barely a year later, in October 1990, left a country full of material remnants abruptly divorced from their former cultural and political meaning. The political changes were enormous; but in the arena of everyday life, it was the change in the value of common objects that most poignantly marked an era as irredeemably past.

As if on cue, untold households emptied their lives into the trash in the unification year of 1990. West Germany produced 428 kilograms of garbage per capita; the East threw out 1.3 tons per person (Ahbe 2005: 7). "Everyday culture had been indiscriminately tossed overboard like ballast," recalled a stunned Westerner wandering through this landscape, "from work brigade books and Party insignia to coming-of-age gifts and many other things." Former GDR citizens, he observed, "could not get rid of their everyday stuff fast enough" (Verein zur Dokumentation der DDR-Alltagskultur e.V. 1997: 9). For years after reunification, the material everyday of a nation kept dissipating into dumpsters and clustering in attics, garages, cupboards, and closets.

Two decades later, many hundreds of thousands of these items have become exhibits. The major state-supported history museums were, from the beginning, among the largest collectors. Among the most prominent state-supported institutions are the Deutsches Historisches Museum (DHM), or German Historical Museum, in Berlin and the Stiftung Haus der Geschichte der Bundesrepublik Deutschland (HdG), or House of History Foundation for the Federal Republic of Germany, which operates museums in Bonn, Leipzig, and Berlin. These museums often emphasize themes of repression and resistance in their portrayal of the former East. They construct what comes across to some former East Germans as an oversimplified Western perspective that showcases East Germany's indigenous revolution against a background of inexorable decline (cf. Berdahl 2010: 112–15).

These state-sponsored museums form an essential part of the memory landscape in Germany. They have a high number of visitors: over one million per year for the HdG museums. They conduct extensive outreach to schools, universities, and military populations. They see themselves as helping to forge a postwar narrative of Germany's division and unification. They follow, in effect, what curator Gottfried Korff saw as a welcome turn in unified Germany toward "the recollection of grand structures, questions, and legacies." This approach shifted the conversation away from a "false strategy" of "small worlds" that devalues both everyday culture and museum work itself (Korff 2002: 136).

In keeping with this privileging of macrohistory, it is possible to discern the workings of an official story: the ineluctable failure of socialism together with the inevitable success of democracy and capitalism. These museums are run by a highly professional staff that strives for accuracy in their historical facts and authenticity in their objects; but the stories they tell are necessarily smoothed into a larger narrative of German history that depicts reunification as a form of victory. Missing from this grand narrative are precisely the kinds of fragments that stand at the center of this book—the variety of unruly experiences of the everyday.

These state-sponsored museums are not the focus of this chapter, but we need to consider what they do because they form the background against which the alternative cases in this chapter emerge. As national museums with primary funding from the German federal government, they reflect both the pressures of a broad educational mission and the legacy of their founding under Helmut Kohl's conservative administration in the 1980s. As a historian, Kohl was particularly committed to these projects, which he saw as complementary. In 1982, before reunification even seemed remotely possible, Kohl called for a museum in Bonn—then the capital of the FRG—that would tell the story of German postwar history. This project became the House of History (Haus der Geschichte, or HdG).

But it was not until 1989 that work on the site in Bonn began; and the doors to the HdG opened in 1994, just as the government was preparing to move to Berlin. In 1987 Kohl also announced—on the occasion of divided Berlin's 750th anniversary celebrations—the creation of a Berlin-based German Historical Museum to be endowed with the broader mission of German history from the first century BCE onward. Originally this museum was to occupy a new building in the West to be built near the Reichstag. In response to the fall of the Berlin Wall, however, the DHM scrapped plans for a new building and moved into the historical building on Unter den Linden that had, until 1990, housed the East German national history museum—known as the Museum für Deutsche Geschichte, or Museum for German History. In a literal way, the West German version of German history occupied the East German one. It opened for exhibitions one year later, in 1991.

Despite acquiring some high-quality artifacts relating to GDR everyday culture, these museums had neither the mission nor the inclination to give its *Alltag* more than a passing notice in their permanent exhibitions. The German Historical Museum has in fact held a number of special exhibits devoted to the everyday, but the GDR is a theme on the margins of its exhibitions. The House of History in Bonn was initially criticized for its minimal portrayal of the GDR. Despite an expanded section on *Alltag* in the GDR in its 2011 revised permanent exhibit, the HdG delegates the everyday as a topic primarily to its eastern Leipzig location, opened in 1999, which incorporates the everyday significantly into its permanent exhibit. Focusing on the "civil courage" of nonconformity and resistance in the GDR, the Leipzig museum embeds the objects in a story line that depicts the Wende as the outcome of popular opposition to the SED regime. This moral clarity serves as a source of civic empowerment and has a legitimate place in a democratic public sphere.

As we learned from our chapters thus far, however, both individuals and families struggled to integrate their experiences and interests into the normative expectations of their societies, a struggle that had both failures and successes. In the case of the GDR, self and family were not politicized solely by force from the outside. Communism and socialism were sources of power for artist–activists and members of families; indeed, both artist–activists and family were embedded in socialist politics from the beginning of the workers movement. Though unreliable in many ways, both were still partners in building socialism. This multifaceted story fits poorly into a straightforward narrative of the GDR *Alltag* in which opposition and resistance are the main or even the only motif. And yet there is a certain irony, given the struggles of fitting self and family into the GDR's version of history; for now it is the socialist everyday that does not seem to fit comfortably within the political narratives of reunified Germany.

One concern involved in sharing this full range of everyday experiences under socialism lay in the risk of making the SED regime look less evil and thus relativizing its repression and glossing over its crimes, especially for a general public increasingly ignorant of history. For instance, the HdG in Leipzig described the self-proclaimed goal of the permanent exhibit as to work "against all tendencies of trivialization and justification of the SED dictatorship" (ZFL 2007). In 2011, the HdG in Berlin began to address the everyday more directly by opening an exhibit on divided Germany in the Tränenpalast—the hall on the former inner-German border in Berlin, nicknamed the *Palace of Tears*, because it was there that East Germans had to say good-bye to departing families and friends.

Only in 2013, when this book was already well under way, did the HdG open a permanent exhibit explicitly devoted to the everyday in Berlin's Cultural Brewery or Kulturbrauerei. Significantly, these initiatives came only after the smaller, privately funded museums devoted to the socialist everyday established themselves in the memory landscape. The state funding institutions view these collectors' museums as firmly outside the mainstream: *nicht museumsgerecht*, as one director put it in private conversation, which could be translated as *not befitting a museum*. It is to these unruly museums that we now turn.

Eigensinn in the Museum

These state-supported institutions are often the first port of call for museum visitors who seek to understand recent German history. The audience for these museums goes beyond tourists to include, most importantly, school groups,

Bundeswehr service personnel on state-organized visits, and visiting delegations from abroad. These latter groups are in a sense captive audiences, presented with the quasiofficial narrative of German history. The state-supported exhibits are impeccably professional and smooth to a fault, absorbing different voices into overarching narratives. In contrast, the over twenty-five stand-alone, privately funded museums devoted to everyday life under socialism found by 2016 in former East Germany seek, often explicitly, to strike a provocative, discordant note in a memory landscape that they see as being defined by the big, state-funded players. We call them *collectors' museums* to emphasize the personal approach that the owners often adopt and the way most of these museums evolved out of personal collections.

Taken as a whole, they seek to consciously expand, subvert, supplement, and sometimes openly oppose what they perceive as dominant state narratives about East Germany that present the everyday only in the context of repression and resistance. The motives vary, but a common sentiment across the museums is captured in the comment by former East German novelist Ulrich Plenzdorf: "You don't shoot at dead dogs." He was using the German equivalent of the English metaphor concerning beating a dead horse. "And still, the dog named GDR remains the focus of the hunt—with cannons firing words like 'criminal state' (*Unrechtsstaat*), 'dictatorship,' 'barbed wire,' 'border deaths,' 'minefields,' 'automatic-fire traps,' 'SED regime'—until, finally, the dog lies still" (2005: 119).

But the dog still gasps, writes Plenzdorf, and therein lies the problem. We see the private museums as a loud part of the gasping.

These collectors' museums are usually run as membership associations or *Vereine* and supported by admissions, donations, and gift shops. They range from little more than overcrowded basements run by retired individuals to large commercial operations with a side business in GDR nostalgia products. One regularly encounters families taking their children to show them "how things were" for their parents or grandparents as well as mixed couples from the former East and West, with the Westerners driven by curiosity and a desire to understand their partners. The often ragtag nature of these museums belies the large audience response.

While no official aggregate statistics for all the museums are kept, individual museums report large number of visitors, from 50,000 a year in Radebeul in Saxony to 500,000 a year in Berlin. They have become increasingly visible, listing themselves with local chambers of commerce and visitor's guides to the town or area. In conscious opposition to the state-supported museums, they locate their value as a supplement or corrective to what some directors expressed bitterly as a hegemonic, Western, self-serving, state-supported "demonization" of East Germany. The conceit, as the museum motto in Langenweddingen in Saxony-Anhalt puts it, is "to remember, not to provoke"

(*Ostalgie-Kabinett*). As these museums gained self-confidence and began to announce that they could show what life was really like, they used the authority of authenticity to enter the highly politicized terrain of German memorialization (Bach 2015).

The core issue that dominates discussions of these museums is also the relationship between dictatorship and everyday life. Most of the collectors' museums, though not all, draw a sharp distinction between lived experience and politics. As a concept paper for the GDR museum in Radebeul near Dresden put it, they are concerned "not with the overly common portrayal of the GDR and its mechanism of repression" but with "real" life (*Zeitreise*). Referring to the German neologism for n*ostalgia* for the East, the Tutow museum in MV rhetorically asks its visitors on its homepage: "Is it *Ostalgie* to long for the scents of childhood?" This formulation seems devised to rankle the establishment, as it combines privileging of the everyday with distrust for professional history.

Professional historians have gladly taken up this debate. Sabrow responded in the introduction to a major exhibit on everyday life and dictatorship at the state-supported DHM: "It would not be the first time in the history of Germany's grappling with dictatorships that the self-validation of one's own experience represses a regime's violence" (2009: 13). Here Sabrow was hinting at the debates among historians in the 1980s about the history of everyday life and the risk of normalizing the Third Reich by relying on the experiences of Germans who lived through this period (Augstein 1987; Baldwin 1990; R. Evans 1991). Echoing the work of Lüdtke, Sabrow also wrote, "The everyday is not the opposite of dictatorial rule but its complement" (2009: 13). To deny it is foolish, Sabrow insisted, and he cast those who do in poor historical company. We have taken this point as a leitmotiv for our work, focusing on how status, power, and even violence are implemented in everyday life.

From this perspective, the stacks of Mitropa menus, furniture units, cameras, and children's toys that one finds in these museums are not innocent; it matters how museums operationalize these objects in exhibitions for visitors. Professional historians and curators worry that the haphazard storage and display of these objects in collectors' museums—like the GDR-era telephones seen in Illustration 5.2—not only does injustice to their intrinsic value as historical artifacts but also undermines the ability of a democratic society to maintain its professional and critical standards. That is, the critique of the collectors' museum as essentially manipulative, and therefore *not* authentic, is closely linked with the ability of the name *museum* itself to retain, as Susan Crane (1997: 45) put it, its "trustworthiness … as a memory institution." The very use of the word is contentious, for most of these collectors' museums make no pretense to following the standards of the International Council of Museums (ICOM) in the preservation or cataloging of their material.

Illustration 5.2. Display of GDR-Era Telephones, GDR-Geschichtsmuseum, Perleberg, 2010. Photo: Jonathan Bach.

In this vein, Sabrow took to task the staff of the Berlin GDR Museum in a 2008 critique. He found that they did not follow standard museum procedures when objects were accepted by the museum. They did not consistently solicit full information about their origins or catalog all the objects individually. They stored the objects in environments where they could be subject to damage over time from environmental conditions; and especially, they made them available on display to be touched by the viewers. Furthermore, Sabrow found that the exhibits lacked critical distance and were too affirmative of life in the GDR.

This problematic affirmation was only intensified by the museum's explicit focus on experience and feeling, which he found inhibits reflection and artificially separated the everyday from dictatorship. By encouraging a good feeling—in German, *das Wohlfühlen*—Sabrow claimed that the museum effectively crossed the line into entertainment. This approach to managing memory not only ran the risk of trivializing the GDR past but also implied the subtle undermining of the legitimacy of democracy in united Germany. The museum's aura, Sabrow concluded, needed correction to avoid being a decontextualized *Jahrmarkt der Alltäglichkeiten*—an amusement park of quotidian things (2008: 12).

Such unprofessionalism is undeniable; yet this type of critique fails to fully capture the phenomenon. With the notable exceptions of the larger museums in Berlin, Eisenhüttenstadt in Brandenburg, and Radebeul in Saxony, the GDR *Alltag* museums tend to take the form of a personal shrine usually presided over by a charismatic individual with little clear plan for the disposition of the artifacts after they close the museum. In the context of the rapid transition from socialism to capitalism and democracy, these collectors' museums are literally transitional: their existence is tied to the biography and biology of their founders, most of whom came of age during the Cold War and whose relation to the objects displayed is visceral and intimate. These museums represent generational and epochal memories that form the kind of *we identity* that is often associated with the political memory of nations (J. Assmann 2006). In this case, it is perhaps more accurate to call these museums manifestations or assertions of a collective memory.

In the exhibits, the visitor encounters large numbers of objects from the GDR era primarily from the 1970s and 1980s. On the one hand, this selection represents a certain kind of reduction of the GDR experience to the Honecker era from 1971 to 1989. These objects reflect that period when the East German regime sought to better address the consumer needs of its citizens, resulting in more readily available mass production items, before leading up to collapse when economic frustration again took a firm hold (Rubin 2008).

On the other hand, these same objects are primarily those products and materials that, after 1989, became culturally obsolete while remaining functional: clothes, books, magazines, cleaning supplies, bottles, bandages, condom packages, toothpaste, eggcups, blenders, radios, televisions, flags, badges, old IDs, sewing machines, schoolbooks, toy soldiers, stuffed animals, cars, powdered pudding packets, soap, telephones, toasters, and alarm clocks. Many of these objects have intimate associations, like bathroom products and condoms. The appeal to the private and personal in its own way enhances the aura of authenticity by establishing an indirect connection between the object and the viewer's own body.

But neither of these considerations are made clear by the collectors. Usually left with little in the way of framing or signage, the visitor is left by default to self-curate and in the process to self-authorize the histories of the everyday. The kitchen display photographed in Illustration 5.3 shows the degree to which the visitor must make sense of these objects for themselves. The sheer amount and assortment of the objects prompt a visceral reaction to their simultaneously banal and sacred status between relics and exhibit items, between a voyeuristic glimpse into the private lives of others and an eerie sense of familiarity.

That these museums exist at all is thanks to the passion of amateurs. Avid collectors laid the foundations for them through their personal salvage missions. East Berliner Jan Faktor specializes in GDR era instruction manuals. Faktor was driven by the collectors' urge: "Most of all it's important to hoard,

Illustration 5.3. Display of GDR-Era Kitchen, GDR-Geschichtsmuseum, Perleberg, 2010. Photo: Jonathan Bach.

hoard, hoard, because time flies and much too much is disappearing into dumpsters … I want above all to brutally collect everything and unsystematically hoard it" (Verein zur Dokumentation der DDR-Alltagskultur e.V. 1999: 7). His goal was to collect as much of the past as possible before it disappears. In the process, he established strong affective relations with these objects.

These sentiments were common among self-appointed collectors who engaged in this hard work that Faktor called "brutal and unsystematic." Their salvage operations became a way of rescuing the Eastern everyday from "the fringes" (Sheringham 2006: 20) to where it has been consigned. Such operations are deeply related to the actor's selfhood, since in effect it is the objectified life experiences of the collectors that they are collecting. As French cultural theorist Jean Baudrillard reminds us, such personal collectors are in essence challenging the death of their past and their own mortality by seeking control over signifiers that otherwise run roughshod over experience; "for what you really collect is always yourself" (1968: 97).

Today, however, most of the items in museums come not from collectors but from donations, so much so that museum directors complain constantly about how they cannot keep up with the inflow. Former East Germans have come to see the collectors' museums as a fitting resting place for some of their own objects that did not make it into the first round of trash because they were still needed, sentimental, or simply ignored. Now they often are given to museums, which actively solicit donations. That is, the museum reauthorizes an affective relationship between the donor and the object that even the donor may have abandoned at some time. The donor is little different from the curator–collector in terms of the way they are establishing affective relationships to these remnants from their past. Indeed, the donor now gains the satisfaction of not only adding to the collection but also being able to visit it on display in the museum.

The collections of GDR material culture are presented as thematic assemblages interspersed with dioramas. Rooms or walls are devoted to particular species of objects such as clocks, toasters, toys, typewriters, printed matter, cars, watches, and radios, as seen in Illustration 5.4; or they are devoted to events or institutions like school, home, and vacation. As an aside, we note that it is not unlike the way we organized the features of the everyday in this book. In both cases, the seemingly incongruous assemblage of objects demands critical engagement and thus represents a challenge, perhaps even a provocation, to use objects and the experiences with which they are associated to make sense out of the German *Alltag*. These collectors' museums do not really rise to this challenge. Their displays are more or less ordered; they are sometimes labeled, though more often not.

Illustration 5.4. Display of GDR-Era Radios, GDR-Geschichtsmuseum, Perleberg, 2010. Photo: Jonathan Bach.

Sometimes they are protected behind glass, and sometimes they are explicitly available to be picked up and held. Dioramas range from kitsch to very serious recreations. In Apolda in Thuringia, mannequins complete a meticulous schoolroom, dentist offices, a party office, Trabant garage, and other scenes from GDR life. In Lutherstadt Wittenberg in Saxony-Anhalt, the local, privately run House of History—not to be confused with the state-funded museum in Bonn—allows only guided tours through lovingly crafted apartments as the visitor moves from the immediate postwar to the 1980s. In many cases, the presentation of quantity is the overwhelming trope of the exhibition. The museum in Apolda proudly advertises over 12,000 objects as if to convey both the scale of the lost past and the comprehensiveness, and hence authenticity, of the collection (*Olle DDR*).

From their emergence on the scene starting in the mid-1990s, the GDR *Alltag* museums have served at least three operations in trying to shape memory. The first is that of symbolic burial. Here we are referring to a ritual of separation in which former GDR citizens can reencounter the past while simultaneously taking leave of it. The curators often represent this taking one's leave as a belated response to the sense that the GDR collapsed, and then was erased from memory, so suddenly. As the title of an *Alltag* exhibit in 1995 put it, "No time remains for a real good-bye"—in German *Zum Abschied bleibt keine Zeit*. It does not strike us as surprising that former GDR citizens have invented this innovative way to mourn the loss of the past, given the way that they dynamically adopted and adapted burial practices during the GDR to negotiate the personal and the political.

The second operation is a form of asserting agency through identity akin to other practices of self. In this case, these unruly acts represent forms of coping with the widespread aura of second-class citizenship that many East Germans perceive in the wake of unification. The museums allow a connection to what the collector Jürgen Hartwig (1994) called the "reservoir of memories deeply anchored in the consciousness of the ex-GDR citizen about the positive side of the GDR and one's own lived past," which forms, he claims, an "East German identity." As Hans-Joachim Stephan, the director of the Radebeul GDR Museum Zeitreise, explained in a 2009 interview with one of our authors, what we call *Ostalgie* "is the term for home [*Heimatsbegriff*] for the East German."

Implicitly, asserting a will to participate in a lost GDR community is also a critique of their sense of alienation from their current FRG society. This operation involves the active contestation of the current German state's institutionalization of memory. It constructs a counternarrative that can include a sense of betrayal, lost opportunity, and socialist achievements.

What makes these examples of the management of memories particularly interesting for us in this study is the way they draw our attention to the objects of these operations. These negotiations of society/community, self/ world, public/private, past/present, and so on involve representing the everyday through material culture. This circumstance prompts the question: *Why do objects take such a central place in the memory of this particular* Alltag? In general, the everyday is a difficult, even treacherous subject for museums to represent. The more scrutiny we give the banality of the everyday, the more it points to chains of signification beyond itself. Eli Rubin (2008) thoroughly describes this issue in terms of the GDR.

At the start of the chapter, we mentioned the now popular, innocent plastic eggcup from the GDR. It is part of a culture of plastic that connects historically to a technological utopianism, with regard to both plastics and modernist aesthetics, shared by both East and West. It connects in turn to the postunification debates about n*ostalgia* for the communist past and criticism of contemporary consumer society (Bach 2002, 2015). Both the plastic eggcup and egg garden chair belonged to the East German everyday in which the home was presented as a "machine for living" (Le Corbusier 2007).

Where, then, do plastic eggcups and egg garden chairs belong in stories about modern Germany? They cannot be reduced to one state, one community, or even one story. Thanks to the many different wills directed at them, these objects acquire multiple associations with different modern Germanies. The eggcup and egg garden chair belong simultaneously to an economy of scarcity; to socialist crusades against allegedly decadent consumptive practices in the West; to a longer history of a German fascination with synthetics as a substitute for natural resources that could otherwise be used for waging war and building autonomous economies; and to the ongoing contest between functionalism and kitsch as true expressions of national character and good taste (Rubin 2008). Indeed, these objects also belong to the post-Wende political culture of memory about how the GDR *Alltag* was created, how it looked, and how it is remembered. Their belonging is limited only by the intentions to which people apply to them.

What this chapter on objects has underscored is the politics inherent in the plasticity of everyday objects. The layers of meaning, associated with the many intentional uses to which these objects are put, are not forgotten per se. Which intentions, uses, and meanings are given normative authority is a matter of politics. These objects therefore elude neat appropriation. They invite multiple sites of authority, asking, *Who is empowered to tell the story and from which vantage point? Who, or what, can speak for others?* The phenomenon of private museums thus indexes a range of issues that resonate beyond these particular objects or even their GDR or German context.

Objects point to what the receding past, of any kind, leaves behind—things and experiences. Within everyday life, these things are most commonly perceived as tools for use; we often experience them in the direct and limited sense of practicality. But afterward, when extraordinary events divorce this everyday from the present, that primary connection between things and experience is overlaid with a secondary one, now mediated by ruptured memory and the new *Alltag* in which those memories are operating.

These things and experiences, now aspects of something called *the past*, become subject to representational strategies that attempt to close the circuit between the material and the semantic in order to tell one story. The purpose of such acts is to assert control over one's experience, both individual and collective, to smooth over the ruptures in the everyday, but at great cost to our appreciation of it. Those strategies sacrifice the essential plasticity of the eggcup and garden egg chair by forcing the many fragments of experience with which they can be associated into one coherent tale of the self.

Still, these attempts to manage memories are always only partially successful. Objects shape a visual language that is prone to endless chains of signification, experiences, and intentions. Contrary to the very concreteness of museum exhibitions, the material remnants of past regimes do not provide the fixed foundations for answers to the—ultimately ethical—questions about everyday experience. The plastic eggcup and the egg garden chair from the socialist *Alltag* only make them more complicated.

The East Goes (Far) West

Could one imagine a museum that draws attention to these qualities of everyday life? On the West coast of the United States, divorced from the personal connections to the lived experiences of dictatorship and repression, collective demonstrations and leisure activities, the WM has emerged as a place to explore and engage with the cultural and personal histories of the GDR as well as Cold War era Eastern Europe and the Soviet Union. Unlike conventional museums that aim to document and represent the GDR past in a unifying and authentic narrative, the WM attempts to capture the lived experience beneath the ideological battles and geopolitical struggles of the Cold War. In line with its name, *the Wende*, the museum collects objects associated with the historical transformations caused by the toppling of the Berlin Wall in 1989 and the progressive dissolution of the Soviet Union in 1991. These political events led not only to the reunification of Germany but also to the spread of democracy in Eastern Europe and the growth of the European Union.

To inform and inspire a broad understanding of the period and its enduring legacy, the WM collects not only consumer goods and state insignias but also individual or private memorabilia such as photographs and photo albums, letters and daybooks, and personal stories captured in home movies and oral histories. The museum also acquires unexpected objects such as lottery tickets, consolation prizes, insurance documents, and educational films, along with other things that reveal aspects of everyday life.

In this way the museum brings together objects that suggest to its visitors a socialist way of living beyond stereotypical notions of socialist life and culture. It conceives of itself as a laboratory for the rethinking of Cold War era Eastern European and East German cultural history and material culture, allowing its users to explore the various ways in which cultural, political, and everyday objects characterize the past and transmit collective memories. This approach enables the museum to function as a place to examine and question how history as a professional discipline has developed a history—a set of commonly accepted narratives—about East Germany and the Eastern Bloc.

The museum's conception of history making, and its broadly contextual approach, sets it apart from its German peers. Its GDR collection emphasizes how the will to document political, social, and everyday practices already existed during the GDR era, both on national and local levels across cities and regions. The producers and preservers of these artifacts, found throughout GDR society, are owed much gratitude for their persistence in preserving a visual and artefactual record of a cross section of life in the GDR. The WM seeks to preserve and make accessible this record. It is manifested through many kinds of individual memories related to family life and friends as well as collective memories associated with mass organizations such as the Free German Youth (FDJ), Pioneers, and the SED; with industries such as VEB Robotron; and with the state, as exemplified by the Palace of the Republic (PdR).

These materials are infused with a sense of identity, authenticity, and normalcy as representative of individual and collective memories. Consequently, the museum preserves evidence of how everyday life became the focus of the GDR regime, complementing a growing scholarly literature on the everyday in the GDR (Fulbrook 1995; Wolle 1998; Berdahl 1999; Ohse 2003; Sabrow 2007; Pence and Betts 2008; Ludwig 2012). In a material analogue to critical scholarship, the museum staff's intention is to collect objects that can lead to questions about the seemingly seamless, allegedly natural condition of GDR existence in order to reveal the conditions of complicity in contemporary society. *How were GDR citizens able to speak critically through material and visual forms of expression?* Everyday objects help scholars (like Blaylock 2013) to pinpoint the operations of complicity in GDR society: that knowing compromise between the party and citizens, opportunities and conditions; and the entanglement of private and state interests, individualistic action, and state control.

This museum started somewhat later than the others. The WM's founder and executive director, Justinian Jampol, began to collect and preserve objects that were at risk of disappearing or critical for scholarly investigation in the late 1990s and early 2000s. Fueled by the need to find evidence for the transformation of the political iconography in the GDR for his master's thesis and doctoral dissertation, Jampol set about collecting artifacts and documents that he could only find in flea markets and through individual GDR citizens, as museums and archives in Germany rarely collected or made accessible such artifacts. These included both individual objects and entire collections.

By 2002, he had amassed two shipping containers full of materials and had to decide whether to establish an institution in Germany or in America. It became clear that it would be far easier to fund a museum through donors and grants in the United States. With the help of his professors and friends, Jampol located this large collection initially in a business park in Culver City, California, in a building that was once the storage space for Christie's Auction House.

Within a short time the second-floor rooms of the Culver City location were renovated into gallery spaces, dotted by offices. The exhibition space accommodates less than 1 percent of holdings, which now exceed 100,000 objects, so these galleries were designed to function as a finding aid to the collection—providing highlights from the collection to inform visitors about the rest of these holdings. One small gallery, off of the main gallery, was used for collection exhibitions that rotate every three to four months and focus on a collection, such as textiles or diplomatic gifts, or on a theme.

Two recent themes include *Claus Bach's Views of Weimar* (April–June 2013) and *Music of the Imagination: Jazz behind the Iron Curtain* (July–November 2013). Since 2013, the museum has begun using main gallery space for rotating exhibitions. The first was titled *Dinner with Communism: Commemorative Plates from the Wende Museum*. Along with the growth of the museum emerged an internal consensus that it should strive to address the material culture of the whole Eastern Bloc and its relationship to the Soviet Union. The museum's mission became one of preserving Cold War era Eastern European and Soviet artifacts and cultural history, making resources available to scholars and applying historical lessons of the past to the present.

In this context, the museum evolved into a research-based and educational institute that takes seriously the changing historiography of the GDR and critically assesses this history. It does so, initially, through what it chooses to collect. The museum salvages items of historical value that are threatened with destruction, such as an eleven-foot, one-ton Lenin monument from Latvia. This Bondarenko monument, almost melted down for its bronze, remains in its shipping crate, signaling its dislocation from its place of origin. It is suggestive of an archaeological find and indicative of the Soviet influence upon East German everyday culture, for example, the Soviet Lenin monument in Leninplatz in East Berlin.

Similarly, in 2009, the museum organized a conference called Germans' Things and published a selection of the conference papers in the German

Historical Institute's Bulletin (2011): *East German Material Culture and the Power of Memory*. The majority of the scholarly papers drew their sources from the museum's collections. At times, the museum collected material for the specific needs of some of the scholars, such as Paul Freedman, whose research on food and politics benefited from the WM collecting for him a platter full of GDR menus. Here it is worth noting that the U.S. perspective does not bear the same cultural and political burden as the German perspective. The museum's location thus allows scholars to address more openly and critically cultural and political issues. Yet the operations of the museum—its collecting and scholarly practices—actively promote an effort to think about everyday life beyond the simple dichotomies of authenticity or trivialization.

The WM is used by a wide range of people—not just the general public and local community but also artists, writers, filmmakers, historians, anthropologists, scholars, and journalists. In serving them, the staff considers the diverse array of objects to be their most important resource, including personal memorabilia such as brigade scrapbooks and photo albums, state-commissioned artifacts, home movies, documentary and educational films, and artworks in all media. This panoply of objects allows the visitors to the WM to explore how the past was constructed as it happened through personal experiences, artistic work, and official events in a politically neutral setting.

They allow, as seen in Illustration 5.5, a contemporary photographer such as Peter Holzhauer to capture the stylistic plurality of socialist realist painting in the GDR as it is displayed every day on the art rack in the museum's vault. Moreover, these objects are not located solely in a German context but intentionally embedded within a framework of Eastern European material culture and the Cold War more generally. This multilevel approach to the quotidian practices of East Germans, told from a transatlantic and cultural–historical perspective, allows a different outcome in Los Angeles than either the state-supported or private institutions of Germany. Its approach—at once transnational and quotidian—makes it possible for contemporary scholars and the public in this present–future continuum to explore and interpret cultural memories of the GDR from unexpected vistas and in terms of its global resonance.

The WM approaches its collection as uncharted territory. Its staff sees objects as overlooked stories and individual memories that address the experiences of normalcy, the ruptures caused by luck and chance, as well as the continuity of social conventions and folk traditions between pre-GDR and GDR cultures. Serendipity leads the scholar to find unexpected and forgotten objects, such as brigade books and signage written in the old German script form known as Sütterlin or a vinyl album titled *Das andere Amerika* (The Other America), featuring Paul Robeson singing a Hassidic chant in English.

Such artifacts provide strong visual evidence for exploring how East Germany shaped different kinds of identities—collective, national, social,

134 ᛰ *Ruptures in the Everyday*

Illustration 5.5. Peter Holzhauer, *Art Rack in the Wende Museum's Vault*, 2013. Digital photograph, courtesy of the photographer Peter Holzhauer. Top, Heinz Drache (1929–1989), *Das Volk sagt 'Ja' zum friedlichen Aufbau* (The People Say "Yes" to Peaceful Construction), 1952; Bottom Left, Lothar Gericke's *Stadtlandschaft mit Liebespaar* (Cityscape with Lovers), 1978; and Bottom Right, a Painting by Lutz Voigtmann (1941–1997), *Düstere Stadt* (Dismal City), 1978.

political, and cultural—through both vernacular and professional objects as well as official and private objects such as albums, scrapbooks, lottery tickets, handcrafted Erzgebirge toys, and artist portfolios. These artifacts illustrate the complex status of material culture in the GDR as an instrument of power, a cultural commodity, and a repository of individual communications.

Read against each other, private photo albums, home movies, and dissident artwork suggest how seemingly contradictory forms of collective memory coexisted within the official narrative of solidarity. These artifacts show what the historian Marc-Dietrich Ohse (2003: 379; cf. Mallmann and Paul 2000) refers to as the "reluctant loyalty" that characterized the GDR, where identification with the regime could paradoxically coexist with open hostility or simply disgruntlement. As a window into the past, they show how individuals, friends, and families sought to hold on to traditions from pre-GDR times or carve out spaces for a life they envisioned.

But that past is never divorced from the present. These materials also represent fragmented biographies in the aftermath of the GDR's dissolution, reminding us of how material culture serves as the basis for both the loss and recovery of identity. That is, such diverse artifacts allow the various users of the museum's collection—collectors, curators, donors, scholars, tourists—to discover for themselves the linkages between everyday practices and shared intergenerational experiences, between personal memory and normative conventions. These particular interactions among the museum's users shape the meaning of everyday objects. Through the WM, they are adding their own intentions to these objects, restoring their original plasticity in a very different context of an *Alltag* museum.

These new intentions on the part of visitors to the WM, and the kinds of dialogues that ensue about the socialist *Alltag*, provide the bridge between normative and personal meanings, past and present experience, as well as local, regional, national, and transnational contexts. Consider the example of the family photo album. The reoccurring memories of travel to favorite vacation spots, first days of school, personal and political anniversaries, and coming-of-age ceremonies, among other important life events, reflect shared common cultural experiences. Yet the family photo album could also be a space where individual expression had the license to be less guarded and more playful and where the private self was openly documented over time.

In Illustration 5.6, we see the album of a man who documented himself through self-portraits for most of his adult life. At the same time, the commemorative practices of awarding certificates and medals to outstanding workers and producing commemorative plates and flags for political anniversaries and workers festivals speak to official memory operations that sustained a collective culture of labor.

Illustration 5.6. Brigade Karnatz Scrapbook, 1969. Title Page, "Kampf um den Staatstitel, Kollektiv der sozialistischen Arbeit," 2008.273.001. Courtesy of the Wende Museum of the Cold War, Culver City, California.

The juxtaposition of these objects make evident the social conventions and everyday rituals that constituted the characteristics of the East German collective society. Another form of commemorative object are miniature books about churches, which feature images of Sorbians in their folk attire (*Tracht*) and other local folk traditions associated with the church. These can be read against films about *Volkstänze*, a term that cultural bureaucrats used for folkloric dances around the world and their official role in GDR socialist culture. These cultural artifacts document the influence that reoccurring acts of commemoration and ritual have on successive presents and across the generations. These objects bear double witness to the ways in which folk traditions served to ground a people's collective culture in the incommon folk practices sanctioned by the state, even though associated with the church, and at the same time contribute to a more dynamic understanding of GDR everyday life and history as shaped not only by utopian dreams but also by folk traditions.

The memoryscape of any given society is determined by the relative agency of its authorities, individuals, and groups to determine what memories remain relevant or become irrelevant over time. The staff at the WM use their materials for *interactive memory operations*, which refers to capturing the traces left behind by everyday activities and ritualized events, which, in this case, took place over the course of two generations in the GDR. These traces communicate to the contemporary viewer how authorities, both state and elite organizations, attempted to steer individuals and groups toward approved goals, while individuals and groups walked their own paths and engaged in their own memory operations.

The point of this exercise is not to reduce these diverse intentions and actions to one story but to work with the objects and visitors in such a way as to maintain the complicated diversity of this fragmented incommon. As carriers of a subjective presence and experience of a particular place, these artifacts help us to explore the relationships between museums and their publics, between German and non-German citizens, and between the master narratives of German history writ large and the stories of former GDR citizens. In conveying the features of the GDR everyday, they define the characteristics of an extinct everyday culture shaped by mass organized activities as well as private moments and personal encounters. And yet those features do not restrict the terms of experience. After all, they communicate an experience of everyday life in the GDR not only to tourists from Germany and Eastern Europe, who visit this museum to the East located in the far West, but also to a diverse contemporary American audience.

We do not want to claim that the WM's transnational approach is somehow unique. By 2016, there was one small collection north of Amsterdam in the Netherlands comparable to the WM: a private, specialized collection in Monnickendam that focuses on the everyday culture of East Germany. In Germany, the Documentation Center for GDR Everyday Culture in Eisenhüttenstadt was a comparable institution; in 2013, however, it lost funding and ceased its professional operations. The DHM in Berlin also shares curatorial interests with the WM. Because of its geographic, cultural, and psychic distance from Europe, however, the WM provides a broader, less insular view of former East Germany. It also addresses the GDR's relationship to the rest of the former Eastern Bloc and Soviet Russia rather than viewing it solely in relationship to a German–German history. The WM therefore is able to draw attention to the global context in which German events and experiences are given relevance by Germans and non-Germans alike.

But the everyday context in which the WM operates changes the nature of remembering. The WM has garnered support in Los Angeles from local immigrant communities, and former East Germans living in Los Angeles have especially sought out the museum. Their initial interaction with the museum has triggered a desire to engage with its collections and its public to share their GDR experiences. This interest has led to their participation in tours, programs, and filmmaking based on a relationship to particular collections, their donation of personal effects, or a role on the board of trustees.

Their activities draw attention to issues of social justice, feminism, and dissidence, for instance, and contribute to a shared perception of identity, symbols, and memory across cultures and transatlantic relationships such as that of the United States and Germany. They have meaning for the diaspora of East Germans in Los Angeles and in the world as well as for German and non-German scholars, who wish to preserve and further the understanding of East German cultural history for future generations. The WM offers as a result a wider range of options for creating meaning out of GDR everyday objects encountered outside of Germany proper.

Beyond this diaspora, these collected objects also influence scholarship—including this book. The WM provides sociologists, anthropologists, and cultural historians with primary source material on the shaping of a socialist people's culture and the contribution citizens made to the nation, social solidarity, and recreation. The more propagandistic artifacts contain a wealth of evidence for the cultural historian to analyze how media treated historical memory and how all media of communication were employed to disseminate and sustain the socialist system of belief. Other materials propose an approach to GDR cultural history through their achievements in industry, architecture, and urban planning.

At this point, we should admit that the primary authors of this chapter were an anthropologist, a political scientist, and a museum curator trained in art history. Their interdisciplinary experience is trumped only by the transnational nature of their biographies. Operating intentionally or unintentionally as ethnographers, they have observed and participated in the work of these various museums in various capacities: development, collecting, curating, promotion, visiting, and critiquing. Here in particular, we cannot divorce our scholarly *Alltag* from the German one we seek to study. More to the point, our intent to participate in this scholarly project is only one of many motives for contributing to this debate about the East German *Alltag* and how to remember it. And we are only a few voices among many.

The WM allows for considerable influences from the outside. Cultural historians are increasingly moving toward the study of material culture, and the museum seeks to adapt its resources to changing scholarly needs, expanding the idea of museum and archive to that of research and educational resource. To break down the boundary between depot and exhibit space, the WM invites guests, donors, and the public directly into the inner workings of the museum. It makes the storage area a focal point for its programs, for example, letting the theater troupe Los Angeles Poverty Department (LAPD, playing on the initials for the Los Angeles Police Department) stage a theatrical performance about the Cold War in the main vault. In this case, the programming process—exhibitions, events, screenings, performances, and other forms of civic engagement—is inspired by the collections but driven by contemporary issues.

The staff similarly tries to embed the museum within a local and a global *Alltag*. On the twentieth anniversary of the toppling of the Berlin Wall, the WM organized a commemorative celebration along and across Wilshire Boulevard, a main artery in Los Angeles. The museum received international press coverage in response, in particular in Germany. This moment marked the beginning of many articles on the progress of the WM that have appeared in the German press. At the same time, the local papers cover the large events that the museum has organized and the *Los Angeles Times* has reported extensively on the museum's move to its new home in a former National Guard armory since 2014.

Germans, too, discover their Eastern histories and memories in the far west. Vacationing in California, German curators, German scholars, and Eastern Europeans have made the WM a destination on their travel itineraries. They come out of curiosity and interest in seeing how an institution such as the WM can exist. Recently, graduate students and scholars of GDR history have found the exploratory and experimental nature of the museum an interesting case study in the process of remembering and rethinking GDR cultural history (McLellan 2011; Blaylock 2013; Paver 2013; Schmidtmann 2013). Scholars look at how the museum collects just as much as the way it presents its artifacts. Though on nearly the other side of the globe, the WM has been incorporated into the German cultural landscape through the things that museum visitors have done with its objects: studying, discussing, and authoring meaningful stories about the German past.

The Temporality of the Everyday

This chapter draws attention to the way that objects come to acquire status, power, and meaning in everyday life. In spite of the way they are presented in many museums, everyday objects do not have the fixity or the authority we ascribe to them. They absorb the many intentions of their users. Plastic in nature, they can move dynamically between states of fluidity and solidity. As such, they offer a model for how to think about the characteristics of the everyday in general that respond similarly to the multiplicity of people's intentions and uses. The traces of this plasticity can be reconstructed through careful study and is best undertaken in everyday incommon settings, where those operations are most evident.

This multiplicity of intentions and uses is quite evident in the memory of the GDR. For the state-funded museums whose task it is to weave a national narrative for as broad an audience as possible, GDR artifacts are relevant as long as they can be incorporated into the political institutions that produce our contemporary everyday. They thereby become an extended argument for a narrative of fall and redemption for particular state and national forms. This narrative, among other things, justifies the decisions surrounding unification and strengthens the social contract underlying today's democratic market society.

By contrast, the collectors' museums, existing outside the system of state funding, are embedded in a kind of double counternarrative. First, they target the dominant contemporary narrative of a unified Germany that they feel minimizes East German identity. Here the collectors' museums appear as a form of regional self-assertion. *We were not just cogs in the wheel*, the exhibits seem to say. *We lived as one always does—autonomous lives that nonetheless required adapting to and navigating the patterns of everyday life.* The presentation of objects in the German collectors' museums seems to offer some kind of solace that fills a postunification gap and at the same time exemplifies a deep sense of loss, of being a personal relic from a time gone past.

The second target, however, is the GDR official culture itself. Both kinds of museums rely on vernacular forms of remembering the past more akin to what Aleida Assmann (2006) terms *communicative memory* than the rigid and removed *cultural memory* that the GDR itself tried to inculcate through lugubrious memorials and official commemorations. Today, this official construction of cultural memory in the GDR appears mostly as ironic references on the margins of the vernacular memory of everyday objects.

The resulting operation is complicated when it is applied as an alternative to both the present and the past. The collectors' museums assemble memory from the ruins of the GDR by constantly reframing their intentions and their selves within the GDR past; at the same time, they insist on a similar autonomous expression of the self in the FRG present through implicit critiques of unified Germany and the unification process. The multivocality of the German present comes through this larger effect of montage and rupture, of the constant shift between self and other that superficially seems to dwell in undifferentiated n*ostalgia;* but upon closer examination, it creates an assemblage that demands that the visitor confront at least the possibility that objects are not innocent storytellers but conveyors of complicated pasts and implicated presents.

The WM speaks more directly than the German-based museums to a global audience less directly connected to the GDR through national narratives or personal recollections. By relocating the GDR in a history of Eastern Cold War material culture, the GDR becomes, in effect, a window into the Eastern version of postwar modernity writ large. Through its efforts to convey diverse kinds of memories, the WM eschews both the grand narrative approach of the state-funded German museums and the counternarrative agenda of the collectors' museums. It produces instead multiple narrative paths for visitors and scholars to follow through the paths of the Eastern everyday—a multiplicity appropriate to both the wider range of visitors and the wide range of intentions in the everyday itself.

Meanwhile, our study of the material culture of the GDR highlights several facets of the everyday. The first is *authenticity* (Bendix 1997). The state-funded German national museums and the WM both take great pains to authenticate the provenance of their artifacts and thereby elevate authenticity to a fixed foundation for history and memory. In contrast, the amateur collectors' museums assert authenticity not through careful documentation and preservation but through operations of intimacy (Bach 2015). They achieved this intimacy for the viewers through a seemingly carefree approach to the objects themselves, which are often available to be touched and lack information as to their origin. This points to an original familiarity with the objects as embedded within their lived experience and as pragmatic tools for daily living. Used in this way, this form of authenticity is not a fixed foundation for history or memory.

This chapter also reminds us of the utility of normalcy as a way to legitimize the everyday. These GDR objects are controversial insofar as they seem to both represent the banality of the socialist everyday and, in so doing, highlight the extraordinary political constellation that conditioned it. Objects such as homemade television antennas that could bring in West German television reception are examples of the dual nature of objects that are simultaneously of the system and outside the system. Or to put it differently, these antennas always served multiple purposes: for GDR citizens to watch only GDR programming and for GDR citizens to watch forbidden programs from the FRG, the United States, and other Western countries. These two kinds of practices, even within the same home and using the same television, constitute two very different kinds of normalcy: one is the normalcy of normative behavior, while the other is the normalcy that integrates and incorporates lived experience, in all of its disruptive varieties, into the ordinary.

This perpetual negotiation between the ordinary and the extraordinary often evokes a sense of *irony*. It is a characteristic motif of the GDR *Alltag* but also of many others (Bergerson et al. 2011). It appears in double form in the representation of the GDR everyday. There is the ironic presentation of GDR era official culture as kitsch, such as the winking digital triumvirate of Marx, Engels, and Lenin on display in the Berlin GDR Museum. Then there was ironic knowing during the GDR, which is expressed through the representation of subcultures such as rock music and jokes in museum exhibits making fun of the Trabant cars and other products.

An old GDR joke could be found, it is rumored, written in the restroom of the museum-like Osseria Restaurant in Berlin-Weißensee that claims to offer an authentic taste of the GDR (*Ossaria*). We liked this widespread joke so much that we started this chapter with it: "Why is the GDR 'Rondo' coffee brand similar to a neutron bomb? The person dies, the cup remains" (Rigney, 2011, "Commie cooking", also "Alte DDR Witze"; our translation). Irony, perhaps, allows the everyday to oscillate between the ordinary and the extraordinary without fully belonging to either. Perhaps too, irony allows Germans to author stories of rupture about the past without wholly authorizing them for the present.

Most of all, though, the case of the GDR highlights the role of temporality in the encounter with the everyday. If the everyday provides a place for its operations, the case of the GDR is one in which its everyday culture very rapidly found itself out of place after the Wende. Everyday life itself became culturally obsolete, while remaining present in myriad ways. This confounding temporality is perhaps particularly evident in the case of the GDR, and yet these kinds of ruptures have happened repeatedly in the case of modern Germany, undermining the ability of Germans to create coherent stories of their self or consensual stories of themselves. It responds to a need to simultaneously disavow and retain the everyday while also struggling to integrate those memories of rupture into the new normal of unified Germany.

Here we do not wish to authorize any one representation of these modern Germanies. The process of defining what is German takes place not only in the national museums of Berlin, Leipzig, and Bonn but also in provincial Perleberg and distant Los Angeles, where different actors collaborate on producing and maintaining the multivocality of the everyday. The collectors' museums and the WM should be seen as contributing to a transnational German self-understanding that should stand alongside, rather than in unmitigated opposition to, the state-funded museums. That these stories often sound contradictory is a reflection of the many different voices that are now actively making sense of these everyday objects.

Jonathan Bach, Cristina Cuevas-Wolf, and Dani Kranz

Note

Parts of this chapter previously appeared in the chapter "Object Lessons: Visuality and Tactility in Museums of the Socialist Everyday," in *Exhibiting the German Past: Museums, Film, and Musealization*, edited by Peter M. McIsaac and Gabriele Mueller © University of Toronto Press, 2015. Reprinted with permission of the publisher.

CHAPTER 6

Institutions

I wish to suggest that one must analyze institutions from the standpoint of power relations, rather than vice versa.
—Michel Foucault, "The Subject and Power," 1983

In our everyday lives, we can hardly avoid institutions. They matter to us because we are embedded in them. Our identity is shaped, for instance, by our citizenship. We are constantly subject to the rule of laws that prevent us from killing our neighbor or force us to find a legal parking spot. Some of us serve in military or patriotic organizations, others join clubs and associations as part of their professional or private lives. In one form or the other, we all must pay taxes.

Throughout our lives, we move through a complex and overlapping network of institutions that mold who we are and the world around us. Most of us are born in hospitals, spend our childhood in schools, study in trade schools or universities, work as adults in companies or factories, and, having grown old, live in homes for the elderly. Institutions are there when we express our most meaningful emotions: when we celebrate a marriage or the birth of children, if we divorce, and when we grieve the passing of a loved one. Some of us may donate our belongings to museums or our documents to archives, weaving our experiences into the fabric of shared memories. In sum, institutions are ubiquitous in the modern *Alltag*, and arguably we cannot live outside of them.

It is difficult to define the boundaries of institutions, as the sociologist Emile Durkheim insisted as early as the end of the nineteenth century. Institutions can sometimes manifest themselves as buildings such as factories and prisons, or they can be associated with particular social constructions, like families or gender. We begin this chapter with a quote from Foucault (1983: 222) to make the claim that the study of institutions should not end at their walls, but that institutions should be analyzed in terms of their inner logic in order to understand the power relations that constitute them.

For Durkheim (2002) writing in 1895, institutions consist of crystallized manners of acting, feeling, and thinking—which he saw as more or less constant, constrained, and distinctive to a social group. But as we have argued about self, family, and other features of everyday life, we should also not define institutions too rigidly. We are more interested in the microsocial interactions that shape how they operate. It is one of the main contentions of this chapter that there is an everyday life to institutions. We wish to investigate how people inhabit them on the ground.

Writing about institutions means writing about commitments to authority, cooperation, and solidarity. At the same time, it also means to write about rejection and mistrust, as the anthropologist Mary Douglas noted (1986). Lüdtke discussed the emotional challenges created by the birth of modern bureaucracy in early nineteenth-century Prussia (1982). We follow this anthropological viewpoint in acknowledging that institutions touch intimate feelings of loyalty and the power of social bonds. Institutions are core sites in everyday life that encourage individuals to act in common. They help us to focus our individual energies into collective enterprises with particular goals in mind. They are inherently political. They thus extend beyond the walls of their buildings, if they have buildings and walls at all, precisely because we use them as sophisticated tools for remaking our world. In this sense, institutions, both public and private, often serve as pillars of a modern self, society, and state.

Focusing on everyday actions uncovers no small degree of collaboration and compulsion. Institutions are normative organizations. They require some measure of force, power, and violence. Paul Steege described this approach in a forum on everyday life in Nazi Germany: "While acknowledging how structures of power, and the people who inhabit them, can limit the room for maneuver available to individual actors, [the history of everyday life] also leaves room for their mutual complicity in producing those same structures of power" (Bergerson et al. 2009: 562).

Designed to transform society, institutions typically target, for example, particular clients, consumers, customers, patients, participants, or prisoners. Human beings create and run these institutions, sometimes in an attempt to realize their own visions of a better world. Humans working in and for these institutions become agents who execute policies more or less according to given guidelines. Institutions and their workers thus influence the everyday as a result of both their external processes and their internal ones.

We conceive of the *Alltag*, and everyday institutions in particular, as a coproduction of the powerful and powerless. For twenty years political scientists, anthropologists, and historians have debated whether institutions shape their representatives or vice versa (e.g., Lacroix and Lagroye 1992). Only in everyday life can we discover the actual relationship between policy and practice, ideology and implementation. Understanding the everyday operations of institutions is equally relevant for communist, fascist, or liberal–capitalist societies. Ethical questions emerge about responsibility for violence, intentional or not, that are inherent to various degrees in many of our modern institutions.

The Nazi regime is an instructive case study of everyday ruptures because institutional violence took on such extreme forms of terror, mass violence, and genocide. On closer inspection, Nazi institutions helped both to create those ruptures and to ameliorate their effects. To be sure, the same institution had radically different impacts on different people (Lüdtke 1998). A rupture for one person could mean security and continuity for another. Inherently political, the effects of Nazi institutions differed dramatically depending on one's position of inclusion in or exclusion from the *Volksgemeinschaft*—the National Socialist vision of a fascist and racist community of Aryans. Making sense of these ruptures for us as scholars of the everyday thus requires understanding how these institutions operate on the ground.

To that end, this chapter extends our discussions about the institutions of the museum, family, and self to new cases. Using a combination of archival and ethnographic sources, we will study an atypical assortment of everyday institutions that share a common association with the Third Reich: the German charity association Deutscher Caritasverband (DCV), the Nazi leisure organization Kraft durch Freude (KdF), and the concentration and extermination camp Majdanek. To these institutions operating in the Third Reich, we will add two German schools in the cities of Leipzig and Hamburg that struggled to educate young people about that Nazi past at the turn of the twenty-first century.

Each of these very different institutions aspired to influence everyday life in different ways, and those goals were embedded in different, sometimes even contradictory contexts. We normatively associate leisure time with entertainment and sports, charity with compassion and care, concentration camps with terror and extermination, and contemporary German schools with education and tolerance. Putting them in the same chapter, we do not want to imply that they are all violent institutions imbued with the same kinds of politics. By juxtaposing them, we are not setting them equal to one another in political, ethical, or normative terms. Rather, we seek to uncover their operations as everyday institutions. This heterogeneity in our case studies may seem jarring to some of our readers, but identifying underlying microsocial interactions will help us to better understand the relatively independent dynamics of everyday life.

Moreover, our chapter is organized around three different kinds of agents involved in the lives of institutions: institutional policy makers, institutional actors, and the objects of institutional policy. *Policy makers* may be inside or outside the nominal structure of the institution per se, but they set strategic goals for institutions as well as norms for institutional practices. Or more accurately, they claim the authority to achieve specific goals by encouraging or forcing institutional agents to act on the world in particular ways.

In this chapter, we will not devote much of our attention to these familiar protagonists of many studies of modern Germany. Instead, we focus on *institutional actors*, the subordinate workers who are tasked with the implementation of those policies. They matter because their tactics for implementing policies on the ground do not always conform to the instructions given from on high.

We are also interested in a third group of actors: the people who these institutions seek to influence. It is far harder to find a single term for them because of their diverse character. Leisure institutions provide entertainment to consumers; charity organizations help the needy; concentration camps police, torture, and exterminate prisoners; schools educate students.

A common term for all of them would seem to erase the ethical differences in the goals and impact of these various institutions. The absence of such a term in our vocabulary seems to suggest a cultural attachment to these distinctions, as if some institutions are worth trusting while others are not. Yet all of these people did become the *object* of institutional policy, by which we mean the focus of institutional attempts to make their lives better or worse by helping, educating, entertaining, penalizing, or murdering them—according to prevailing norms. In what follows, we will pay close attention to how dynamic interactions between all three kinds of actors shaped the institutions and their outcomes.

One of the criticisms of an everyday approach is that focusing on the experiences of so-called ordinary people artificially isolates them from the formal institutions of the German state and German society. Scholars of everyday life have insisted, conversely, that there is an *Alltag* within institutions that can help us to understand how they operate as supporting pillars for the constructs of self, state, and society. A microanalytic approach (Magnússon and Szijártó 2013) complements a macroanalytical perspective because it offers insights into the underside of these institutions—the incoherent, fractured, and shifting side of institutions where multiple discourses and practices intersect.

Rather than treating institutional norms as preexisting and internalized, our approach explores the everyday mechanisms of institutions to uncover the interactions whereby the making, remaking, and unmaking of conventions in social practices became possible. A microsocial perspective also encourages scholars to recognize that institutions are places of labor: both in the high-minded, ideological sense of reshaping the moral fabric of the world and in the practical, literal sense of paid or unpaid employment in actual workplaces. Here, multiple agents encounter each other and their objects on a daily basis, with multiple intentions, acting, and reacting. But the microscopic and macroscopic perspectives are really not distinct. By studying how institutions do their work on the ground, we can observe the worlds they build in the process.

Institutions are tools. Their purpose is to remake individuals and collectives on the basis of certain ideological or normative rules. But the agents who work in institutions and even the human recipients of institutional policies and practices can be unruly. Actors often attempt to enter and reshape the everyday of institutions, reappropriating resources and even rules for their own purposes. This unruliness is always about both fulfilling and inhibiting institutional aims to various degrees. We cannot truly understand the quotidian dynamics of institutions, or any of the ruptures in the everyday discussed in this book, without taking these ambiguous actions into consideration. It is our conviction that institutions are best understood as the locus of both normative rules and unruly actions. Accordingly, we argue that unruly actions often served to not only help the institutions work but in fact help them work *well*.

Getting at this unruliness is not always easy precisely because institutions are designed to impose normative behavior. Consider the example of schools. Like museums, schools are modern institutions that construct discourses about the past; but they do not always operate as intended. When confronted with the history of the Third Reich, for instance, adolescents quickly learn how to behave properly (Gudehus 2006); but normative behavior does not keep them from using the Nazi past in ways neither planned nor desired by their teachers. The latter often complain about these deviations from the norm, for instance, when students laugh or make jokes about genocide.

For this reason, it would be a mistake to focus our attention solely on their instructional activities. Historical discourse also emerges in the schoolyard where children play during recess. Goffman (1956) refers to schoolyards as the secondary scenes of the institution where the students challenge institutional rules. Spaces and times like these capture the unofficial power relations that contribute a great extent to the functioning of the institution. Both normativity and unruliness comprise the *Alltag*. Our point is that it is in microsocial interactions that we discover the actual impact of everyday institutions.

We begin by first investigating the normative goals of two such institutions. The Nazi leisure organization and the twenty-first-century German history classroom were set up to shape the everyday lives of members of the working classes and students. On the ground, practices rarely if ever took place without friction with regard to meeting the aims of the institutions and the efficiency of their functioning.

Second, we will illustrate how institutions were shaped by the everyday practices of the institutions' agents and objects. Here we will combine examples from the KdF with the charitable actions of the DCV and the genocidal practices of Nazi extermination camps. We will explore how institutional agents and even the objects of institutional interventions reappropriated discourses and practices in unruly or unexpected ways under Nazi rule.

We will end by looking at the ironies of efficiency in many of these situations. Though technically deviations from originally formulated goals and guidelines, these acts of *Eigensinn* could sometimes help these institutions to work well—at least when measured according to the values of that particular German *Alltag*.

Institutional Aspirations

We begin with the implicit goals of institutions: to alter habits, beliefs, or circumstances; to reform self or society; and to change the contours of the everyday. These interventions into the lives of others have been used for both German nation building and fostering a postnational *constitutional patriotism* (Sternberger 1990; Habermas 1992). But whether they are used for good or ill according to our values today is largely irrelevant. These two institutions in particular—one for leisure and the other for education—remind us of the ambitions of modern German states to reform their citizens for the sake of new and better societies.

Within the Nazi regime, KdF was responsible for arranging leisure events for Germans, especially workers. Its various branches covered the sectors of tourism, after-work entertainment, education, folklore, and the beautification of work sites. In terms of policy, the leisure organization was driven by the goal of reaching Germans in the private sphere. It strove to shape the leisure-time activities of the German people with the ultimate aim of broadening popular support for Nazism, strengthening the *Volksgemeinschaft*, and rooting both in their everyday lives. This Nazi organization seemed to have recognized the importance of the *Alltag* in achieving its goals for the sake of Nazi ideology. With its entertainment offers, KdF embarked on a kind of colonizing mission to co-opt happiness for political purposes (Baranowski 2004; Timpe 2017).

Twenty-first-century German schools also have political agendas. After several troubled generations of *Vergangenheitsbewältigung*, or working through the Nazi past, history teachers by the turn of the century tended to take proactive roles to teach the Third Reich and the Shoah to a younger generation. Prior scholars have studied this issue in terms of memory, discourses, or places (Nora 1984–1992; Borries 1995). We look at transmissions of history here as a social practice embedded in the everyday of an institution. Our insight into this phenomenon comes from fieldwork conducted by one of our authors in two German schools at the beginning of the millennium (Oeser 2010). Like the activities of the KdF, teaching German history, too, involved the use of emotions.

KdF envisioned collective leisure activities as a way to create and reinforce their vision of a "pure" society based on one's racial heritage. In this context, KdF saw sports as a means to improve Germans' bodies for the sake of the *Volksgemeinschaft* by strengthening the German national body or *Volkskörper* (Malitz 1933: 18; cf. Diehl 2002, 2006). School programs in reunified Germany fulfill a similar function by relying on education curricula to develop within young people a civic-mindedness grounded firmly in tolerance and democracy. Teaching the history of Nazism in particular is designed to reinforce the belief in the democratic constitution of the Federal Republic as a solid bulwark against dictatorship. Thus, although these two institutions are antagonistic politically, both are similar in that they were designed to help transform society. *What techniques* (Certeau 1984) *did these two institutions develop and deploy to reach their divergent goals?*

KdF started its manifold activities in the realm of leisure, sports, and entertainment in the prewar years and continued, wherever possible, during most of World War II. Its main purpose was to entertain so-called racially pure Aryans in their free time. Focusing specifically on the leisure of private individuals, it tried to replace individualistic practices with collective ones. Even though the institution was founded by a dictatorial regime with the purpose of furthering its ideological goals, participation in the institution's program was officially voluntary. Overall, KdF can be seen as one element of a larger, serious effort of the Nazi regime to win and keep the support of the German population.

One way that the KdF sought to meet this goal was to beautify the sites of labor for workers. According to KdF statistics, over 600 million reichsmarks were invested in renovating and beautifying German factories. From 1933 to 1938, they were able to "improve or newly construct 20,741 workrooms, 13,122 maintenance areas and parks, 15,595 cafeterias and lounges, 20,455 security complexes and dressing rooms, 2,557 community houses and holiday homes, [and] 2,107 sports facilities" for workers in and around the factories (Busch 1938: 76ff.). No doubt these numbers are exaggerated for propaganda purposes, but they show the effort on the part of KdF to win over the workers (Smelser 1988: 214ff.).

The KdF deliberately brought its programs—such as sports activities, inexpensive entertainment events, cultural programs, and travel offers for workers—directly into German factories and other workplaces. Workers attended classical concerts in manufacturing halls, visited so-called factory exhibitions that displayed visual arts on the shop floor during their breaks, and joined their colleagues after work in KdF-organized sports classes taking place on factory grounds. The Nazi regime sought to get German workers more involved with their place of work as well as to improve the experience of work in order to increase their productivity.

In the same vein, KdF sought to make elite practices available to groups that previously had no access to them. For instance, they offered sports such as tennis, golf, riding, and sailing—normatively associated with the upper classes—to less affluent and less sophisticated—also known as "simple"— workers. The political agenda here was coordination, or *Gleichschaltung*. This term generally refers to the enforced political unification of previously divided social groups. Until the Weimar Republic, social clubs, including sports associations, were divided not only by class but also by religion. To be sure, the Nazis introduced new social hierarchies along racial and eugenic lines, excluding Jews and others from these organizations; but the coordination of associational life created unified organizations for Aryans. In the case of the KdF, however, this political process of coordination was also fun, which can help us to explain why this institution worked well.

The Nazis sought to subsume all of these activities under Nazi-controlled institutions. On the one hand, the Nazis did so for the control it afforded them. They sought to reduce class conflict or potential resistance to their regime by subordinating all groups to singular Nazi organizations for various demographics, such as women, youth, and workers. On the other hand, this coordination of society was presented in Nazi propaganda as bringing a new degree of equality to Aryans. KdF contributed to both policies by trying to use collective activities and emotions as a kind of social glue. Specifically, the organization aimed to use the happiness evoked for participants in its programs as a means to create and strengthen the *Volksgemeinschaft*—one could call this strategy *joy production* (Timpe 2017). As a result, KdF activities deliberately favored entertainment over competitive training in sports. As KdF's leader Robert Ley put it, "It is not about how far somebody jumps—but that he jumps" (qtd. in Busch 1938: 162).

German schools provide another example of institutional techniques designed to create a better society by altering human behavior, in this case, the behavior of students. By the new milennium, many German teachers explicitly tailored their history lessons about National Socialism as a way to create democratic citizens. For teachers, this goal meant denouncing the Nazi regime as well as contemporary neo-Nazi movements and extreme right-wing political thought. Not only did teachers distance themselves from previous generations that were implicated in the Nazi regime, but they also took explicitly political positions conditioned by the time and place of their formative development.

Teachers who entered the teaching profession in the 1970s and 1980s tended to orient their politics according to their experiences as adolescents and students in the 1960s and 1970s in the former GDR or the FRG. On both sides of the former inner-German border teachers turned to a specific pedagogical approach termed *Betroffenheitspädagogik*. This term literally translates to *pedagogy of affect*, referring to instruction that both emerges from and targets emotions. In practice, it means using emotion to teach history (Schiele and Schneider 1991; Mütter and Uffelmann 1992; Gies 1995: 127–41).

Pedagogues distancing themselves from a cognitive approach to learning have promoted teaching through emotion since the beginning of the twentieth century. Yet the use of emotions specifically to teach the Nazi past can also be understood as a political critique and practical response to the lack of empathy for the victims of the Shoah typical of the FRG in the 1950s and 1960s (Lüdtke 1993: 542–72). Having empathy with victims is thought to have a twofold political and pedagogical role. On the one hand, it demonstrates one's understanding of the suffering of the victims (Wenzel and Weber 1989). On the other, it presents an alleged bulwark against neo-Nazism among young people by creating identification with the German constitution, the political regime, and, ultimately, the act of voting.

The generation of history teachers working at the turn of the millennium saw the study of National Socialism as a particularly efficient technique for the civic education of students and the promotion of democratic values. In an interview conducted by one of our authors in February 2003, Mr. Schultze, a history teacher in his early sixties at a university–preparatory high school (Gymnasium) in Hamburg, described his instruction about the Nazi past as resembling "religious lessons." As he put it, "talking about Social Darwinism and the *Völkerprinzip*," by which nations and their peoples are divided eugenically into races, "always means talking at the same time about the opposite world: the values [*Gegenwerte*] we believe in. In general, [the students] understand quickly: why is Social Darwinism impossible to defend? What does that mean in our world today? How would we treat the handicapped?"

Setting up these binaries was intended to serve democracy. Their pedagogical approach created "two opposite worlds": the fascist and racist community of Nazism in contrast to a society based on human dignity and the constitution of the Federal Republic, called the *Grundgesetz*, or Basic Constitutional Law. In constructing a fundamental antagonism, the teachers seemed to imply that the rejection of one led almost automatically to the adoption of the other. They proposed that, by teaching the history of genocide and identifying with the victims, instructors encouraged students to support the rule of law in general and the German constitution in particular (Oeser 2009).

Often the teachers sought to transmit to their students a much broader system of beliefs including both tolerance for difference and active rejection of anti-Semitism and racism. This set of beliefs sometimes included criticism of discrimination against homosexuals and the handicapped, though less frequently. Behind these beliefs, we find values that are expressed in the United Nations Declaration of Human Rights. Some teachers, like Mr. Gerste, made explicit reference to human rights and their relevance to teaching the history of Nazism (Interview. February 2003).

"Accept others as they are," Inge Müller explained in an interview from October 2003, "even if they are different from us." Applying the past to the present, teachers hoped to encourage students to become more tolerant in their everyday practices, notably toward ethnic minorities. If the teachers were particularly ambitious, they may have hoped to inspire concrete acts of civil courage and the active protection of the rights of others. They wanted children not only to ask questions but also to question authorities and state administrations if their actions seemed arbitrary. According to their beliefs, the ideal citizen was not just tolerant. They also had to be courageous and capable of defending human rights even under a dictatorial regime.

These pedagogical ambitions were utopian in many ways. These teachers believed that progress could and should be made possible by state-sponsored educational institutions, or at least they tried to believe in it. That is to say, embedded in their discourse about pedagogy was a faith in the efficiency of schools as institutions that could change not only human minds but also society as such. The Nazi leisure organization and the German schoolteachers thus had opposite goals in terms of the directions of their politics but both strove to be state-supporting institutions.

KdF wanted to shape German workers' lives and attitudes in a way that would ensure they fit in and strengthened the Nazi-envisioned *Volksgemeinschaft* and the dictatorship of the Third Reich. Especially when it comes to the teaching of the Nazi past, German teachers and schools in the early twenty-first century wanted to educate students in a way that would not only fit them into democracy but also prepare them to fight against dictatorship and discrimination. What both institutions also shared was a commitment to shaping their members, as consumers of leisure or recipients of education, into proper members of their society based on prevailing norms. And not by accident, both used emotions to do so.

Institutional Agents

Institutional ambition, however, is quite different from lived reality. It would be wrong to assume that institutions always accomplish the goals they set for themselves. Everyday life almost always gets complicated. In the case of institutions, their operations are made more complicated by competition between institutions and the relative autonomy of institutional agents upon whom they rely to implement their policies. Goals can also be subverted when the services provided by the institution are used in ways that contravene their guidelines. That is to say, goals can be challenged at all three levels: by policy makers, by institutional agents, and even by the people institutions are designed to entertain, help, correct, or control.

Despite various attempts of institutional coordination, the Nazi regime actually promoted a proliferation of institutions with overlapping authorities and objectives. This *polycratic* quality of the Nazi regime led to permanent institutional competition (Broszat 1981). Embedded in redundant institutions with overlapping responsibilities, Nazi bigwigs fought repeatedly with each other for control over regime policies and public sectors—a struggle for wealth, influence, power, and status that led to a progressive radicalization of the regime's policies. Each institution and its agents strove to meet and even anticipate the presumed aspirations of the Nazi regime in advance of their competitors.

The Deutscher Caritasverband is a prime example. The DCV enjoyed considerable political and social influence during the Weimar Republic. When Hitler took power in 1933, Nazi policy makers restructured social relief networks by changing both relief practices and organizational structure. The Nationalsozialistische Volkswohlfahrt (NSV) was tapped to be the official welfare organization of the Third Reich, while all other organizations were forcibly disbanded. Only three of the formerly private charity institutions were allowed to operate under Nazi rule: the DCV, the Protestant Inner Mission, and the German Red Cross. Yet they were all subordinated to the NSV. *How did the DCV respond to these new obligations and reshaped social expectations?*

Many high-ranking officials of the DCV lamented the Nazi takeover of charity and social relief. Director of Youth Welfare Gustav von Mann condemned the officials from the NSV as "new people with a lack of expertise" (Wollasch 1996: 154). For many DCV officials, the newness of NSV policies and structures threatened the considerable social and political influence that the Catholic charity had established during the Weimar Republic. In response the DCV's leadership tried to establish continuity with the practices, symbols, and images of the past. We see this move as a self-preservation tactic, as the DCV sought to confirm its place within the competitive arena for social relief in the new Third Reich.

This commitment to tradition, however, created antagonism between the workers and administrators of the DCV and the new NSV officials. Members of the Hitler Youth (HJ) and the League of German Girls (BDM) clashed directly with the DCV in the streets as the organizations competed for potential donors. In a letter dated 9 May 1934 (ADCV 236.40.025), a Catholic priest from Karlsruhe wrote to the Central Office (Zentrale) of the DCV in Freiburg to complain about unwanted youth volunteers wearing Nazi uniforms while collecting on the DCV's behalf.

The priest referenced a decree issued on 6 April 1934 that stated youths under eighteen could only collect in uniform if they did so on behalf of national associations. He even went as far as phoning the Baden branch of the BDM to complain about the transgressions of their members. His complaints fell on deaf ears at the BDM, which shows to what degree the Nazi organization was able to efficiently appropriate the legitimacy of charity from the DCV. At the same time, this letter documents the active engagement of this leading member of the Caritas organization in protecting his institution's unique Catholic vision of charity. It reveals the anxiety about the fragility of the image of the DCV. These and similar incidents gave the impression that the DCV was unwilling to accept the authority of the NSV over their operations and was reluctant to be represented by the iconography of National Socialism.

There was not just competition between different social relief institutions. At times the DCV explicitly challenged expectations placed on it from above. In one striking example, they ignored what was arguably the most sensitive policy of the Nazi regime: the racial and eugenic boundaries of the *Volksgemeinschaft*. In one hospital in Branitz, a borough of the city of Cottbus in northeast Germany, DCV caregivers accepted Jews during the Third Reich (Wollasch 1996: 181). Nurses and doctors administered the same services to them that they offered to Protestant and Catholic patients.

Along with medical services, hospital workers also enabled Jews to continue their religious practices. The Branitz hospital maintained two kitchens to accommodate Jewish dietary practices in addition to providing Jews with sufficient time to observe religious holidays and rituals. In doing so, the DCV both implied that Jews deserved care and explicitly acted on these beliefs. Through their charitable expressions, DCV agents revealed that they would not easily yield to the new racial definitions of the *deserving poor* imposed by Nazi policy makers. They continued to make decisions that confirmed their own traditions in caring for those in need and clung desperately to a sense of their own authority.

It is tempting to read these unruly acts as a form of resistance. For our purposes in this chapter, these acts of *Eigensinn* are best understood as a reappropriation of institutional rules by the agents responsible for implementing them. The agents of the DCV chose between two conflicting sets of principles, both of which informed their institutional practices; and as a result, they helped some of the victims of Nazi persecution. But it is not always true that these kinds of reappropriations resulted in resistance to Nazi policies; they could also help facilitate collaboration (Bergerson et al. 2011). Perpetrators often took this process one step further. As examples from the Shoah illustrate, their reappropriations of institutional rules surpassed the original intentions of the policy makers, though perhaps not their aspirations. Nazi concentration and death camps thus bring us to the violent heart of Nazi institutions.

Consider the concentration camp at Majdanek. It was located outside of Lublin in the General Government, the Nazi name during World War II for what was left of occupied Poland. Between fall 1941 and summer 1944, Majdanek fulfilled many different functions: it was a POW camp for Soviet soldiers, a labor camp for Jewish as well as Polish prisoners, and a hostage camp for the local rural population. Majdanek was also one of the main killing sites for Aktion Reinhardt—the multisite, mass murder operation designed to exterminate the 1.35 million Jews living in the General Government (Pohl 2012). In this capacity, Majdanek combined the functions of a concentration and extermination camp, where Jewish women, men, and children were systematically murdered. As an institution, Majdanek thus harbored an enormous potential for abuse of power and brutality.

But we doubt: *do the goals, structure, and organization of the camps as institutions really provide an exhaustive explanation of their violent nature?* A closer look at the women's camp at Majdanek and its female guards, called SS-Aufseherinnen, complicates our understanding of how such institutions operated. The institutional setting of the women's camp certainly shaped the everyday for both its inmates and the guards. Here, we are not referring simply to the physical infrastructure of the camp but also to the regulations and ideology that informed the concentrationary universe (Rousset 1946: 17).

Scholars of the camps tend to emphasize these elements of camp institutions: their formal structure and organization. A few scholars deal with social practices and situational dynamics (Sofksy 1997; Herbert, Orth, and Dieckmann 1998; Caplan and Wachsmann 2010; Wachsmann 2015). We do not ignore the former; but to understand the German *Alltag*, we want to highlight the latter. To be sure, the guards, as institutional agents, were tasked with implementing policies. Yet the massive violence perpetrated by them is best understood, we argue, as a result of a complex interplay between structure and agency, global and local dynamics.

In Majdanek, the camp commander and his immediate staff managed exterminatory violence in close cooperation with the central camp administration located in Berlin. The latter, including both the Wirtschaftsverwaltungshauptamt (WVHA) and the former Inspektion der Konzentrationslager (IKL), administered the camp system as a whole. This central camp administration issued guidelines for proper behavior for the local camp administration with the intent of determining the framework of violence in the camps. Some kinds of violence were thus ordered from above. Guards regularly selected, gassed, and shot prisoners or injected them with poison. These kinds of violence were further encouraged by distributing decorations and rewards to the guards for their service, including narcotics, alcohol, and extra rations of cigarettes (Mailänder Kolsov 2009, Mailänder 2015). So we certainly find what one might call an *official* kind of genocidal violence operating here.

Yet, sometimes, the camp's local management far exceeded the expectations defined in Berlin. Camp guard Luzie Halata testified in court about a selection of children in the camp in summer 1943 during which the Schutzstaffel (SS) tried to separate Jewish mothers from their small children. The fact that she was known as "nice" and rather "mild" in comparison to her fellow guards and that she was the only one among them willing to collaborate and testify during the Majdanek trial makes her example particularly strong. Interviewed by the documentary filmmaker Eberhard Fechner in the late 1970s (1984: pt. 2), Halata described her behavior in this stressful situation:

> I wanted them [the mothers] to shut up and be quiet. I saw the chief guard Else Ehrich coming. So I started to scream and shout at the mothers to keep them quiet. But only for the sake of the chief guard. I wanted to do my duty. And she walked past and whispered to me: "*Frau Aufseherin*, have some sympathy for the women." Do you hear, I assumed that she wanted me to maintain order.

Halata no doubt thought that she did a good job as a guard and sought advancement in her career. But that meant that she had to meet the expectations of her superior, Else Ehrich, who was known to be particularly severe and pitiless. Halata showed her toughness by being particularly harsh with the prisoners. In fact, Halata anticipated a degree of brutality that the chief guard did not even demand. We consider this kind of violence to be a form of *vorauseilender Gehorsam*, which translates as *anticipatory obedience*. It is a good example of reappropriating the official rules of the institution. Anticipatory obedience certainly met the aspirations of the institution but far exceeded its guidelines. Effectively overfulfilling institutional expectations, Halata took it upon herself to extrapolate from the official guidelines into new degrees of persecution.

The everyday violence at Majdanek shows us the challenges facing institutional officers when they try to harmonize and streamline the practices of their subordinate agents. Guidelines are not sufficient to govern an institution because lower-level institutional officers either do not fully accept institutional goals or do not do so consistently. Along with the other guards, Halata contributed to the creation of *locally relevant* norms for violent behavior that actually exceeded expectations from Berlin. (As such, it is an example of what social scientists call a *principal–agent problem*.)

The particular horror of this informal kind of brutality lies in no small measure in the fact that the vast majority of these institutional functionaries came to a pragmatic kind of consensus about it, above and beyond the bureaucratic dimensions of mass murder (Mailänder 2010). The point is that this *excessive* brutality did not emerge from orders from Berlin but in working contexts where power, force, hierarchies, and peer-group relations were permanently renegotiated through interactions among guards. The concentrationary universe depended on both kinds of violence: the bureaucratic mechanisms of extermination and the innovative expressions of excessive brutality. It was shaped by microsocial interactions on the ground among institutional policy makers and agents (Lüdtke 2002).

What does this comparison between Nazi institutions of charity and extermination teach us? In spite of their official obedience to homogeneous rules and procedures, institutions, insofar as they are able to operate efficiently at all, rely centrally on the actions of workers on the ground to implement their goals. Yet these institutional agents at times contravene those very rules and procedures. This unruliness can be oriented in many directions: harkening to former traditions or anticipating implied aspirations. It would therefore be more accurate to say that agents throughout the hierarchy of the institution, from the highest administrator to the lowest worker, contribute not only to the functioning of the institution but also to the formulation of its written and unwritten guidelines for its day-to-day operation. They do so as much through their formal adherence to guidelines as through their informal adaptation of policy to particular circumstances.

But we can go further: institutions can even be subverted by the very people who these institutions were designed to serve, reform, or control. Consider the example of the German workers who participated in KdF's leisure activities. In the mid-1930s, KdF had founded so-called Factory Sports Communities or Betriebssportgemeinschaften (BSG) in German factories. Before the Nazis' rise to power, many German workers had been active in working-class sports clubs closely affiliated with the Catholic, Communist, or Social Democrat milieus. As part of the concerted effort to coordinate the workers into Nazi-run organizations, the Nazis outlawed these older organizations in 1933. Inside German factories, KdF-run BSG came to function as a substitute. However, some workers adhered only to the letter of this new rule. An investigation "from below" reveals that they used these KdF-sponsored activities to continue to meet with their former comrades from their old sports clubs (Teichler 1987: 240; Frese 1991: 403).

The irony here is rather rich. In its constant attempts to control the everyday lives of German workers, KdF unwittingly created an institutional space that allowed some continuity for the workers' milieu that the Nazis had sought—and largely managed—to destroy. Sometimes this circumstance even meant that KdF's leisure programs could become sites for acts of clandestine oppositional activities against the Nazi regime. In other words, these anti-Nazi acts occurred within an institution initiated and led by the Nazi regime.

One local Nazi party official, Notter, lectured on this matter on 24 January 1938, outlining the "Guidelines and Practice of the Communist International for the Destruction of the Factory Community" (BArch NS 5/IV/94). He described how Communists acted as undercover participants in KdF events and in some instances even became their organizers. Their goal was to meet with large numbers of German workers in an inconspicuous manner or set up small circles, which they hoped might become the sites of future resistance work.

In his memoirs (BArch SgY 30/2058), activist Alfred Nothnagel described establishing such a sports group for working-class youth. This youth group, "disguised with leather trousers, colorful shirts and skirts respectively, and musical instruments, undertook trips through the urban hinterland of Leipzig." To avert the danger of inspections and possible arrests as a "wild group"—that is, not authorized by the Nazi regime—he decided to have one of his participants apply for a KdF hiking license. This license then allowed him to mask the group as a KdF hiking club. His plan worked.

On several occasions, the KdF license prevented the arrest of members of the group. Nothnagel's hiking group was not unique in this regard; we know of adult hiking clubs populated by former Socialist Youth members and of folk dance groups led by a Marxist (see the report *Bund Niederdeutscher Heimatwanderer* in BArch NS 5/IV/39: 35; and the report *Volkstanzkreis 215 Guben*, in BArch R 58/316: 37f, discussed in Timpe 2017). A survey conducted by Hans Joachim Teichler after World War II among former members of Weimar era working-class sports clubs (1985: 199f.) revealed that about a third of them continued to do sports during the Third Reich by using KdF's institutional frameworks of sports classes and communities.

We are reminded of Alexander Morawitz, who was able to create an alternative space for hip-hop culture in the GDR by obtaining an official license as a musician. We tend to evaluate these kind of actions as resistance. But by investigating the German *Alltag*, we discover a more contradictory and controversial scene.

On the one hand, camouflaging an illegal Communist youth club as a KdF hiking group is not an example of direct resistance against the Nazi regime. It did not directly attack or sabotage a leading member or agency of the Nazi state. (Some useful distinctions here can be found in Geyer 1992: 217–41.) Additional motives for creating these Communist institutions within Nazi ones included meeting old friends, participating in sports, simply having a good time, or even getting drunk at the regime's expense during evening entertainments called *Bunte Abende*. On the other hand, these Nazi institutions clearly did not work as planned. Reappropriated to preserve social relations with former members of a Communist milieu, some workers subverted KdF's institutional goal of helping to build a Nazi *Volksgemeinschaft*.

There is one more twist to this story, however; in the long term, these subversions in the realm of sports eventually did help to further the KdF's aims. The workers may not have joined the Nazi leisure organization for its own sake. Once active within the KdF, however, the older socialist side of their sports activities faded in most cases. And even if they did not, even if these activities were indeed foremost embraced by the workers as a way to continue meetings in socialist or even anti-Nazi circles, sources suggest it took too much energy to continue the KdF masquerade, and some workers lacked the ability to engage in actual resistance activities. We wonder whether these subversions might have served the Nazi cause in the end.

We could make similar arguments about these other institutions. Acting in unruly ways that were neither intended nor anticipated, people sometimes disrupted the everyday of institutions. But even these disruptions did not always function as intended or anticipated. Ironically, they may have contributed, in dynamic and complicated ways, to the institution's functioning. Here we see the benefit of viewing these institutions from the perspective on the ground, for the actual ways they reshaped self, state, and society were determined by these microsocial interactions between historical actors.

Bending the Rules

We would be mistaken if we evaluated institutions solely in terms of the goals for which they were created. We cannot assume that this goal is ever reached directly. The power of institutions to do and to make in everyday life does not simply move in one direction from the policy makers through agents to the people. Often, agents and even the objects of institutional policies influence in unexpected ways the outcomes of institutional policies.

Yet we contend that this unruliness actually helps institutions to work. Looking at the everyday of institutions, we see people both bending and adhering to rules, challenging de jure processes but in the process inventing de facto ones. What matters here is not to focus on the rules of the game, which are constantly changing, but the fact that they are playing along. The institution might consider these innovations to be disruptive, but the reappropriation of its goals, rules, and resources is often productive in helping the institution to achieve aspirations that exceeded its current expectations.

Caritas is a good case in point. DCV workers sought to maintain their institutional individuality through images and symbols. They sought distance from Nazi symbols, like uniforms, in order to inject their own imagery into their caring practices. To be sure, these workers were not simply preserving the traditional operations of their institution. They were also openly criticizing the new forms of behavior in the face of massive pressure to conform.

In DCV correspondences, for instance, only seldom did DCV workers sign letters with *Heil Hitler!* They appear to have used this greeting only in an official capacity when addressing Nazi authorities (for more on greeting, see Bergerson 2004; Allert 2005; Fritzsche 2008). Instead, most DCV members chose to sign intradepartmental and personal letters with their own Catholic valediction *Mit caritativen Gruß*, meaning, roughly, *with a charitable greeting*. By contrast, its Protestant counterpart, the Innere Mission, quickly adopted the Nazi phrase in all correspondences.

The reluctance on the part of DCV to conform to Nazi codes for behavior created the appearance of two institutions at odds with one another and perpetuated the perception of a divide between Nazism and Catholicism. The ability to marshal institutional authority rested, in the eyes of its members and administrators, in their capacity to continue past practices under Nazi rule. Administrators like von Mann, whom we encountered above, believed that the DCV's tradition afforded its members a sense of expert authority that the NSV did not have. Moreover, he believed that his volunteers and workers maintained and injected that tradition into Nazi Germany's public sphere through their everyday practices.

But even though the DCV insisted on maintaining its own traditions, symbols, and imagery, we should not automatically assume that the DCV somehow conspired to rid itself of the Nazi regime. DCV workers and volunteers very easily imagined themselves functioning within a fascist system. Klaus-Michael Mallmann and Gerhard Paul (2000) conceptualized this kind of ambiguity as "loyal reluctance" (*loyale Widerwilligkeit*). In an article dated 16 May 1935 titled "From the Diary of a Caritas People's Day Collection Box Nr. 223" (ADCV 236.40.025), we read that a woman, after being asked by a DCV charity collector to give a donation, refused to contribute because she claimed she needed the money for her "sick dog." The collector remarked, "The Führer must hear [of these refusals]! How would Hitler respond to this?" In this case, the charity collector policed some of the most important principles of the Nazi regime: denunciation and the Führer principle.

But there were also more subtle ways in which the DCV supported the Nazi system. Ironically, their pronounced public acts of Catholic spirituality may have made some Catholics feel more comfortable with the Third Reich. By insisting on maintaining its own traditions and practices, the DCV may have helped to generate a more diverse and holistic image of the *Volksgemeinschaft* such that a wider range of Germans could come to accept the German *Alltag* under the Third Reich. Thus the same institution and the same acts of unruliness often have multiple meanings and consequences, which makes it difficult to determine retrospectively their precise political valence. More to the point, these acts both satisfy and discourage different and sometimes contradictory institutional aims at the same time.

A similar story could also be told about Majdanek, though it is a much more extreme example. Here it is worth considering the definition of the term *work* in the context of the camps. Leading Nazi authorities considered collective mass killing to be an official and highly appreciated form of labor on the part of the guards. Yet the opposite was the case when it came to individual acts of violence or personal abuses of prisoners. These spontaneous acts of brutality were not considered part of their job description (Mailänder Koslov 2009: 571, Mailänder 2015). When guards were first trained for these difficult assignments, they had to swear to the fact that only the Führer and his Berlin administration could decide the life and death of an inmate.

While the central camp administration in Berlin expected the systematic extermination of inmates, official guidelines expressly prohibited guards from abusing any of the inmates individually. Any such autonomous assault on prisoners was formally forbidden and punished, although the guards never faced the death penalty for such acts. This distinction between legitimate and illegitimate forms of killing on the part of the guards, and therefore also legitimate and illegitimate forms of work, might seem astonishing to us today in light of the brutality of the camps. But we need to view this issue from their institutional perspective: senior administrators in Berlin considered this kind of individualized violence to be *counter*productive insofar as it created chaos. They wanted disciplined employees who killed when it was necessary and ordered. In a sense, the central camp administration in Berlin issued instructions like the traditional Prussian bureaucracy. They wanted institutional orders—in this case, mass murder—to be executed according to centralized procedures and regulations.

As Michael Wildt has argued (2012a, 2012b, 2013), the dynamism of the Third Reich lay precisely in the tension between these traditional state institutions responsible for order and the popular violence of the Nazi movement. In this reading, the camps were effective as killing institutions because of the dynamic relationship between officially sanctioned, bureaucratic murder and unofficial expressions of excessive violence. The brutality of the guards was therefore individualized but never isolated. It so permeated the everyday life of the camps that it became part and parcel of the system of extermination and central to its efficient operation. The central camp administration reluctantly recognized this fact. They admitted that this kind of spontaneous and individualized violence could also be productive insofar as it motivated and empowered the guards in an emotionally stressful situation.

Ultimately, the innovative brutality of the guards worked in conjunction with the organized procedures of mass murder to make the camps run more efficiently, as both institutions of mass murder within the camps and institutions that by reputation terrorized the larger civil society. Here it is important to remember that, initially in the 1930s, the Nazi regime used concentration camps primarily as a weapon to break—or, as they put it, to reeducate—political enemies. This terror function was communicated largely through the press (Gellateley 2002; Wrocklage in progress). But the camps themselves had to operate as systems of excessive violence within complex social dynamics in order for that message to have clout.

Once the war started and the camp system expanded in the east, the communication politics and purposes of persecution changed. In the 1940s, the central camp administration and high-ranking politicians did not want to diffuse information about the ongoing brutalities against POWs and inmates from the occupied territories in the camps. They did not want to publicize the extermination of the European Jews. Their motives lay not only in ensuring the cooperation of their victims but also in avoiding protest on the part of the Aryan population and insulating them from responsibility.

Nevertheless knowledge about those activities circulated among the personnel on the ground and eventually reached the *Altreich*, as the pre-1937 boundaries of Germany were called. This diffusion of knowledge about the camps and their extreme violence had an unintended side effect. The seemingly total power of the camp guard over life and death served the regime insofar as it reinforced the fear of the Nazi regime among the population, increasing its position of authority.

We suspect that something similar has contributed to the persistent image of the Nazi regime in the postwar era as a regime commanding authority through terror. As instructors in German studies, we find that many of our students have been fascinated by the Third Reich and the Shoah because of this image of terror. This dynamic seems as true in Europe as in the United States and among both university and high school students. Yet this legacy makes teaching these subjects more difficult. What often frustrates high school teachers, for instance, is that students do not always cooperate with the teacher's attempts to provide a more complex and critical vision of Nazi Germany.

The high-school students of Hamburg and Leipzig at the turn of the millennium also fit this model. In these schools, the people who were supposed to be changed by the institution instead reappropriated its resources in unruly ways. Specifically, the students often resorted to humor when confronted with the history of Nazi terror and genocide. Officially, this subject was not suitable for jokes; and yet, in the schoolyard and classrooms, students made jokes about it. In her field work, one of our authors observed young people laughing in a broad range of situations: in the classroom, when a male student confronted his teacher with a casual "Heil Hitler"; when the class clown told a joke about Hitler or Jews; and when one of the boys started to laugh out loud during the screening of the Holocaust movie *Schindler's List*. These different situations evoked different kinds of laughter (Oeser 2015).

In part, students relied on various coping techniques when confronted with extreme violence. It also helped them to endure institutional rules by transgressing or sublimating its norms. What surprises us, however, in reviewing this ethnographic evidence, is that students applied material they learned in class to everyday interactions both inside and outside of school. Facing the constraints of the institution, students adapted them while they adapted to them. They accepted, avoided, confronted, or ignored them, appropriating times and spaces for themselves and creating new rules of the game by taking positions relative to their adult instructors (Oeser 2010).

But more than anything else, the students positioned themselves in hierarchies of status and power within the group of their adolescent peers.

Jokes—and, in this case, controversial ones about Germany's Nazi past—represented one mode by which students negotiated the power dynamics at school. Such jokes contained a plethora of meanings that signified a student's relationship with the teacher and with other students. Karsten, a fifteen-year-old middle school student from Leipzig, played this game on two different levels. On the one hand, he understood the institutional language that restricted his behavior. He said, "I thought it was quite evident, really," after his teacher explained to him and his classmates that these jokes were inappropriate. That is, institutional rules that defined such jokes as taboo clearly resonated with Karsten.

On the other hand, Karsten recognized the implications of such jokes within his social circles. Karsten made jokes about Jews in order to gain acceptance with his classmates. Interestingly, he claimed to not make the same jokes as some of the other students—the "really bad ones." As he stated: "I admit, I also make jokes about [Jews], a little with them. But not, 'Out with the Jews,' or things like that—what they say. I do not say things like that." Karsten condemned the excessive and systematic transgression of institutional rules. Yet he seemed to draw a careful distinction between the institutional spaces of school and the social spaces embedded within it.

Like many people embedded within and the objects of institutions, Karsten was sensitive to the guidelines for his behavior. He was able to carefully parse the nuances that existed within his own peer group in terms of whose unruliness was acceptable and who took the joke too far. Those who continuously went beyond the bounds of legitimacy faced punishment and ultimately exclusion from the institution by their teachers, which led to exclusion from the peer group as well.

His lucidity as to the risks involved in transgressing institutional rules allowed Karsten to play two different games. By staying attentive in class, he played the role of student well, so he could pass his professional graduation exams, called the *Fachabitur*. Nevertheless, his jokes allowed him to play the game of his peers and to take his place among the deviant in the classroom and in the schoolyard. Through his unruliness, he set his own rules for behavior; but they were still ultimately dependent upon the strategies established by the institution. Thus he also respected certain limits: he refused to participate in a xenophobic discourse, even if he tolerated it from his peers.

Karsten moved adroitly between these two interdependent, yet distinct institutional topographies. But his practices of self also had consequences for others. His tactics (Certeau 1984) also helped shape the everyday for his peers. They too inhabited the times and spaces made distinct by these different practices. They had to decide how to respond to his jokes in different settings, both in the presence and in the absence of the teachers. Such practices undermine institutional rules and are thus partly directed against the institution.

At the same time, they very often contribute to its functioning. For example, laughing after a joke permitted students and teachers to calm down and get back to work; breaking the boundaries of propriety in the schoolyard marked the limits of propriety in the classroom. These practices also created parallel worlds, spaces within the institutions, different social scenes, which allowed agents space and time for more autonomous action. But those independent actions also marked, through difference, the normative behavior expected in other situations.

A fascinating process of misdirection is implicit in many of these practices of self. They are sometimes, but not always, socially excluding, verbally insulting, or physically abusing vulnerable third parties, but with an intent to communicate something about themselves to their peers or superiors. That is, the victims of this abuse—directly present or indirectly the butt of the jokes—became a medium for a social message (Gleason 2001). In the context of microsocial interactions, their suffering seems almost a side effect.

In many of these cases, the audience for these actions was peers or superiors. Charity workers chose how to greet other workers; guards demonstrated their brutality primarily to other guards; and schoolchildren made jokes about the Shoah in school primarily for the benefit of fellow students. Within all of these institutions, then, unruly actions challenged or exceeded official guidelines for behavior. Indeed, they seem to have stood at the heart of how these institutions worked.

How Institutions Work Well

In this chapter, we took a close look at four German institutions. They all sought to impose homogeneous ways of being, believing, and behaving. And to some degree, they did so in a way that reflected the political context in which they were operating. If exercising the Aryan body and providing charity to Aryans in need fit the politics of the Third Reich as much as brutalizing Jews in camps, teaching adolescents to reject that past in support of democracy fit the politics of the Federal Republic at the turn of the millennium. These institutions were designed to transform some combination of self, society, and state, or at least to buttress existing forms more effectively. Institutions are a crucial site for the making of incommon worlds—an overarching theme of this book.

These efforts evoked reactions inside and outside these institutions. Our analysis has tried to draw attention to the complexity of these interactions among agents at various levels of these institutions. More to the point, these boundaries of inside and outside, above and below, while crucial in terms of hierarchies of power and force, can distract us from the interactions that take place across them. What strikes us about all of these cases is that these institutions served not only as places where people were educated, entertained, provided charity, coordinated, terrorized, or exterminated, but also as places where people lived and worked.

Their functioning as institutions cannot be understood in isolation from the everyday life they were designed to alter or improve. Viewed on the ground, we are struck by the degree to which the domains of private and professional were intertwined. Following the experiences of our historical subjects as they moved across this quotidian terrain allows us to discover the *art of in-between*: the familiar and creative way of negotiating the features of everyday life that allowed them to deal with contradiction, complexity, human behavior, and institutional settings.

But never in isolation: examining the everyday of institutions requires that we reintegrate them into the actual sociopolitical environments in which they operated and consider how embedded agents shaped and were shaped by their surroundings. Our insight here is that people are always both the subjects and objects of institutions, operating between rejection and affirmation of them. This dynamic tension between obedience and transgression can be found in settings of terror and exterminations such as concentrations camps as well as in institutions like schools in the twenty-first century. We encountered it in organizations like the KdF, focused primarily on winning supporters through joy production, and the DCV, with its concern for helping others. The actual everyday emerged between these microsocial processes.

In some of these cases, institutions generated particular times and places for quasiautonomous activities. Workers could use KdF groups to practice sports among like-minded comrades. These spaces, embedded within the larger institution, were not entirely off limits to Nazis but were largely removed from the influence of the institution and the regime. Students similarly appropriated recess on the schoolyard, embedded within the institution and yet effectively removed from the authority of the teachers, as a time and place for testing the limits of anti-Nazi orthodoxy through jokes. These distinctions of time and space constituted the solid, if plastic, boundaries of partial life worlds. Creating these spaces of relative autonomy required engaging with the circumstances of everyday life while also manipulating them to one's own ends.

The tight focus on everyday lives similarly blurs the distinctions between the inside and outside of institutions that seem so reliably clear in a wider lens. When viewed on the ground, institutions provide the framework for both the adoption and the adaptation of normative practices, rules, and goals. DCV workers or volunteers may have understood themselves as political opponents by, for example, attempting to distance their institution from the NSV. Yet they also legitimated the Nazi regime by evoking Hitler's authority to justify their actions. In these institutions, German people were given new roles to perform—as caregivers, workers, guards, and teachers. They had to perform those roles on an institutional stage that was likewise embedded within a larger lived reality that included the Nazis. Perhaps this point is the irritating crux of the matter. There was no avoiding some degree of compromise with everyday life.

It may appear inappropriate to speak of an everyday of Nazism in light of its seemingly extraordinary violence, especially of a concentration or extermination camp. Yet to scrutinize the everyday does not mean to treat it as banal. On the contrary, in these exceptional institutions distinct experiences of the everyday emerged. The guards' autonomous expressions of unofficial violence were a way to show off and distinguish themselves from other coworkers. This behavior shows striking similarities to the students of twenty-first-century German schools who developed ways to affirm themselves, to pass time, and to amuse other members of the peer group.

For some students, the Nazi past, when expressed through a joke, carried a certain social currency. These claims to power and status among one's peer group, which involve staking out a particular self in public for the benefit of oneself and others, could also be extended to charity workers insisting on extending their colleagues a caritative greeting and workers preferring to engage in sports with their old communist comrades. Here the everyday directs our gaze to the social practices of the agents, the ambiguity of their actions, the creation and destruction of social solidarities, and the formation of social norms.

The point of this chapter is that the people embedded in institutions also helped shape those institutions by participating in their operations. Some of them were more powerless than others, but all of them used available resources to reshape their life worlds and, indirectly, the larger world. The same could also be said of the people who were the objects of institutional policies. As individuals struggled to adapt to rules of the institutions that served or oppressed them, they were also able, at times, to appropriate or subvert those rules. They altered the rules of the game while playing them. We might tentatively conclude that these institutions all worked according to normative guidelines, but they worked *well* thanks to this dynamic relationship between normative rules and unruly actions.

This reading of everyday institutions is pessimistic in terms of the ultimate impact of *Eigensinn*. Each of these institutions developed a variety of strategies designed to control their own operations, to get the agents and objects of these institutions interested in obeying the rules, to make them participate complicitly in the activities of the institution, to prevent them from disturbing those operations, and to incite them to adequately position themselves toward the rules. Yet on every level of the institution, the people involved in these institutions carved out spaces and times to reappropriate those institutions using the very ingredients of institutional rules imposed on them. Unruliness created parallel world within institutions, but at least in the case of these four institutions, that space of quasiautonomy contributed to the institutions' functioning. In Steege's words (Bergerson et al. 2009: 562): "Acts of independence work to articulate and reinforce structures of hegemony," which, in the case of the Nazi regime, meant fascist terror and racist extermination.

This chapter offers an account of everyday institutions that could be extended, no doubt with caveats, to many others of self, state, and society. On the ground, the functionality of institutions seems to derive in part from the many ways in which people conform to some rules in order to gain maneuverability vis-à-vis others. Here again we see that ruptures are not extraordinary breaches in the *Alltag* but part and parcel of the everyday itself, not least the everyday of institutions. Yet the point is not that institutions are *inherently* functional. Institutions are functional *as a result of what human beings do with them*.

Elissa Mailänder, Alexandra Oeser, Will Rall, and Julia Timpe

CHAPTER 7

Anti-Semitism

Illustration 7.1. Erich Bloch, *Bloch/Begall*, 1946. Reprint from Kläre-Bloch-Schule 1992: 9.

Anti-Semitism has been a feature of everyday life throughout the long history of German-speaking Central Europe, but never so central as during the Nazi regime from 1933 to 1945 (Benz and Bergmann 1997). In the span of twelve short years, the Nazi leadership tried to transform German society into a violent *Volksgemeinschaft*. We use this Nazi term as an analytical tool to describe the attraction that many Germans felt to the social inclusion promised by the Nazi regime, an inclusion that not only proved to be illusory for many so-called racially pure Aryans but was also always predicated on anti-Semitic and racist exclusions (Bajohr and Wildt 2009: 8–12). As a result of the latter, six million Jews and 200,000 Sinti and Romanies across Europe were murdered and many more were persecuted, along with opposition politicians, homosexuals, resistance fighters, and many other people in Nazi-occupied Europe. These murders marked a rupture in the everyday lives of both Jews and non-Jews.

Most of the Shoah took place outside of the borders of Germany proper (Hilberg 1961; Benz 1991). Yet even in the *Altreich*, the Jewish minority was disenfranchised and ostracized; many fled the Third Reich, and many were murdered. In 1933, more than 500,000 Jews lived in Germany; by 1945, there were some 15,000. *How was this process possible in a modern society and within such a short span of time? Who was responsible for this radicalization of anti-Semitism into genocide?* These questions continue to inspire the wider public's engagement with the Nazi past, just as it is a central theme of interdisciplinary German studies.

The radicalization of anti-Semitism was not a simple and direct effect of the Nazi regime's policies from above but involved a large number of actors on different levels. The aim of this chapter is therefore not to offer an overarching history of anti-Semitism in the Third Reich but to provide the reader with stories of people negotiating relationships in the context of everyday anti-Semitism, social exclusion, and mass violence.

Our approach draws attention to the impact of microsocial interactions on these macrosocial policies. We explore the *room for maneuver* of three non-Jewish women, all of whom were German but who held very different positions in the racial hierarchy of Nazi-occupied Europe. Here we are referring to the concept of *Handlungsräume* used by Kirsten Heinsohn, Barbara Vogel, and Ulrike Weckel to describe "the complexity of the social connections in which human beings operated" while also recognizing that they "did not just passively accept their fate but also actively helped to shape it" (1997: 10). In myriad ways, they tried to assert control over their lives and their circumstances in order to make the best lives for themselves and their loved ones in the given situation.

Most of the people who participated in crimes during the Shoah were men—especially the mobile killing squads (*Einsatzgruppen*) of the SS and soldiers of the German army (Jureit 2002; Angrick 2003). Yet the main characters of this chapter are women. German women were confronted with the Nazi policies of anti-Semitic persecution in many arenas and participated on various levels (Harvey 2003; Steinbacher 2007; Lower 2013). They had radically different options for action at their disposal, depending on their relative life situation and profession as well as their location in the Nazi racial hierarchy. As Birthe Kundrus so incisively formulated, "There is no singular history of all women in National Socialism" (2003: 15).

To capture this wide range of experience among women, this chapter investigates the biographies of three non-Jewish German women who exemplify very different positions in the racial hierarchy of Nazi-occupied Europe. One was a concentration camp guard who then married into the SS-Sippengemeinschaft, meaning *SS tribal community*, but was conceived by the Nazis in racist terms and as a new racial elite (Schwarz 2001). Another was a rescuer who disguised herself as a good German *racial comrade* (*Volksgenossin*) while hiding and protecting Jews. She appears in the drawing at the beginning of this chapter along with a Jewish man she helped to save.

Yet another was a German woman who married a Jewish–German man and who, in spite of desperately trying, could not protect him from being murdered. Juxtaposing these three very different stories allows us to view the ruptures of everyday anti-Semitism from the ground of the same Nazi Germany. It also helps us to recall the variety of potential actions available to Germans under Nazi rule—both successful and unsuccessful, remembered and forgotten.

Wherever possible we make use of ego documents produced by the actors themselves—sources that express their subjective perspective. It is not our intention to create artificially coherent stories from the fragmentary nature of these sources or make linear explanations of events. Instead, we want to read these fragments closely to uncover the many ambivalences and contradictions of their particular historical situation. This complexity allows us to think critically about everyday life as a byproduct of never completely determined human interactions.

We present these women's biographies in four sections, each corresponding to different chronological periods. The social positions of our three main figures changed over the course of their lives and in relation to the persecution that they faced. Correspondingly, their options for action changed as well. First, we describe the paths they took through life until the genocide began in 1941. We identify the social spaces in which they moved both before the Third Reich and during the early stages of its racial policies. We explore how each of the three actors reacted to everyday anti-Semitism, what choices they made, and how those decisions changed their everyday lives.

Second, we address the systematic mass murder of the Jewish population from 1941 onward, during which anti-Semitism began to disrupt the biographies of our actors far more dramatically. We are particularly interested in the circumstances in which they experienced the first murders and deportations as well as how they responded to this violence. We interpret their biographies in terms of the constraints, ordinances, and practices of social exclusion that shaped their lives from above and especially the ways in which they sought to improve their lives and the lives of others on the ground.

Following from the work of the other chapters, we observe practices of self as individuals, within the framework of families, interacting with objects and people, and forging memories from those experiences. We expand on the discussion of institutions by exploring how Germans negotiated the intense pressures and high stakes for inclusion and exclusion in Nazi Germany. In doing so, we are concerned with how both men and women negotiated the gendered relations between Aryans and Jews in the context of persecution. In the third section, we therefore discuss these operations in terms of their gender-specific qualities. Moreover, the history of everyday anti-Semitism does not suddenly end in 1945. In the last section, we investigate how anti-Semitism continued to play a role in the lives of these women in the postwar era. At each stage in the history and memory of the Third Reich, it is instructive to relate these three cases to one another; for their three very different positions, when taken together, help us to understand the everyday dynamics of the Shoah.

Everyday Anti-Semitism

Between 1933 and 1945, the Nazi regime issued new anti-Semitic laws and ordinances almost every week. So for instance, beginning in 1933, Jews were effectively forbidden to work as professionals such as artists, doctors, lawyers, teachers, professors, and bureaucrats. In 1936, they were no longer permitted to use public parks or swimming pools. By 1938, Jews had to add either "Israel" or "Sara" to their given names and had to have a large red "J" stamped on their passports (Walk 1996). Along with these governmentally sanctioned and police-enforced mechanisms for ostracizing Jews came manifold local initiatives on the part of Nazi Party formations, communal institutions, interest groups, businesses, and private individuals, which massively impaired the quality of life for Jews in Germany (Gruner 2002; Büttner 2003; Bergerson 2004).

In response to massive discrimination, many Jews decided to leave their homeland and go into exile. At the start of Nazi rule, approximately half a million Jews lived in the German Reich; but due to these policies and processes of discrimination, some 250,000 Jewish men and women had already chosen exile by the end of 1938 (Benz 1988: 733). Around 100,000 more Jews followed until the fall of 1941, when all emigration was officially suspended. In sum, two-thirds of all German Jews had left their homeland before systematic deportations began (Kundrus and Meyer 2004: 11).

On 9 November 1938 during the Night of Broken Glass, as it came to be called in popular usage, hundreds of synagogues, thousands of Jewish stores, and many houses and apartments were destroyed; tens of thousands of Jewish men were arrested and incarcerated in concentration camps; and hundreds of Jews were murdered (Steinweis 2009: 1; Wachsmann 2010: 25). Afterward, the situation got even worse for the remaining Jews. Their shops and real estate were expropriated. They were compelled to participate in forced labor and relocated into so-called *Judenhäuser*: living in Jewish houses isolated them from the rest of the German population (Gruner 1997; Wojak and Hayes 2000; Willems 2002; Steinweis 2009).

The situation changed dramatically with the invasion of Poland in 1939. Within the *Altreich*, it was in October 1941 that the Nazi regime began to systematically deport German Jews to ghettos and concentration camps in the Nazi East (Gottwaldt and Schulle 2005; Strnad 2011). In 1942, it began to institute mass murder in death camps (Hilberg 1961; Aly 1995). In total, some 130,000 Jews were expelled from Germany and murdered during the Shoah and many millions more from Eastern Europe (Kwiet 1988: 651). The few Jews who survived Nazi rule within the territories of the *Altreich* were typically protected by marriage to a non-Jewish partner prior to the deportations or succeeded in staying hidden (Benz 1991; Kosmala 2004).

These policies formed the context in which our three figures lived and made their choices. We are able to reconstruct the story of the first family through collections of their papers bequeathed to the town archive (StadtA MM, NLG and Personalmeldebogen Alfred Guggenheimer; Strnad 2013). Annemarie Guggenheimer was born to a bourgeois Catholic family on 7 April 1896 in Munich, Bavaria, under the name Anna Maria Meitinger. In June of 1922, she married a Jewish horse trader named Alfred Guggenheimer who was twenty years her senior; and she moved into his home in Memmingen. The Guggenheimers had lived there since 1866. Their horse-trading business was successful, the family well off. Six months after the wedding, Annemarie gave birth to a daughter, Ursula Elisabeth Guggenheimer. Although Annemarie maintained her own social contacts independent of her husband and with non-Jews, it was Alfred's Jewish circle of acquaintances and relatives that most shaped her everyday. In Illustration 7.2, we see Alfred, Annemarie, and Ursula among their Jewish relatives and friends.

We researched the story of Hertha Ließ, by contrast, using official documents preserved by the Federal Archives (BArch RS/B 0125 Heiratsgesuchakte Hans-Joachim Ehlert, 2 April 1893; BArch B162/ AR-Z 77/72: 1.17f.). Ließ lived more than six hundred kilometers from

Memmingen in Berlin. She was born there on 26 March 1905 and, after the death of her thirty-year-old father in 1909, was raised by her mother and her stepfather along with two half siblings. She graduated from a high school for girls, studied home economics for one year, and completed her education with a three-year vocational program as a salesclerk. Ließ started working as a salesclerk by the mid-1920s and later became branch manager. By the 1930s, she was a young, unattached woman who had already been working for several years and had the first advances in her career to show for it. She is our second case study.

We know a lot about the life of Kläre (officially: Klara) Begall, our third, thanks to the work of several historians who have conducted interviews with her and collected biographical information that can be accessed in the archive of the German Resistance Memorial Center (ArchGdW, Dossier Kläre Bloch). Begall was also born in Berlin but was three years younger than Ließ. Her father was the owner of a taxi business, her mother a housewife. Begall left school after the eighth grade, completed vocational training at a trade school, and worked afterward as a stenotypist. As the unemployment rates rose at the end of the 1920s, she decided to retrain as a taxi driver and worked temporarily in her father's company. Like Ließ, Begall was, by the 1930s, a young, unattached, financially independent woman.

But more akin to Guggenheimer, Begall had maintained intensive friendships with Jews since the mid-1920s. She became acquainted with many of her Jewish friends at the leftist intellectual Romanisches Café on the Kurfürstendamm—a locale that became an important point of reference in her life (Haider 2006). In a 1986 interview some sixty years later (ArchGdW), she described the café in terms of a rupture in her autobiography:

> The bohemians socialized there back then, and for me that was like falling into another world. I will say it this way: that is where I first learned to walk. All of my worlds were destroyed there, filled as they were with all of the dopey attitudes that I got from home ... And in those years—the end of '28, '29—there was such enormous unemployment. I too was unemployed. And there, I began to become a little more interested in politics and was enlightened.

It was in the Romanisches Café where Begall met a Jewish journalist with whom she entered into a romantic relationship early in the 1930s.

We have only limited information about Ließ at this stage of her life. The surviving documentary evidence reveals very little about her private contacts prior to 1933—whether Jewish or not. It is impossible to determine whether she had even ever met a Jewish person. The reason lies in the nature of the sources. These files were created by the British and West German officials in charge of her criminal prosecution to determine if she was guilty of war crimes, ill treatment, or murder as an SS guard at the women's concentration camps in

Illustration 7.2. The Guggenheimer Family, Unknown Location, Mid-1920s. Alfred Sitting in Front, Annemarie to His Right, Their Daughter Ursula Standing behind. Courtesy of Stadtarchiv MM, NLG.

Bergen-Belsen and Ravensbrück (Cramer 2007: 107, 2011: 119, note 61). For the investigators, no other questions were relevant.

We know far more about the private relationships of Annemarie Guggenheimer. Her postwar case involved a series of administrative hearings before the reparation authorities to determine the amount of her compensation. It was centrally concerned with her so-called mixed marriage and especially with the character and circumstances surrounding her divorce. That is, the nature of her relationships with Jews was important for the case. The same could be said of the documentary evidence for Begall. She is well known for her efforts as a rescuer, so her relationships with Jews have been studied several times in the context of historical research projects. Still, the unevenness of the documentary evidence reminds us of the role that the surviving remnants of material culture played in the postwar construction of memory. Its fragmentary character influences what we can know and how we can represent the German *Alltag*.

The Nazi seizure of power in 1933 and its anti-Semitic program for ruling Germany had differential impacts on the lives of these three women. The Guggenheimer family felt the consequences of Nazi anti-Semitism most clearly. Together with other Jewish inhabitants of Memmingen, Alfred Guggenheimer was arrested in April 1933 for "spreading horrendous, treasonous lies" (*Verbreitung staatsfeindlicher Gräullügen*). He sat for one month in what the Nazis euphemistically called *protective custody*, or *Schutzhaft* (StAM, SpKA 1734, Wilhelm Schwarz).

According to Nazi racial theory, Jews did not belong to a religious group but a racial one. While German non-Jews were imagined to be *Übermenschen*, members of a master race, the Jews were conceptualized as *Untermenschen*, members of an inferior race. In September 1935, the Nuremberg Laws redefined citizenship based on race, so that Jews became second-class citizens; and it forbade sexual relations and marriages between Jews and non-Jews. Those non-Jews who had previously married Jewish Germans now legally were in mixed marriages in the eyes of the law. The non-Jewish spouse was reviled as *jüdisch versippt*, which means *closely related to Jews*.

In this political context, the Nazis successively destroyed the Guggenheimer family's livelihood. They made less and less money by buying and selling horses because as Jews they were being expulsed from business. Then the regional commercial organization in charge of the horse trade, the Viehwirtschaftsverband Bayern, permanently withdrew the license from the Guggenheimer firm on 30 November 1937 (StadtA MM, NLG). Alfred Guggenheimer and his family fell into serious financial difficulties. Within a few years, their firm, which had been the largest to sell horses in the Allgäu region of southern Bavaria, was driven into the ground.

For the family, however, it was the events of the Night of Broken Glass that represented the most profound and irreversible rupture in their everyday lives.

On 10 November 1938, the perpetrators ravaged twenty-three residences and three businesses of Jewish residents in Memmingen. During the postwar trial against Wilhelm Schwarz—the NSDAP district leader (*Kreisleiter*) in Memmingen—and others, the judge listed in his verdict what the perpetrators had done:

> The interior in the residences was smashed to pieces with axes, picks, and hammers. Furniture, pianos, radios, and so on were smashed; cabinets were bashed and knocked over; their contents flung out. Porcelain, mirrors, lamps, window panes shattered; leather chairs and sofas cut open; pictures sliced up; beds ripped open until the feathers flew all over the place. (StAM, SpKA 1734)

In the home of the Guggenheimer family, even their clothing was torn to pieces. During these trials, one witness recounted his impressions with these words: "If a grenade had hit, it could not have looked more dire" (idem).

The valuable items filling the Guggenheimer's six-room apartment—furniture, carpets, and porcelain as well as other household effects and valuables—were either destroyed or stolen. Alfred was arrested once again and released only ten days later. The perpetrators thus violated the Guggenheimer's last refuge—their home, the place into which they had retreated to protect themselves from Nazi persecution and discrimination. Moreover, this invasion of their private sphere held grave consequences not only for Alfred, for whom this arrest was the first step toward deportation and death, but also for Annemarie and Ursula, who were left behind. In 1939, the Guggenheimer family was forced to sell the property at Herrenstraße 7 for a greatly undervalued sum. The gross income from the sale was just enough to pay off their accumulated debts. And they accumulated more. For a time, the family was allowed to remain in their apartment, but now they were paying rent.

The family's social life also changed completely. Many non-Jewish acquaintances turned their backs on them. The anti-Jewish policies of the Nazi regime influenced the behavior of a wide range of social strata; Germans adopted the official anti-Semitism and made it part and parcel of their daily practices. Annemarie faced open hostility on the streets. People of her hometown even spat upon her (Holstein, Interview, 2 July 2012). Here it is worth mentioning that the Nazi regime did not require the people of Memmingen to spit on their Jewish neighbors. They chose to overfulfill Nazi principles of their own accord and even innovatively (Bergerson 2004; Walser Smith 2004; Wildt 2012a). These small acts of violence helped translate the concept of a racist *Volksgemeinschaft* into daily practice by excluding Jews.

Kläre Begall similarly experienced the anti-Semitic measures of the Nazi regime point blank. Shortly after the seizure of power, her Jewish partner was warned of a looming arrest and fled in a mad rush to Paris. Begall stayed back alone and for the time being without any further information. In the interview conducted in 1986 (ArchGdW), she recalled that they were able to manage one final secret rendezvous in Bulgaria before breaking off all contact. Yet it was not just her romantic life that was so systematically destroyed by the regime's anti-Semitic policies; it was also her circle of friends. The milieu of the Romanisches Café collapsed, as many of her friends and acquaintances emigrated. The clientele changed to Nazi storm troopers. The old regular tables, called *Stammtische* in German, remained empty (Haider 2006: 167).

But Begall responded to this situation very differently than the Guggenheimers' neighbors. During this crucial early phase of segregating German society, Begall took great pains to stay in contact with those Jewish friends who remained in Berlin. She continued to call on a family living on the famous Kurfürstendamm and provided them with groceries every now and again. When she started to receive suspicious looks from their neighbors, as she described in the same interview (ArchGdW), she decided to sneak in to see them from then on. In the place of a friendship between equals, their relationship thus became badly asymmetrical, with a kind of dependence and one-sidedness that neither party desired.

In accordance with or against her will, Begall found herself suddenly with more power and status in relation to her Jewish friends. Contrary to them, she was now classified as a racial comrade. From this position of relative privilege, she could substantially influence the living conditions of her Jewish friends, positively or negatively, depending on how she chose to act. Begall courageously decided to provide both emotional and material support to her Jewish friends. However, it is noteworthy that she did not openly protest against anti-Semitism to stop the public assaults on Jews that people like the Guggenheimers faced. Rather she made use of private spaces for her acts of compassion and friendship. Opting for this strategy, she was able to stem the tide of persecution and alienation among the Jews that she knew personally, but her actions did not change the everyday anti-Semitism in the public sphere.

Hertha Ließ made very different use of Nazi rules. In a resume of her life written on 4 July 1941, Ließ wrote that she had worked in various firms in Berlin, first as a salesclerk and later as a branch manager, before she became an SS guard in the women's concentration camp at Ravensbrück (BArch RS/B 0125 Ehlert). After the war, she explained to a British tribunal that she was "called up for S.S. on 15th November, 1939, through the Labour Exchange" (Philips 1949: 227). At this point in time, however, the employment offices did not place young women under any kind of pressure to work. They functioned more like an employment referral service. Only starting in the middle of 1944 were unemployed single women from the lower classes obliged to take part in "war service." Still, they did not have to carry out this service in concentration camps; they could have selected any other form of work so long as it was "critical for the war effort" (Oppel 2007: 88).

Ravensbrück was, by May of 1939, the only concentration camp in the German Empire designed solely for women. The camp was run by a camp commander who had five men serving under him as department heads at the rank of SS-Führer (Strebel 2003: 52–65). They were all issued women guards to perform various functions in the women's camp. These women guards were defined as the "female retinue of the Waffen-SS" according to Nazi regulations—a position, in other words, with a modest measure of status in the Nazi regime. Women SS guards wore field-gray uniforms with trouser skirts. They were deployed in a very wide range of arenas for guarding and controlling the female inmates of the camp (Erpel 2007: 20–30; Mailänder Koslov 2009: 172–88). When Ließ began to work at Ravensbrück in November 1939, there were around two dozen of them responsible for guarding some 1,900 female prisoners.

On February, 20, 1942, there were all in all 7,216 female prisoners in Ravensbrück, including 691 Jewish women, according to the status report on the number of inmates in the women's concentration camp (MGR/StBG, KL 17/9). Over the course of a typical day, the Jewish inmates worked together with non-Jewish prisoners on so-called mixed work details, but at night they were housed in segregated prison blocks. Although few Jewish inmates were assigned to Ließ directly, she had regular contact with Jewish prisoners thanks to her duties supervising the work details and her daily presence in the camp. Directly next to Block 10, to which she was assigned, was a barracks in which some 320 Jewish prisoners were detained. As in most concentration camps, Jewish prisoners in Ravensbrück were subjected to especially harsh working conditions, humiliating punishments, and arbitrary violence on the part of the women guards (Apel 2003: 152).

The expansion of the Nazi apparatus of persecution opened up new possibilities for Ließ. To be sure, she had supervised staff as a branch manager in the business world; but her new professional status as an SS guard provided her with a much better opportunity for advancement and for far greater authority to control and to oppress other human beings. For this work, she required "no professional training, since it was only a matter of watching the prisoners," as the camp commander at Ravensbrück replied in a letter to a woman applying for a position as a guard (BArch NS 4/Ra Bl. 7). Ließ could also advance socially thanks to her new position in the SS.

Together with her future husband Hans-Joachim Ehlert, a certified forester and also second lieutenant in the SS (*Untersturmführer*), she submitted an application to the SS Main Office for Race and Settlement (RuSHA) in hopes of being accepted into the SS-Sippengemeinschaft, the organization recognizing membership in this imagined new racial elite among the already elite Aryan race (BArch RS/B 0125 Ehlert). Her photo for this application can be seen in Illustration 7.3. On this application, she proudly presented herself to the Nazi officials in Berlin as a "Block Leader in the Women's Conc[entration] Camp Ravensbrück." The SS doctor, tasked by the RuSHA to examine her, determined that she belonged to the "Nordic race" and had a "muscular, athletic frame" as well as a "well vaulted rib cage." He expressed no "medical concerns that might prevent her from getting pregnant" (ibid., S. 6) Under the heading "special," he emphasized additionally that she "felt very happy in the exercise of her profession" (ibid., 6 July 1941).

Ließ was accepted in this way into the SS-Sippengemeinschaft and, in their terms, became officially a member of the "eugenically valuable tribe of the northern Germanic type" (Schwarz 2001: 24). At the wedding itself, she had to promise to devote herself, together with her husband, "to a collective life and effort on behalf of the nation" (ibid.: 56). These actions were designed to improve her future both materially and symbolically. That is, the Nazi

Illustration 7.3. Hertha Ließ, Profil, Ravensbrück, 1941. Photo attached to her application forms for the SS-Rasse- und Siedlungs-Hauptamt (RuSHA) in order to marry SS-Unterscharführer Hans-Joachim Ehlert, BArch RS/B 0125. Courtesy of BArch.

seizure of power did not disrupt her life. Rather, she used it successfully to promote her career. From then on, she was both engaged professionally in the uniformed, hierarchical association of the Waffen-SS and integrated privately and socially into a racially and politically elite SS organization.

The anti-Semitism of both the Nazi regime and a large part of German society fundamentally transformed the lives of these three women. Begall and Guggenheimer experienced it above all else as a threat to themselves, their friends, and their families. Begall was confronted after 1933 with the loss of her lover and the destruction of her social circle from the Romanisches Café. This transformation burdened her emotionally but did not cause her financial losses or endanger her personally. Guggenheimer was herself persecuted for being married to a Jew, and she suffered drastic losses in financial and social capital. By contrast, Ließ used this racial social order for her own social mobility. She was, we suppose, not directly affected at first by the anti-Semitic measures. But after November 1939, when she chose to build her future strategically within the SS exterminatory apparatus and its racial community, she made the Nazi regime's racial anti-Semitism into the economic and social foundation for her daily life.

None of these women were the passive objects of persecutory policies imposed from above. They noticed the changes in everyday anti-Semitism and responded to them. They did so either to try to protect themselves and the people they cared about or to profit from that new situation. Guggenheimer stood loyally at the side of her Jewish husband—a choice she made public to acquaintances and neighbors simply by still living with him. Begall too stayed in contact with her remaining Jewish friends. Though she restricted her solidarity to secret acts performed in private spaces, her interventions ameliorated the official ostracism of Jews from German society. Where Begall and Guggenheimer tried to limit the degree to which institutionalized anti-Semitism penetrated their everyday lives, Ließ reinforced its authority by joining an SS institution and supporting its principles.

Maneuvers

Thus far, we have shown that these three women chose very different options for how to act and that they did so in very different operational spaces. In this part of our chapter, we describe how their room for maneuver, and thus the maneuvers themselves, changed in the context of the worsening anti-Semitic measures of the Nazi regime after 1941.

Since the beginning of the war in the fall of 1939, the Nazi regime increased the pressure of persecution on the Jews of Germany. Jewish property was confiscated. Jews were compelled to participate in forced labor and, from

September 1941 on, they were forced to wear a yellow star on their clothes. In February and October 1940, over 7,500 German Jews were deported to the concentration camp in Gurs in the south of France and to the Lublin district in occupied Poland. When the systematic deportation of German Jews to the east began in the fall of 1941, the implementation of this policy involved a large number of agencies and workers—and not only the staff at the Reichssicherheitshauptamt (RSHA) and the Geheime Staatspolizei (Gestapo), the secret police.

Mayors, their local police forces, the train personnel who accompanied the transports, the bureaucrats in charge of liquidating Jewish property, the staff at the employment agencies responsible for the Jewish forced laborers, the concierges, and the neighbors who helped to locate Jewish residents—they too were all involved in the social organization of deportation. Many other people profited from these deportations because Jewish residences and furniture at bargain prices were suddenly made available for non-Jewish use. The Nazi regime thus successfully mobilized a quotidian kind of interest in the implementation of their anti-Semitic policies.

While various Germans profited from the exclusion of their Jewish neighbors, these same anti-Jewish measures meant a worsening for the Jewish people along with those Germans who still maintained contact with Jews. Since 1941, Begall and Guggenheimer lived with the constant fear that their friends and family members would be deported. In this situation, however, both women acted in order to ameliorate, each in her own way, some of the effects of the Nazi persecution. By contrast, the escalation of the persecution opened new opportunities for Ließ in the changing dynamics of war and genocide. Let's consider her story first.

In the fall of 1941, the first preselections began in Ravensbrück for Aktion 14f13 (Strebel 2003: 322–24). This term refers to a murder campaign in which 1,701 female and 298 male inmates—many of them Jews—were selected, deported to a killing institute in Bernburg, Saxony-Anhalt, and murdered (Apel 2003: 296–316; Strebel 2003: 329; Schwartz 2013: 289). Confirmation from multiple survivors has since verified that women SS guards also conducted selections (Schwartz 2013). In an undated report written at the end of the 1950s or the beginning of the 1960s, the survivor Erna Krafft described Ließ's activities in the course of this murder campaign in great detail (BArch B162/AR-Z 77/72: 1.2–4). Krafft recounted how Ließ promised several Jewish inmates that she could free them from the camp.

Ließ suggested that, if they would give her their valuables, she could bribe "the crucial people." Many Jewish women took her up on her offer. So for instance, the Jewish inmate Alice Chajetwitsch had hidden valuables in Berlin with some friends. After Ließ got her hands on the valuables, however, she completely ignored Chajetwitsch. That was the story for several other women in the Jewish block. Then, in March 1942, the camp staff "put together a transport of the sick and the emaciated" with the promise that "they would be transported to another camp" (BArch B162/AR-Z 77/72: 1.3). In fact, these women were murdered during the 14f13 action in the T4 facility for forced euthanasia in Bernburg (Strebel 2003: 334f.). Crucially, Krafft drew a direct connection between this murder campaign and Ließ's private practice of enriching herself. She suggested that Ließ used the murder campaign to "eliminate her confidants in a completely legal way" (BArch B162/AR-Z 77/72: 1.3).

After studying this report critically, historian Linde Apel (2003: 306) has come to the conclusion that Krafft's account draws our attention to the "dependency and hopelessness of the Jewish inmates" at Ravensbrück. It shows, moreover, that the murder operation 14f13 opened up new and previously unfamiliar space for maneuver for SS women guards. Krafft described the situation of the Jewish women as if they believed every lie and deception by woman SS guards, if only to preserve a small bit of hope for survival and freedom. At the same time, Krafft imputes absolute power to Ließ, using it in a merciless way in order to extract from these Jewish inmates their few remaining valuables in exchange for a false promise to free them—while anticipating that the witnesses to her corruption would soon be eliminated. In Krafft's report, Ließ is portrayed not as the helpful executor of governmental plans and interests but rather as someone who exploited the official murder campaign to maximize her own financial interest.

Above all, the report's ground-level perspective deserves our attention because of the way it challenges our understanding of everyday anti-Semitism. Historians have heretofore depicted 14f13 as if this murder operation had been initialized by Heinrich Himmler personally and "directed centrally by the IKL," the inspectorate of concentration camps in Oranienburg (Friedlander 1997: 237f.; Orth 2002: 115; Ley 2009: 37, 49; Klee 2010: 280; Wachsmann 2010: 28). Krafft's report reveals far more room for autonomous operations at the lower levels of the SS hierarchy among women guards. It depicts a woman guard who transformed her career at Ravensbrück by abusing prisoners and who reinforced their persecution by destroying their last shred of hope for survival.

There are, of course, problems with some of these fragmentary sources in terms of their reliability (Apel 2003: 306); yet many other memoirs and testimonies bear witness to the fact that corruption and graft were everyday practices among both men and women SS personnel as well as among *Kapos*—the fellow prisoners who assumed administrative and disciplinary functions in the camps (Buber-Neumann 2002: 323; Strebel 2003: 98f.; Schwartz 2007: 69). These local initiatives on the lower levels of the concentration camp hierarchy supposedly stood in opposition to the plans and regulations of the central concentration camp office in Oranienburg. According to historian Ian Kershaw, however, these kinds of "radical initiatives from below" were typical of "Hitler's personalized form of rule" (Kershaw 1998: 530, also 1993; Mailänder Koslov 2009; Bergerson et al. 2011; Wildt 2012a). As we argued in the last chapter, this unruly behavior helped these institutions to work well.

We would like to emphasize that this corruption changed face-to-face social relations in the camps. On the one hand, it bound the SS personnel together in a new way. They were aware that they were all exceeding the official rules in terms of abusing prisoners for their own enrichment; this collusion bound them together across hierarchies of gender and rank. On the other hand, this same corruption left the inmates in a position of extreme dependency and, ultimately, with even fewer resources available to them for survival. That is, these scams had the dual function of both creating more solidarity among the guards and making it easier for them to control inmate society (Sofksy 1993: 152–77). Ließ's actions, together with those of her fellow guards, thus demonstrably shaped the outcomes of anti-Semitic policy; in this sense, Ließ and her fellow guards shared in the process of policy making.

Around the same time as the murder campaign in Ravensbrück, the Guggenheimer family was ripped apart. In the spring of 1942, Alfred was compelled to move into a *Judenhaus*, where Jews were forced to live isolated from society and often in crowded conditions. Just one month later, Alfred was deported to the nearby village of Fellheim along with other Jews living in mixed marriages. This action was part of the *Säuberung*, meaning cleansing, of Jews in Memmingen. The next measure took place at the end of May 1942 in which Annemarie and her daughter had to come to accept yet another major transformation in their lives. On the orders of the NSDAP district leadership, they had to leave their residence in the span of just a few days (StadtA MM, NLG: certificate of Georg Kolb, 18 February 1949).

It was in this situation that the Guggenheimers decided to divorce—at least technically and only for tactical purposes. According to several later witnesses, they never in fact separated emotionally, only officially to make it seem like they had split up. To make their separation as believable as possible, the couple relied upon anti-Semitic stereotypes. In court, they claimed that, "in the last five months," Alfred had "often insulted, physically abused, and threatened to bribe and kill" his non-Jewish wife. The divorce became official by the decision of the Landgericht of Memmingen on 11 June 1942 (StAM, OFD 12596).

Alfred was assigned sole responsibility for the failure of his marriage. On the advice of her lawyer, Annemarie began to once again use her maiden name in order to underscore her separation from her former husband (StadtA MM, NLG: Schreiben Dr. Laube, 29 June 1942, 18 August 1942). Here we find another scam—and it is interesting in itself that Nazi-occupied Europe created a situation in which such scams became a common feature of everyday life. But this one was quite different in its objectives. Where Ließ apparently feigned being a friend to Jewish inmates in order to trick them out of their last resources, Annemarie tried to protect her Jewish husband and half-Jewish daughter by testifying to anti-Semitic stereotypes.

By comparison, many couples in mixed marriages had chosen to get divorced during the early years of Nazi rule. Often it was the non-Jewish partner who pushed for this divorce in order to avoid persecution and return to the proclaimed *Volksgemeinschaft* (Meyer 1999: 68–91). But with the start of systematic deportations in 1941, the divorce rate among mixed marriages declined. It became apparent that survival was made more likely if you stuck together as an intact family. In fact, until close to the end of the war, a preexisting mixed marriage usually protected Jews from deportation. That is how some 10,000 Jews survived while living in the *Altreich*. Conversely, a divorce was life threatening for the Jewish partner.

Why did the Guggenheimers choose to divorce? They did so in order to try to relieve the growing pressure on their family from the Nazi persecution (Meyer 1999: 68–91). They were hardly the only couple to opt for this survival strategy. Mixed marriages between Jewish men and non-Jewish women disproportionately ended in divorce because the persecutory pressure was higher than in cases of marriage with an Aryan man (Kundrus 2003: 18–19). In contrast to many other cases, however, the Guggenheimer's divorce was intended above all to salvage what remained of their property from plunder. They hoped to ensure some financial security for their daughter Ursula and to remove her and her mother from the line of fire, ignoring the danger of deportation. As part of the plan, Alfred transferred the last of his real estate to his wife and daughter. Moreover, the separation was only supposed to exist on paper. In fact, according to later testimony, they stayed together in secret.

Unfortunately, the divorce did not have any of the desired results. The transfer of ownership of their property was not approved. It was confiscated at Alfred's deportation on the basis of the 11th Ordinance of the Reich Civil Law for the Benefit of the German Empire (11. Verordnung zum Reichsbürgergesetz). His assets were auctioned, and his wife was compelled to purchase some of them back if they did not wish to lose them. Their relative penury is attested by the inventory list from their case file regarding the withdrawal of assets (StAM, OFD 12596).

In public, Annemarie behaved in ways expected of a proper German woman in the Third Reich: she did so as if she had implemented the politically imposed separation in her everyday. Secretly, however, she circumvented Nazi policies by attempting to continue her marriage. The Guggenheimers' long-time family doctor, Kraemer, attested to the following before the Reparations Offices (Wiedergutmachungsämtern) on 15 April 1948 (StadtA MM, NLG):

After the divorce, Mr. Guggenheimer stayed in almost daily contact with his wife. I often met him there [at his wife's flat] in person and never had the impression that anything had changed for any of them in terms of their family life as a result of the divorce. I know that he frequently slept there overnight and that Ms. Annemarie Meitinger-Guggenheimer often met with him on the bridge in Fellheim.

Other evidence can be found in the archival bequest of the Guggenheimer family, such as the testimony of Theo Grünfeld, a man who lived in the *Judenhaus* in Fellheim to which Alfred was moved in 1942. These materials all bear witness to the ongoing and intensive contact of the divorced couple (StadtA MM, NLG).

It is important to appreciate the risks that they were taking by getting divorced in the first place, and those risks only increased thereafter. Once divorced, every private meeting between the Guggenheimers was defined, in the terms of the Nuremberg Laws, as *Rassenschande*, a criminal act that defiled the race. This law did not stop the divorced couple from meeting in secret anyway—but obviously at enormous risk. The Guggenheimers decided to accept these risks because of their tremendous financial need.

They were still hoping for a secure future in Germany, at least in material terms and at some time in the future. Instead of financial security, however, the divorce further undermined their ability to survive in Germany. Above all, the Guggenheimer family divorced in an effort to restore some room to maneuver in their private sphere. They thought that they needed an operational space in which they could circumvent the everyday dangers of anti-Semitism. The institutional attacks on their private lives—by both the Nazi regime and their anti-Semitic neighbors—necessarily pushed them into this kind of parallel world.

That parallel world existed in a tentative, liminal state. As we saw in the previous examples of the workers who used Kraft durch Freude events to preserve their pre-Nazi socialist milieu, such parallel worlds have to adapt to, and therefore continue to be shaped by, the institutional frameworks in which they operate. In a similar way, the Guggenheimers were repeatedly forced to invent new tactics to keep this parallel world intact. The local authorities—especially the district leader of the Nazi Party, Wilhelm Schwarz—were in no way convinced that the de jure divorce was a de facto one. Leading Nazis like Schwarz continued to reach into practically every part of both public and private life. This dynamic left its Jewish victims, along with those non-Jews associated with them, with almost no path for escape.

Much like Annemarie Guggenheimer, Kläre Begall attempted to circumvent the dangers of the official anti-Semitic policies of the Nazi regime, though under very different conditions. She witnessed how long-time acquaintances from the Romanisches Café were arrested, brought to collecting points, and deported. Her friend, Erich Bloch, was spared from deportation at least at first. Bloch was born in 1893 in Berlin, was Jewish, and had been married to a non-Jew since 1920. He was trained as a goldsmith and began his career as a manager in his parents' wholesale glass company. Starting in 1924, he worked as a commercial artist and press caricaturist. Under the Nazis, he was forbidden to work in these professions.

One of the things that we learned from the sworn statement of Erich Bloch, taken on 9 November 1955 as part of his reparations lawsuit, was that he was hardly able to provide for his family through the sale of his private property and by giving private drawing lessons to Jews who sought emigration (LaBO, Entschädigungsakte, 5379: 2). Begall remembers that his non-Jewish wife suffered badly in this situation. She decided to flee bombed-out Berlin for the mountainous countryside of Tyrol. Bloch stayed in Berlin alone.

In contrast to the Guggenheimer's case, his marriage was—due to the absence of children—not classified as a privileged mixed marriage. Beginning in September 1941, Bloch had to wear a yellow star on his clothes. The situation became threatening for Bloch at the end of February 1943, when a raid—directed by the Gestapo and with the collaboration of SS and police forces—was executed on the few Jews who still remained in Germany. During the so-called factory action (*Fabrikaktion*), several thousand Jews went underground in Berlin alone (Gruner 2005: 11), among them Erich Bloch.

Throughout the two years of his illegality, he relied heavily on the support of friends and acquaintances. According to a letter written by Erich Bloch to the restitution office in Berlin dated 1 December 1953, some friends had given him timely warning of the raid (LaBO, Entschädigungsakte 5379: 2). They also took him into their homes on a rotating basis. At first, Begall hid him sporadically. But after June 1944, as she explained in her declaration from 1 February 1952, he lived on a long-term basis in her two-room ground-floor apartment on Horstweg 28 in the Charlottenburg neighborhood of Berlin (ibid.: 1).

Through Bloch, Begall was introduced to two Jewish women who had already lived illegally for some time. According to her 1986 interview (ArchGdW), Begall supported these two women in their search for a new place to hide. She also declared having maintained contact with yet another Jewish friend who had gone into hiding after the death of that woman's non-Jewish husband. Shortly before the end of the war, Begall added yet another resident to her apartment: a deserter from the German military. In her diary on 23 April 1945 (ArchGdW), she described her small residence as overflowing. "Six people are now sleeping in my apartment," she wrote. "My skull is throbbing."

The private sphere of Begall's apartment was certainly the asset that most enabled her to provide assistance to her friends. The boundaries of this sphere underwent considerable transgressions and transformations. During the Nazi period, the Nazi regime and its formal and informal agents tried to make normatively private spaces and practices into tools for realizing their concept of *Volksgemeinschaft*, but not without challenge from individuals and families (Bergerson 2004; Steuwer 2013).

Begall succeeded in using this boundary to temporarily withdraw herself and her friends to a large degree from the controls of both state and society. In her apartment, she hid her friends, listened to enemy radio stations, and conducted political discussions. In this way, the private spaces of one's residence could be used to carve out a space for self-fashioning, unruliness, or both. Again, the private sphere was an unreliable partner of politics; it was in this parallel world that politically undesirable relationships could be pursued against official rules and proclamations.

Yet the private sphere in no way comprised a secure realm: it was in fact consistently under siege. In the previously quoted interview from 1986 (ArchGdW), we learn how Begall's own family responded to the fact that she was hiding Bloch in her apartment: "They shut up. But they were not happy about it." Her mother beseeched Begall to end her support for Bloch: "Throw the Jew out! You are exposing our whole family to danger." Clearly, it would be a mistake to reduce the social unit of the family either to a parallel world insulated from politics over and against a violent Nazi regime or to an obedient executor of Nazi political policies. Rather the family functioned much more as a mediating institution in which political demands and individual interests were negotiated in everyday life. In this situation, Begall succeeded in defending her unruly use of her apartment against the demands of her family.

Relatives were not the only danger for Begall and Bloch; the local *Blockwart* also closely monitored all new residents and pressed them to be registered. The block warden was a low-ranking political officer of the Nazi Party charged with keeping his neighbors under surveillance and denouncing them when they engaged in politically oppositional activities. The block warden did so with the assistance of neighbors, for people listened in on conversations, inquired about the latest news, and denounced transgressions.

According to Begall's later testimony, "a bunch of Nazis" lived in the house. A man living on the second floor denounced his roommate for defeatist statements. Fearing denunciation, Bloch avoided the apartment's air raid shelter (Begall 1984: 17, 26). When the air raid sirens sounded, he went instead to the nearby shelter in the subway on Sophie-Charlotte-Platz. Unfortunately, when Bloch returned home after the alarm, "these German Nazis were still standing there in front of the door to the house, spouting forth. And I would then give him a signal with a flashlight: 'you cannot come in now'" (ArchGdW, Interview Bloch, 1986). This practice—of giving Bloch a signal with her flashlight—served to secure a boundary between public and private spaces that their Nazi neighbors tried to penetrate. On 6 March 1945, Begall wrote in her diary (ArchGdW):

> I cannot help but get scared, when I sleep too long, that my dear neighbors in the house will denounce me for it; for if I do not shutter during blackouts, the people see that I am still sleeping. Speaking my opinion out loud in my own apartment is also something I do not dare to do, for someone outside my window could hear; how many times have I run out to see whether or not someone is listening in on me.

Clearly, she felt that she needed to actively defend her private space from intrusion by neighbors. By taking these security measures, Begall was able to successfully preserve her apartment as a space to maneuver personally and a place to hide Bloch.

Her actions were in no way excessive, as a very frightening incident illustrates. One day, the caretaker came to Begall and declared, "This note was just put into my pocket! It alleges that you have hidden a Jewish man!" (Begall 1984: 17). In this anonymous note, Begall was also insulted as a "Jewish sow." Yet the caretaker confronted her with the note without bringing the matter directly to the Gestapo. This courtesy opened a little elbowroom that Begall exploited to protect herself and her friend. During the interview from 1986 (ArchGdW), she described her reaction in this way:

> I went down to the cellar and began to scream: "I got this note here. I am a German woman. This pig—[who wrote] this note, [saying that] I have a Jew in my apartment—I will get him arrested! I will find it out! I will figure out where you all work, get the typewriters checked, and then denounce. I am an upstanding German woman." And they all grew silent, embarrassed. And then the custodian came and says: "This thing here, I am tearing it up, such nonsense." As you can see, we were always in danger of and fearing for our lives.

Begall defended herself among her neighbors not with humanistic arguments but with her honor as a proper German woman. She presented herself as a *Volksgenossin* who seemed to be deeply affronted by the accusation of contact with Jews.

Still, we are once again confronted by a tragic inversion. To protect her parallel world as a vehicle for nonconformity, Begall publically conformed to the normative discourse of Nazi politics. Like Guggenheimer, Begall had to veil her help for Jews in anti-Semitism. She went so far as to play with the fears of her neighbors: she threatened them with an investigation, denunciation, and even prosecution. In effect, she reappropriated the very terror of social surveillance with an attack of her own. By preventing Bloch from being deported, she successfully sabotaged Nazi politics with its own weapons.

On the one hand, this performance served to protect her private sphere from social and political control. On the other hand, Begall's parody of Nazi behavior (Bergerson et al. 2011) reproduced the normative consensus among her neighbors in the apartment building. It confirmed the notion that contact with Jews should be considered an offense against propriety and morality. Ironically, her act of sabotage against anti-Jewish principles and policies involved an act of conformity to the very same principles and policies.

The number of Germans who protected hidden Jews from deportation was decidedly small. Lacking accurate documentation, scholars vaguely estimate that several tens of thousands rescuers were operating in the *Altreich* (Benz 2006: 48; Kosmala 2007; Beer 2014). Their primary task was to provide the persecuted with a place to stay and help them to get their hands on false papers. Secondary tasks consisted of providing food, clothing, and information—especially about imminent raids—as well as sometimes providing support for illegal border crossings to Switzerland. Unlike in occupied Eastern Europe, rescuers in the *Altreich* did not face the death penalty (Kosmala 2002: 207; Benz 2006: 30–40).

Indeed, there was no law on the books forbidding Germans to help Jews (idem). Still, non-Jewish rescuers could be and were charged for facts related to the case, like illegal trafficking across borders or the falsification of documents. But most of the cases uncovered by the Gestapo never made it to court: the Gestapo dealt with them through arrest and interrogation followed by punishments ranging form reprimands to internment in a concentration camp (Benz 2006: 39–40). Incomparably worse were the consequences for the so-called submerged Jews. If discovered, they were typically all deported and murdered. Of the approximately ten to twelve thousand Jews who tried to survive by hiding illegally, as Erich Bloch did, only some five thousand were alive by the end of the war (Kosmala 2004: 106).

Gender Relations

The relationship between men and women in the Third Reich was characterized by a marked inequality, but it was also partially disrupted at least on two levels. First, although women were prevented from serving in leadership positions in the economy or polity, they "took active part in the public arena to a greater extent—a participation that transgressed the limits of predominant gender politics" (Kundrus 2003: 22). Thus the numbers of women gainfully employed rose after 1933, as did the percentage of women enrolled at universities and engaged in academic professions (Bock 1997: 264). Second, traditional gender hierarchies lost some of their significance as a result of priority being placed on racial hierarchies (Lanwerd and Stoehr 2007: 31). As anti-Semitic practices became more prevalent in German society, the racial status of Aryans over Jews subordinated patriarchal hierarchies. This transformational process was operative even during those moments when the actors tried to sabotage anti-Semitism, whether for real or for show.

This point can be illustrated in terms of the relationship between Begall and Bloch. During the 1986 interview (ArchGdW), Begall recalled her friend's decision to go into hiding in spring 1943:

> He had [removed] the Jewish star ... that he was supposed to wear, and I came for him. Then we took the streetcar to my apartment. He used to say: "Can't you tell from my appearance that I am a Jew?" I said, "No one can tell just from looking at you."

Bloch feared that he would be recognized as a Jew. By contrast, Begall kept a cool head and tried to calm him down. She represented herself as a strong woman who placed herself at the side of a weak Jewish man, serving as his support.

A retrospective graphic, reprinted at the beginning of this chapter, conveys a similar impression. Drawn by Bloch in 1946, it depicts the pair standing before shopwindows. Their silhouettes are visible from behind. Bloch appears small and fragile in the image; Begall in contrast seems large and strong. She is observing the menu that has been hung on the pane of glass at her eye level, while Bloch looks at the display of the bookstore next door. This image both subverts and adheres to stereotypes. Contravening gender norms, Bloch depicted his female friend as stronger than him, a man. He also depicted the man in normative ways as inclined toward spiritual things, the woman toward bodily ones. Moreover, the image plays with the racial stereotypes of the down-to-earth *Übermensch* and the overly intellectual *Untermensch* (A.G. Gender-Killer 2005: 15–18). This image thus illustrates one crucial aspect of their shared experience: the racial hierarchies of the Third Reich had undermined traditional gender hierarchies.

Still, the figures walk arm in arm. They do not face off against each other antagonistically but stand next to each other affectionately. The caption describes them as "comrades"—an allusion on the part of Bloch to their shared communist ideals. That is, Bloch depicted not only the new asymmetry that had crept into their relationship but also how they overcame it—through friendship.

The gender dynamics of the Guggenheimer family also changed as a result of persecution. In spite of the divorce, they tried to continue to exist as a family. Yet from then on, the daily life of their family was heavily impaired. Right after the divorce, Alfred's name was put on the deportation list. What emerges from a letter dated 11 August 1942 is that Annemarie was able to obtain a last-minute postponement through the spokesman at the Reich Association of the Jews in Germany (Reichsvereinigung der Juden in Deutschland) who was responsible for the village of Memmingen. This postponement was in turn supported by an official directive from the RSHA in Berlin, the agency that was in charge of the deportations. It stated that, at this time, Jews in existing or dissolved mixed marriages should not be deported, though the agency implied *not yet* (StadtA MM, NLG, Schreiben, Vertrauensmann der Reichsvereinigung; also Gottwaldt 2005; Meyer 2011).

It is worth noting here that Annemarie was forced by the Nazi persecution to assume more and more of the roles that had formerly been the responsibility of her Jewish husband. The experience was true of many other women in a similar situation. Along with communicating with government agencies, which was forbidden to Jews, these women were also increasingly preoccupied with the family's financial affairs, including, not uncommonly, earning the family's upkeep (Kaplan 2001).

On 12 January 1944, Alfred was deported to the concentration camp of Theresienstadt after all. In his last letters, he expressed concern for the security of his family. On 10 January, he asked several friends to take in his wife and daughter (StadtA MM, NLG). His ability to care for his family in his traditional role as provider and protector had, since 1933, been circumscribed more and more—an experience that most Jewish husbands in Germany shared. The divorce can be interpreted as a final attempt on his part to win back some room to maneuver and to redirect the fate of his family in a positive direction.

The deportation closed off all of his remaining options for influencing future events. Once he had been deported, the fate of Annemarie and Ursula lay wholly in the hands of others, few of whom had any sympathies for their plight. Instead, the mother and daughter tried to ensure Alfred's survival in the concentration camp. In spite of the catastrophic situation with regard to the food supply at the end of the war, they sent regular food packages to Theresienstadt. The postcards with which Alfred gratefully acknowledged the packages have been preserved (StadtA MM, NLG). In spite of their efforts, Alfred did not survive the camp. He died on 13 August 1944 in Theresienstadt, according to a letter dated 19 March 1945 from fellow inmate Laura Eisfeld, as a result of a chronic bladder ailment that was not adequately treated (StadtA MM, NLG).

The case of the SS guard Hertha Ließ can verify similar findings even if in a completely different way. In her case, we cannot trace how her relations to the Jewish inmates of Ravensbrück changed because these inmates were killed during the murder campaign 14f13. Nevertheless, we can trace her career within the camp system until May 1945 and show how her career was closely related to the course of both the genocide and the war. Both led to a substantial rise in the status and power of those women SS guards. By 1942, they could look back on many years of experience in the system of women's camps.

When the RuSHA processed the marriage application of Ließ and Ehlert, it did so solely in consideration of their goals of breeding a racial elite. The agency's medical investigation sheet requested information with regard to criteria such as the ability to conceive and to give birth as well as physical constitution (BArch RS/B 0125 Ehlert). They reduced the role of a woman to her function in reproducing the race. The fact that Ließ, in May of 1941, had a miscarriage at five weeks served as proof to the SS physician of her ability to conceive.

Yet these considerations, of motherhood and playing the housewife, soon played little or no role in her life; her career as a woman SS guard took precedence in the eyes of the camp administration. Ließ was just too necessary, and too experienced, for them to force her to take on the traditional gender role as a mother. After the murder campaign 14f13, Ließ continued her career as SS guard in the exploitation of camp inmates in the German war industry. According to the job allocation lists from this period, she worked by mid-July 1942 as the squad leader of the Central Naval Laundry Camp and by the end of August 1942 as squad leader in the Siemens workshops in Ravensbrück (MGR/StBG, KL 18/10–15; Schmolling 2006: 588).

On 2 January 1943, the central camp administration in Oranienburg rated her as "suited" to be sent, together with four others, to support the team of ten woman SS guards already stationed at the women's concentration camp Lublin-Majdanek (APMM, XX-26: 16) in the General Government— formerly Poland. Their task was to guard female camp inmates who worked in the Used Goods Recycling Plant at the airport clothing factory. There they sorted, disinfected, and prepared for shipment the clothing that had belonged to the Jewish people who had been exterminated in Aktion Reinhardt (APMM, XX-26: 258; Mailänder Koslov 2009: 66).

On 21 January 1943, Ließ left Ravensbrück and was reassigned to Lublin-Majdanek. In July 1943, there were 7,821 female prisoners in the women's camp, of whom 5,371, or more than two-thirds, were Jewish (Kranz 2008: 49). Moreover, the majority of the Jewish women and men deported to Majdanek were murdered as soon as they arrived, either in the gas chambers or by being shot. Within the framework of the extermination of the Jews, the camp at Majdanek had "a hedging function for the overburdened camps of Aktion Reinhardt," as historian Dieter Pohl formulated it (2004: 103). On 3–4 November 1943, the remaining Jewish inmates in Majdanek were murdered as part of the so-called *Erntefest* operation, meaning Harvest Festival (Kranz 2008: 51–53).

When viewed biographically, a very important part of Ließ's career, especially her transfer to Majdanek, took place in relation to the Nazi regime's developing anti-Semitic policies of deportation and extermination. Only one month after arriving at Majdanek, Ließ was already filling in for the guard supervisor (*Oberaufseherin*) Elisabeth Ehrich (BArch B162/AR-Z 77/72: 1.19). We encountered Ehrich in the last chapter as the superior officer to the SS guard Luzie Halata. According to her own account, Ließ served in Majdanek as the squad leader at the laundry—no doubt because of her previous experience in this area at Ravensbrück.

Her experience within the camp system was so valued that she was transferred, one after the other, to the women's camps at Płaszów, Auschwitz, Rajsko, and Bergen-Belsen in the wake of the advance of the Red Army (Philipps 1949: 227–28). Since January 1944, there were all in all nine concentration camps for women on the sites of the main concentration camps of the Nazi camp system at the same time (Schwarz 1994: 38). In addition, each main concentration camp had subcamps exclusively for women (Ellger 2007; Buggeln 2009; Schalm 2009; Rudorff 2014). In total, there were some 4,000 women employed in this network of camps as SS guards (Schwarz 1994: 32). Among them, Ließ belonged to the small elite of twenty-four women who had garnered previous professional experience in the camp system since 1939. That is why she finally took over the responsibilities of *stellvertretende Oberaufseherin*, or deputy chief guard, this time in Bergen-Belsen (Philipps 1949: 236).

Ließ's career in the camp system was thus characterized by a high degree of mobility, personal independence, and professional success. Her husband seemed to have played no role in her professional advancements; she moved up and around within the concentration camp apparatus in keeping with the tides of war and genocide. Her gender played a central role in facilitating this career in the first place because the camp system continued the established prison tradition of assigning women guards to the task of directly guarding women prisoners.

An independent hierarchy developed within the camp system of female personnel that expanded enormously as a result of the escalating use of camp inmates as forced labor in war industries. But beyond her gender, it was her professional experience that mattered. Ließ was badly needed, and she was frequently transferred to where she was needed most in the expanding camp system. In sharp contrast to these professional challenges, her role as a wife and her contribution as a mother to the breeding of an elite SS racial community played little if any role in her everyday life. Her career fit poorly into the official role to which the RuSHA ascribed her gender.

In the final years of the war, the German defeat at Stalingrad and the persistent advance of Allied forces in no way led to an amelioration or the disappearance of the camp system. The Nazi push toward the so-called final victory or *Endsieg* led in fact to both more economizing within the camp system and an explosion of its scale and scope. In the words of historian Bernd Weisbrod, Germany "encamped" itself (1998: 354). All of the concentration camps from outside the borders of Germany proper, whether in the East or in the West, were evacuated into the interior of the Reich. During these death marches, more than one-third of all the concentration camp prisoners lost their lives (Blatman 2011). Women SS guards like Ließ followed the inmates back to the *Altreich*. They could thus continue their careers right to the end of the war. That is, they could continue to fulfill their gender-specific professional obligations, which had become central to both the Nazi regime's war aims and its ability to continue to fight.

Postwar Anti-Semitism

The year 1945 marks the so-called zero hour, or *Stunde Null*, when, thanks to total defeat and mass destruction, Germans had to rebuild their lives again. It was, in many ways, the most fundamental rupture in the everyday lives of many Germans at that time. Yet there has been considerable public and scholarly debate about the degree to which this image of a complete disconnect across 1945 is accurate. The Allies certainly transformed the everyday life of the German people when they defeated the Third Reich and liberated the concentration camps. They occupied Germany, broke Nazi power, and, at least officially, proscribed anti-Semitism. Still, many objects, memories, prejudices, and resentments from the Nazi period, including anti-Semitism, survived in the everyday life of Germans.

The Cold War strengthened this development. In the Soviet occupation zone, punishment was harsher but enquiries about the persecution of the Jews only played second fiddle to the compensation of persecuted communists (Illichmann 2007; Joseph 2010). In West Germany, by contrast, the denazification process was already finished by the beginning of the 1950s, and many Nazi perpetrators were let off without conviction. Rather than punishing the persecutors and granting full compensation to the victims, the government of the FRG, founded in 1949, prioritized restoring state sovereignty and social stability. As a result, the process of coming to terms with the past failed to a large extent (Reichel 2001: 24–26).

In the offices of many government agencies sat bureaucrats who had helped execute the policies of the Nazi regime. Many former Nazi judges, state attorneys, and other bureaucrats continued to sit in high offices, even though they had awarded death penalties for small crimes during the Third Reich and kept the Nazi system of injustice operational. Only in the 1960s was there a public debate about the continuities in the judicial system between the FRG and the Third Reich, and even this debate remained largely ineffective in creating change. Former Nazi judges now protected their compromised colleagues from prosecution while continuing to pass legal judgments over the surviving victims of the Nazi system (Miquel 2001: 221).

The legal system is only one example of the continuing and active role of collaborators and perpetrators within the postwar social consensus of the Federal Republic. It is emblematic of the persistence of anti-Semitism both inside and outside of the major institutions of postwar West Germany. These continuities in anti-Semitism are one reason why the process of reintegration into postwar society for Jewish victims badly miscarried. The administration and the majority of the population were indifferent toward the postwar problems of former victims of Nazi persecution (Brenner 1995: 77–87). Most Germans concerned themselves first and foremost with themselves. Those surviving victims of the Nazis, still unloved and unwelcome, often fell victim once again to persecution.

A different but parallel story could be told about the persistence of anti-Semitism in East Germany (Haury 2002; cf. Pätzold 2010), but all three of our figures lived in the FRG so we focus our attention there. Officially, it seemed that the situation of these women had been inverted in 1945. Annemarie Guggenheimer and Kläre Begall finally escaped from the constant threat to life and limb. Hertha Ließ lost not only her regular income but also the social status she enjoyed as a woman guard in the SS. From that moment on, she had to reckon with criminal prosecution. Yet if we take a closer look at how each of their lives unfolded, it will become clear that their situations in fact did not change as might have been expected after Allied victory. On the ground, the practices of anti-Semitism persisted.

Consider first the case of the Guggenheimers. "My mother's condition in terms of health is that of a complete psychological breakdown," wrote Ursula on 30 July 1949 to the Bayerisches Hilfswerk, a quasipublic charity institution that sought to address the needs of the victims of the Nuremberg Laws (StadtA MM, NLG). Mother and daughter were marred both physically and psychologically by the murder of their husband and father and the persecution they all suffered. According to their family doctor, W. Stuermer, writing a report to the local court of Memmingen on 25 April 1974, they lived very isolated lives after the war and suffered from a persecution complex (Sammelakten zu den Sterberegistern, Sterbefallanzeige Ursula Elisabeth Guggenheimer, 1981). According to an application of their landlord, the Memminger Wohnungsbau e.G., to the court of Memmingen from April 25, 1974, they did not allow strangers to enter into their apartment, even handymen working for the building manager (StadtA MM, NLG, Gesuch).

The ruptures experienced during the Nazi period also continued to influence their postwar lives in material ways. Her former school confirmed on 19 January 1955 that Ursula was unable to complete her education during the war (StadtA MM, NLG). Any attempt on her part to reintegrate herself into the postwar economy and society failed. The family's property had all been stolen from them. With the murder of father, husband, and breadwinner, they also lost their economic livelihood. That is, the November Pogrom of 1938—when their residence, their private refuge from the Third Reich, was violated—continued to shape their everyday lives even in postwar Germany.

On top of these hardships, mother and daughter also faced continued anti-Semitic persecution. In Memmingen, Annemarie Guggenheimer found herself exposed to the libel of Ludwig Bach. A local profiteer from Aryanization, Bach had been issued the Guggenheimer family's former apartment during the Nazi period with the help of the NSDAP district leader Wilhelm Schwarz. On 27 May 1949, Bach wrote a letter to the administrative court in Augsburg claiming that Annemarie had indirectly caused the deportation and even the death of her husband by divorcing him. He essentially made use of anti-Semitic arguments in order to forestall having to return the apartment to them.

We do not know whether Annemarie reproached herself in the same way for the divorce. But such accusations amounted to psychological torture insofar as they blamed the victims for their persecution. At the very least, Ursula rebuffed this calumny directed at her mother. She corrected Bach by saying that her father's deportation "coincided with that of the other couples in Memmingen who were still living in mixed marriages" (StadtA MM, NLG).

One thing was clear, however: the divorce continued to make their lives difficult in the postwar period. At first, the court refused to recognize Annemarie as Alfred's widow and, by extension, refused to recognize her as his legal heir, a status that devolved to the daughter. This decision badly disadvantaged her. Fortunately mother and daughter maintained a very close relationship until the end of Annemarie's life and even lived together, so that she in fact could benefit from compensation granted to her daughter. Yet this decision must have been extremely humiliating for her.

Even the reparations authorities questioned their claims. In 1949, the Landesamt für Soforthilfe, which was the provincial office responsible for emergency aid, briefly canceled Annemarie's already approved monthly allowance from the Bayerisches Hilfswerk on the premise that her divorce was the reason for her husband's deportation. Only after she could verify that her marriage had been ended consensually did the complaint commission revise on 10 July 1950 the decision from 1949 (StadtA MM, NLG, Entscheidung). In 1958, she was finally granted a small annuity. Even in this, the divorce made itself evident in the relatively low amount of the pension that she had to accept. Overall, the process of seeking and receiving reparations transpired over an extremely long time and hardly ameliorated the dire conditions in which the two women lived. They remained alienated from society after the war.

Annemarie died in Memmingen on 2 February 1975, and her daughter died seven years later—both alone and completely impoverished (StadtA MM, Sterberegister, Ursula Guggenheimer).

Hertha Ließ was better able to reintegrate into postwar German society. On 17 September 1945, the British military court in Lüneburg indicted her for jointly committed war crimes and maltreatment resulting in death in Bergen-Belsen and Auschwitz (Cramer 2011: 119). During the trial, she admitted that she had struck prisoners in the face with her hand (TNA War Office/235/15: Bl. 78). On 17 November 1945, she was finally declared guilty of prisoner abuse in Bergen-Belsen and sentenced to fifteen years imprisonment (Cramer 2011: 249–51). On 7 May 1953, she was paroled from the Werl prison. In 1970 she worked in Bad Homburg as a switchboard operator (BArch B162/AR-Z 77/72: 1.17). She later remarried, became a housewife, and took the name of her new husband, thus becoming Hertha Naumann.

When, in May 1974, the Frankfurt state attorney questioned her about Erna Krafft's report, she admitted freely that she had served as block leader in Ravensbrück at the time and had even enjoyed her own office (BArch B162/AR-Z 77/72: 4.690). But she vehemently disputed all other accusations. She was concerned first and foremost with her own well-being, which she ensured by once again conforming to the norms of the existing society. In none of the surviving testimony did she demonstrate any sense of guilt or regret for her work as an SS guard in a concentration camp. She repeatedly claimed that she had nothing whatsoever to do with either murder campaign—14f13 in Ravensbrück and Harvest Festival in Majdanek—in spite of the fact that she was a SS guard in these camps at the precise moment when these campaigns took place (BArch B162/AR-Z 77/72: 1.20, 4.689). To her death on 4 April 1997, she was able to successfully avoid any further criminal investigations with regard to her activities in the concentration camps.

Kläre Begall remained in close contact with Erich Bloch after his liberation. Until 1946, the two lived together in the ground-floor apartment at Horstweg 28. In the summer of 1945, Bloch opened an art school, and Begall supported him in this endeavor by working in the school office. An anonymous text from this period threatened Begall with death because of the help she had provided to Jews. "If you think that you were very clever to have hidden Jews during the war—we are still living. For people like you," it read, "there will be a reckoning at the right time. For you, a bullet has already been cast. We will return!" (Kläre-Bloch-Schule 1992: 43). Threats like this one suggest that anti-Semitic practices outlasted the fall of the Nazi regime.

Bloch and Begall both fell into financial hardship. Due to the currency reform of 1948, Bloch lost his financial security. He had to close the art school. From then on, he lived for several years without an income before he managed—after a long dispute with the Berlin reparations office—to receive a reparation pension. In a resume that Bloch produced on 25 July 1949 for the magistrate of Berlin, he claimed to be 75 percent handicapped. Among other things, he suffered from a heart condition that resulted from the strains of his illegal life in the Third Reich (LaBO, Entschädigungsakte 5379: 2).

While perpetrators like Ließ were being released from Allied incarceration by the 1950s—if they were charged at all—enabling them to reintegrate themselves into the postwar society of the Federal Republic, the municipality of West Berlin still refused to provide Begall with financial aid in 1957 because she was a member of the Society for German–Soviet Friendship (Gesellschaft für Deutsch-Sowjetische Freundschaft) as well as the communist-related Democratic Women's Union for Germany (Demokratischer Frauenbund Deutschlands; Kläre-Bloch-Schule 1992: 42; Marpe 2014: 17–18). The Senate of Berlin also excluded active Communists from a decoration campaign that took place during the late 1950s and 1960s to honor those who had rescued Jews (Riffel 2007: 205–10). The reasons Begall still managed to be decorated by the Senate as an "unsung hero" in 1960 are not quite clear.

The relationship between Bloch and Begall intensified again in 1955, when Bloch suffered from a stroke. In her 1986 interview (ArchGdW), Begall traced the origins of the attack to his psychological suffering during the Nazi era. "It was a consequence of the fear, the terror, and so on. He was in [such] a state of despair that he had a stroke." He was paralyzed on his right side and required extensive care. A letter from advocate Emanual Bloch to the Berlin reparations office from 18 November 1955 explained that Erich Bloch was incapable of "completing the most minor actions" and suffers, moreover, from very great pain (LaBO, Entschädigungsakte 5379). Begall took care of him until his death in 1965. Shortly after his stroke, they decided to marry. Thanks to this marriage, Begall received 60 percent of his reparations pension after Bloch's death (Szepansky 1983: 200). In the end, this acquaintance from the Romanisches Café became not just her good friend but her long-term companion.

Begall remained in Berlin until her death from cancer on 4 November 1988. Even after her death, she was the object of anti-Semitic attacks. After printing Begall's obituary, the *Berliner Tagesspiegel* received an anonymous letter in which the deceased was denounced for her "shameful actions" and the Jews were defamed, once again, as "Germany's misfortune" (Kläre-Bloch-Schule 1992: 43). In public, however, Begall was honored for her deeds. In 1992, an adult education center in Charlottenburg was named after her. Twelve years later the District Assembly of Berlin-Charlottenburg decided to rename a small square in the neighborhood of Begall's former apartment in her honor (Marpe 2014: 20). These contradictions in memory mark the persistence of rupture in the everyday lives of Germans.

Conclusion

In Nazi Germany, anti-Semitic policies were not implemented from above by the regime alone; many Germans on the ground practiced anti-Semitism in their everyday lives, though for many different purposes (Mallmann 2002). This dynamic process of self, state, and society almost succeeded in completely eradicating Jews and Jewish life from Germany.

For many, anti-Semitic practices opened new doors and new opportunities. Germans denounced their neighbors, took over Jewish companies, and bought Jewish property at auction at great discounts. They benefited from upward mobility in terms of social, professional, and financial status. They denounced their neighbors, took over Jewish companies, and bought Jewish property at auction at great discounts. They did so not only to gain access to Jewish wealth and residences but also to lay claim to authority in everyday life: it amounted to a Nazi seizure of power in the neighborhood (Bergerson 2004). As seen in the case of Ließ, the persecution of Jews opened new possibilities for professional success for non-Jewish Germans. Her career as a camp guard exemplifies the way many Germans profited from the persecution of Jews by making their careers in party organizations, private industry, and public institutions.

The official policies of persecution increasingly penetrated into both the public sphere and private lives. Yet the crucial step in the Shoah took place when the vast majority of Germans made anti-Semitic principles and policies into everyday practices. There is even a tragic irony at work here when it comes to those people who wanted to help the Jews. In many cases, they needed, for strategic reasons, to perpetuate some of the mechanisms of anti-Semitic ostracism, even if they did so to preserve a little room for maneuvering to protect themselves or the people they cared for from the worst parts of Nazi policy.

With differential degrees of success: while Begall could create a safe space for hiding Jews by performing publicly as a loyal member of the proclaimed *Volksgemeinschaft*, the Guggenheimers' divorce was not able to save the family property and resulted in the deportation and murder of the Jewish husband Alfred. Given the social isolation of potential helpers and the lack of any coordinated, public protest against anti-Semitism, Jews and the people trying to help them could only make use of the very limited private spaces at their disposal. This situation made their actions particularly fragile and vulnerable, especially since the border between private and public was itself an object of negotiation and conflict. Solidarity with Jews thus became a lonesome undertaking. It helped to save the lives of a few thousand Jews, though it was unable to prevent the deportation and murder of the vast majority.

After defeating the Third Reich, the Allied effort at denazification was intended to be comprehensive and accomplished some restructuring of the German landscape. In addition to reintroducing democracy, human rights were reestablished, in that Jews could no longer be persecuted in Germany as such. Still, anti-Semitism persisted in German society and determined the operations of certain public authorities after the war. For Annemarie and Ursula Guggenheimer, for Erich Bloch and Kläre Begall, as for many others, this postwar experience of everyday anti-Semitism was extremely disappointing.

The implementation of Nazi racial and genocidal policies required the participation of many Germans on the ground. Their actions in the neighborhoods of Memmingen and Berlin were linked—as part of a pattern and a system—to many similar practices in many other places both within the *Altreich* and beyond its borders. As the Third Reich conquered the bulk of Europe and parts of Africa, German occupation forces spread the dynamic of violence from the *Altreich* to these conquered territories (e.g., Korb 2013). Almost all of the ministries of the German state and branches of the German economy as well as many of the organizations of the Nazi Party were present in the occupied territories. Yet it was not just Nazi policy makers who imposed the new order on occupied Europe. Within this framework, other Germans, including women, were dispatched to the occupied territories. Hertha Ließ was one of these women—but there were many, many more.

Susanne Beer, Johannes Schwartz, and Maximilian Strnad

Note

Parts of this chapter previously appeared in the chapter "Manche Spuren menschlicher Existenz verblassen schneller als andere: Die Geschichte einer 'privilegierten Mischehe' in Memmingen," in *Allgäuerinnen: Ein Lesebuch*, ed. Barbara Lochbihler and Sabine Schalm (Berlin: Ebersbach & Simon, 2013), 171–189.

CHAPTER 8

Violent Worlds

Monsters exist, but they are too few in number to be truly dangerous. More dangerous are the common men, the functionaries ready to believe and to act without asking questions.
—Primo Levi, Interview for the *New Republic*, 1986

In terms of both direct control and indirect influence, the German Empire grew tremendously during the Nazi era, in large part through violence and war. Men, women, and children, Jews and non-Jews, were displaced, confined in ghettos, or subjected to forced labor under brutal circumstances. Millions were murdered, starved to death, or died due to utterly devastating living conditions in the German-occupied eastern territories. German men and women bore responsibility for those consequences. Given the massive impact of the Nazi regime on the occupied territories of Poland and the Soviet Union, we refer to them collectively as the *Nazi East*, a phrase coined by historian Elizabeth Harvey (2003; also Snyder 2010). This chapter explores the everyday in the Nazi East not merely as an extremely violent society (Gerlach 2010) but also as an extraordinarily violent space (also Christ 2011; Fulbrook 2012; Lower 2013).

It may seem strange that, in a book about the German *Alltag*, we are dedicating a whole chapter to the everyday in Poland and the Soviet Union—especially after a chapter on anti-Semitism. But we have good reasons. First, it is impossible to isolate the story of Germany per se from the events that took place in the Nazi East. Fundamental transformational processes took place there during World War II for both the occupied and the occupiers. Ubiquitous violence executed by the German military and civil administration as well as the reactions to the terror by the local population radically and rapidly changed the social, cultural, and political landscape in both Eastern and Central Europe; indeed, those policies and practices had repercussions around the world.

For the many different peoples of Eastern Europe conquered by the Nazis, this violence marked a fundamental rupture in their everyday lives in terms of basic civility and sociability, infrastructure and institutions, self and family, meaning and memory; and tens of millions lost their very lives. The Shoah marked a rupture for the conquering Germans too, whether they took an active part in it or not. They assumed the role of a racially superior Aryan overlord even if they only benefited from that status indirectly, and they bore responsibility for this war of extermination even if they personally were not perpetrators. Both the hardships facing the German people at the end of the war and the postwar reconstruction of civility, infrastructure, institutions, self, and memory took place in the shadow of this earlier violence. The prior chapter focused on the microsocial interactions in the *Altreich* relating to anti-Semitism; in this chapter, we follow Germans into the expanding German Empire in Eastern Europe.

Our second rationale for moving into the Nazi East derives from our belief that it offers special insight into the everyday. The consequences of German occupation politics were existential for the vast majority of people. Particularly in situations that are steeped in violence, it is useful to study the microsocial interactions through which this violence actually took place. As Primo Levi, the Jewish–Italian survivor of the Auschwitz extermination camp system, reminds us (1986), it would be a mistake to blame the monstrous leaders who devised this system of genocide at the expense of those common functionaries who implemented its policies. We frame this chapter with his warning. What may seem to be extraordinary or monstrous became ordinary for those who experienced it at an astonishing speed. In this context, we use the term *ordinary* in the sense that men and women learned rapidly, and according to their social position, how to arrange their lives within the new living conditions, which included adopting an extraordinary kind of violence.

At the same time, the ordinariness of this extraordinary violence provokes the troubling question of who precisely was responsible for making these worlds so very violent. Over the last several decades, scholars have struggled to explain Nazi atrocities in the East and elsewhere. In a series of controversies, they have debated the relative significance of different causal factors in the Holocaust: Hitler's racist and murderous intentions, the increasingly chaotic conditions on the ground, and the economic and racial considerations of population planners, wartime barbarity, peer pressure, group dynamics, and socialization in anti-Semitic ideology.

Scholars now generally agree that different factors were more or less important to different actors in varying situations. For policy makers, for instance, explicit motives may have played more of a role than for those who were constrained or mobilized to kill at the front line. This chapter does not seek to rehearse, let alone resolve, these wider debates. We prefer instead to explore some of the ways in which Germans practiced and accustomed themselves to everyday violence and, in doing so, created violent worlds.

Our aim is not merely to redescribe or recount the violent, racist, and anti-Semitic character of this particular German *Alltag* for a general reader but also, in keeping with our critical inquiry into the everyday as such, to inquire into the causal connections between microsocial and macrosocial changes. *How did microsocial interactions on the ground help to shape the everyday lives of the various people who inhabited the new territories of this German Empire? And with what consequences for the Nazi system of violence as a whole?* To address these questions, we will focus less on what people believed and more on the self that they practiced on their own and with others. The fantasies and ambitions of Germans who went east did not radically vary.

For the most part, they were shaped by the dominant nationalist, imperialist, and racist ideas of the Third Reich. Moving east, German men and women brought these everyday *frames of reference* with them. This analytic term, developed by the sociologist Erving Goffman (1974), refers to the normative setting in which people organize their actions. In the case of many German functionaries and facilitators, these frames in themselves were not a sufficient cause for murder. But they implemented Nazi policies and practices nonetheless, creating the conditions in which mass murder was possible (Browning 1992; Walk 1996; Kaplan 1998; Bankier 2000; Bergerson 2004; Welzer 2005; Fritzsche 2008; Bergerson et al. 2011; Wildt 2012a, 2012b, 2013). To explain these contradictions, we will draw attention to the ambiguous ways in which the act of authoring narratives of self in memory are connected to authorizing—in this case, particularly violent—social relations historically.

The same can be said about gender roles. Most German men and women who went east held certain perceptions about what it meant to be a strong male or female in a colonial and wartime setting. They were expected to assert themselves as elite members of the Aryan race, for which lording over the inferior Slavs and Jews required distinctly gendered roles. In this chapter, we once again pay particular attention to how women practiced a self in terms of career, gender, family, and race. The consensus in Holocaust and genocide studies is that the systems that make mass murder possible required broad societal participation; and still many histories of the Holocaust leave out the majority who populated that society, as if women's history happens somewhere else (Lower 2013; Allen 1997).

There is a debate over women in Nazi Germany, and there are studies of female perpetrators (Koonz 1987; Bock 1989, 1997; Grossmann 1991; Schwarz 2001; Stephenson 2001; Kraus 2008; Mailänder Koslov 2009). Our knowledge remains limited, however, with regard to women's room for maneuver and the many ways in which they were integral to the Holocaust. As we have already seen in the examples of Luzie Halata and Herta Ließ, German women were more than cheerleaders for the Führer, loyal wives, and baby machines (Lower 2013). The actions of women are key to understanding how a society can emerge in which violence and anti-Semitism permeate daily life and otherwise ordinary people opt for cruelty, sadism, and murder.

Documenting the actions of female perpetrators helps us to understand the difference between a warring state and a genocidal one.

To be sure, the implementation of the so-called *Endlösung*, or Final Solution to the Jewish Question was a male-dominated affair. But the outstanding cases of female witnesses, accomplices, and mass murderers reveal that most women had little trouble adapting to the wild East that was often seen as a man's world. Many young women were attracted by the nationalistic fervor of the movement and the chances for traveling abroad. Hundreds of thousands used this opportunity to liberate themselves from familial and societal constraints.

They moved to Poland, Ukraine, Belarus, and the Baltics, placing themselves directly in the genocidal war zones of the expanding Reich. Many of these self-styled Aryan pioneers and patriots ended up adapting their ethics to the Nazi moral code along the way. Female professionals posted in the Nazi East encountered a wide range of native populations; and they exploited and abused them to advance their own careers, personal desires, and relationships with men. It is this story we wish to tell: how they helped make the territories they occupied into violent spaces.

Changing Spaces

Going east was different from staying home in Germany proper; yet many of the young men and women who did so imagined a future home there. The women who were attracted to life in Ukraine, Poland, and Belarus were already of a certain character and ambition. If they did not join their husbands in the SS, then they were single women seeking a career path. In both cases, these were women with ideological convictions and gumption who saw the newly conquered territories as a place of opportunity and advancement (E. Harvey 2003). These young women comprised an entire generational cohort. Born between 1919 and 1925, they were the baby boomers of World War I. They made the Nazi war machinery possible by serving not only practically within the legions of administrators required to sustain the machinery of destruction but also ideologically as steadfast patriots who were more politically minded than they cared to admit (Lower 2013).

The Nazi regime viewed the East as Germany's Manifest Destiny and wild frontier: a roughrider, cowboy culture fused with the disciplined Nazi one of racial hierarchies. German colonizers, including women among them, referred to Ukrainians as their slaves and sought to eradicate the Jews like the Americans had the Indians (Gröning and Wolschke-Bulmahn 1987; Grill and Jenkins 1992; Trevor-Roper 2000; Aly 2005: 230–44; Lower 2010a; Baranowski 2011; Kakel 2011: 1). Repressive laws, bourgeois mores, and social traditions that made life in the Reich regimented and oppressive were shed when one went to the East. There, the decrees and whims of a motley crew of lower-class, newly minted regional governors and SS chiefs ruled the day. Looking back after the war, most German women who went east were proud of their contribution to the war effort.

As German men and women moved east, they radically changed the spaces they inhabited; and in the process, they changed themselves and others. The reference here to space signifies not only the topographical place but also the social relations of the people who live there. The evidence suggests a reciprocal dynamic between people and their lived environment: spaces mold violence and violence imprints spaces. How violence was executed depended on the kinds of spaces in which it took place; equally, violent behavior changed the spaces in which it occurred and the character of the people involved. The Eastern spaces that Germans invaded and inhabited were transformed radically and rapidly by their arrival. These transformations took place along roughly similar lines, although on very different timescales, depending on location.

We begin in the Silesian borderlands that were annexed to the Reich, where German functionaries faced the major challenge of Germanization. Consider a small town such as Będzin. It was situated in the so-called eastern strip that ran along the eastern frontier of Silesia. It was also located some twenty-five miles north of Auschwitz. Będzin had a prewar population of around 55,000, of whom nearly one half were Jewish, the majority Polish, and only a few hundred German. From February 1940, the civilian administration stood under the leadership of the chief executive, or Landrat, Udo Klausa.

The policy of Germanization meant immediate immersion in a project of colonial racism. Jews were ousted from their houses in the better areas of town and forced to move together into ever more cramped conditions; they lost their livelihoods as businesses were expropriated; their rations were progressively reduced; and they were subjected to increasing restrictions on movement, punctuated by so-called raids and forced labor duties (Fulbrook 2012). This radical, brutal appropriation and transformation of space was made possible only because of the colonial mentalities and assumptions about German superiority of the new civilian administration. The same held true across vast areas of former Poland, now incorporated into the expanded German Reich; it held true, for instance, in the Warthegau under Reich governor Arthur Greiser and in the city of Łódź, from 1940 home to the second largest ghetto after Warsaw (Horwitz 2008; Epstein 2010). For the inhabitants, the ruptures in their everyday lives were systemic, violent, and rapid.

But these transformations were far more rapid in the territories farther east that had been occupied by the Soviet Union until 1941. One of those radically changing spaces was the city of Berdichev, in northern Ukraine. Some 30,000 Jews resided there before World War II—that comprised half of the city's population. For centuries, the city was known as a center of Jewish cultural life.

The initiation of the German occupation of Berdichev in July 1941 marked the beginning of the end of this era. The Nazi occupation, and the murder of Jews connected to it, changed the urban landscape; they transformed the Ukrainian *Berdichev* into the German *Berditschew*.

During the invasion of Russia in summer and autumn 1941, the Nazis restructured the city space in ways similar to Będzin but much more rapidly (Christ 2011). Berdichev was situated farther to the east and not occupied until much later in the war. Still, this transformation did not begin only after the first soldiers drove through the city streets on their motorcycles, announcing the supremacy of the German Armed Forces. In fact, Berdichev had already begun to transform itself even though the front still lay several hundred kilometers to the west. Hundreds, perhaps thousands of Jewish refugees fled to the city—the exact numbers are impossible to reconstruct from the available sources. Situated on the crossroads of two important transport routes and on one of the main railway tracks to the east, the city was a way station for many mainly Jewish people heading farther into the inner regions of the country. They were escaping the anti-Semitic violence that typically began immediately after the German troops marched into the city.

Refugees had an important function in the social order of the city as well as for the dynamics of the violence process. Refugees brought news to Berdichev. They talked about the Germans and their crimes against Jews. Their presence itself was informative. The fact that they needed to flee, and barely escaped, demonstrated to those beyond the pale of German control just how the social order of a place would change as soon as the Germans came to power. It was mainly Jews who fled to the east. Their presence showed all of the inhabitants of Berdichev who was going to be in what kind of danger once the Germans had arrived. Thus the social situation of the Jews had already become fragile and unstable before the actual occupation. This influx of people and information had certain structural similarities to the anticipatory obedience we observed among the agents of Nazi institutions, although in the case of the victims it was geared toward quite different ends, namely self-preservation.

At the beginning of July 1941, a few days before the German takeover of the city, not only civilians but also the soldiers of the Red Army sought their luck in flight (Epelfeld 2004: 110). Mikhail Vul, like other survivors, called those few days between the Red Army's withdrawal from the city and the arrival of the German troops "days of anarchy" (SFI, Code 25159, 1996). His and more than 50,000 other survivor memoirs are available through the Shoah Foundation Institute for Visual History and Education at the University of Southern California. At that time, the vulnerability of the Jewish population of Berdichev became especially clear. The closer the front got to the city, the more chaotic the city became. Thousands of Berdichev residents—most of them Jews—left the city and turned into refugees themselves. Many left the city on their own; others were part of an escape effort more or less organized by the Soviet authorities.

The latter were especially interested in preventing the town's industrial plants from being seized by Germans. Entire factories of equipment were loaded by their workers onto freight trains and transported east. The retreat of the Red Army and the Soviet administration, which could no longer effectively defend or keep order in the city, also stripped the space of its last vestige of protection. The town now lacked the institutions and the personnel not only to maintain order among the city's residents, guarantee their safety, and protect their property but also to represent the interests of the local populations in negotiations with the invading Germans. This panic-stricken escape was also a clear sign for the remaining citizens: the city and all its inhabitants were now summarily dispatched to the approaching enemy.

For the most part, it was women, children and elderly people, Jews and non-Jews who stayed in Berdichev. They faced an unknown future. Innumerable abandoned buildings, dwellings, businesses, and industrial plants stood in the city in disarray. Remaining residents began to plunder these buildings. This wave of plunder again changed the power structure of the city—to the detriment of the Jewish population. Mostly Jewish homes remained empty and unguarded because Jews formed the majority of those who had left the city. So it was mainly Jewish homes that were looted after the inhabitants, now refugees, had left the city.

This change was observable even before the arrival of the German army. Naum Epelfeld, a teenager at that time, described the "days of anarchy" in a postwar memoir (2004: 111) as a lawless time: "On July 7th robbery and bodily injury reigned: doors were kicked in, locks broken off, everything that was not nailed down was taken away." Those days without regulatory power provided the opportunity for some to enrich themselves in places where the owners were still present. Mariia Beizerman, a young girl in 1941, recalled a situation where a man attempted to steal a pigeon from her brother. She described it in a postwar interview:

> My brother bred pigeons and our neighbor had also grown pigeons. Before the arrival of the Germans, some people just took a few of my brother's pigeons. This guy also wanted the pigeons. My father ran out of the house and threatened him. Then the neighbor said: "You kike, I'll show you." And so it was: as the Germans began killing, he turned my father and brother in. (SFI, Code 27766, 1997a)

Within a few weeks of the German takeover of the city, the situation intensified acutely. Yet the residents of the town anticipated German rule in the days before they arrived.

So it was not only the name that changed. *Berditschew*, as the city was called by the Germans, was soon characterized by its anti-Semitic atmosphere. The Germans—as they did everywhere in the newly conquered territories—established a set of formal administrative laws and rules as well as informal norms and values that excluded Jews from public life. Both German military administration and soldiers then implemented these policies and practices. Even the non-Jewish population contributed to the drastic and sudden transformation of the city. Their contribution often consisted of relatively small or subtle gestures.

These seeming secondary operations laid part of the foundation for the massive violence that was to break out shortly thereafter. In the smallest possible time, then, the men and women, soldiers and civilians, in and around Berditschew succeeded in establishing this new frame of reference. Jews had no place in this new framework. Implementing it in practice proscribed almost every form of interaction with the Jewish population of Berditschew other than their social, psychological, or physical destruction.

One of the first measures that made a big impression on the image of the city was the burial of German soldiers who had fallen in the battle over Berditschew. Wehrmacht soldiers turned a park in the middle of the city into a German war memorial cemetery. That a military cemetery would be positioned in Berditschew was not unusual at this time. The Wehrmacht needed to bury the dead quickly due to both their continuing advance and the summer heat, which led them to transform parks into burial grounds in many cities of the newly conquered territories. In one part of this site, however, stood an old Jewish cemetery in a state of disuse. The German occupiers sanded down the gravestones and probably reused them for construction elsewhere in the city. Gestures like these symbolically and publically announced the dominance of the victorious Germans in the town and the arrival of a new order based on Nazi principles.

As a reward for their service and their sacrifice, Germans claimed the right to reorder the space of the town to suit the representational needs of the Nazi empire. The dead were not quickly buried by the roadside. Rather, Wehrmacht soldiers laid out graves in the form of memorials and sites of remembrance, and they decorated these two hundred graves thoughtfully with crosses of birchwood (Volksbund Deutsche Kriegsgräberfürsorge, Archiv, GN 1.2. Lr 1992/93). Located at the summit of the local landscape, the cemetery lay at the crossroads of two important trade routes; it was impossible for anyone to ignore, resident or guest, who passed through the city.

By doing so, German soldiers intended to honor their dead. But in the process, they also—presumably unintentionally—announced that the new rulers of the city were settling in for the long term. To use Lüdtke's expression, it was *Herrschaft* as a social practice (1991b). In our terms, the functionaries and soldiers within these units of the German occupation were laying claim to authority over the people and spaces of this town as part of a larger project of imperial conquest and racial reorganization.

These powerful gestures transmitted their signals by restructuring the social space, but it would probably be giving the occupying forces too much credit if we were to assume that those signals were always intended from the beginning. It would be more accurate to say that they were the not unwelcome, practical consequences of their intentional actions (Barlösius 2003). These practical consequences in turn became the practical conditions for what came next. Said in another way, the Germans transformed the space in which they operated deliberately but also to a certain degree incidentally. By contrast, the people who found themselves under German rule experienced those changes as both fast-paced and ineluctable.

The German forces also took other more direct measures to transform the space of the Nazi East. Immediately after the beginning of the occupation, the military administration demanded the registration of Jewish residents. This procedure served to quickly establish their number and domiciles. It also ensured that the Jews followed the new regulations of the occupiers, since the order to wear the so-called Jewish star was connected with registration. All those who came to register were obliged to wear a yellow six-pointed star visibly on their clothes. If Jews were caught who did not adhere to this rule, they were severely punished. As survivor Mikhail Aronowitsch Vanshelboim recalled in an interview (SFI, Code 27225, 1997b): "The ordinance also stated that when someone was discovered without a star, one would be immediately shot. These ordinances were hung all around the city." The ordinance was designed to make the Jews more readily recognizable as Jews at first glance to the Germans.

At least officially, the *Kennzeichnungspflicht*—that is, the mandatory identification as a Jew by wearing the yellow star—divided the city into two social and topographical halves: Jews and non-Jews. This forced obligation to label cleaved the city into places allowed and forbidden to Jews. They were, for instance, not allowed to use the tram or do their shopping at the marketplace. But they did not just avoid forbidden areas. The Jewish residents of Berditschew avoided appearing in public at all if they could manage it. They did so to protect themselves from attacks by their neighbors or by the German occupying forces, either with official sanction or, as we have seen in earlier chapters, independently working toward the aspirations of the regime for genocide. Formally and informally, then, the star denied them the free, unlimited use of the space of the city. The local German military functionaries thus continued the process of restructuring the territories under their control to suit the needs of the German Empire in Eastern Europe.

By the end of August 1941, only six weeks after the beginning of the occupation, Berditschew had irretrievably lost its former character as a Jewish city. The German military administration forced the Jewish residents to move to a particular area beyond the city center. Documents of the local German civil administration prove that the Germans gave public notice to relocate through newspapers and posters (Grossman 1994: 62). Again, Vanshelboim recalled (SFI, Code 27225, 1997b): "It stood there in black and white that all Jews and their children should move from the other parts of the city to the old downtown: Staromestna Street and a few others. It was called the ghetto. Yes, everyone was supposed to move there."

Several thousand Jewish people left their houses and apartments and moved into the prescribed area. Many places stood empty there—abandoned by those who had escaped from the city. Those who could not move into the ghetto for health reasons or refused to leave their homes were shot. The forced move lasted for days (Grossman 1994: 62). As in all cities occupied by the Germans, the local German authorities chose the locations for the ghetto. In Berditschew the military administration considered the districts of Jatki and Pisski to be appropriate choices. These satisfied in many ways the criteria for quickly closing off the area without too much expenditure. Nonetheless it was not pragmatic reasons alone that convinced the authorities in charge to locate the ghetto there. Rather, this decision represents yet another example of how Nazi ideology found its expression in daily social practices of the German politics of occupation.

Simply put, they moved the Jews to the worst corner of town. In doing so Germans—by intention or coincidence—symbolically ascribed to them the lowest place in the social hierarchy. Directly on the bank of the river, the air in this part of the city was always humid and the ground moist; the construction material was rotten; the houses small, miserable, and dilapidated. By contrast, the German occupiers settled in the center of Berditschew, laying claim to the less destroyed and most beautiful buildings and places. They left the in-between spaces to the local non-Jewish Ukrainians, who were similarly in between the Aryans and Jews in terms of the new racial hierarchies. By making residence congruent with social status, the city's topography became a way to transparently map the social hierarchies of the new racial order.

These policies and practices created and then reinforced transparent distinctions between Germans, Jews, and Ukrainians. The more the Jewish residents of the ghetto sank into poverty, the more clearly the German occupying forces demonstrated their superiority. These local measures were thus hardly secondary to the planned colonization of Poland, Belarus, and Ukraine; rather they were central to the process of building the Nazi East. They laid the foundations for a new Nazi *Alltag*, where anti-Semitism and race shaped the microsocial interactions on the ground.

Women outside the Office

The German colonization effort was no small matter. At least a half million young German women went east through the German Red Cross, the Reich Labor Service, and a plethora of private and public agencies. Tens of thousands worked in SS and police offices, in prisons, assisting with interrogations as well as typing up arrest reports and death notices. In Nazi-occupied Minsk, a five-day rally was held to recognize the work of about 1,800 female German occupiers in the city and surrounding area (Lower 2013). As Germanization enthusiasts, female welfare workers and educators labored on behalf of the Nazi Party and the *Volksdeutsche*—the ethnic Germans imported by the Nazi regime from more distant parts of Eastern Europe to settle on Polish and Jewish properties. These female pioneers also exploited Polish and Ukrainian Jewish laborers and toured ghettos such as those in Łódź and Warsaw (E. Harvey 2003).

These and other German women, including the wives and lovers of SS and policemen, witnessed the Holocaust and were heavily involved in implementing the Final Solution. In their postwar testimonies and memoirs, German women relate how the Holocaust crossed into daily activities in the workplace and around their homes. The boundaries of family, school, and office proved quite permeable; living and working as part of these institutions in the Nazi East, German women participated in routine and ad hoc ways in the violence connected to those institutions just as they often tried to safeguard their life world from it. As both history and memory, their practices of self normalized this violence.

Consider one example from Romaniv in Ukraine. The secretaries of the District Commissar prepared orders for shooting actions. They had access to top secret documents and to office forms such as labor passes that were lifesaving documents for Jews. Outside of the local offices, German women discovered the actual crime scenes. Florentina Bedner, a kindergarten teacher, recalled in her postwar testimony for the Bavarian criminal investigative bureau that many Jews lived in the forests nearby (BArch B162/76-K 41676, Koe, 29 November 1976).

She admitted that the Jews were shot there and that she herself saw the two large pits where their bodies were buried. She described the grave as follows: "It was as big as our house, about 10 meters wide ... I occasionally passed by there." On the one hand, this teacher stated that she did not actually witness the mass shootings being carried out. On the other hand, she does not deny involvement in the preparatory measures, such as the gathering of the Jews at the local school, where she worked as a teacher (idem).

Most women found themselves face-to-face with the horror of the Nazi war of extermination. They found various means of adaptation to it. In the Nazi capital of Rowno (Rivne) in Ukraine, the secretary Ilse Struwe—later writing under her married name of Schmidt—was stationed with fifteen other young women as a clerk in the operations office of a Wehrmacht sentry. A Jewish girl worked in their office. Her name was Klebka. One day Ilse decided to visit Klebka in the "fenced, miserable ghetto, where the Jews were forced to live. It was horrible, ramshackle, dirty houses ... 'Filthy Jewish nest' was the term often spoken around Rowno" (Schmidt 2002: 73–75).

The same derogatory term for Rovno's Jewish community appeared in the testimony of the commander of the Order Police for Ukraine, Otto von Oelhafen (NARA, Record Group 238, roll 50, M1019, 7 May 1947). It was clear from the sight of the ghetto that the Jews were in a desperate, bleak situation. But Ilse carried on with her work. She found comfort in the company of her female colleagues in the special dormitory where they lived together (Schmidt 2002). Here we see how practices of self supported the regime's policies by emulating its frame of reference.

To be sure, these postwar narratives of self may be creating only an artificial sense of distance in retrospect, but two factors at least mitigate this interpretation: the continuities in anti-Semitic practices that we identified in the last chapter and the many other sources in this chapter that confirm the construction of these social and spatial hierarchies. Still, there were limits to distancing oneself from genocidal violence in the East. The house for the German female staff was situated across the street from the cinema. In the summer of 1942, German SS and policemen decided to use this cinema as a gathering point for Jews who were being relocated from the ghetto to the mass-shooting site at the outskirts of town. Ilse's room faced the street, across from the cinema. In her memoir, she described being "awakened by the hubbub of voices, banging tin cups and soldier commandos." She looked out of her window and saw:

> A crowd of people stepped out of the open door of the cinema onto the street, and under the guard they led away. It was between three and four in the morning. I could clearly recognize men, women, children, elderly, and youths. On their clothing I could see that they came from the ghetto. Since September 1941, it was mandatory for all Jews to wear the star ... These persons, according to my estimate numbered about 300, later I learned that it was much more, and they were being led by a handful of soldiers ... And I had a good look until the entire column disappeared. Then I lay down again on my bed. These persons will be killed. I knew it ... The next morning in the office it was made known that these Jews had been shot a few kilometers from Rowno. We never saw Klebka again. (Schmidt 2002: 74–75)

Schmidt's story is in many ways representative of what most German women experienced in the East. They were witnesses to the genocide as discrete events in certain localities. They lacked a larger view of the entire machinery of destruction, but they still worked in it. Schmidt often received reports on her desk, as well as photographs, of the atrocities against civilians and POWs in Ukraine and in Serbia. She asked her boss about them, but she was told to keep quiet. These institutions poorly insulated their workers from the violent worlds in and on which they worked, in spite of efforts to do so (Lower 2013).

For some of the Germans going east, however, these new worlds were in fact already familiar territory. For example, Udo Klausa, the *Landrat* of Będzin, had family roots in this region; and his wife maintained connections with friends such as the Henckel von Donnersmarck family living in Tarnowitz just to the northwest on the other, more German, side of the police border. Klausa's wife—who, unlike her husband, had been born and brought up in the capital city of Berlin—had initially held high hopes for establishing a secure family base here.

Yet her first reactions on seeing her new home were not favorable; and during the three years that she lived in Będzin, she never came to like the place, often seeking the opportunity to stay for extended periods with friends or relatives. She finally left in the summer of 1943 to stay with relatives on an estate in East Prussia before fleeing, in the course of 1944, to the relative safety of the west. Her distaste for life in the Nazi East seems to make the Klausa family an unreliable partner for Nazi politics. But inner distaste was perfectly compatible with outward conformity. This probably widespread combination allowed the Nazi regime to function to the end.

In the context of the war for living space, the very presence of her German family in Będzin was part of a violent occupation. Her assumptions about the cultural superiority of the Germans meant that, however shocked and disgusted she was at the sight of the Jewish population of the area, she apparently failed to make any connection between their state and the policies of the Nazi regime that were implemented by, among others, her own husband. She did not seek to ameliorate their conditions, preferring to look away and not have to witness the violence all around, which she found distressing if it took place too close to her home.

Benefitting from the economic expropriation of the Jews and managing to acquire furniture at knockdown prices, her family sustained the racial hierarchies and genocidal dynamics of this war of extermination through both action and inaction. While Klausa performed his duties with exemplary efficiency, he registered a degree of discomfort as it became ever more murderous. He nevertheless continued to play his role in implementing policies of ghettoization and degradation of the local Jewish population, effectively paving the way for others to implement the Final Solution in the region around Auschwitz. The separation between inner doubts and outer conformity was typical of many who were involved in sustaining the Nazi project. Conformity in a role, not inner commitment and ideological motivation, were sufficient to keep the Nazi machine in operation.

There was also a gendered form of anti-Semitic thinking and expression specific to women's roles and their place in the Nazi system and society as secretaries, wives of officials, nurses, and teachers. Women rarely expounded in wartime records and postwar accounts on their views of Jews and the Holocaust. This circumstance raises difficult challenges for historians as to how to interpret these silences in the sources. More common was a colonialist discourse about the stupid, dirty, and lazy locals, referring to Poles, Ukrainians, and Jews; veiled language from the time, references to the dark terrain infested with criminals and partisans; and references to the infantilized native who is clever but inferior and dispensable. One way to address this methodological problem is to look at the ways in which Jews were routinely exploited and killed in the same matter-of-fact, everyday manner.

Though some German women were just witnesses to violence in the east, others were actively involved as accomplices, plunderers, and administrators of anti-Semitic policies. As part of the process of being dehumanized, Jews were labeled as inanimate objects, detested animals, colonial subjects, and a source of booty. In the Nazi East, they became material commodities in a culture of consumption, trade, and profiteering; and German women, as household managers, were in many ways at the center of this culture (Lower 2013). When transports of Jews arrived in Minsk, the Gestapo office staff enjoyed an abundance of delicacies. The secretaries in the office referred to the food taken from Jewish deportees before they were killed as *Judenwurst*. German women in the East organized and distributed Jewish goods and property. In the offices, they handled this so-called Jewish sausage, prepared it, served it, and ate it with their male colleagues (BArch B162/1682, Testimony Erna Leonhard, 14 December 1960; Lower 2013).

Of the accounts that place German women directly at deportations and mass shootings as onlookers and even revelers, most include details about banquet tables and refreshments provided by them such as cake and coffee. As historian Claudia Koonz discovered in her work about German women at home in the Reich, German women in the East also contributed to the normalization of the mass murder directly at the scenes of the crimes. Here too we see one example of how Germans profited from the Nazi war of extermination.

Annette Schücking-Homeyer recounted the following story on 28 January 2010 in an interview with *Spiegel Online International* ("'They Really Do Smell Like Blood'"; Interview 30 March 2010; Lower 2013). In Novhorod Volynsk in Ukraine, at the end of 1941, she went to the warehouse established by the NSV. She went there to find clothes for the Ukrainian kitchen helpers in the

Soldatenheim, a retreat for soldiers that she ran for the German Red Cross Aide. It was piled high with Jewish clothing.

She was struck by the piles of children's clothing. As they picked through the clothes, some of her German female colleagues were uneasy and did not take anything; others enthusiastically thanked the German officials who opened up the warehouse to them, declaring *Heil Hitler* when they saw all the booty. Schücking-Homeyer wrote home to her mother about the clothing collected by the NSV and told colleagues at home not to accept clothing from the NSV since it was from murdered Jews (idem). This autobiographical account—a practice of self with dimensions of both history and memory—suggests that many Germans abroad and at home were in fact receiving plundered goods from murdered Jews.

German functionaries often demonstrated insatiable greed when it came to such goods, and it sometimes generated critical reports and investigations during the war. Jewish belongings were officially Reich property and not meant for personal consumption. There were many cases of theft committed by officials from the highest ranks, such as Greiser in the Warthegau and Odilo Globocnik, police leader in the Lublin district, down to the rural chiefs and gendarmes. There are also cases of excessive plundering by women. See, for instance, the extensive Schenk report of the Office of the Commander of the Security Police and Security Service for District Galicia from 14 May 1943 (ITS archive; also Aly 2005; Epstein 2010).

These acts of plunder connected the German occupiers, and even the Germans back home, to the system of exploitation and extermination throughout Nazi-occupied Europe. The distribution and consumption of Jewish goods near the mass murder sites were part of a ritual of triumph and compensation. The killing was a form of labor, of hard work that could be rewarded. It is an example of how new practices of self transformed not only the occupied but also the occupier.

Responses to Terror

Ever tighter restrictions made life increasingly difficult for Jews. Some—particularly those active in Jewish youth organizations—continued to explore the possibilities of resistance or escape. But the majority, with decreasing options available to them, simply sought somehow to survive in the hope that this state of affairs would be temporary and things might improve again if they could just sit it out. Meanwhile, Jewish councils often still pursued policies of close cooperation with the institutions of the German occupation, while attempting to mitigate the sufferings of members of the Jewish community through a range of welfare measures. But the balance was hard to get right.

Not knowing what ultimate fate was in store for the entire Jewish population in due course, many cooperated with delivering up Jews. There was thus a relatively broad spectrum of responses to the ever more restricted conditions of everyday life.

Such responses were not merely increasingly restricted by the growing constraints on the physical freedom of Jews; they were also rendered ever more difficult in light of the physical and psychological consequences of radically altered conditions of life. Jews faced illnesses exacerbated by low immunity, unsanitary housing conditions, and overcrowding. They suffered from constant hunger and malnutrition because of the inadequate food rations allowed by the German administration. They were emotionally afflicted by separation from and worry about loved ones. And they were beaten down by hard work in conditions of forced labor as well as daily experiences of random acts of brutality and terror. These pressures combined to diminish or destroy the will or capacity for resistance on the part of most Jews subjected to German rule in this area.

Many Jews in the Będzin area at the same time held the view that, in eastern Upper Silesia, Jews still lived and worked under better conditions than Jews in the ghettos of Łódź and Warsaw. This notion also had the effect, for many Jews, of believing that the best strategy was to work hard and try to sit it out rather than risking not only one's own life but also those of many others. Despite the severe penalties for being caught without the correct papers, Jews from the General Government and elsewhere in the Nazi East often still sought to gain access to this eastern strip of the enlarged greater German Reich.

Paradoxically, those taken for forced labor at the time thought they had a worse deal than those staying at home; but those in labor camps were the ones who ultimately had a slightly higher chance of surviving the war, unlike those remaining in the last trap of ghettoization prior to deportation for gassing. In the meantime, those remaining at home were unable to find enough food to survive; and if caught dealing with ration cards or on the black market the penalty was death, sometimes by hanging as a public ritual of retribution. In this violent world, the victims faced an absurd situation in which rational choices and personal politics failed to result in reasonable outcomes (Bauman 1989).

The Jewish residents of Berditschew reacted similarly to the policies of the occupying forces. They tried to make rational choices in a situation that offered hardly any choice. Nina Kordash, a young girl at the beginning of the occupation, recalls in a postwar interview (SFI, Code 38524, 1997c): "It was not allowed to sell food to Jews. They should starve. We were at home the whole time and had nothing to eat. Four children. We sat at home, did not go out. What should we do?"

The non-Jewish residents also tried to protect themselves from the violence. For instance, they nailed wooden crosses on the doors of their houses—an orthodox Christian symbol that signified that Christians and not Jews lived there. As Mariia Beizerman recalled (SFI, Code 27766, 1997a):

> Everywhere the Russians lived, all over the place where they had lived, crosses were hung on the doors before the shootings, before the Pogrom. They made crosses out of small boards and hung them on the walls not to be accidentally mistaken; so that the Russians would not be taken in place of Jews. They already knew that a cross here meant that Russians lived there, no cross: *here live Jews*.

German violence was mostly but not exclusively directed at Jews. Although non-Jewish Ukrainian men, women, and children were not targeted for extermination, they also suffered from the occupation. There were millions of them; and although they had not yet been degraded to forced laborers in the beginning of the occupation, they were seriously affected by the German occupation regime as it strove to feed and dress its military personnel—mainly by exploiting the occupied space by taking what it wanted to have (Pohl 2012). From this anecdote about wooden crosses, however, we see that non-Jewish residents also took measures to protect themselves from violence, thus distancing themselves from their Jewish neighbors.

This seemingly rational choice to avoid immediate danger had perhaps unintended nonrational repercussions. In the context of the Nazi occupation and its excessive violence, both Jewish and non-Jewish residents of Berditschew adapted to a violent society in which life and death were determined by membership in racial groups imposed by the occupying forces. While the scope for action for the Jews of Berditschew was extremely circumscribed by the Germans, they did act; and in making choices, even between equally bad options, they too helped shape the experience and events of everyday life.

As we saw in prior chapters, these attempts to insulate the private sphere from politics, to create a parallel world apart from violence, were only partially successful. What these particular examples demonstrate, however, is that these individual choices have systemic consequences for the people who share this life world. In the case of Berditschew and many other similar places in the Nazi East, the new practices left the Jews even more fearful and socially isolated. The microsocial interactions between German occupiers and Jewish and non-Jewish natives contributed to the remaking of Berditschew into an anti-Semitic place, even if anti-Semitism was the intent of only some of those involved.

Mass Murder

On 15 September 1941, the Nazi officials closed the ghetto in Berditschew. These operations were conducted by German police officers as well as members of a task force made up of special units of security services, the SS, and

Ukrainian auxiliary police. They were all under order from Martin Besser, commander of Police Battalion 45. In the early morning hours, these units drove the residents out of their houses.

The remaining residents were mostly women, children, and the elderly. From a central gathering place, the Germans, with the help of Ukrainian auxiliary police, led long columns of people out of the city to a nearby airfield. Those who could not yet or no longer walk were taken on trucks and driven to the execution fields just outside town. In the days prior, Besser ordered Soviet prisoners of war to excavate five big pits. German and Ukrainian policemen and SS men instructed people to undress and hand over their valuables. The victims had to position themselves on the edge of the pits in small groups of about twenty people and were shot dead. They fell into the pits. Not all were dead immediately; many fell in injured. They were buried by the fall of those who followed. The execution was finished in the late afternoon. Altogether, around 12,000 people were killed that day. This kind of systematic murder was the most radical strategy employed for transforming Berditschew from a Jewish and Ukrainian city into part of a German Empire in the East.

And yet some survived. After the fact, the pits with the dead and the living were filled with earth. For several days, the earth above the graves kept moving. Some of those who had not died did manage to dig a way out from among the corpses. Similarly, only a few people managed to escape the place of execution in advance. They succeeded in running away, bribed the police to let them go, claimed to be Ukrainians, or some combination of the above. Others knew a Ukrainian policeman who, for one reason or another, felt sympathy for them and helped them to survive the killing by hiding themselves in the piles of clothes. Almost none of the victims could leave the execution site without the help of at least one of the executioners. In this context, help could mean intentionally turning one's gaze aside to avoid looking in a particular direction.

Killing on this scale was harder than it seemed. The perpetrators had not brought with them anything other than the weapons they already had, so they had to improvise on the spot. In contrast to the murders that took place in the concentration and extermination camps, the murder of Jews in Ukraine was not embedded in institutions and sites specially selected and devised for mass murder. Rather the institutions—the German Wehrmacht and its auxiliary units filled by Germans and many other Europeans, the SS units, and the police battalions—adjusted their operations in an improvised and irregular way to direct their workers toward new goals, fitting their institutional practices to the Nazi frame of reference. Still, the particular murder actions themselves were carefully thought out and planned. The perpetrators developed or acquired all of the tools they needed to kill masses of people on-site.

As a result, in Berditschew, the majority of the Jewish population died in meadows and fields around the city. After the end of the killings, after the pits were filled in again, nothing remained that could remind one about the dead and the crimes. The pits were neither graves nor cemeteries. The memory of these killing sites was designed to disappear like the bodies of the people exterminated. This approach to the dead and their corpses is yet another example of the ways in which the German occupiers intended to Germanize this social topography.

In Będzin, the process was slightly different. The Nazi occupation had lasted for more than two years before the implementation of the policy of mass extermination; as a result, systemic violence preceded mass murder and helped to make it possible. The effects on the Jewish population of the policies implemented by the civilian government over the proceeding years were horrendous. Losing their family homes, their means of livelihood, and their freedom of movement, local Jews were progressively moved into ever worse accommodations and forced to live on inadequate rations in overcrowded and unhygienic conditions.

Humiliated and degraded in everyday life, they had to wear the Star of David, observe a curfew, and avoid areas forbidden to Jews; they were restricted and then prevented from using public transport; they were increasingly kept under surveillance and control; they progressively fell prey to illness and premature deaths due to malnutrition and brutal maltreatment, including severe retributions for even minor infringements of the numerous, newly imposed restrictions and regulations. Even before the deportations to the gas chambers, Jews lived in constant fear of raids and deportation to slave labor camps. While some Poles helped those Jews with whom they already had good personal and emotional connections, others profited from the Jewish plight or simply took delight in denunciations. They betrayed Jews in hiding or drew the authorities' attention to any Jew seeking to pass off as an Aryan in order buy forbidden foodstuffs.

The last stage of ghettoization in Będzin, inaugurated in the autumn of 1942 and completed in the spring of 1943, was explicitly designed as a form of incarceration pending deportation to extermination. Jews were brought to the selection points in August 1942 under the pretext of an identity card check, but that deception could no longer be used once the murderous meaning of deportations to Auschwitz had become clear. In September 1942, the minutes of a meeting of Gestapo official Hans Dreier with Będzin local officials state quite clearly that the last stage of ghettoization was designed as preparation for what they euphemistically called the *final evacuation of the Jews.*

Within the Jewish community, a few predominantly young Jews became actively involved in resistance movements, partially in conjunction with people from the Warsaw Ghetto. Others, particularly resourceful and resilient, devised strategies for escape or for survival in hiding. The vast majority of Jews were sent to their deaths with the liquidation of the linked Będzin–Sosnowiec ghettos in the final roundup of August 1943. Those Germans who had held significant roles in local government and the economy—including Landrat Klausa, Sosnowiec police chief von Woedtke, the city mayor of Sosnowiec Schönwälder, and notable local industrialist Rudolf Braune—later professed to have known nothing about it.

They effectively chose to reduce the ethical problem of genocide to the actual task of execution—that is, to acts of physical violence and direct killing—while failing to acknowledge their role both in the brutal rule of colonial racism and in creating the preconditions for genocide. Rossner was the one local industrialist who, along the lines of the much better known Oskar Schindler, seems genuinely to have tried to save large numbers of his employees along with members of their families. He was eventually arrested by the Gestapo and ultimately found dead in his prison cell.

Although Klausa may never have intended to contribute to the machinery of mass murder, as Landrat he played an active role in the stages of ghettoization along the way, which aided this ultimate outcome. But in his narratives of self, Klausa was unwilling to put the different sides of the story together. His wife's letters to her mother at this time betray clear evidence that, particularly during the summer of 1942, he was suffering from "nerves," but the archival records show only that he continued to fulfill his official role with customary efficiency (Fulbook 2012: ch. 11).

It does seem likely that he had growing scruples—or perhaps fear of being in some way actively associated with what were clearly criminal acts—in the course of 1942, when the first major deportations to the nearby gas chambers of Auschwitz took place. But what Klausa may have been thinking at the time and what he actually did were sufficiently far apart for him to receive confirmation of his previously only probationary appointment as Landrat; and he suffered no obvious adverse consequences in his career. Klausa himself later repeatedly asserted that he had made every effort to leave the area because, as he frequently put it in his memoirs, he did not want "innocently to become guilty" (Fulbrook 2012: 8); but he was never able to fully face up to the extent to which he had, in effect, already become guilty.

By compartmentalizing his feelings from his behavior as a bureaucrat, Klausa could later represent himself as a man of inner decency and honor. Still, the historical records show that he played an efficient part in the destruction of the Jewish community for which he held responsibility. Klausa baulked somewhat at the final stages of extermination; but even the everyday anti-Semitism of a Nazi functionary prepared the conditions for genocide. For many people who acted to sustain the Nazi regime, inner feelings and outer behavior did not always match.

Failure to make connections between interior and exterior worlds—between internal hesitations and self-distancing, on the one hand, and actual behaviors and their systemic consequences, on the other—has analytic significance beyond this particular case. At stake here is the possibility of playing a specific role in a genocidal system while still assuming that one could remain fundamentally a decent human being and registering a degree of inner doubt. It was sufficient for Nazi goals—to destroy the Jewish community one way or another—if Germans like Klausa conformed to the Nazi frame of reference and acted, for the most part, according to its precepts (more generally Fulbrook 2011; McMillan 2014). These particular practices of self helped the complex institutional machinery of genocide to work well.

Similar tales could be told about so many other Germans. For many, it was only in the course of 1942 that everyday anti-Semitism and the more radical, murderous, so-called eliminationist anti-Semitism (Goldhagen 1996) parted company. At this stage, many functionaries, facilitators, and beneficiaries of Nazi racial rule became uncomfortable, realizing the ends to which policies had led; and yet they still felt constrained to continue to conform, or appear to conform, to the scripts required of them. Different people of course responded in different ways, and some were clearly more committed than others. But their possible inner feelings of unease often figure more prominently in retrospective accounts than in any archival evidence of the time. And it does not really mitigate the fact that most continued to do their jobs, which was, in the end, all that was necessary for the genocide to continue.

There were also gendered aspects of the ways in which different roles could demand varying degrees of conformity or elicit different kinds of practice. The logic of involvement seems to have worked somewhat differently for women, who did not themselves have official roles but were present at the front line of violence, for example, the wives of SS officers. If the actions of a Nazi functionary such as Klausa can be explained in terms of a combination of careerism, cowardice, and possibly a degree of courage in seeking to get out of an increasingly unbearable situation, the same is not true of a few outstanding female perpetrators who seem in some ways to have relished the chance to mimic the brutal actions of male perpetrators who were close to them.

In 1942 when SS officer Gustav Willhaus was offered an opportunity in the East, he brought his wife Elisabeth and child with him. He was assigned to the Janowska camp near Lviv, where he quickly gained a reputation as the "bloodthirsty camp commandant" as survivor Stepan Yakimovich Shenfeld recollected in 1943 (2008). The Willhaus family lived in the special SS settlement at the camp's perimeter in a custom-built home. Elisabeth requested a large balcony, which provided a view of her husband's workplace. Janowska was situated at a former machine factory and had a good railway connection to Lublin and the newly established gassing facility of Belzec. Hundreds of thousands of Polish and Ukrainian Jews died in Janowska or passed through it on the way to Belzec and Sobibor, making it the biggest Jewish labor and transit camp in

Ukraine according to today's borders. In effect, her family inhabited a porous border, along an axis of traffic, for the institutions of genocide.

Yet it is how she chose to interact with the people in that situation that contributed most directly to making her world part of this larger system of genocidal violence. From the balcony of their family home, Elisabeth Willhaus observed the laborers at work in the camp and in her garden below. In fact, according to survivor testimony and the foundational research of historian and survivor Philip Friedman, Willhaus and his family killed the prisoners for the "'sport' of it" (1980: 311; Lower 2013).

> Willhaus's wife, Otilia [sic] also had a pistol. When guests came to visit the Willhaus family, and sat on the spacious porch of their luxurious house, Otilia [sic] would show off her marksmanship by shooting down camp inmates, to the delight of her guests. The little daughter of the family, Heike, would vigorously applaud the sight.

One account has Heike shooting at "Jewish targets" with a pistol supplied by her parents as a birthday gift (Yones 2004).

Liesel (i.e., Elisabeth) Willhaus displayed an utter lack of regard for the value of a Jewish life. Her behavior in the East seems to have been shaped by Nazi frames of reference that included both anti-Semitic premises and individual ambitions. She was raised a Catholic and wished to baptize her child in the Catholic Church, against the wishes and orders of her husband's SS superiors. It is possible that her anti-Semitism combined traditional religious and modern racial ideas.

In the biographical information in her SS marriage application, it is also clear that she and her husband came from working-class backgrounds and saw the Nazi movement as their chance for social mobility. Her husband Gustav's post at Janowska was a promotion. He wielded enormous power over the victims who passed through this camp, the largest one in Ukraine. In fact Gustav was extremely sadistic, entertaining his colleagues and showing off his power by concocting various forms of torture that became local spectacles of Jewish suffering. Liesel followed her husband's lead; but in the setting of their home, she shot from her balcony, a space where everyday rituals of meals and afternoon coffee and cake became staging areas for murder (Lower 2013).

What normalizes this system of genocidal violence is precisely the fact that these perpetrators, including women, embedded it within their everyday practices of self. A similar scene took place at the home of Gertrude and Felix Landau. Not far from the Willhaus villa, the Landaus established their home in Drohobycz in eastern Galicia. According to the testimony of a Jewish survivor, on Sunday afternoon 14 June 1942, the Landaus were playing cards on the balcony. Gertrude wore a bathing suit. A small group of Jewish men and women worked in the garden below, spreading soil.

At one point Felix got up abruptly and grabbed his rifle. He started to shoot birds. Gertrude also gave it a try. At this point either Gertrude or Felix turned the rifle down on to their Jewish gardeners and shot a worker named Fliegner. According to Marjan Nadel, who was working in the garden, Felix wanted to show off in front of his lover. They laughed as they left the balcony and reentered the house. Additional testimony against Gertrude revealed that she ordered the deaths of three maids and also trampled a Jewish child to death (Schwarz 2001: 205–6; Judgement, 16 March 1962, qtd. in Rüter and de Mildt 2010: 364–65).

The balcony of a villa was also the setting for an incident with another SS couple in eastern Galicia. When the SS wife Erna Petri served coffee and cake there, she overheard the SS police officers, her husband's colleagues, as they discussed the mass shootings of Jews. They explained the proper method. Erna later experimented with her own pistol when she shot six Jewish children who had fled a transport headed to a gassing center. They were hiding on her SS estate. After the war, she explained to East German interrogators on 19 September 1961 why she had killed them:

> In those times, as I carried out the shootings, I was barely 23 years old, still young and inexperienced. I lived only under men, who were in the SS and carried out shootings of Jewish persons. I seldom came into contact with other women, so that in the course of this time I became more hardened, desensitized. I did not want to stand behind the SS men. I wanted to show them that I, as a woman, could conduct myself like a man. So I shot 4 Jews and 6 Jewish children. I wanted to prove myself to the men. Besides in those days in this region, everywhere one heard that Jewish persons and children were being shot, which also caused me to kill them. (BStU 000050-57)

Note that this story, itself a practice of self, focuses attention on the storyteller: it concerns the murder of Jewish children only insofar as those actions said something about Erna. Here narrative strategies of memory reflect the earlier practices in which she shot Jewish children in order to prove herself to the SS men including her husband. When pressed by the East German prosecutor during her interrogation about how she, "as a mother of 2 children, could shoot innocent Jewish children," Erna replied:

> I am unable to grasp at this time how in those days that I was in such a state as to conduct myself so brutally and reprehensibly—shooting Jewish children. However earlier [before arriving to the estate in Ukraine] I had been so conditioned to fascism and the racial laws, which established a view toward the Jewish people. As was told to me, I had to destroy the Jews. It was from this mindset that I came to commit such a brutal act. (BStU 000050-57)

Whereas we certainly believe that she fit her actions into the Nazi frame of reference, the evidence from these various stories, when taken together, suggests a more convincing explanation for how that adaptation to Nazi norms took place: through microsocial interactions as ordinary as sunbathing, playing cards, eating cake, drinking coffee, shooting birds, and shooting Jewish children.

When it comes to these violent acts of self-fashioning, we are reminded of the case of Luzie Halata. She too wanted to prove herself to the authority figures she wished to impress. Beating, even murdering Jewish children became equated with a form of self-expression as much as it was a demonstration of loyalty and conformity to Nazism. And in this unusual case, Erna also displayed a desire to exceed what was expected of her as a woman. Erna's father had given her his World War I pistol out of concern for her safety in the wild East. She was supposed to use it to protect herself. Instead she used it, like the men around her, to shoot defenseless Jews. In this case, overfulfilling her role helped the entire system of genocide work well.

Building Empires

In the Nazi East, a new, violent world was built with remarkable speed. In it, the Germans could, with local help, escort thousands in broad daylight across cities and villages to nearby fields, where they were murdered, or deport them to dedicated sites of extermination—and then erase the traces of these crimes thereafter. But what from hindsight seems like a well-orchestrated system was, when observed from close proximity, the result of a far more complex process of appropriation and allocation. What made the Holocaust so effective as a system of mass destruction is the fact that the perpetrators coordinated their efforts independently and in excess of central instructions.

This account of a genocidal *Alltag* in the Nazi East does not ignore the role of policy making at the centers of power—a story familiar to many contemporary readers. Rather, we view these violent policies first and foremost in terms of how they were implemented on the ground. This perspective draws our attention to the complex interplay between what was possible at any given time and the consequences of everyday practices that, though apparently small in themselves, cumulatively produced a continual deterioration in the living conditions and social circumstances of Jews. There were of course many other factors that contributed to genocide; but what we notice most in the evidence presented here is the role played by face-to-face social relations.

The Third Reich was designed with the inherently political goal in mind of fashioning a racially pure German nation–state supported by the resources of a racial empire. Hitler's Germany legitimized mass murder; and in an everyday, even intimate manner, the interactions of ordinary German men and women effectively normalized it. Thus, the division of labor among male and female workers, policy makers, and administrators as well as the dynamic of personal relationships, liaisons, and marriages were all part of the sociopolitical fabric of the *Volksgemeinschaft*—an inherently political, and ultimately criminal, enterprise.

The Holocaust marked a rupture in very many ways, but not least because of the way that its violence was embedded in everyday life. The murders described in this chapter were not isolated incidents but part and parcel of a violent world created in the Nazi East. That system of violence interrupted the lives of millions of people and engulfed the globe in a war of extermination. Yet it was grounded in the acts of German men and women who chose to authorize themselves not just to dominate and expropriate but to murder others they deemed less than human. Even those who benefited only indirectly from this system of violence, through plunder for instance, still embedded that genocidal violence in their everyday lives.

In a remarkable contradiction, these self-authorizations allowed both for self-fashioning and for denying their own agency in the process of making themselves into what they became. These practices of self thus marked a disruption in history and memory that created lasting challenges when postwar Germans tried to make sense of their individual biographies and collective prosopography. The rupture lay not simply with destruction and loss per se, but with the fact that the practiced self was now tied inextricably to genocidal violence—as its object, its subject, or some of both.

The violence of the Holocaust developed in explicit and intimate as well as direct and indirect ways. The power and status that the Aryan pioneers in the East possessed over the life of a Jew—branded an enemy of the Reich, an odious racial defect, and a contemptuous creature—was enormous and for many irresistible. One could impress a mate, friend, neighbor, or co-worker by laying claim to this authority over life and death. In the killing fields of Ukraine, Belarus, Poland, and the Baltics, humiliating and brutalizing Jews became a public spectacle. It was in its basic form an expression of anti-Semitic hatred, but the life and death of a Jew also became a function of everyday desires, needs, and ambitions. In retrospect such petty motives are easy to dismiss when compared with anti-Semitic hatred, Nazi ideology, or sadism. But the mundane and the grandiose intermingled on the ground.

We zoom in on those moments when Germans and their collaborators first took action on the ground. They drew social and spatial distinctions between human beings as a precondition for both exterminating some of them while also claiming to know nothing about those crimes—indeed for seeing themselves in some sense as victims of the system. These reorderings of the social space sometimes took place, surprisingly, in anticipation of the German invaders or their policy aspirations; yet they were always worked out through microsocial interactions. Herein lies the benefit of viewing events like the Holocaust on the ground. An *Alltag* approach shows how Germans, with the help of many collaborators, located and then normalized genocidal violence in particular places and, in the process, connected their small biographies to big wars of extermination.

Michaela Christ, Mary Fulbrook, and Wendy Lower

CHAPTER 9

Taking Place

If it were up to the fanatics, I couldn't even see my friend that I went to school with for years. I believe the craziness in our village doesn't approach what's going on along the rest of the zonal border. But we already know to help ourselves. We did not want this stupid border!
—A West German in divided Mödlareuth, quoted in Hilmar Pabel, *Quick*, 1951.

In the preceding chapters, we explored the microsocial interactions that produced a variety of German institutions, policies, and worlds. Many were violent. Many were authorized in part or in principle by others. But the key to making them work *well* was the fact that people authorized themselves to fulfill or even to overfulfill those tasks, with both conformist and nonconformist motives, in coordination with and resistance to larger systems. In this chapter, we continue our exploration of the ways in which Germans coordinated their actions in their life world with global dynamics. We focus on how the practices of laying claim to and challenging *authority*—which the authors of this chapter understand as power with legitimacy—transforms abstract space into an everyday place.

As we noted in the chapter on interpersonal relationships, we understand *place* as created when particular spaces are invested with a specific meaning. We now take up that issue again but with attention to this question of authorization. Effective authority must *take place* in the sense of inscribing the everyday with its symbolic and material effects. Insofar as certain features of the everyday are authorized, they all must take place on the ground. For us, taking place means both the happening of a historical event on the ground and an often-contested process of colonizing particular spaces for purposes of power.

Authority presents itself normatively as providing a fixed foundation for everyday life in terms of law and order, so people often experience insecurity as an extraordinary and temporary rupture in its smooth functioning. Yet ruptures in themselves are not always evidence of the failure of authority. Ruptures can also derive from authorized political initiatives, as we have seen in prior chapters. So it would be more accurate to understand ruptures as part and parcel of the everyday political process. Disruptions arise on the ground as individuals, social groups, and states struggle for status, power, and resources.

We treat everyday spaces as sites where authority is chronically insecure. Our three examples of this process are strange bedfellows, particularly in contrast to the last chapters, in which the examples all seemed to fit naturally. Our new examples include tense negotiations at Atlantic trading posts, violence along a militarized border, and the sociability of informal gatherings on the margins of socialist society. Given their normative expectations for what authority should look like, Europeans experienced a sense of disruption when trading in West Africa in the seventeenth century; daily life seemed similarly disrupted by the new inner-German border after 1945; and changes in gay and lesbian self-understanding seemed to disrupt life in East Berlin in the 1970s and 1980s. As we will demonstrate, however, these microsocial interactions in fact ensured that authority worked well in all of these cases.

Viewed globally, the disruptions at these sites seem to have been caused by wider geopolitical and social processes: the rise of the early modern Atlantic economy, the Cold War, and social movements of identity and liberation. Viewed from close up, however, these disruptions seem to have arisen from personal interactions among those claiming, legitimizing, and contesting authority. It is a mistake to prioritize one of these perspectives over the other. Authority is exercised, experienced, and disrupted in local spaces through microsocial interactions; yet these local events are also part and parcel of larger macrosocial dynamics. *How then do we make sense of everyday life simultaneously from these multiple perspectives?*

Our response to this question has been to treat everyday life as a product of multiple wills and multiple acts of apprehension. We reject the notion of a single objective perspective or authoritative account. This statement holds true for scholarly interpretations of the *Alltag* as well. Two of the ways that scholars view events—the *micro* and the *macro*—map roughly onto the distinction between the *life world* of our apprehensions and the *larger world* beyond them. But they are only two, and we cannot presume in advance that either is better.

To our growing list of options, we would like to introduce another set: *insiders* and *outsiders*. These terms are similar to the ones used by ethnographers to distinguish between the *emic* perspective of people within a culture and the *etic* perspective of the scholar who participates and observes that culture (Harris 1988: 131–33). In the way we are using them here and now, however, insiders do not necessarily share a common culture and outsiders are never truly objective. In our usage, insiders are simply those who inhabit the life world while making sense of it—a life world that outsiders view from elsewhere.

Policymakers, bureaucrats, and officers of public and private institutions can be outsiders, insiders, or both. Their perspective depends on the positions they take to these events: not just on their physical location in core or peripheral offices but also on their intentions and practices. Like all features of the everyday, these categories are both dynamic and porous.

We have seen that it was not sufficient for outsiders to explore or conquer a territory in order to have effective control over everyday life. Military, political, or economic invasion was only the first step toward making a space into a place where they could exercise legitimate authority. We have also seen how outsiders inhabiting a larger world required the cooperation of insiders in the life world for their policies to be effective. Policies manifest themselves in everyday life as much when nonconformists make use of them temporarily for their own purposes as when supporters implement them directly.

Insiders understand these everyday dynamics from experience. Sometimes they use their hands-on knowledge to assert control over their life world or create parallel worlds of security and autonomy. Sometimes they report the events they witness to distant outsiders, enabling the latter to respond to them. Those responses from outsiders may or may not be practical responses to the realities on the inside.

A crucial aspect of asserting one's authority over, and perhaps also one's autonomy within, a space is therefore phenomenological: acts of apprehending, imagining, and depicting that space as a place imbued with particular characteristics. Events take place in this sense: of being represented by an insider for the benefit of outsiders. Yet the forms taken by these *representations of space* (Lefebvre 1991) are as important as their content. Maps can serve as a *technology of power* (Harley 1988); the same can be said of reports, dossiers, memoranda, charts, statistics, and images.

These forms both connote authority in their normative status as objective representations and facilitate authority through what they enable authorities to do to space. Social processes further authorize these forms: the fact that they are sent, stamped, published, sold, and archived, not to mention found by scholars and turned into scholarship. These representational strategies allow outsiders and insiders to take place in the more subtle sense of asserting control over the unruly life world to which these texts refer.

In our case studies, we will be reading documents written by officers of state bureaucracies in various degrees of development. They exerted authority over unruly spaces by adopting an allegedly external, objective, and rational perspective about it. Moreover, they imagined, described, and depicted it in purportedly authoritative texts—in our cases, official travel accounts, military police reports, and secret police dossiers. These official accounts are certainly useful as evidence of what may have happened on the ground, but we are more interested in what they tell us about their anxieties concerning the disruption of authority and their attempts to reassert it over that space. Outsiders often relied on these multiple layers of authorization in order to feel a sense of control over an everyday life that stubbornly refused to conform.

We should not overstate the significance of local disorder. Not all instances of peripheral disorder matters for the core. Or more precisely, authorities sometimes chose to ignore much of the unruliness of everyday life—because it contributes to authority working well, because they do not wish to recognize the gaps in their legitimacy, or for both reasons. Disruptions in local settings are only dangerous to larger systems of power when insiders or outsiders make those connections. Sometimes it was the insiders who give these events larger significance while the outsiders played it down; other times these roles were switched. Yet there were few settings in the modern Germanies that were not being actively shaped and transformed—sometimes violently—by global processes. What makes these three sites appropriate for study here is that they were also being treated as events with larger ramifications.

How did these insiders or outsiders make these connections between the local and the global? They did so, simply, by mapping local issues onto broader ones and vice versa. They read the contours of everyday life on their local map as the same contours inscribed on global maps. It was the same ground after all; they were just looking at it using a different scale (Herod 2010). Our proposition: we too can see these complex connections between local and global interactions in everyday life if we view the life world and the larger world as the same topography on different scales, so that we do not have to make a distinction between micro and macro, life world and larger world. This way of viewing the everyday recognizes that the same contours are always present on both the global and the local scales. Viewing them on the ground allows us to see them for their own sake and in relation to one another.

In order to demonstrate this multiscale approach to the practices of authorizing a self, we provide examples for the reader from three very different times and places. Including an example from early modern Germans in Africa is perhaps the most jarring juxtaposition in a book that is mostly focused on the twentieth century. But including earlier practices will enable us to identify some continuities and changes in the way state authority takes place.

These three spaces are German only in a transnational sense. As we did in places from Mecklenburg-Vorpommern to Berlin, and from Los Angeles to Berditschew, we follow Germans as they move beyond the borders of Germany proper; along external, interstitial, and internal trajectories; and as they navigate borders of German states, nations, and empires that are porous and dynamic. Moving to less familiar sites may in turn encourage the reader to test our approach on other examples in German studies and beyond. Our guiding question: *how do authors—authorized by states, authorizing themselves, or some combination of both—imagine the spaces over which they are trying to exert authority?*

Unstable Claims

In the authoritative accounts of these sites, a clear theme emerges: unease over the absence of clear contours of authority. This anxiety led to attempts to articulate how authority should appear and function in daily life. In response, insiders and outsiders not only described these places but also inscribed their authority onto these contested spaces. These events certainly took place historically, but we have access to them thanks to these practical efforts to extend authority into everyday life. These practices took place not only in the sense of boots on the ground but also by authoring written texts and visual images that asserted authority over an unruly geography.

The first such text was the 1682–83 travel account of the Prussian Junker Otto Friedrich von der Groeben of Brandenburg-Prussia. Based on his official report of 1683, Groeben recounted his journey to the Gold Coast in a 1694 publication titled *Guineische Reise-Beschreibung*. Contemporaries used the term *Guinea* to refer to the Grain Coast, Ivory Coast, Gold Coast, and the Slave Coast, that is, the West African coastline from Sierra Leone to the Bight of Benin. In his text, we see a taste for adventure and colorful description as well as a certain cavalier interest in sex, gender, and marriage. Groeben also liked to ascribe certain customs to Africans in order to comment on and criticize supposed European shortcomings. Foremost in Groeben's narrative, however, are questions of secular or political authority.

This focus on authority should come as no surprise. He came from an early modern German territorial state, Brandenburg-Prussia, itself in the process of building a stronger central authority. It is also important to remember that this principality is the classic example of state building in the early modern period. In the early eighteenth century, shortly after this publication, Prussia emerged as a Great Power on the European stage. His interest in authority also makes sense given the fact that Groeben entered into an interstitial area of contact between African and European states where political authority was dispersed and disputed. It is therefore an ideal case for understanding how authority took place in the early modern world.

In regard to trade, the contrast between home and away was even sharper. The Brandenburger African Company (BAC) was born of *mercantilism:* the economic system in which European states claimed the authority to regulate trade and commerce both internally and with their colonies. Among the diverse societies of the West African coast, however, trade was extraordinarily difficult for African or European rulers to control, tax, or direct. As the BAC officials instructed Mattheus de Voss—captain of the frigate *Churprinz von Brandenburg* that brought Groeben to Africa—on 17 May 1682:

> When they arrive, they shall see if there is any trade to be done quickly on the Grain and Ivory Coasts and buy what they think fit. They shall then run on to the Gold Coast and, keeping a mile away from all Dutch, English, French, Danish, etc. company forts, trading posts and castles, shall anchor and trade there in peace. (A. Jones 1985: 19)

Trade was self-regulated, based on trust and mutual advantage. Merchants could appeal to no certain authority in cases of conflict.

For the Africans with whom he traded, Groeben was of course an outsider; but for the Europeans who read his book, he was an insider who spoke about events in Africa from his life experience. Early on, Groeben described his sense of insecurity in the absence of state authority. On the advice of his captain, de Voss, who was experienced with trade in West Africa, Groeben and a trading party went ashore unarmed at Cape Mesurado in Sierra Leone. After "trading amicably" with the people there, Groeben began to fear that he and his men would be captured and held for ransom—or worse: "Indeed, they could have also cut off all our heads (after receiving the ransom) and no one would have cared less" (1694: 39).

To Groeben, this place in Sierra Leone seemed devoid of authority: no one would have raised an alarm if the party had been attacked, and no authority would enforce any laws against robbery or murder. Groeben's party did not actually experience such disturbances—at least not yet. Yet Groeben clearly expected to find a space permeated by authority, and his account captures his sense of surprise at its absence. He chose to represent this encounter with a reworked image of New World cannibalism titled *Tractirung der Blancen* (*Treatment of the Whites*), as seen in Illustration 9.1.

A week later, Groeben finally found some semblance of authority. He reported with evident relief his encounter with an actual king in the Sestos River region. "We went ashore in the longboat and found the king (who called himself Peter) by the river, sitting within a hut of the Blacks … He was a venerable old man, in whose eyes one could read something great." This ruler wielded the kind of authority Groeben expected to see in everyday life.

Yet the king's authority was not marked by any symbols that Groeben recognized. "Otherwise," Groeben wrote, "he was not to be distinguished from those other Blacks by anything (for the clothing was all the same), except the respect which those sitting around and all his subjects paid him." Groeben described the disjuncture between symbols and the exercise of authority: "Indeed, his [King Peter's] authority was so great that when a bottle of brandy was stolen from our boat by the Blacks and we did not know who was the

Taking Place ›~ 233

Illustration 9.1. *Treatment of the Whites*. Illustration in Groeben, *Guineische Reise-Beschreibung*, 1694. Staatsbibliothek zu Berlin—PK, http://resolver.staatsbibliothek-berlin.de/SBB0001027B00000000.

thief among so many hundreds, a single word from the king restored it to us" (Groeben 1694: 45).

Groeben was so impressed by King Peter that he included an engraving of him in the published edition of the *Guineische Reise-Beschreibung* (Illustration 9.2). He depicted Peter in classic imperial garb based on his own

Illustration 9.2. *King Peter of Rio Sesder*. Illustration in Groeben, *Guineische Reise-Beschreibung*, 1694. Staatsbibliothek zu Berlin—PK, http://resolver.staatsbibliothek-berlin.de/SBB0001027B00000000.

sketch. Here at last was authority, expressed in direct and personal terms. By portraying King Peter like a Roman emperor, Groeben brought the possessor of authority back into line with symbols recognizable to a European. Finding himself again in a place structured by authority came as an immense relief to Groeben. Though an outsider, he felt he understood his place.

Groeben's authoritative narrative of his travels reinscribed authority into this interstitial borderland of European and African interaction. That he did so in terms of his own culture befits his position as outsider; still he presented it to his European audience as an insider. These events took place as historical events thanks to this authorial narration and aesthetic representation; it also enabled him to reassert at least discursive control over a geopolitical place that contravened his expectations for authority. Even so, early modern states almost by definition struggle with asserting authority.

Let us compare this case, then, to a modern borderland in a similar state of disorder to see if the same dynamics are true of modern states. After the defeat of the Third Reich in 1945, the Allies occupied Central Europe and divided Germany into zones of occupation. Both the Soviet Union and the United States more or less formally colonized their respective sides of Central Europe. The middle of Germany became a new frontier (Berdahl 1999; Port 2007; Sheffer 2007: 307–39, 2011: esp. 17–117; Eckert 2011; Hauptmeyer, Schmiechen-Ackermann, and Schwark 2011; Henke 2011; Schaefer 2011a, 2011b, 2012: 116–31, 2014: 18–57, esp. 56; J. Johnson, 2017, esp. ch. 1), a frontier of two Cold War empires.

In 1949, the 800-mile inner-German border between the Soviet and the Western zones also became the boundary between the two German states, the FRG and the GDR, as well as the *Länder* of Thuringia in the GDR and Bavaria in the FRG. Between 1945 and 1949, part of this border even ran along the frontier between two German counties—Hof County in Bavaria and Schleiz County in Thuringia. That is, the same border distinguished social and geopolitical spaces on multiple scales.

Consider the village of Mödlareuth, which was divided in half by this border. This farming community of around one hundred people was split down the center such that it was shared by both counties, both German states, and both Cold War empires. Thuringian and Bavarian border troops guarded their respective sides, supported and supervised by American and Soviet occupation troops. For these foreign troops, this posting was remote. They found themselves stationed in the hinterland of the border zone, and a hinterland of these two Germanies. Meanwhile, local German residents—Bavarians in the west in Hof County and Thuringians in the east in Schleiz County—found themselves living on either side of this new so-called Iron Curtain. Both strangers and natives to Mödlareuth were insiders when it came to witnessing how the Cold War played out on the ground.

Precisely because the locals did not always respect this remote stretch of the inner-German border, it became the subject of reports written by local authorities in both counties to two kinds of outsiders: their German administrative superiors in the county seats as well as the two occupying powers. We looked at the records from 1945 and 1952, when Schleiz County along with Thuringia was absorbed into new administrative units as part of a general reorganization of municipal and regional government. As in West Africa, we found evidence in Mödlareuth of microsocial interactions involving outsiders and insiders that suggested a fluid and dynamic border. Also as Groeben discovered far from home, both insiders and outsiders discovered in Mödlareuth a disturbing lack of authority along this major geopolitical frontier.

The records of the Bavarian Border Police—called the Landesgrenzpolizei or Grenzpolizei (GrePo)—are housed in Munich (BayHStAM). There, one of our authors studied reproductions of reports submitted to the Präsidium der Bayerischen Grenzpolizei (PrBayGrePo) by the local Hof County GrePo that patrolled the western side of the border. These documents were often translated into English and forwarded to the U.S. military government in Bavaria, which had reformed and reestablished the state's border police in November 1945 (Herger 2004). The GrePo accounts describe everyday life on the border as a series of violent disturbances. In these authoritative reports, police reasserted control over this unruly space.

As far as the Hof County GrePo were concerned, the Soviet occupation troops guarding the eastern side of the frontier were responsible for many problems (Naimark 1995; Satjukow 2008; Sheffer 2011: 39–41). Consider their report from 23 April 1946 to the PrBayGrePo (Nr. 1365). The Russian troops used the distance from their commanders in order to get drunk, "plunder," and run amok along the frontier. On 25 May 1948, the GrePo reported another incident (1366). A Russian soldier had showed up drunk in a county borderland village, part of the American zone of occupation at the time, shooting his pistol. A resident described the incident:

> At 7:30 p.m. on May 9, a Russian soldier appeared with a stick and with the stick knocked sharply at the fence whereby he shouted at the top of his voice. When I heard this I went to the yard and asked him what he wanted. He did not reply. When the soldier came into the yard the dog barked at him. The Russian drew his pistol and fired three shots at the dog without hitting him. Then the Russian entered the house, took my bike, and rode away on it.

The drunken, trigger-happy Soviet soldier then proceeded to another residence, where he entered the yard, wanting to enter the home. He drew his pistol at the resident's dog and "wanted to shoot at the dog." The resident, with the help of a few others, was then able to detain the drunken soldier until American officials arrived.

Meanwhile the Cold War was growing tense. The following month, in June 1948, Western authorities instituted a currency reform. Introducing the deutschmark as the new currency for the three Western zones dramatically revived the German economy and helped consolidate these three zones economically. Because the Soviet zone refused to participate in this currency, it also increased economic division between East and West along the border and further heightened illegal crossing (Sheffer 2011: 53–54).

Soon after, Soviet authorities began a blockade of the sectors of Berlin under Western Allied control that continued until mid-May 1949. The Western occupation powers launched an airlift to supply the residents of West Berlin. This crisis—at once of local, national, and global significance—contributed to the rapid deterioration of relations between the Western Allied powers and the Soviet Union, and it helped usher in the creation of two postwar German states. In this global context, a trigger-happy Soviet soldier wreaking havoc on the Western side of the border was cause for more than just local concern.

Another problem for borderland residents was rape by Soviet soldiers. The GrePo reported (1366) that an American soldier brought a fleeing Thuringian border policeman to a GrePo post in the early morning hours of 11 February 1949. The latter recounted this story to explain his flight: while he and a fellow Thuringian border guard were patrolling in the village earlier that night, they heard cries. They rushed to the scene to find two Soviet soldiers. One of them was raping a girl who had come over from the American occupation zone. The two East German guards pulled the Soviets away from the girl; but the Soviet soldiers then responded, with imperial authority, by confiscating the Thuringian policemen's weapons and wallets and forcing them to walk to the Soviet headquarters in a nearby village. It was then that the two Thuringian policemen tried to flee across the border at the edge of Mödlareuth, but the Soviets also crossed the border and, according to one of the Thuringian border guards, "They fired several shots at me while on Bavarian soil."

Soviet soldiers were not the only source for disruptions along the borderland. A U.S. occupation soldier also appeared in the GrePo reports as a troublemaking outsider. The GrePo post in Kirchgattendorf reported on 26 March 1951 how the intoxicated American soldier entered a Hof County GrePo post demanding beer (1367). He then proceeded to the GrePo commander's adjacent private apartment, where he poked his gun into the stomach of the commander's fourteen-year-old son. Authorities arrived soon after, and the soldier was arrested. In May, the Hof County newspaper published that, as a result of the incident, the officer was demoted to the lowest rank, forced to pay a monthly fine of fifty-eight dollars for six months, and assigned to perform hard labor for ninety days.

These incidents show that the inner-German border remained contested. Moreover, these disruptions were not simply a matter of East versus West but were complicated by conflicts between occupiers and the occupied. The local GrePo felt sufficiently harassed by their own allies that they saw fit to report the transgression, a rather risky act given the German position vis-à-vis the Allied forces. Yet if the border zone documented in the GrePo reports was a space of disorder, reporting these events to the outsiders was one way to begin to assert control over them—or at least to call for the outside authorities to do so. Reading between the lines, perhaps they understood that the failure to maintain order had larger implications. Unruly behavior on the border implicated them in multiple crises of authority: for their police units, for their county administrations, for the two new German states, and for the occupation armies. Magnified in this way, these local incidents had the potential to exacerbate a geopolitical conflict.

We find it interesting that the descriptions of the borderlands by Western journalists followed closely along the lines of interpretation offered by the Western border police. Consider the article from 1951, nearly two years after the creation of the two postwar German states, that appeared in the West German magazine *Quick: Illustrierte für Deutschland*. It featured divided Mödlareuth as a case study about life along the inner-German border. The title itself suggests the main point: "Insanity—1,358 km long!" (Pabel 1951: 533–35). In the wake of the currency reform and the blockade of Berlin, East German authorities had increased security along the inner-German border, tightening the Iron Curtain (Sheffer 2011: 50–94, esp. 50, 88–90). The article's author and photographer, Hilmar Pabel, used words such as "inhumane" to describe this border that had led the German people to be "torn" (533). To Pabel and many of his German readers, the border was wrong because it divided the German nation into two different states.

Yet more than anything else, Pabel found confusion along this illegitimate border. The magazine piece included two photographs from Mödlareuth. The first pictured a pair of Volkspolizei—the East German People's Police—chatting in a friendly manner with a couple of West German border guards, presumably GrePo. "In the quiet of this remote place," the caption read, "sometimes a strict ban is transgressed: People's Police talk with the Western police." Pabel went on to report that the Eastern police had said to the Western authorities that they did not believe there would be a war; regardless, "You can rely on us! We certainly will shoot at no Germans!"

These declarations of solidarity with a likely enemy were unruly not just because they were treasonous but also because they posited a German nation that trumped the two competing German states. The first photograph showing cross-border chatting was titled "Rely on the People's Police!" The second was "Don't Rely on the People's Police!" In sharp contrast to the growing polarization between East and West on a global scale, the boundaries between East and West in Mödlareuth were not only porous and transgressive but also elusive and hard to pin down for actors on the ground.

The East Germans and the Soviets imagined the borderlands in very different terms. As the division of Germany began, Schleiz County authorities acknowledged difficulties along the border relating to Soviet troops. As the 1940s came to a close, however, the authors of these reports shifted the responsibility for these difficulties to external and internal antagonists: the West, on the one hand, and perceived opponents within the Soviet zone, on the other. This attempt to shift blame for local problems shows the influence of changing macrosocial relations: the Cold War getting hotter as well as a transition in their thinking toward victimhood. State bureaucrats used their reports and memoranda as weapons in the struggle against those insiders and outsiders intent on threatening the emergent socialist way of life.

In the East, the relevant documents can be found in the State Archive of Thuringia in Greiz (ThStAG). In response to an inquiry from Thuringian officials in Weimar on local conditions, the administrator of Schleiz County (KrLkS) wrote on 7 September 1945 (Nr. 44), "Great difficulties are occurring in the communities that lie along the Bavarian border." He described, for example, that the Soviet border soldiers refused to allow farmers with property in Bavaria to cross the frontier to manage their fields. Interestingly, this county administrator was defending the porousness of the inner-German border against the desires of the occupying force to maintain them more strictly.

Addressing a follow-up inquiry from the Thuringian State Office for Communal Affairs (Landesamt für Kommunalwesen, or LaKw) five months later (KrLkS Nr. 44), the county administrator wrote again (23 February 1946) to declare that the problems still continued. Six days prior, he reported, he had held a meeting of the mayors in the county. A Soviet representative from the commandant's headquarters promised that everything possible would be done to remedy the problems. "I do not believe, however, that the county's local Soviet commandant will succeed," the county administrator wrote. He then requested that the matter be presented to the Soviet Military Administration of Germany in Weimar.

The issue, however, was largely resolved a few months later, or at least that is how the administrator in Schleiz County depicted it. By 11 June 1946, he wrote to the LaKw, saying, "The difficulties created by the [Soviet] border troops and the NKVD [Narodnyy Komissariat Vnutrennikh Del; or People's Commissariat for Internal Affairs] are no longer frequent. There are encroachments here and there which lead to unpleasant consequences." He outlined cases of borderland farmers who needed to cross the border for work-related purposes, but he claimed that overall there were only "minor problems" that could be handled locally.

The Eastern bureaucratic image of the borderland contrasted sharply with the Western. In the East, the authorities noted initial problems caused by the

Soviets but depicted them as having decreased. Overall, the Eastern authorities seemed to represent the border as more secure and orderly than the West did. Perhaps the local administrator censored his report in order to avoid appearing too critical of the Soviets. Or perhaps the difference lay in the relative claims of legitimacy of the two German states: the Western authorities treated the border as disorderly in order to delegitimize the GDR, while the Eastern ones represented it as orderly to show the viability of the GDR.

By early 1948, in the context of the Cold War getting hotter, top Thuringian officials began to shift blame for local border problems to the Western authorities (Sheffer 2011: 41). Here we turn to documents located in the Thüringisches Hauptstaatsarchiv Weimar (ThHStAW). A statement from the Thuringian Ministry of Interior titled "Criminal Machinations on the Zone Border" appeared in late March 1948 in the *Thüringer Volk* (ThHStAW Nr. 1129), the regional newspaper of the SED, which would soon be the ruling party of the GDR.

In it, the minister described interviews with those who had illegally fled into the Soviet zone. These interviews revealed that they came east because the Western zones were in a constant state of social and economic emergency. The minister added that, between December 1947 and March 1948, the Soviet zone border troops reported that more than 74,000 people had fled from the British and American zones. Though most of these people came to the East to find food and work, some, the statement claimed, came to wreak havoc in the Soviet zone.

This Thuringian administrator suggested that the West was responsible not only for disorder on the border but for threatening the stability of the Soviet zone. If there were dissenters in the zone who questioned its legitimacy, his report implied, at least some were saboteurs infiltrating from the West. This representation of everyday life was factually specious. It was contradicted by the ministry's own internal activity report, called a Tätigkeitsbericht (ThHStAW, 1131). During the ten-day period from 1 to 10 June 1948, it calculated, the Thuringian Border Police apprehended a total of about 9,500 illegal border crossers, but roughly 87 percent of them were living in the Soviet zone. The Eastern authorities seemingly represented the disorder on the border as connected to the West in order to bolster their fledgling authority.

These administrative and journalistic reports about the border came at a crucial moment, when these two Germanies were emerging as independent states; and we should read them in terms of those state-building projects. At the end of July 1949, in the wake of the creation of the FRG and two months before the establishment of the GDR, the Schleiz County administration sent instructions to the roughly one hundred community mayors and local councils across the county. Officially, it concerned "the participation of the population in the administration of Schleiz County" (ThStAG, KrLkS, Nr. 98), but there was more at stake. A high degree of participation by the population in municipal government would have sent the message that the county population recognized the legitimacy and supported the functioning of the GDR state on the ground and where it mattered most—along the border.

Unfortunately, that is not the feedback that the center in Schleiz received from the periphery. One mayor from Raila wrote back on 9 September, "The involvement of the population in the meetings of the municipal council is on average very low" (ThStAG, KrLkS, Nr. 98). He offered this explanation: "The reason probably lies in the fact that the population is predominately engaged in agriculture and is not interested in other daily issues" (idem). On 7 September, the mayor of Oberböhmsdorf gave a similar report: "The population participates very little in the local administration. They have no interest in doing so" (idem).

On the same day, the mayor and community council of East Mödlareuth responded briefly. In Mödlareuth, they characterized "the cooperation" between village officials and residents as "good." Still, there "are no concrete suggestions made" (idem). Many reports read simply *Fehlanzeige*, which translates roughly as *no returns* and means that they too have nothing to report. These villagers were making it clear to the county administration that they wished to keep the GDR at a safe distance.

It makes sense that the insiders in places like East Mödlareuth wanted to keep the party, state, and occupation authorities off their back. Yet in order to attempt to negotiate this border, they had to at least formally recognize its existence. By 21 March 1952, the Schleiz County administration issued a "confidential" internal report to the mayors of the county that bore the title "New Work Methods of the Opposition" (ThStAG, KrLkS, Nr. 96). Accordingly, the Schleiz County authorities continued to monitor perceived enemy activity in the borderland. The upper echelons of the GDR and Soviet administration knew how to read these local reports for the more effective policing of the inner-German border that they officially authorized as well as the unofficial unruliness they disguised.

What can then be said of boundaries within the state? Consider the gay and lesbian scene in East Berlin in the decade before the fall of the Wall. It is useful to us for comparison precisely because of its position at once solidly within and yet also dangerously outside the boundaries of state authority. During the 1980s, the East German Ministry for State Security (MfS) launched a program of intense surveillance of gay and lesbian activity in East Berlin (McLellan 2011). This program was not an attempt to prevent same-sex sexual activity, which had been decriminalized in 1968 (Grau 1999, 2002; J. Evans 2010). Rather, it was a reaction to a wave of renewed gay activism under the auspices of the Protestant Church.

The state had demarcated spaces for the Protestant Church and, on a much more limited scale, for gay men and lesbians. A handful of bars had been tolerated since the 1960s. It was the confluence or overlap of these two spaces and the collision of two different scales—one for a large institution, the other for seemingly isolated individuals—that caused concern to GDR authorities. They feared that gay and lesbian citizens were creating networks, organizations, and activities outside state control. This new cooperation between the Protestant Church and gay men and lesbians disrupted the state's understanding of everyday space in East Berlin. They responded with efforts to police the internal border of the state.

Curiously, the MfS files on gay and lesbian East Berlin contain pages of photographs of deserted streets, devoid of the very people the MfS were attempting to observe. Discos and church meeting rooms were mapped in pedantic detail. Yet all this documentation seemed to miss, spectacularly, the human dimensions of these spaces—and the reason they were considered to be so threatening to the socialist state. For the activists who found and claimed such spaces, they were sites of sociability, community building, political consciousness raising, and potential sexual connection. Instead, MfS officers produced a picture of an oddly depopulated city.

Consider for instance the images in Illustration 9.3. They come from the surveillance of the Bekenntniskirche in Berlin-Treptow, which was the meeting place of "gays in the Church," as well as the youth club on Veteranenstrasse, Berlin-Mitte, which was the meeting place of the "Sunday Club" (BStU, MfS-HA XX/9, Nr. 1680). Such photographs and diagrams were mirrored in the lifeless prose of the reports of the MfS officers. They conceived of these places solely in terms of their material dimensions and of their potential to yield further surveillance opportunities. These maps hardly seem a technology of power: they appeared to serve little purpose, beyond the activity of mapping itself. Here the forms of power have become formalities, intended only to reassure authorities of their authority. Through surveillance, the MfS attempted to control the city—yet the objects of their attention remained curiously elusive.

Across these disparate spaces—hybrid urban sites of surveillance, a Cold War borderland, and precolonial West Africa—the absence of authority is seen as a fundamental problem by those who sought to describe and control these spaces. The view from the outside focused on a shared expectation of authority and an uneasiness at its absence. Even those whom one might assume to be in control of the situation felt the need for authority to structure and show them their place in the game. Yet it would be a mistake to divide too rigidly between the authorities and their subjects, the outsiders and insiders, the authors and the objects of these reports. These people all moved dynamically between these positions in response to changing local and global

Illustration 9.3. Surveillance Photographs, Area around the Youth Club at Veteranenstrasse, Meeting Place of the Sonntagsclub, Berlin-Mitte, 1986. BStU, MfS-HA XX/9, 1680, Foto 46. Courtesy of BStU.

conditions. Authority arose in this context: in the turmoil and uncertainty of everyday life.

The Local and the Global

A small village like Mödlareuth seems to epitomize the local. Stalin, Churchill, and Truman had almost certainly never heard of Mödlareuth or its neighboring villages. Here, though, among the fields and forests, a deadly border emerged, one that disrupted centuries-old economic and social ties in these ancient little communities. Philip Shabecoff, a journalist from the *New York Times*, traveled in the summer of 1966 to West Mödlareuth. It was some two decades into the community's division and only weeks after the GDR built a nine-foot-tall concrete wall through the community. He reported the comment of a local teacher in a nearby Hof County borderland community to a global readership: "But then I must let [the schoolchildren] draw their own conclusions [about Germany's division]. What else can I say? I can't tell them to do anything about it because the only ones who can do anything about it are the important people in Bonn and Washington and Moscow" ("Country Cousin of the Berlin Wall," July 10, 1966).

As we stated at the beginning of this chapter, we expect that outsiders made these connections between the life world and the larger world; but as an insider, this schoolteacher was more complicated. On the surface, he adhered to the normative assumptions about ordinary people who lived in the local political periphery. They acted as if they were the objects of policies set by elites in the political cores of states, nations, and empires. Yet this Western villager had grown keenly aware of the global connections of the border that ran through his everyday life.

These insiders also responded to the disruptions in the life world by seeking to control it. They did so in part by articulating their own vision of what that space should be. But did they "think globally/act locally," as the contemporary American bumper sticker reads? *Did they try to influence global affairs through their local actions?* In keeping with our critical reassessment of the category of *ordinary* throughout this book, we are wondering to what degree ordinary people are really as ordinary as they claim to be. Our evidence for this point thus far has also been more indirect than direct. *Were our informants aware of this interplay? Did they explicitly include global considerations in their local calculus? Did they employ global forces tactically for local purposes? Did they also seek to influence those global situations strategically by taking local places?* Possible answers to these questions hinge on how Germans represented everyday life and the ruptures in it.

Authority remains our key category; but as the example of this West German teacher illustrates, it becomes more a question of self-authorization when we are discussing the practices of German people on the ground. This teacher from Hof County authorized himself to publicly question the authorities responsible for division. Here we are once again grounding the process of taking place in practices of self, specifically the act of laying claim to status or power in everyday life. Our approach allows us to track how our German figures tried to construct a ground for their self-fashioning and to show that they viewed their everyday topography on multiple scales. They acted with an astute, calculated awareness of these multiple scales. Indeed, their claims to authority made sense in the life world only in these larger contexts.

From the Sestos River in modern-day Sierra Leone, the BAC ships continued to the Gold Coast, dotted with the forts and trading posts of the other chartered European trading companies. The Brandenburgers were, after all, the last European state to establish an African trading company during the era of slavery. Calling first at Axim, the westernmost Dutch fort on the coast, Groeben noted "all the nations which have any forts or lodges on the Guinea coast, namely the French, Danes, English, Portuguese and Dutch" (1694: 64). These outposts served as symbols of European authority. Averaging one every ten miles along a 300-mile stretch of coastline, they formed the borderland of interaction between Europeans and West Africans.

These outposts reflected the mercantilism of the age. Each national trading company sought to maximize its trade and profits at the expense of the others. Groeben found himself on an insecure global frontier where the theory of mercantilism diverged from the practice of trade. On arrival on the Gold Coast, even before reaching Axim, Groeben and the two BAC ships met up with a Dutch interloper. It was an unauthorized ship trading outside the monopolies claimed by the national chartered companies. This interloper was a clear sign of the absence of state authority on the coast. With no central authority on land to limit European presence, and no ability by any European power to drive out rivals, interlopers and pirates were free to sail.

Another danger came from the authorized representatives of rival states trying to build mercantile empires—by force when needed. Contrary to their instructions, the BAC ships continued east along the coast and anchored in sight of both the English trading post at Commenda and the main fortress of the Dutch Chartered West Indies Company or Geoctroyeerde Westindische Compagnie (GWIC) at Elmina. After a day of brisk trade, the BAC ships "had received quite a quantity of gold." Yet the representatives of the GWIC in the Elmina fortress did not appreciate this new rival trading right in their face, so to speak, and dispatched the chief factor and two assistants to the BAC ship. These men explained to Groeben that the BAC ships "were doing great damage to their trade and in fact had no right to trade on the coast." The Dutch claimed to have authority over the entire coast based on their seizure of Elmina from the Portuguese. If the BAC ships refused to leave, the cannons of the Elmina fortress would "apply the laws of nature" and drive them away by force.

Groeben and the ships' captains "held a council of war." They responded by first citing the authority by which they acted. "It was our duty," he declared, "to live in accordance with the orders of His Highness the Elector of Brandenburg." Groeben then pointed out the gap between the Dutch representations of authority and the actual limits of Dutch authority:

> And since they [the Dutch] called themselves lords of the whole Guinea coast, we would be quite content if they forbade their subjects to trade with our ships; but since they could not do this, it was evident that it was a free territory, in which everyone was allowed by the natives to trade. (1694: 64)

Groeben denied Dutch authority on the Guinea coast not for any legal reason or treaty claim but simply because the Dutch could not enforce it. This relationship between representation and authority was the reverse of Groeben's encounter with King Peter. The West African king bore no visible symbols of authority recognizable to Groeben, but his commands were immediately obeyed. The Dutch had visible signs of authority, but Groeben refused to recognize their claim—not because they were unable to effectively enforce their will on the ground but because he did not wish to recognize it. In effect, Groeben decided that the Gold Coast was a "free territory" in which trade was open to all by the true insiders—the local African authorities. He made these distinctions between legitimate and illegitimate authority strategically with both the local and the global situation clearly in mind.

International political developments help explain the actions of the Brandenburgers on the Gold Coast—particularly their search for treaty partners. Groeben described the concerted efforts of the Brandenburgers to locate the three Axim men who signed the first treaty with Elector Frederick William in May 1681. As it turned out, only one, Apani, had survived a recent attack by the neighboring Adom people. More importantly, Groeben described the successful search for new treaty partners to confirm the BAC alliance with the Axim people in the coastal region called Cape Three Points. On 5 January 1683, the Brandenburgers succeeded in signing a new treaty with "the *caboceer* [local leader] called Apani," Groeben recounted, and "also with many other caboceers" (1694: 82). These local leaders agreed to help the BAC build a fort, defend it, trade with no other Europeans, and allow no other European powers to settle in the area.

Such treaties were common in European expansion; but for representatives of Brandenburg-Prussia, these treaties held an added significance. As Heinz Duchhardt has noted (1985: 372–74), principalities within the Holy Roman Empire were given the *jus foederis*—the right to make international treaties with other sovereign states—by the Peace of Westphalia. To be real, this right had to be exercised; and after 1648, many principalities of the empire signed treaties with France, the United Provinces, Denmark, Sweden, and other powers acting as sovereign equals to these European states.

Thanks to the signature marks of Apani and his fellow caboceers, Brandenburg-Prussia was alone among the principalities of the empire to exercise the *jus foederis* with sovereigns *outside* of Europe. The treaties signed in Guinea thus accomplished something quite significant: it elevated Brandenburg-Prussia above the other territorial princes of Germany to parity with Portugal, Spain, England, France, the United Provinces, and the other sovereign European states engaged in overseas trade and colonization.

Groeben and the other representatives of the BAC found what they were looking for in Guinea. Beyond gold, ivory, and slaves, they found authority—or at least something they could fashion into authority and present as a sovereign treaty partner. They imagined in Apani and his fellow caboceers a distant but recognizable reflection of the relations of authority they experienced in their own daily lives. As they linked the local to the international, the signatures of these Gold Coast caboceers grew to signify Brandenburg-Prussia's claim to preeminence in the Holy Roman Empire.

Groeben did not change the borders of Brandenburg-Prussia, but he altered its relative standing in the world. By securing this treaty, reporting his activities to the elector, and publishing his account of his travels in Guinea, Groeben also presented himself as an especially loyal and capable noble servant of the elector. The mission to Africa was central to Groeben's self-image, and he noted it carefully in the design for his tomb, prepared many years later.

The inner-German border was also a place filled with both danger and potential authority. Consider this incident from 1951, when the border had already become a firmer reality of the German *Alltag*. The second photograph in the West German magazine piece discussed above (Pabel 1951: 533–35) pictured a West Mödlareuther hurrying back from the border. Pabel, the West German journalist, captured the image by hiding in a village barn. The reporter asked the young woman what was going on, the answer to which the journalist published in the photograph's caption:

> Nothing special! I have only visited a friend on the other side—and I'm not actually allowed to do this, even for fifteen minutes! We here in the West have a border pass, but it's only valid for fieldwork since our fields are also on the other side. So we always just wait until the police are not looking or until someone on duty turns a blind eye. (Idem)

This young woman clearly did not recognize the legitimacy of the border and authorized herself to contravene it as needed. But she also framed her everyday activities in an understanding of their larger context.

> If it were up to the fanatics, I couldn't even see my friend that I went to school with for years. I believe the craziness in our village doesn't approach what's going on along the rest of the zonal border. But we already know to help ourselves. We did not want this stupid border! (Idem)

Her willingness to speak her views openly to the press is further evidence of self-authorization.

But such behavior elicits responses from the authorities. In the context of the Cold War getting hotter, this photograph and its caption prompted a response from the GDR. GrePo reports (BayHStAM, PrBayGrePo, 1367) shortly thereafter stated that "presumably" the Volkspolizei got ahold of this edition of the magazine; for an officer of the organization soon lured her to the border, handcuffed her, and dragged her to his local headquarters. There she was detained for nearly a week, "searched bodily," and accused of espionage. No doubt she also understood that she had become the victim not simply of local but also of global forces.

In this borderland, contestation of authority and control of and access to place were inextricably intertwined (Steege 2011: 140–63 esp. 154). During the spring of 1952, the GDR carried out an action to remove from the area along the frontier individuals deemed hostile to East Germany. This action represented the political effort of outsiders to assert control over this disorderly life world; it was also a key moment in the hardening of the division of Germany (Bennewitz and Potratz 1997; Wolter 1998; Wagner 2001; Sheffer 2011: 97–117). Schleiz County residents used their proximity to the border to express their objection to the GDR in the strongest way possible.

During the 1952 operation, numerous East Mödlareuthers fled permanently to the West. In abandoning the GDR just in time, the East Mödlareuthers were not only seeking to improve their everyday life for themselves but also contributing to a mass movement with larger political implications. Just after the operation, East German authorities built a wooden fence through the village. The GDR gradually further militarized the border through the community and carried out a second relocation action in October 1961. By 1966, a concrete wall divided the community, much like the Wall in Berlin.

Local places were not shaped just by absence—such as that of GDR citizens who had flown—but also by presence. While Cold War spaces could be physically demarcated, they were far from hermetically sealed. Both ideas and people passed through the so-called Iron Curtain. As we saw earlier, Alexander Morawitz created his performative persona TJ Big Blaster Electric Boogie around the available information on American hip-hop. He remade his life world in Dresden into how he imagined the Bronx. At the same time, he hoped to change the cultural landscape of the GDR through his performances. What Alexei Yurchak (2005) called "the Imaginary West" played a vital role in how postwar Eastern Europeans configured and constructed their own spaces.

It is equally impossible to understand gay and lesbian East Berlin without taking into account the influence of the wider world. Activist Peter Rausch played a central role in founding the Homosexual Interest Group Berlin (HIB), a pioneering gay rights organization in the GDR. In an interview with one of our authors on 28 June 2010, he made clear how intimately gay lives in the GDR were bound up with the West. Rausch first deduced the existence of cruising sites after watching a Western television program about the "lowlife" around West Berlin's Bahnhof Zoo. "If something like that's possible in the toilets over there," he thought to himself, "it must be in the East too" (idem).

Through a friend, he got to know West German gay visitors, who had easily found their way to the gay-friendly bars near the border crossing at Friedrichstrasse. Via such contacts, they heard of the birth of the West German gay and lesbian liberation movement (*Schwulenbewegung*), prompting the idea that something similar was needed for the GDR. The conversation went like this: "So, we have to do that now," Rausch said. "A group like that, a gay group: we have to do that in the East!" (idem).

West German media also played an important role in spreading ideas. A revelatory moment for the nascent activists of the GDR was the TV screening of Rosa von Praunheim's *Nicht der Homosexuelle ist pervers, sondern die Situation, in der er lebt*, or *It Is Not the Homosexual Who Is Perverse, but the Society in Which He Lives* (McLellan 2011: 120). In the same interview from 2010, Rausch remembered reading Wilhelm Reich (1971) as well as Martin Dannecker's influential West German publication on male homosexuality (1974). But when he wanted to explain "how much fun our lives were," he emphasized the importance of "Afro-American Disco … Disco was our music naturally. You know, Fifth Dimension and Gloria Gaynor and all the rest." Just as Morawitz made himself into part of an international hip-hop community, Rausch connected his life world in the GDR to a transnational gay community.

It is important to recognize that each person's imaginary West was shaped differently by personal experience, interest, and creativity. TJ Big Blaster Electric Boogie was at pains to emphasize the fact that US hip-hop was only a starting point—what mattered was one's own original and authentic adaption of the genre. One example serves to show the gendered nature of such influences. In 1987, Karin Dauenheimer published *Breaking through the Silence* in samizdat format: self-duplicated typed manuscripts transmitted by hand clandestinely as a way to circumvent official censorship and police surveillance. Dauenheimer took as her subject the relationship of lesbians to the church and the broader gay rights movement. Within a handful of pages (400, 402, 396), Dauenheimer cited Adrienne Rich, Simone de Beauvoir, the "myth of the female orgasm," and the radical slogan "feminism is the theory, lesbianism is the practice." Hers was a very different mental universe and intellectual context than that of her male peers, even gay men activists.

This different way of making sense of her larger world resulted in a different experience of her life world. Dauenheimer called for spaces that were not necessarily women-only but were where women and lesbians could be in the majority and could express their ideas and experiences without the threat of male dominance. "The frequently heard accusation that we are sealing ourselves off is inaccurate, insofar as we are all 'in [real] life' the rest of the time: in jobs, housing associations [*Hausgemeinschaften*], families, and circles of friends" (1987: 403).

The influence of Western feminist consciousness raising and radical lesbianism is easy to recognize here. These East German social and cultural activists sought to create spaces and identities that were appropriate and authentic to the GDR—as shown by Illustration 9.4. These actions acknowledged a certain GDR reality, while in the process of undermining its authority. To do so, they drew on a global repertoire of political and cultural practices. Like Groeben and the residents of the Cold War borderlands, they conceptualized *Alltag* in the context of both global and local spaces. Their strategic practices made explicit and calculated connections between them.

Illustration 9.4. Lesbians in the Church at the Friedenswerkstatt, Berlin Erlösergemeinde, n.d. (1980s). BStU, MfS-HA VII/Fo/445 Foto 31. Courtesy of BStU.

Viewing disrupted places on the ground allows us to glimpse the creation and destruction of everyday places. A key part of gay and lesbian activism was the creation of a semipublic, but entirely unofficial, sphere of life within socialism. The state had decriminalized homosexual sexual activity, but it was not prepared to authorize the extension of public gay and lesbian spaces beyond the handful of bars that had been tolerated since the 1960s. To compensate for this absence of meeting places, individuals turned their apartments into *Partywohnungen* where large groups of people could get together. At the Müggelsee on the outskirts of Berlin, gay men set up a gay nudist beach on the edge of the official bathing area. A wooded hinterland provided a convenient cruising spot in summer afternoons and evenings. These practices of self generated a parallel world.

We have seen in the earlier chapters how self often had a spatial dimension. Families were the sites of both politicization and efforts to insulate oneself from politics. Couples in mixed relationships during the Third Reich tried to use the home to retreat from persecution during the Third Reich. The deliberate destruction of this parallel world and its attendant privacy was a key part of the Nazi assault on Jews and the people who aided them. Kläre Begall, who hid a number of Jews in her home, felt unable even to sleep in without fear of surveillance by her neighbors. Place was also central to the development of gay and lesbian identities.

On 14 April 2011, one of our authors conducted an interview with Michael Unger, a key member of the 1970s gay activist scene. In his autobiographical narrative, he contrasted his home village, "where I could hear the birds singing" with his first impressions of Berlin, "particularly on Schönhauser Allee, where there is an elevated train with a tram underneath and it's really loud." For the Unger of 2011, remembering his seventeen-year-old self, the sounds of the city crystallized his feelings of anonymity and excitement. The physical sensations of his arrival to Berlin became part of his narrative of becoming and his sense of self as an openly gay man.

It is in this embodied sense too that we understand taking place. A sense of place is not just about its physical dimensions but also its smells, sounds, and impact on the human body: sausages sizzling under the S-Bahn arches, the whistle of the wind on an exposed hillside, or the touch of a hand in a cruising site. The figure we cut is always tied to the ground in which it is performed. Borders can evoke fear, sadness, longing, and rage. Not for nothing was the departures hall at Friedrichstrasse station, where East Germans said good-bye to guests from West Germany, called the Tränenpalast—the Palace of Tears.

What did East German gay and lesbian activists hope to achieve? Unlike other actors in this book, who sought privacy and freedom from state interference, they deliberately engaged with state institutions in an attempt to move out of social and often sexual isolation. The concept of *Öffentlichkeit*, meaning public sphere, recurs frequently in both contemporary writings and retrospective accounts. Rather than attempting to distance themselves from authority, the members of the HIB repeatedly approached the state and its actors during the 1970s in the belief that they would be able to achieve more from within the system. The disappointment of these hopes meant that some 1980s activists took a more radical view: yet they still worked within the restrictions of the 1978 church–state agreement. They effectively recognized the authority of both the Protestant Church and the SED in everyday life in order to create room for them to maneuver as gay men and lesbians.

Did this pragmatism mean that GDR institutions worked well as we have argued in other cases? The evidence suggests not. The photographs of empty streets and deserted buildings in the MfS surveillance files seem like an empty and mechanical exercise, which added little or nothing to the sum of official understanding. The SED's failure to listen and respond to initiatives on the part of gay and lesbian activists merely delayed the inevitable—the more open discussion of homosexuality that finally began to take place in the late 1980s was a little too late. This is not to say that there was a causal connection between the authorities' obstinacy and the decline and fall of the GDR. Yet the SED's inability to answer the demands of its citizens—not just gays and lesbians but also other youth groups and disaffected segments of society—was symptomatic of the dysfunctional relationship between the regime and the population. Over time, these niggling symptoms accumulated into a more significant threat to the health of the GDR.

Self-Authorization

It seems, then, that the authority figures we have studied in this chapter were right to be anxious. Ordinary people contested the control of space and sought to create new spaces for social and political activities. Taking place refers to this kind of assertion of their own priorities in the process of appropriating authority, whether it was imposed on them by the more powerful or they disrupted it. Whether an official of the Brandenburg African Company, a resident of a borderland village, or a zealous convert to the nightlife of Schönhauser Allee, they all acted strategically in life worlds that they understood to be connected to larger realms.

The everyday is multidimensional. Modern Germans negotiated skillfully between topographic scales for their own purposes. Even the selection of differently shaped worlds to inhabit was itself a strategic act that facilitated the fashioning of a particular kind of self. The everyday conditioned and constrained those practices; but modern Germans, like all of us, also reshaped it in a calculated manner to create a better context for self-fashioning. In spite of itself, everyday life leaves open this opportunity for self-authorization.

Jason Johnson, Craig Koslofsky, and Josie McLellan

CHAPTER 10

Telling Stories

That's it. Now you get to decide on your own authority.
—Harald Jäger, East German Border Police Officer, 1989

In this book, we (ATG26) have invited you to enter the interdisciplinary study of modern Germany through this different doorway: not of leading figures, collective groups, ideal types, or abstract forces, but of everyday Germans. Ruptures, large and small, were part and parcel of their everyday lives. We told their stories to draw attention to how Germans created, experienced, and responded to them. Meanwhile, the trajectory of this book has taken us through ever-larger forms of social complexity: from self, interpersonal relations, family, objects, and institutions to policies of anti-Semitism, the creation of violent worlds, and the taking of place on borderlands. By the last chapter, we had shown how their actions played out on different scales at the same time.

Just like the Germans we study, we have tried to make sense of everyday life, to tell meaningful stories about its ruptures, and to do so incommon. This task was as challenging as it was ordinary. For, telling stories about everyday life requires moving between two seemingly incommensurate perspectives: fragmentary experiences in everyday life and some kind of shared, pragmatic understanding about it.

Over the course of these many anecdotes, however, we were slowly able to develop a set of four analytic concepts that seem to connect them into a single tale. In this conclusion, a smaller group of seven authors offer these loosely fitting components as a tentative model for how one might approach the everyday from a new interdisciplinary perspective. But this chapter cannot really meet the expectations of a traditional conclusion. It cannot propose a way to study everyday lives abstracted from the actual experiences of people in everyday life. Similar to the first chapter, we ground our thoughts in several kinds of evidence.

First, we derive our concepts from the chapters that preceded this one: their evidence and their analyses. Second, we add some more material from the Wende, returning us to the theme of the first chapter. And finally, we include some ethnographic evidence of our experiences while writing this book. We wish to draw more explicit connections between the everyday lives of modern Germans that we scholars interpret and our academic everyday as scholars engaged in researching and writing German studies. As always, our examples are neither exhaustive nor representative; they serve to illustrate how these four concepts might begin to work together as an integrative approach to the everyday.

Each of these concepts was proposed by our authors with respect to case studies in their respective chapters. Only through the long process of collaborative writing and thinking did they emerge as useful tools for the monograph as a whole. They are *microsocial interactions, plasticity, self-authorization,* and *consensus*. We use them to make the following provisional claims: that the everyday is inherently dynamic in nature; that it acquires this quality thanks to the way people interact with one another and lay claim to the right to shape its features as they see fit; but that, nonetheless, people come to a provisional kind of common understanding about its nature in order to get on with the business of living. The act of telling stories about ourselves and others seems to serve as a particularly viable strategy for living and dealing with these paradoxes of everyday life.

We make these claims with many caveats, of which we mention only two. Just as any one person cannot wholly dictate the nature of everyday life for others, the seven primary authors of this conclusion do not speak for all of the authors of this book. Moreover, everyday consensus should not be misunderstood as agreement, harmony, fixity, or certainty. The everyday lives studied in this book must remain, at some level, disaggregated fragments if we are to depict them accurately.

Microsocial Interactions

Almost by definition, autobiographical stories focus on particular people and the things that they do. The same goes for this book. At its core stands the problem of human agency: what people do within the constraints of given circumstances. In this book, we use the concept of *microsocial interactions* (following Revel 1996; Magnússon and Szijártó 2013). But there are of course many more options for describing these phenomena.

In the literature on everyday life, there is considerable emphasis on the concept of *Eigensinn*; and many of the authors of the preceding chapters have picked up on it explicitly or implicitly. First coined by Lüdtke (1995: 313f.; Lindenberger 2014), it is often translated as *unruliness*. On the one hand, it refers to acts of appropriating power and giving it one's "own meaning." On the other, it represents a form of "willfulness" and "spontaneous self-will" which can even become "a kind of self-affirmation"—the kind that often accompanies interactions with authority. *Eigensinn* often draws attention to not only how people in various degrees of authority negotiate power but also how they ascribe meaning to those interactions. It is as much a comment about authority as an interpolation of the self in and out of its hierarchies.

Eigensinn is neither resistance nor collaboration per se; it thumbs its nose at efforts to define it as either conformist or nonconformist. Subscribing to ideologies, obeying the law, and following regulations rarely correspond perfectly to subjective intentions, attitudes, or experiences. Nominal or partial obedience can be used to make good on unruly claims to alternatives; conversely, a posture of unruliness can also veil sufficient conformity to secure the benefits of it without the responsibility for its consequences (Lüdtke 1991a: 9–63; Lindenberger 1999: 22–24, 2007: 33, 2014; Bergerson 2004; Davis, Lindenberger, and Wildt 2008: 18; Bergerson et al. 2011). Its motives and consequences are therefore more inconsistent and paradoxical than neat and logical.

This slippery term has become popular among scholars and not just of Germany. One reason perhaps lies in the fact that it reflects something about our scholarly lives: that academics too must negotiate complicated, ambiguous, and even paradoxical situations vis-à-vis authority, or at least that we like to imagine ourselves as nonconformists. But there are also solid intellectual reasons for our interest in unruliness, for scholars have long struggled to better account for the ambiguity, abruptness, and incoherence of human actions. Consciously or not, people typically imbue their actions with multiple, sometimes even contradictory meanings; those meanings may become apparent only after some reflection; and they often change over time. Like our other terms, unruliness is inherently unstable—but in this case, it is intentionally so in order to preserve maneuverability in everyday life.

As useful as this term has become, it can also be abused. Unruliness does not exhaust the scope of everyday actions and interactions, and framing all forms of agency as unruliness runs the risk of overstating its significance. There is a wide range of other terms that scholars have developed in order to capture different qualities of everyday actions. In terms of authority, one can also speak of *resisters, perpetrators, collaborators, bystanders, victims*, and *rescuers*. Scholars use terms like *strategies, tactics, negotiations, maneuvers,* and *appropriations* to emphasize the calculated manipulation of circumstances; concepts of *habit, praxis,* and *practices* to draw attention to the ritual reiteration of meaningful action; and phrases like *spatial practices* and *room for action* to foreground relationships to the lived environment. One could also speak of events *taking place* in everyday life as a way to recognize the relationship between multiple dimensions of time, space, and scale. These terms, and many others like them, seek to address a similar need to think in less dualistic and more dynamic ways about the relations between structure and agency (Lefebvre 1974, 1991;

Bourdieu 1977; Certeau 1984; Lloyd 1991; Butler 1999; Reckwitz 2003; Foucault 2005; Sewell 2005; Gudehus and Christ 2013: 9–10).

This wide range of vocabulary is available to characterize how people act and interact in face-to-face situations. The twenty-six authors of this book used it variously based on their applicability to the specific cases in question. Throughout this book, however, we placed them under the common rubric of *microsocial interactions* because this general term draws attention to several features of everyday life that we consider crucial.

Everyday life takes place between human beings. Even when people are alone, they operate in social contexts that presume and implicate larger audiences in their story. The term *interactions* corresponds to our metaphor of viewing everyday life on the ground. To the vertical–political axis that views the *Alltag* either from above or from below, it adds both a horizontal–social and temporal–historical axes. Actions are always necessarily also interactions, for they involve individuals in direct or indirect negotiation with others about the world they share incommon. Actions also always imply contexts and consequences; and when embedded in stories, they have a past, present, and future.

Life in the GDR offers a good illustration of this multidimensionality. Under the communist-led SED, the political system was organized around the principle of *democratic centralism* (Le Blanc 1993). But recent scholarship shows (Carter 1992: 184–189; Fulbrook 2005: 12; Geisel 2005; Straughn 2005; Port 2007; Richter 2007; Johnson 2008; Riley 2008; S. Jones 2011) that everyday life operated in fact as a kind of *participatory dictatorship*. The GDR allowed ordinary citizens to have a degree of input into the making of their own lives while simultaneously preserving the authority of the SED. Over the course of the 1980s, everyday forms of indirect subversion—political jokes, informal conversations, and small group dialogues in more or less safe spaces—grew into direct calls for structural reform within the GDR. These dynamics were not limited to face-to-face relationships.

Peace movements on both sides of the Berlin Wall, protesting the deployment of medium-range nuclear missiles, called for the demilitarization of the two Germanies and "beating" these nuclear "swords into plowshares." Some courageous GDR citizens even called for a transition to some kind of *democratic socialism*—a so-called third way between Western-style capitalism and Soviet-style socialism in which citizens would be afforded more civil liberties within a socialist system. Recounting stories of everyday life thus prompts interpretive questions about the consequences of these microsocial interactions: *did they somehow contribute to the collapse of the GDR?* The payoff of studying these interactions is that they help us to follow the trajectories of everyday lives in multiple dimensions at once.

In emphasizing the microsocial qualities of these interactions, however, we are not artificially isolating local events from the larger circumstances in which they take place and that can, and often do, influence events on the ground. We do not see the *Alltag* as a choice between a narrow and a broad focus or a local and global perspective. Rather, we see the everyday as a way to address large questions in small and sometimes even intimate settings. Consider our analysis of Dieter, the unemployed former East German who we met in the first chapter. Focusing on how he responded to the Wende gave us far more insight into how everyday life works on the ground than viewing the Wende from the perspective of the capitals of the two Germanies or of the two superpowers. Placing interpersonal interactions under a microscope lets us study the relatively independent dynamics arising on both of these scales as well as the ways in which they interconnect (Lepetit 1993; Klein 1995; Revel 1996; Lüdtke 2006; Herod 2010; Magnússon and Szijártó 2013).

Our method has been to follow the microsocial interactions in the life stories of our subjects wherever they led, while also filling in the relevant contexts that they ignored, intentionally or not. In the chapters, we followed these leads from local places, like divided Mödlareuth, to global dynamics, like the Cold War and back again. Their stories led along intricate pathways within the fashioned self of artists, divorced partners, SS families, communist neighbors, high school friends, museum visitors, mercantile trading partners, and co-workers in charity organizations.

These autobiographical accounts brought us into rooms where German women hid Jewish men, apartments for gay and lesbian subcultures, garages of amateur collectors, schoolyards of joking children, anonymous streets and cinemas, working-class neighborhoods, sports activities at factories, racially divided towns, cities of celebrity encounters, and entire regions transformed into genocidal landscapes. Indeed, all of these places were connected to larger markets, systems, states, nations, empires, and continents. We connected these levels both structurally and interpretively, following the lead of our informants.

That is, we told stories. In the case of Dieter, what made his personal crises particularly powerful was the degree to which the many pivots in his life played out on multiple levels at the same time. Not only did he blame the Wende for the fact that he lost his job, but he tied his unfortunate circumstances causally to the structural changes of the Wende. Commentators also made this link for Dieter by labeling him a Wende-loser and member of the declining East German workers' milieu. Meanwhile, Dieter himself struggled to fit his personal story of failure into the official national story of successful reunification. There is, therefore, a striking similarity between what happens within everyday life and what we as scholars try to do with it. We all try to make sense of everyday experiences by connecting them to—often multiple and messy—frameworks of meaning.

Plasticity

No doubt, the scale of the problem reinforced Dieter's sense that he could not alter his circumstances. But the everyday is not as solid as it seems. In one moment, it can seem stubbornly resistant to change; but in the blink of a historical eye, its seemingly resilient features can suddenly change. The deceptive permanence of everyday life returns us to the problem of pinning it down with the kind of precision expected of scholarly work. Dieter expressed this disturbing paradox with appropriately circuitous logic: "Then things fell apart afterwards just as before."

In this book, we have referred to this dynamic quality of everyday life with the term *plasticity*. At one moment the features of everyday life can appear as preexisting structures that resist or impede our actions; and in the next, the form, meaning, or functions of those structures can become pliable in response to the things we do to and with them. The features of the everyday are also more porous than they seem. Modern institutions and interstate borders certainly give off the impression of being impermeable, sealing off an inside from an outside and vice versa; but as we have seen, neither institutions nor borders are nearly as solid as they claim to be. They are more like subcultures or private spheres: normatively bounded but negotiated in practice.

We are not being naïve here. We recognize that human beings are not the autonomous beings that they like to imagine they are. We cannot simply author a new biography for ourselves. Structures condition much of our lives—like the cumulative mess facing Dieter after 1989, when persistent unemployment turned into alcoholism, divorce, and a suicide attempt. Their solidity restrains and constrains human agency more often than not. We recognize as well that many of the things we encounter in our daily lives have considerable degrees of physical, social, and cultural resilience. The GDR no doubt felt that way to many Germans up to 1989: quite resistant to change. And then, suddenly, its feet turned to clay. The Berlin Wall fell, the two Germanies reunited peacefully, and the GDR was simultaneously integrated into what subsequently became the European Union.

Clearly, we need to better understand the plasticity of everyday things if we are to fully appreciate such ruptures in the lives of modern Germans. *What kinds of things have this plastic quality?* If we were to look for examples, we might ironically begin by more closely considering just about any aspect of our *Alltag* that we encounter as a fixed condition of our lives. It could be an object like an egg chair, an institution like family, a composition like a memoir or a photo album, a habitual way to walk through a city, or even an analytic term like *Alltag* itself. In Dieter's story, many things turned out to be more plastic that he supposed, including his village, his career, and his marriage.

Take the Iron Curtain, for instance. It no doubt served its function as a border even in rural MV, even if Dieter never personally crossed or even visited it (Major 2009). In our accounts of everyday life, however, we cannot define its features too precisely, as if to fix them once and for all as the foundation for drawing conclusions about Dieter's everyday life, because they are too dynamic in nature. Part of the shock of the Wende no doubt derives from the fact that Dieter himself believed in the resilience of the GDR, and he was not alone in this misapprehension. Erich Honecker, general secretary of the SED, and the rest of the politburo of the GDR celebrated the fortieth anniversary of the Republic in East Berlin on 7 October, only one month before the Berlin Wall fell. But as the Wall itself underscores, it would be more accurate to say that the persistence of everyday objects is both a norm and a myth—a claim about the world that actually disguises and shapes how it operates. Ordinary people may ignore the plasticity of everyday things at their risk, but it would be a mistake for scholars to take those things at their word.

The Wende made this plasticity painfully apparent in rural MV. The member of our authorial team who conducted the interviews with Dieter was born and raised in the former GDR. Like so many others who left this region after graduating from high school, he moved in order to study in West Germany; but in 2010, he returned as a sociologist and ethnographer, traveling along the Polish border.

As soon as he left the recently completed highway, he felt like he entered a lost world (Straughn 2016). He saw production and industrial facilities of the former East German state economy in ruins. He took the photograph seen in Illustration 10.1. It records the apartment houses of workers who had been employed at the local agricultural production cooperative (LPG), now abandoned and falling apart. Traveling through the former GDR after twenty years, he could no longer recognize the places he once knew quite well. He found it hard to imagine that they would ever be able to recover to provide their inhabitants with a good quality of life. The persistence of rupture disclosed this underlying character of everyday life itself—its inherent malleability and historicity.

The approach we are proposing to everyday life is *poststructural*. This book's authors certainly want to draw attention to many of the structures of everyday life, but our recognition of the ways they shape our actions and interactions cannot stifle our appreciation for how they also empower them. More to the point, we do not treat their forms, meanings, or functions as fixed or discrete. They cannot form the stable foundations for knowing about or acting with everyday life as a closed, complete, and coherent system. These things can change depending on the relationships into which they are placed and the uses to which they are put. Any new application or operation only adds another layer of meaning, experience, and memory (Rorty 1967;

Illustration 10.1. Abandoned Apartment Building, Mecklenburg-Vorpommern, 2010. Photo: T. Gurr.

Lyotard 1984; Caplan 1989; Comaroff and Comaroff 1992; Derrida 1997; Butler 1999; Foucault 2005).

Consider the institutions of Dieter's world. In addition to the decaying physical infrastructure, village life had fallen apart. It required considerable fantasy to envision the inhabitants enjoying local cultural institutions or clubs, going shopping in their own stores instead of traveling to distant cities to acquire even their most basic requirements for daily life, or zipping around town on their mopeds the way young people used to do. When asked, the local people talked more about the good old days in the GDR, but those days were good primarily because work was secure, it provided a source for recognition, and it even substituted for family.

Everyday life typically had strong rhythms. But unemployment disrupted them (Jahoda, Lazarsfeld, and Zeisel 1960). The unemployed could not maintain the expected divisions into workdays and holidays, weekdays and weekends. They experienced this loss of firmly established rhythms and routines as a caesura. With the loss of established rhythms of time, the unemployed also lost hope for finding a way to reintegrate into society. As social relations and daily rhythms broke down, this place lost many of its distinguishing qualities as a home for its residents and a foundation for personal identity.

What is so disturbing about the experiences of Wende-losers is the degree to which the features of their everyday lives seemed simultaneously resistant and compliant to human agency. Taken together, the myths they lived by—that everyday life in MV could never change, that it then changed in 1989 abruptly and radically, and that it thereafter could never change again—appear contradictory; but in the moment, each story seemed completely convincing. Focusing on the plasticity of everyday life allows us to engage critically with its myths. Taking its "slipperiness" seriously does not prevent scholars from utilizing the features of everyday life in analytic ways for the same reason that it does not prevent people from deploying those features in practical ways in everyday life (Bennett 2006: 9). They are useful to them, as they are to us, precisely because of their plasticity.

Self-Authorization

The plasticity of everyday life raises the question of power—bringing us to one crux of the matter. It is perhaps not too great a leap to imagine the everyday as a realm of microsocial interactions and these dynamics as helping to shape those features. We have seen, after all, many examples of precisely this dynamism with regard to German borders and institutions, spaces and places, families and their memories, communities and societies, artistic personae and their charisma. But *who can determine the nature of everyday life? How are these determinations made?*

These questions are inherently political because plasticity involves shaping a world that we share with others. Established authorities certainly play their part in making things appear self-evidently and naturally what they seem to be, but they can never do so on their own. They are in fact dependent for their authority on the very microsocial interactions that open the possibility for change. It is thus far more relevant to the study of the *Alltag* to investigate how people and things gain and lose that authority.

To address this issue, we have proposed the concept of *self-authorization*. In the preceding chapters, we have used it to refer to the social processes by which individuals lay claim to the legitimacy to act in and on the *Alltag*, regardless of whether they actually have that legitimacy. And we speak here of social processes because these acts of authoring and authorizing always take place directly or indirectly through microsocial interactions. Self-authorization opens the door for individuals to try to determine the nature of plastic things that are part of a world held incommon.

Our understanding of self-authorization begins with its opposite. For many people, their sense of self feels determined for them: by religion or metaphysics; by their communities, families, or critics; by culture or language; by political or social polarities; or by any other structures beyond their control. Self-authorization by contrast claims the freedom of self-determination, to construct an identity free from those constraints. For art and literary critics, that process takes place first and foremost through acts of self-expression—writing, painting, filming, composing, drawing, and so on. But for other scholars, this process could just as well take place through acts of representation that seeks to depict everyday life accurately, such as charting, mapping, documenting, observing, informing, reporting, policing, and so on. Indeed, almost any act in everyday life necessarily involves an act of representation if those acts are to hold any meaning.

These representational acts may be executed by elites, by their agents, or by their subjects; by insiders or outsiders. They may be grounded in intuition or reason, experience or reflection; and those representations, we might add, may be fictional or factual, about the self or about a society. No matter—every representation of the self, whether it is a novel or a memoir, a crime or a habit, presumes an authentic representation of everyday life and vice versa. Representational acts from aesthetic works to police work and even to scholarly monographs are everyday practices that—as attempts to experience, capture, share, control, or even fix the nature of an unruly life world—also help determine the world shared with others.

The degree to which the self is always embedded in everyday life is, in turn, what makes it so fragile. It is fragile first in an existential sense: when actors try to navigate everyday life without secure moorings or in opposition to them. Yet modern society is not without its own dominant forces determining the self. Indeed, one could argue that these forces are far more constraining, and it is everyday practices themselves that give modern structures their authority. So self-authorization is fragile in a second sense as well: as marginalized by the very systems through which it claims autonomy. We see self-authorization in this ambiguous way, evoking *autonomy, authorship,* and *authority* without resolving those contradictions (Greenblatt 1980; Foucault 1991, 2005; Eldridge 2001; Jarraway 2003; Hammer 2006; Elder 2011).

Self-authorization also evokes the familiar multivocality that makes studying everyday life both fascinating and challenging. The divergent histories and memories of the Wende are good examples. Germans describe these events in a multitude of ways (Swibenko 2008; Hensel 2009; Clarke and Wölfel 2011; Laabs 2012; Lahusen 2013; Straughn 2016).

Some Germans continue to draw a stark distinction between Germans from the East and from the West; the often pejorative labels of *Ossis* and *Wessis*, respectively, only serve to reinforce that divide. But some Germans from the former East also laid claim to this label as a positive form of identification—for instance, in order to lament the loss of state-supported childcare, low rents, and job security in the GDR as well as its closer knit communities.

Some go so far as to criticize what they described as the wholesale colonization of social, cultural, economic, and political life by their more prosperous Western neighbors. Meanwhile, some West Germans criticized the *Ossis* for whining. *Wessis* labeled them *Jammerossis*, meaning *whining East Germans*. In giving positive or negative values to this term, these various Germans authored stories about everyday life, both after and even before the Wende, in order to authorize their actions in it: support, protest, reform, criticism.

These labels are not fixed or stable in a way that enables us to define these groups once and for all; they are descriptions of the self that are embedded in stories of everyday life. By calling East Germans complainers, for instance, these hecklers embedded both Westerners and Easterners in particular kinds of stories about everyday life: the assumption, widely shared in the West, that the *Alltag* was inherently worse in the GDR than in the FRG due to the lack of consumer goods and personal freedom. Of course, some *Ossis* contested this point as well as the very premise of it: they questioned whether West Germans really knew anything about their lives in the former GDR. They called them *Besserwessis*: a sarcastic play on words that means *better West Germans* but also sounds a lot like *arrogant know-it-alls*.

Some of the authors of this book have serious misgivings about replicating these pejorative terms. Yet others feel that they have a certain empirical validity. In 1991, *Besserwessi* was named the official word of the year by the Society for the German Language. But the main reason we use these terms is to illustrate what we mean by self-authorization. It was also common among *Wessis* to complain about the fact that they had to contribute large amounts of money to reconstruct the Eastern territories after decades of failed socialist policies. They felt that they had already invested their sweat equity in rebuilding the country after World War II. Here again, West Germans authored stories about everyday lives in the two Germanies in order to authorize particular kinds of actions in it—in this case, the right to refuse financial support for the East, or at least complain about having to do so.

The problem between *Ossis* and *Wessis* did not begin with storytelling per se. They neither share all of the same political interests nor the same experiences. The German *Alltag* was quite different on either side of the Iron Curtain, with different kinds of ruptures resulting in different desires for their future and different ways of viewing the world. And insofar as these ruptures were tied to pain or violence (Gudehus and Christ 2013: 1, 227–31), it may be a challenge to communicate them or even remember them.

We have referred to this situation as a *fragmentation of experience*. It is hardly unique to Germans: we have treated it as a common feature of modernity. It has led some scholars to the pessimistic conclusion that one can never find points of agreement between different subjective experiences. They argue that one must accept the "sublime" meaninglessness of everyday life, past or present, and reduce the scholarly task to depicting, as best one can, the "singularity" of particular stories (Vann 1998; Magnússon and Szijártó 2013; cf. Klein 1995). But this argument seems to us to exaggerate the challenge. In everyday life, people deal with multiple interpretations of fragmentary experiences all the time. They simply authorize themselves to assert an orthodox account of everyday life—in spite of these many alternate accounts.

One way of thinking about self-authorization is as a component of the tactical *bargains* that people strike in everyday life (Sa'ar: 2005). Such bargains are familiar to scholars of the GDR, especially those studying East Germans who cooperated with the Stasi (Fulbrook 2005; Port 2007; Ash 2009; Glaeser 2011; Kowalczuk 2013). These so-called *informal collaborators* were recruited through a number of strategies usually involving various forms of coercion. Sometimes they provided the Stasi with detailed reports about the behavior of colleagues, neighbors, friends, and even family members. Sometimes, as we noted in the case of Ingeborg Erdmann, people's links with the Stasi could be even less direct and formal but still highly damaging.

The Stasi used these autobiographical narratives as one resource for surveillance and denunciation, but that surveillance began in microsocial relationships. Participating in this system, on the one hand, enhanced the social, economic, and political capital of the collaborators. It could spare them from punishment, allow them to attend university, advance their careers, or enable them to enjoy scarce material goods. On the other hand, informal collaborators helped support the state's system of internal political policing. Many citizens of the GDR thus participated in a paradoxical dynamic in which they were busy reporting on each other and, by doing so, making themselves into both the perpetrator and the victim of political surveillance. Collaboration constituted a tactical bargain on the premise that the informants hoped to gain material benefits by denouncing someone else, even if those imagined benefits meant protecting themselves—or, ironically, even the ones on whom they reported—from future trouble with the Stasi.

People rarely live in a world that is wholly agreeable or disagreeable, wholly conducive or wholly detrimental to their needs and desires. The bargaining begins here. In order to challenge or change the nature of some things, to treat them as plastic, one must accept many other things as they appear to be, as the stable conditions of our daily lives. Many GDR citizens, for instance, conceded that the SED, the Stasi, and their network of unofficial informants constituted a natural foundation for everyday life as the payment required for some measure of personal flexibility in their *Alltag*. Informal collaboration can be understood as a form of self-authorization in three senses. Informants claimed the right to act *in* everyday life with social legitimacy. Those actions then involved telling an authentic story *about* everyday life as the framework for those actions. And in turn, those actions and stories legitimized certain features of that everyday life in order to manipulate or alter others.

Implicitly or explicitly, each of these informants insisted that his or her descriptions of everyday life were accurate, even though those accounts were contradictory almost by definition insofar as the one often denounced the other in mutually contradictory reports. This contradiction was perhaps less of a hindrance to the Stasi officers, who were interested primarily in social and political control, than it is to scholars, who sometimes struggle to negotiate between the seemingly contradictory demands in our work for precision and messiness, authenticity and accuracy. These contradictions arose in the lives of police and informants, just as they arise in the lives of scholars, from the simple fact that, through our many deeds and the stories we invent about them, we often make authoritative yet contradictory claims about the same everyday life.

At first glance, success in this regard seems to be directly related to the power of individuals to impose their version of events on others. People certainly command very different resources; the playing field of everyday life is neither even nor fair (Lindenberger 1999, 2014). Institutions provide further leverage to personal authority. The SED leadership in the politburo commanded enormous status and power within the GDR. They lived much better than and largely apart from the rest of its citizens. From the perspective of the citizens of the GDR, these policymakers commanded enormous power to influence everyday life.

Germans lower on the political hierarchy were still able to influence everyday life but from a very different position. Consider a notorious example from the Cold War: the German Border Police, later reorganized as the Border Troops of the GDR. Members of this police force were infamous for shooting East Germans trying to cross the inner-German border illegally. They would without doubt insist that they were just implementing orders given to them by their commanders, but like the Berlin Wall itself, they became a symbol for the Cold War division of Germany and the abuses of the SED regime. For many of the East and West Germans who crossed this inner-German border, the institutions of the GDR not only appeared to have authority but even seemed authoritarian (Sälter 2009).

Yet authority was never fully theirs in the sense of being a condition of their being. No one is actually inherently powerful in the sense of a truly divine ruler. And as for their officers, no one is under orders at all times concerning all possible situations. In any given situation, each person still has to authorize themself to act, here and now, and either according to existing norms or contrary to them. This point is made clear by the events of 9 November 1989, when Germans on both sides of the inner-German border discovered the surprising plasticity of the Berlin Wall.

One key figure in these events was Günter Schabowski—newspaper editor in chief of *Neues Deutschland*, member of the GDR's politburo, and unofficial media spokesperson for the regime. During a press conference, Schabowski conveyed an imprecise order, about which he was inadequately informed, concerning the opening of the Berlin Wall for GDR citizens to inter-German traffic. When challenged on the specifics before an audience of Eastern and Western journalists, he improvised the terms of this order. In effect, he made up a story. He said that the Wall was open "as far as I know—effective immediately, without delay." In the larger scheme of things, this announcement represented a poorly planned response on the part of the regime to mounting domestic and international pressure (Sebestyen 2009).

But this announcement can also be read as an account of everyday life (Schabowski and Sieren 2009: 22–39) that came to define it thereafter. Following Schabowski's press release, Western television stations began reporting that the borders were open. East Berliners began massing at crossing stations, arriving on foot and in cars, creating massive traffic jams. They demanded the freedom to cross into the West, and they used Schabowski's press release to legitimize that demand.

A second figure was Harald Jäger, the East German Stasi officer in charge of controlling passports at Bornholmer Strasse on the northern border of East Berlin. Jäger was uncertain as to how to proceed. He too watched Schabowski on television, but he had received no direct order from his supervisors to implement this new policy or explaining how precisely to do so. When he called his supervisors to report the situation and ask for clarification, they at first refused to believe him—or Schabowski for that matter. They even questioned Jäger's ability to properly assess events on the ground.

Jäger sincerely feared the increasingly uncontrollable crowd. He worried that the guards, the citizens, or both would likely get hurt if the situation escalated. So he decided to raise the alarm—even though he did not have the authority to do so. Also trying to deescalate the situation, his direct supervisor, Rudi Ziegenhorn, instructed Jäger to let the louder and more aggressive people leave the GDR but only after marking their passports as invalid. This impromptu policy, never approved by any higher authority, would have effectively deprived these GDR citizens of their citizenship without their knowledge or agreement.

Instead, this makeshift solution only exacerbated the situation. Observing that the guards were letting the unruly people cross the border, other people in the crowd began to voice their anger and frustration more loudly, if only to get selected. Meanwhile, some GDR citizens were already returning home from the other side of the Wall, only to be told by the border police that they could not. They too grew frustrated and angry. In this worsening situation, Jäger took action once again. Disregarding the instruction from his direct supervisor, Jäger let his fellow citizens back into the GDR. But the crowds just grew bigger still.

Jäger grew increasingly frustrated by the lack of clear instructions from the regime that placed him and his fellow guards in this awkward and dangerous position. Fearing that the masses could seize the guards' weapons, Jäger took matters into his own hands for a third and final time. As he recounted for a 2009 television documentary (Das Erste Mediathek), Jäger said to himself: "That's it. Now you get to decide on your own authority [*auf eigene Faust*]." He instructed the soldiers under his command to close the passport control and open the crossing at his station for all GDR citizens. With this story—a story he only told himself at first but repeated publicly many times thereafter (Haase-Hindenberg 2007: 150–217; *Die Zeit* 2011; Haeming 2014)—Jäger authorized himself to act in and on the German *Alltag*.

Jäger's autobiographical statement about this crucial moment in German and world history seems to capture much of what we are trying to propose here about everyday life with the terms *microsocial interactions, plasticity,* and *self-authorizations*—and for that reason we placed it as an epigraph for this final chapter. It is also fitting that he was an officer of the GDR, for it raises one of the most persistent issues of interdisciplinary German studies. *How then does self-authorization relate to power and force? How do power and force generate systems of violence and terror in everyday life?*

These leaders and officers of the GDR were certainly granted political and military authority by their superiors to police the inner-German border with state violence. Nonetheless, they had to assert and validate that authority on the ground in the face of their fellow citizens and, when necessary, on their bodies. The philosopher Hannah Arendt made this point. She defined *power* as that which "can arise only out of the cooperative action of many people." She contrasted it with *force*, defined as "the means of which … an individual can seize and control" (2005: 99). She admitted that "power and force appear to be identical, and under modern conditions, that is indeed largely the case" (147). She is perhaps thinking of mass dictatorships like the Nazis and Communists. But she would hardly limit herself to only those regimes.

The authors of this book are not marking certain kinds of self-authorizations as *inherently* valid when taken in the abstract. Arendt posits this distinction not to offer us analytical categories that can be used evaluatively, as if we could conclusively determine that "incident X is a case of force and is therefore bad" while "incident Y reflects power and is therefore good." We are, like Arendt, trying to think more deeply about our experience of politics and the demand for judgment in particular circumstances, given the fluid nature of the relationship of force and power in any given situation. So for instance, she wrote, "Wherever force, which is actually a phenomenon of the individual or the few, is combined with power, which is possible only among the many, the result is a monstrous increase in potential force [such that] force, grows and develops at the expense of power" (2005: 147). By treating the relationship between power and force as fluid, she warns us of the danger of reducing any situation of power and force to either one or the other. In everyday life, she seems to be suggesting, social processes of empowerment can become instruments for individuals to compel others, just as individual acts of self-authorization can become mechanisms for social bargains of empowerment.

So even authority itself, it turns out, is as plastic as all of the other features of everyday life. From this perspective, the foundations of everyday life lie not in its features per se but in the process itself of determining them in microsocial interactions. For this reason, it behooves us as scholars to pay close attention to the stories people tell in order to lay claim to the right to define the meanings of inherently plastic things. Why some situations become violent and others remain peaceful depends on precisely these everyday politics.

Consensus

In the end, then, self-authorization is never really the autonomous act of a single author. It always requires recognition in the eyes of others. It is always a performance that implies an audience (Goffman 1956). This fragile dependence on others for validation is one reason people tell stories in the first place. They use narrative to make a more compelling case for their right to lay down the law as they see fit. These stories of our everyday lives can be shared with others; or they can be the kinds of stories that we only tell ourselves to convince us that we are right. They sometimes get shared publicly after the fact, perhaps especially when those actions marked a rupture in the everyday lives of millions of people; or they may only remain private stories that we record in a memoir. The larger the stakes, however, the more we feel the need to justify that authority to ourselves and to others.

Perhaps for that reason, self-authorization has a certain tautological quality to it. It is a claim to act in and on everyday life with social legitimacy—a claim that is its own writ. Rather than reducing it to either individuals or collectives, the preceding chapters tracked the processes by which these negotiations take place incommon. During the Wende, for instance, they did so on multiple scales at the same time from the global to the local. Thousands of Germans of all sorts crossed the Wall in both directions, mounted it, took sledgehammers to it, took pictures while doing so, and told stories to legitimize this unruliness. Not all of the stories in this book are quite so earthshaking or so inspiring, but they shaped the *Alltag* nonetheless. They are the stories that modern Germans told to authorize their actions.

But given that multiplicity of experiences, *how could the Germans, no less the scholars who study them, ever come to consensus on what actually happened? Or to ask this question more pointedly, how is it possible to write a book about the ruptures in their everyday lives when those ruptures draw attention to precisely the incommensurability of diverse and seemingly contradictory everyday experiences?* This challenge is only compounded by the fact that we sought to write a book that spanned the twentieth century. Combining multiple life stories into one book—the stories of so many ruptures, large and small, that characterized the everyday lives of modern Germans—certainly evoked in us a deep sense of humility with regard to the scholarly endeavor. When we began this project, it seemed unlikely that these often radically different perspectives would fit together. Self-authorization gives rise to this fear—of an anarchy of individual subjectivities sharing nothing in common (Hammer 2006).

But people come to a pragmatic, provisional kind of consensus all the time. Our informants did so in the case of each of the features of everyday life that served as the focal point of the preceding chapters from the self to international borders. Conceding to a minimum level of agreement about the general contours of everyday life is a necessary function of it, without which human beings would not be able to interact with one another in meaningful ways.

Our method for writing this book was inspired in part by these same insights—the difference being that the lead authors tried to make those everyday practices into an intentional and self-critical methodology. So we end this chapter, and this book, with some brief comments about consensus: how it happens, in spite of the odds, that people come to accept certain things about everyday life as natural, even if provisionally; and how we, the twenty-six authors of this book, did the same with regard to the everyday lives of modern Germans.

According to the German philosopher, Edmund Husserl, consensus depends on the *intent* to find it (1973: 163–64). Mutual understandings exist embedded in the stories people tell about the world they share in common. They then clarify this knowledge implicitly through their interactions. To be sure, they sometimes also challenge that inherited stock of knowledge through their actions. But people do not need to agree on all things in order to come to consensus on some of them. We agree that walls are walls—for instance, the Berlin Wall—to keep people in or out, to paint graffiti on them, or to tear them down. Intent is always situational and tactical; it can also be complicated and even contradictory. Consensus begins in principle with self-authorizations. People lay claim to the right to make judgment calls about the world they share with others, in the hope that others will agree to some of those claims.

But those claims become social facts only when, as part of the bargains people make with their circumstances, other people agree to treat certain features of the everyday as fixed and valid in order to place others in question or to use them to their purposes. It really does not matter if these provisional agreements are the product of sincerity or calculation, passive acceptance or active approval, sloppy thinking or even self-deception.

Here is where academics can really learn from our informants. Precise definitions, accurate descriptions, and consistent usage are not prerequisites for consensus, since consensus is always temporary—the de facto outcomes of everyday politics. People often agree to disagree on the finer points in order to accomplish their goals here and now, since they reserve the right to change their minds next time.

Consensus is also not the same as compromise. Writing about the period after the Congress of Vienna in 1815, intellectual historian Frank R. Ankersmit (2002: 96) sees European political culture as arriving at a compromise between irreconcilable worldviews in order to maintain a society at relative civic peace. Consensus, by contrast, can only be arrived at when essential principles are shared.

This condition is surprisingly familiar, as we confront it every day. An example is language: without a common word for a thing, it is hard to talk about it, use it, or even destroy it. Yet just because we use the same word does not mean that we agree on its proper usage or underlying meaning. When living together with others, compromise can be hard, given our multiple experiences, intentions, values, and interests. Yet some degree of consensus on everyday life is necessary if we are to even hold that conversation. The intent to come to consensus thus provides the pragmatic foundation even for conflict. People accomplish this minimum degree of consensus all the time and without very much critical reflection, effort, or worry. If people do not look too closely at the details, to see if their terms conform in all ways to actual experiences and definitions, they enable themselves to do what they want in everyday life—that is the whole point.

Some evidence to support these claims comes from our own experience. The twenty-six authors in this book certainly shared some common principles about the study of everyday life. But we differed in terms of many of the details, and these differences created no small amount of conflict. Most of that conflict was productive; some of it was not. Our interactions took place in many different ways, in various settings, and with a wide range of commitments to the project as a whole. In their solo scholarship, the authors in this book reserve the right to interpret the evidence differently than it appears here—a dynamism that fits perfectly with our understanding of everyday life.

Still, a common consensus emerged gradually through the process of collaborative writing—case by case, chapter by chapter, and finally for the monograph as a whole. In effect, it happened in two ways. For the most part, the authorial teams actually listened to the evidence and interpretations that their colleagues were making about everyday life in one case and chose to adopt and adapt those concepts to the others. Sometimes, the lead authors took the lead in this intellectual work by proposing ways to weave themes from one case or one chapter into others.

It is worth mentioning that this process of collaborative writing leaves any notion of individual or even team authorship on rather shaky ground. The names at the end of the chapters often reflect the authors who provided the original scholarly contributions on which the chapters were based, and those authors certainly worked hardest on them. But many other voices from the larger group are present in each chapter, some softly and some loudly. You will also hear echoes in the text of the contributions of the series editor, numerous outside readers, and members of the audiences to whom we presented drafts of this work. And not least, you will hear the interpretive voices of the two lead authors in each of the chapters—to the satisfaction or dissatisfaction of the chapter authors.

In this collaborative effort to tell a coherent set of stories about the German *Alltag*, however, our most important partners were our German informants. We listened to the "voices" of hundreds of Germans—a few in person through interviews, but most mediated through their art, books, memoirs, newspapers, photographs, objects, records, and so on. The participants in these microsocial interactions did not stand as equals in terms of power or status. The voices of our informants were necessarily muffled in contrast to our own; and no doubt to some degree, our selections of particular anecdotes suited our own interests rather than theirs. Yet it would be a mistake to imagine that, as scholars, we could do what we wanted with the evidence. Our sources were unruly in that they often refused to comply cooperatively with our analyses.

Said in another way, we discovered a certain similarity between the everyday process of scholarship and the everyday that we were studying as scholars. Everyday life requires a process of coming to a provisional kind of consensus about its nature, whether you seek to study it or just inhabit it. For the purposes of this book, we had to build that consensus not only among scholarly authors, editors, and reviewers but also with our German informants, who insisted empirically on the validity of their own interpretations of everyday life. Everyday life in turn responded to our efforts at making sense of it with its usual plasticity. It turned pliant in response to some of our self-authorizations, allowing us some leeway for interpretation, while remaining resistant to others, stubbornly insisting on truths that refused to fit comfortably with our claims.

After six years of collaboration, many revisions, and many rounds of internal and external peer review, the primary authors of this conclusion were authorized—some might say we authorized ourselves—to describe our new approach to everyday life as we have now done. These four key terms derived in this way from the preceding chapters, but even so, the definitions you read here did not satisfy everyone. Still, we agreed to this much long before we wrote this conclusion: to use these terms softly and provisionally, with caution and caveats, adapting them to our own individual needs, so that we could at least communicate with each other and you, our readers. This process, by the way, was true of all of the body chapters as well. To some degree, each of the twenty-six authors of this book has chosen, actively or by default, to allow fellow authors to make claims that they believe are misguided, misleading, or downright wrong in order to be able to help say something together about the everyday lives of modern Germans.

Consensus happens. It emerges not in spite of the conflicts, ruptures, multivocality, plasticity, interactions, and authorizations of everyday life, but through them. Consensus takes place in common—referring to how we are when we interact with others, here and now. Coming to consensus about everyday life is thus a political process, both in academia and beyond. Arendt described politics as the world of *"common* sense" (our emphasis, 2005: 30–31). Conflict inevitably arises when we try to determine the forms, meanings, and functions of the everyday world we share with others; but her point is that politics "arises *between men"*—meaning human beings (again, our emphasis, 95).

This everyday kind of politics is both necessary and unavoidable. We need others to verify the meaning of things, including ourselves. Everyday life can have little meaning if those meanings are not shared to some degree with others. Yet the negotiations involved in determining the nature of things give them their plasticity and everyday life its multivocality. The everyday—defined through a process of coming to consensus about its nature while also inhabiting it—is thus always both political and collaborative. The twenty-six authors of this book generated the stories you have read in the same way: in common.

But here we reach the limit of our consensus—and our work together. Consensus presumes neither persistence, agreement, harmony, fixity, nor certainty. The fragments of everyday life will never fully fit together into an artificial order. Our book certainly exaggerates the degree to which the life stories of modern Germans make sense as part of something coherent called everyday life. And these are hardly the only stories that could and should be told about the everyday lives of modern Germans.

As for the four analytic concepts proposed in this conclusion, we suspect that they may not have the same validity in other contexts. Someone will no doubt do something unexpected with them soon enough. They may use them to craft their own stories of everyday life. At least, we hope so.

Andrew Stuart Bergerson, Mark E. Blum, Thomas Gurr, Alexandra Oeser, Steve Ostovich, Leonard Schmieding, and Sara Ann Sewell

REFERENCES

Published Material

Adler, Friedrich. 1906–7. "Friedrich Engels und die Naturwissenschaft." *Die Neue Zeit* 25, vol. 1, no. 19: 620–38.
A.G. Gender-Killer, e.V. 2005. *Antisemitismus und Geschlecht: Von "effeminierten Juden," "maskulinisierten Jüdinnen" und anderen Geschlechterbildern.* Münster: Unrast.
Ahbe, Thomas. 2005. *Ostalgie: Zum Umgang mit der DDR-Vergangenheit in den 1990er Jahren.* Erfurt: Landeszentrale für Politische Bildung Thüringen.
Alheit, Peter. 1983. *Alltagsleben: Zur Bedeutung eines gesellschaftlichen "Restphänomens."* Frankfurt a.M.: Campus.
Alexis, Willibald. 1905. *Erinnerungen.* Berlin: Concordia.
Allen, Ann Taylor. 1997. "The Holocaust and the Modernization of Gender: A Historiographical Essay." *Central European History* 30, no. 3: 349–64.
Allensbach Institut für Demoskopie. "Wertewandel Ost." *Märkische Allgemeine.* http://www.maz-online.de/Lokales/Bildergalerien-Region/Studie-Wertewandel-Ost#p0 (accessed December 2014).
Allert, Tilmann. 2005. *Der Deutsche Gruß: Geschichte einer unheilvollen Geste.* Berlin: Eichborn.
Allinson, Mark. 2009. "1977: The GDR's Most Normal Year?" In *Power and Society in the GDR, 1961–1979: The "Normalisation of Rule?"* Ed. Mary Fulbrook. New York: Berghahn, 253–77.
"Alte DDR Witze," *Witzeland: einfach lächerlich.* http://www.witzeland.de/ddrwitz/druck/DDRWitze01.pdf. Accessed November 2016.
Aly, Götz. 1995. *"Endlösung": Völkerverschiebung und der Mord an den europäischen Juden.* Frankfurt a.M.: Fischer.
———. 2005. *Hitlers Volksstaat: Raub, Rassenkrieg und nationaler Sozialismus.* Frankfurt a.M.: Fischer.
Anderson, Benedict. 1983. *Imagined Communities: Reflections on the Origin and Spread of Nationalism.* London: Verso.
Angrick, Andrej. 2003. *Besatzungspolitik und Massenmord: Die Einsatzgruppe D in der südlichen Sowjetunion 1941–1943.* Hamburg: Hamburger Edition.
Ankersmit, Frank R. 2002. *Political Representation.* Stanford: Stanford University Press.
Apel, Linde. 2003. *Jüdische Frauen im Konzentrationslager Ravensbrück 1939–1945.* Berlin: Metropol.
Appadurai, Arjun, ed. 1986. *The Social Life of Things: Commodities in Cultural Perspective.* Cambridge, UK: Cambridge University Press.

Arendt, Hannah. 2005. *The Promise of Politics*. Ed. Jerome Kohn. New York: Schocken Books.
Arnold, Jörg. 2011. *The Allied Air War and Urban Memory: The Legacy of Strategic Bombing in Germany*. Cambridge, UK: Cambridge University Press.
Ash, Timothy Garton. 2009. *The File: A Personal History*. London: Atlantic Books.
Assmann, Aleida. 2006. *Der Lange Schatten der Vergangenheit: Erinnerungskultur und Geschichtspolitik*. Munich: Beck.
———. 2011. *Cultural Memory and Western Civilization: Functions, Media, Archives*. New York: Cambridge University Press.
Assmann, Jan. 2006. *Religion and Cultural Memory*. Stanford: Stanford University Press.
Augé, Marc. 1995. *Non-Places: Introduction to an Anthropology of Supermodernity*. Trans. John Howe. London: Verso.
Augstein, Rudolf. 1987. *"Historikerstreit": Die Dokumentation der Kontroverse um die Einzigartigkeit der nationalsozialistischen Judenvernichtung*. Munich: Pieper.
Bach, Jonathan. 2002. "'The Taste Remains': Consumption, (N)ostalgia and the Production of East Germany." *Public Culture* 14, no. 3: 545–56.
———. 2005. "Vanishing Acts and Virtual Reconstructions: Technologies of Memory and the Afterlife of the GDR." In *Memory Traces: 1989 and the Question of German Cultural Identity*. Ed. S.A.-d. Simine. Oxford: Peter Lang, 261–80.
———. 2015. "Consuming Communism: Material Cultures of Nostalgia in Former East Germany." In *Anthropology and Nostalgia*. Ed. O. Angé and D. Berliner. New York: Berghahn, 123–38.
Bahr, Hermann. 1914. *Der Querulant: Kömodie in vier Akten*. Berlin: Fischer.
Bajohr, Frank and Michael Wildt. 2009. *Volksgemeinschaft: Neue Forschungen zur Gesellschaft des Nationalsozialismus*. Frankfurt a.M.: Fischer.
Baldwin, Peter. 1990. *Reworking the Past: Hitler, the Holocaust, and the Historians' Debate*. Boston: Beacon Press.
Bankier, David, ed. 2000. *Probing the Depths of German Antisemitism: German Society and the Persecution of the Jews*. New York: Berghahn.
Baranowski, Shelley. 2004. *Strength through Joy: Consumerism and Mass Tourism in the Third Reich*. Cambridge, UK: Cambridge University Press.
———. 2011. *Nazi Empire: German Colonialism and Imperialism from Bismarck to Hitler*. New York: Cambridge University Press.
Barlösius, Eva. 2003. "Weitgehend ungeplant und doch erwünscht: Figurationen und Habitus. Über den Stellenwert von nicht-intendiertem Handeln bei Norbert Elias und Pierre Bourdieu." In *Die Transintentionalität des Sozialen. Eine vergleichende Betrachtung klassischer und moderner Sozialtheorien*. Ed. Rainer Greshoff, Georg Kneer, und Uwe Schimank. Wiesbaden: Springer, 138–57.
Baudelaire, Charles. 1995. "The Painter of Modern Life." In *The Painter of Modern Life and Other Essays*. Ed. and trans. Jonathan Mayne. London: Phaidon Press, 1–40.
Baudrillard, Jean. 2005 [1968]. *The System of Objects*. New York: Verso.

Bauman, Zygmunt. 1989. *Modernity and the Holocaust*. Ithaca: Cornell University Press.
Beattie, Andrew H. 2008. *Playing Politics with History: The Bundestag Inquiry into East Germany*. New York: Berghahn.
———. 2011. "The Politics of Remembering the GDR: Official and State-Mandated Memory since 1990." In *Remembering the German Democratic Republic: Divided Memory in a United Germany*. Ed. D. Clarke and U. Wölfel. New York: Palgrave, 23–34.
Becker, Manuel. 2011. "Die Bedeutung des deutschen Diktaturenvergleich für die politische Kultur der 'Berliner Republik.'" *Deutschland Archiv* 8 (16 August). http://www.bpb.de/geschichte/zeitgeschichte/deutschlandarchiv/53434/diktaturenvergleich-und-politische-kultur?p=all (accessed 3 January 2014).
Beer, Suzanne. 2014. "Aid Offered Jews in Nazi Germany: Research Approaches, Methods, and Problems." *Online Encyclopedia of Mass Violence* (22 September). http://www.massviolence.org/Aid-Offered-Jews-in-Nazi-Germany (accessed 17 August 2015).
Begall, Kläre. 1984. "'Ein Leben ohne Vorurteile, dazu Civilcourage.' Interview von Kläre Bloch (geb. Begall) mit Hans Wienicke." In *Ein Leben ohne Vorurteile, dazu Zivilcourage*. Ed. Kläre-Bloch-Schule. Berlin: Selbstverlag, 14–26.
Bendix, Regina. 1997. *In Search of Authenticity: The Formation of Folklore Studies*. Madison: University of Wisconsin Press.
Benjamin, Walter. 1979. "Theories of German Fascism: On the Collection of Essays *War and Warrior*, Edited by Ernst Jünger." Trans. Jerolf Wikoff. *New German Critique*, no. 17 (Spring): 120–28.
———. 1998. *The Work of Art in the Age of Mechanical Reproduction*. Transcribed by Andy Blunden. UCLA School of Theater, Film and Television. http://www.marxists.org/reference/subject/philosophy/works/ge/benjamin.htm (accessed 20 December 2013).
———. 2002. *The Arcades Project*. Ed. Rolf Tiedemann. Trans. Howard Eiland. New York: Belknap Press of Harvard University Press.
———. 2003. *Walter Benjamin, Selected Writings, Volume Four, 1938–1940*. Trans. Edmund Jephcott et al. Cambridge, MA: Belknap Press of Harvard University Press.
———. 2006a. *Berlin Childhood around 1900*. Cambridge, MA: Belknap Press of Harvard University Press.
———. 2006b. *The Writer of Modern Life: Essays on Charles Baudelaire*. Trans. Howard Eiland, Edmund Jephcott, Rodney Livingston, and Harry Zohn. Cambridge, MA: Belknap Press of Harvard University Press.
Bennett, Judith M. 2006. *History Matters: Patriarchy and the Challenge of Feminism*. Philadelphia: University of Pennsylvania Press.
Bennewitz, Inge and Rainer Potratz. 1997. *Zwangsaussiedlungen an der innerdeutschen Grenze*. Berlin: Links.
Bensa, Alban, and Eric Fassin. 2002. "Qu'est-ce qu'un évènement? Les sciences sociales face à l'évènement." *Terrain*, no. 38: 5–20.

Benz, Wolfgang, ed. 1988. *Die Juden in Deutschland 1933–1945: Leben unter nationalsozialistischer Herrschaft*. Munich: Beck.

———. 1991. *Dimension des Völkermords: Die Zahl der jüdischen Opfer des Nationalsozialismus*. Munich: Oldenbourg.

———. 2006. "Juden im Untergrund und ihre Helfer." In *Überleben im Dritten Reich Juden im Untergrund und ihre Helfer*. Ed. Wolfgang Benz. Munich: Deutscher, 11–48.

Benz, Wolfgang and Werner Bergmann, eds. 1997. *Vorurteil und Völkermord: Entwicklungslinien des Antisemitismus*. Freiburg im Breisgau: Herder.

Berdahl, Daphne. 1999. *Where the World Ended: Re-Unification and Identity in the German Borderland*. Berkeley: University of California Press.

———. 2010. "Expressions of Experience and Experience of Expression: Museum Re-Presentations of GDR History." In *On the Social Life of Postsocialism: Memory, Consumption, Germany*. Ed. Matti Bunzl. Bloomington: Indiana University Press, 112–22.

Berenson, Edward and Eva Giloi, eds. 2010. *Constructing Charisma: Celebrity, Fame, and Power in Nineteenth Century Europe*. New York: Berghahn.

Berg, Christa, ed. 1991. *Handbuch der deutschen Bildungsgeschichte. Vol. 4: 1870–1918, von der Reichsgründung bis zum Ende des Ersten Weltkriegs*. Munich: Beck.

Berger, Peter L. and Thomas Luckmann. 1996. *Die gesellschaftliche Konstruktion der Wirklichkeit: Eine Theorie der Wissensoziologie*. Frankfurt a.M.: Fischer.

Berger, Stefan and Bill Niven, eds. 2014. *Writing the History of Memory*. London: Bloomsbury.

Bergerson, Andrew Stuart. 2004. *Ordinary Germans in Extraordinary Times: The Nazi Revolution in Hildesheim*. Bloomington: Indiana University Press.

———. 2008. "The Devil's Horn in Hildesheim: Or the Space and Time of Everyday Life." In *Alltag, Erfahrung, Eigensinn: Historisch-anthropologische Erkundungen*. Ed. Belinda Davis, Thomas Lindenberger, and Michael Wildt. Frankfurt: Campus, 249–63.

———. 2010. "Raum und Zeit in der deutschen Mittelstadt." In *Mittelstadt: Urbanes Leben jenseits der Großstadt*. Ed. Brigitte Schmid-Lauber. Frankfurt: Campus, 245–60.

Bergerson, Andrew Stuart, K. Scott Baker, Clancy Martin, and Steven Ostovich. 2011. *The Happy Burden of History: From Sovereign Impunity to Responsible Selfhood*. Interdisciplinary German Cultural Studies 9. Berlin: De Gruyter.

Bergerson, Andrew Stuart, Elissa Mailänder Koslov, Gideon Reuveni, Paul Steege, and Dennis Sweeney. 2009. "Forum: Everyday Life in Nazi Germany." *German History* 27, no. 4: 560–79.

Berlin Aktuell. "Jeder Zweite Ostdeutsche fühlt sich als Wende-Gewinner." Berlin. de. 1 October 2014. http://www.berlin.de/aktuelles/berlin/3639179-958092-umfragen-jeder-zweite-ostdeutsche-fuehlt.html (accessed December 2014).

Bernus, Alexander von. 1984. *Wachsen am Wunder: Heidelberger Kindheit und Jugend*. Heidelberg: Heidelberger Verlagsanstalt.

Betts, Paul. 2010. *Within Walls: Private Life in the German Democratic Republic.* Oxford: Oxford University Press.
Black, Monica. 2010. *Death in Berlin: From Weimar to Divided Germany.* Cambridge, UK: Cambridge University Press.
Blatman, Daniel. 2011. *The Death Marches: The Final Phase of Nazi Genocide.* Trans. Chaya Galai. Cambridge, MA: Belknap Press of Harvard University Press.
Blaylock, Sarah. 2013. "Whither *Alltag?* How the Wende Museum Revises East German History (and Why It Matters)." *Verges: Germanic & Slavic Studies in Review of the University of Victoria* 2, no. 2: 1–17.
Blum, Mark E. 2011. *Kafka's Social Discourse: An Aesthetic Search for Community.* Bethlehem: Lehigh University Press.
Blum, Mark E. and William Smaldone, eds. 2015. *Austro-Marxism: The Ideology of Unity. Vol. 1: Austro-Marxist Theory and Strategy.* Leiden: Brill.
Bock, Gisela. 1989. "Die Frauen und der Nationalsozialismus: Bemerkungen zu einem Buch von Claudia Koonz." *Geschichte und Gesellschaft* 15: 563–79.
———. 1997. "Ganz normale Frauen: Täter, Opfer, Mitläufer und Zuschauer im Nationalsozialismus." In *Zwischen Karriere und Verfolgung: Handlungsräume von Frauen im nationalsozialistischen Deutschland.* Ed. Kirsten Heinsohn, Barbara Vogel, and Ulrike Weckel. Frankfurt a.M.: Campus, 245–77.
Bodek, Richard. 1997. *Proletarian Performance in Weimar Berlin: Agitprop, Chorus, and Brecht.* Columbia: Camden House.
Borries, Bodo von. 1995. *Das Geschichtsbewusstsein Jugendlicher: Eine repräsentative Untersuchung über Vergangenheitsdeutungen, Gegenwartswahrnehmungen und Zukunftserwartungen von Schülerinnen und Schülern in Ost- und Westdeutschland.* Weinheim/Munich: Juventa.
Borscheid, Peter. 1986. "Alltagsgeschichte—Modetorheit oder neues Tor zur Vergangenheit?" In *Sozialgeschichte in Deutschland. Vol. 3: Soziales Verhalten und soziale Aktionsformen in der Geschichte.* Ed. Wolfgang Schieder and Volker Sellin. Göttingen: V&R Kleine Vandenhoeck Reihe, 78–100.
Bourdieu, Pierre. 1974. "Avenir de classe et causalité du probable." *Revue française de sociologie* 15, no. 1: 3–42.
———. 1977. *Outline of a Theory of Practice.* Trans. Richard Nice. Cambridge, UK: Cambridge University Press.
———. 1993. "Ortseffekte." *Das Elend der Welt: Zeugnisse und Diagnosen alltäglichen Leidens an der Gesellschaft.* Ed. Pierre Bourdieu. Konstanz: UVK Universitätsverlag, 159–68.
Bowlby, Chris. 1986. "Blutmai 1929: Police, Parties and Proletarians in a Berlin Confrontation." *The Historical Journal* 29, no. 1: 137–58.
Boyer, Dominic. 2005. *Spirit and System: Media, Intellectuals, and the Dialectic in Modern German Culture.* Chicago: University of Chicago Press.
Bredel, Willi. 1981. *Die Prüfung.* Berlin: Aufbau.
Brenner, Michael, ed. 2012. *Geschichte der Juden in Deutschland. Von 1945 bis zur Gegenwart.* Munich: Beck.

———. 1995. *Nach dem Holocaust: Juden in Deutschland 1945–1950*. München: Beck.
Brentano, Franz. 1973. *Psychology from an Empirical Standpoint*. Ed. Oskar Kraus. Trans. Antos C. Rancurello, D.B. Terrell, and Linda L. McAlister. New York: Humanities Press.
Broszat, Martin, ed. 1977–83. *Bayern in der NS-Zeit*. Munich: Oldenbourg.
———. 1981 [1969]. *The Hitler State: The Foundation and Development of the Internal Structure of the Third Reich*. London: Longman.
Browning, Christopher. 1992. *Ordinary Men: Reserve Police Battalion 101 and the Final Solution in Poland*. New York: HarperCollins.
Brunner, José and Nathalie Zajde. 2011. *Holocaust und Trauma: Kritische Perspektiven zur Entstehung und Wirkung eines Paradigmas*. Göttingen: Wallstein.
Buber-Neumann, Margarete. 2002. *Als Gefangene bei Stalin und Hitler: Eine Welt im Dunkel*. Munich: Ullstein.
Buchholz, Kai, ed. 2001. *Die Lebensreform: Entwürfe zur Neugestaltung von Leben und Kunst um 1900*. 2 vols. Darmstadt: Häusser.
Buck-Morss, Susan. 1989. *The Dialectics of Seeing: Walter Benjamin and the Arcades Project*. Cambridge, MA: MIT Press.
———. 2000. *Dreamworld and Catastrophe: The Passing of Mass Utopias in East and West*. Cambridge, MA: MIT Press.
Buggeln, Marc. 2009. *Arbeit & Gewalt: Das Außenlagersystem des KZ Neuengamme*. Göttingen: Wallstein.
Bullock, Marcus P. 1992. *The Violent Eye: Ernst Jünger's Visions and Revisions on the European Right*. Detroit: Wayne State University Press.
Burckhardt, Jakob. 1860. *Die Cultur der Renaissance in Italien: Ein Versuch*. Basel: Schweighauser.
Busch, Karl. 1938. *Unter dem Sonnenrad*. Berlin: Verlag der deutschen Arbeitsfront.
Butler, Judith. 1999. *Gender Trouble: Feminism and the Subversion of Identity*. New York: Routledge.
Büttner, Ursula. 2003. *Die Deutschen und die Judenverfolgung im Dritten Reich*. Frankfurt a.M.: Fischer.
Caplan, Jane. 1989. "Postmodernism, Poststructuralism, and Deconstruction: Notes for Historians." *Central European History* 22, no. 3/4: 260–78.
Caplan, Jane and Nikolaus Wachsmann. 2010. *Concentration Camps in Nazi Germany: The New Histories*. London: Routledge.
Carter, April. 1992. *Peace Movements: International Protest and World Politics Since 1945*. London: Longman.
Casey, Edward S. 1987. *Remembering: A Phenomenological Study*. Bloomington: Indiana University Press.
Certeau, Michel de. 1984. *The Practice of Everyday Life*. Trans. Steven Rendall. Berkeley: University of California Press.
Chakrabarty, Dipesh. 2000. *Provincializing Europe: Postcolonial Thought and Historical Difference*. Princeton: Princeton University Press.

Christ, Michaela. 2011. *Die Dynamik des Tötens: Die Ermordung der Juden in Berditschew. Ukraine 1941–1944*. Frankfurt a.M.: Fischer.
Clarke, David and Ute Wölfel. 2011. *Remembering the German Democratic Republic: Divided Memory in a United Germany*. New York: Palgrave Macmillan.
Comaroff, John and Jean Comaroff. 1992. *Ethnography and the Historical Imagination*. Boulder: Westview Press.
Confino, Alon and Peter Fritzsche. 2002. *Work of Memory: New Directions in the Study of German Society and Culture*. Urbana: University of Illinois Press.
Connell, Raewyn. 1995. *Masculinities*. Berkeley: University of California Press.
Connell, Raewyn and James W. Messerschmidt. 2005. "Hegemonic Masculinity: Rethinking the Concept." *Gender and Society* 19, no. 6: 829–59.
Conrad, Michael G. 1886. "Wagneriana." *Die Gesellschaft* 2, no. 2: 244–47.
Cramer, John. 2007. "'Tapfer, unbescholten, mit reinem Gewissen.' KZ-Aufseherinnen im ersten Belsen-Prozess eines britischen Militärgericht 1945." In *Im Gefolge der SS: Aufseherinnen des Frauen-KZ Ravensbrück. Begleitband zur Ausstellung*. Ed. Simone Erpel, Jeanette Toussaint, Johannes Schwartz, and Lavern Wolfram. Schriftenreihe der Stiftung Brandenburgische Gedenkstätten, no. 17. Berlin: Metropol, 103–13.
———. 2011. *Belsen Trial 1945: der Lüneburger Prozess gegen Wachpersonal der Konzentrationslager Auschwitz und Bergen-Belsen*. Göttingen: Wallstein.
Crane, Susan. 1997. "Memory, History and Distortion in the Museum." *History and Theory* 36, no. 4: 44–63.
Crew, David F. 1998. *Germans on Welfare: From Weimar to Hitler*. New York: Oxford University Press.
Dannecker, Martin and Reimut Reiche. 1974. *Der gewöhnliche Homosexuelle: Eine soziologische Untersuchung über männliche Homosexuelle in der Bundesrepublik*. Frankfurt a.M.: Fischer.
Dauenheimer, Karin. 1995 [1987]. "Das Schweigen durchbrechen: Zur Situation von Lesben und in Kirche und Homosexuellen-Bewegung (Vortrag)." In *Frauengruppen in der DDR der 80er Jahre: Eine Dokumentation*. Ed. Samirah Kenawi. Berlin: GrauZone, 395–407.
Davis, Belinda, Thomas Lindenberger, and Michael Wildt. 2008. "Einleitung." In *Alltag, Erfahrung, Eigensinn: Historisch-anthropologische Erkundungen*. Ed. Belinda Davis, Thomas Lindenberger, and Michael Wildt. Frankfurt a.M.: Campus, 11–28.
Decker, Oliver, Johannes Kiess, and Elmar Brähler. 2014. *Die stabilisierte Mitte Rechtsextreme Einstellung in Deutschland*. Leipzig: Leipzig University.
Demshuk, Andrew. 2012. *The Lost German East: Forced Migration and the Politics of Memory, 1945–1970*. Cambridge, UK: Cambridge University Press.
Derrida, Jacques. 1997. *Of Grammatology*. Baltimore: Johns Hopkins University Press.
Diehl, Paula. 2002. *Macht—Mythos—Utopie: Die Körperbilder der SS-Männer*. Berlin: Akademie.

———. 2006. *Körper im Nationalsozialismus: Bilder und Praxen*. Munich: Fink.
Dilthey, Wilhelm. 1959. *Introduction to the Human Sciences: An Attempt to Lay a Foundation for the Study of Society and History*. Trans. Ramon J. Betanzos. Detroit: Wayne State University Press.
Diner, Dan. 1988. *Zivilizationsbruch: Denken nach Auschwitz*. Frankfurt a.M.: Fischer.
Douglas, Jack D. 1971. "Understanding Everyday Life." In *Understanding Everyday Life*. Ed. Jack D. Douglas. London: Routledge & Kegan Paul, 3–44.
Douglas, Mary. 1986. *How Institutions Think*. Syracuse: Syracuse University Press.
Douglas, R.M. 2013. *Orderly and Humane: The Expulsions of the Germans after the Second World War*. New Haven: Yale University Press.
Duchhardt, Heinz. 1985. "Europäisch-afrikanische Rechtsbeziehungen in der Epoche des 'Vorkolonialismus.'" *Saeculum* 36, no. 4: 367–79.
Durkheim, Emile. 2002 [1895]. *Les règles de la méthode sociologique*. Paris: PUF.
Durst, David C. 2004. *Weimar Modernism: Philosophy, Politics, and Culture in Germany, 1918–1933*. Lanham: Lexington Books.
Eckert, Astrid M. 2011. "'Greetings from the Zonal Border': Tourism to the Iron Curtain in West Germany." *Zeithistorische Forschung/Studies in Contemporary History* 8, no. 1: 9–36.
Elder, Lara. 2011. "Constructing Legitimacy: Strategies of Self-Authorization in Heinrich Heine's Prefaces." *Oxford German Studies* 40, no. 3: 240–52.
Eldridge, Richard Thomas. 2001. *The Persistence of Romanticism: Essays in Philosophy and Literature*. Cambridge, UK: Cambridge University Press.
Eley, Geoff. 1989. "Labor History, Social History, 'Alltagsgeschichte': Experience, Culture, and the Politics of the Everyday—a New Direction for German Social History?" *Journal of Modern History* 61, no. 2: 297–343.
Elias, Norbert. 1978. "Zum Begriff des Alltags." In *Materialien zur Soziologie des Alltags*. Ed. Kurt Hammerich and Michael Klein. Opladen: Westdeutscher, 22–29.
Ellger, Hans. 2007. *Zwangsarbeit und weibliche Überlebensstrategien: Die Geschichte der Frauenaußenlager des Konzentrationslagers Neuengamme 1944/1945*. Geschichte der Konzentrationslager 1933–1945, no. 8. Berlin: Metropol.
Epelfeld, Naum. 2004. "Möge mein Gedächtnis das Vergessen verhindern ..." In *"Nur wir haben überlebt": Holocaust in der Ukraine, Zeugnisse und Dokumente*. Ed. Boris M. Zambarko, Margaret Müller, and Werner Müller. Trans. Margrit Hegge, Renate Meier, and Ruth Vogt. Cologne: Dittrich, 110–29.
Epstein, Catherine. 2010. *Model Nazi: Arthur Greiser and the Occupation of Western Poland*. Oxford: Oxford University Press.
Erpel, Simone. 2007. "Einführung." In *Im Gefolge der SS: Aufseherinnen des Frauen-KZ Ravensbrück. Begleitband zur Ausstellung*. Ed. Simone Erpel, Jeanette Toussaint, Johannes Schwartz, and Lavern Wolfram. Schriftenreihe der Stiftung Brandenburgische Gedenkstätten, no. 17. Berlin: Metropol, 15–36.
Das Erste Mediathek. 2009. "Schabowskis Zettel." ARD-Fernsehdokumentation (2 November). http://mediathek.daserste.de/Reportage-Dokumentation/Scha

bowskis-Zettel/Das-Erste/Video?documentId=8577490&topRessort=tv&bcast Id=799280 (accessed 11 December 2014).
Evans, Jennifer. 2010. "Decriminalization, Seduction, and 'Unnatural Desire' in the German Democratic Republic." *Feminist Studies* 36, no. 3: 553–77.
Evans, Richard J. 1991. *Im Schatten Hitlers? Historikerstreit und Vergangenheitsbewältigung in der Bundesrepublik.* Frankfurt a.M.: Suhrkamp.
———. 2005. "Zwei deutsche Diktaturen im 20. Jahrhundert?" *Aus Politik und Zeitgeschichte* 1, no. 2: 5–9.
Fallada, Hans. 1988. *Jeder stirbt für sich allein.* Reinbek bei Hamburg: Rowohlt.
Fallersleben, August Heinrich Hoffman von. 1868. *Mein Leben: Aufzeichnungen und Erinnerungen.* 2 vols. Hannover: Carl Rümpler.
Fechner, Eberhard and Norddeutscher Rundfunk. 1984. *Der Prozess: Eine Darstellung des Majdanek-Verfahrens in Düsseldorf.* VHS. Waltham, MA: The National Center for Jewish Film.
Feinstein, Joshua. 2002. *The Triumph of the Ordinary: Depictions of Daily Life in the East German Cinema, 1949–1989.* Chapel Hill: University of North Carolina Press.
Fischer, Norbert. 2010. "Von Krematisten und Sozialisten: Zur Geschichte weltlicher Bestattungskultur." In *Humanistische Bestattungskultur.* Ed. Horst Groschopp. Aschaffenburg: Alibri, 66–78.
Fischer, Vanessa. 2014. "Wir sind ein Volk." *Deutsche Rufe,* Deutschlandradio Kultur, 14 July.
Foucault, Michel. 1983. "The Subject and Power." In *Michel Foucault: Beyond Structuralism and Hermeneutics.* Ed. Hubert L. Dreyfus and Paul Rabinow. Chicago: University of Chicago Press, 208–28.
———. 1991. "Governmentality." Trans. Rosi Braidotti and revised by Colin Gordon. In *The Foucault Effect: Studies in Governmentality.* Ed. Graham Burchell, Colin Gordon, and Peter Miller. Chicago: University of Chicago Press, 87–104.
———. 1994. *The Order of Things: An Archaeology of the Human Sciences.* New York: Vintage.
———. 2005. *The Hermeneutics of the Subject: Lectures at the Collège De France, 1981–82.* New York: Palgrave Macmillan.
Frei, Norbert, ed. 2001. *Karrieren im Zwielicht: Hitlers Eliten nach 1945.* Frankfurt a.M.: Campus.
Freidank, Gustav E. 1975. *Alles hat am Ende sich gelohnt: Material für weltliche Trauerfeiern.* Leipzig: Zentralhaus für Kulturarbeit der DDR.
Frese, Matthias. 1991. *Betriebspolitik im "Dritten Reich": Deutsche Arbeitsfront, Unternehmer und Staatsbürokratie in der westdeutschen Großindustrie 1933–1939.* Paderborn: Schöningh.
Freud, Sigmund. 1938. "Psychopathology of Everyday Life." In *The Basic Writings of Sigmund Freud.* Trans. and ed. A.A. Brill. New York: Modern Library, 35–178.
Friederici, Hans-Jürgen and Wolfgang Welckerling. 1975. "Zur Entwicklung des antifaschistischen Widerstandskampfes unter der Führung der KPD in den

Jahren 1933 bis 1935 in Leipzig." *Jahrbuch zur Geschichte der Stadt Leipzig*: 23–46.

Friedlander, Henry. 1997. *Der Weg zum NS-Genozid: Von der Euthanasie zur Endlösung*. Trans. Johanna Friedman, Martin Richter, and Barbara Schaden. Berlin: Berlin.

Friedman, Philip and Ada June Friedman. 1980. *Roads to Extinction: Essays on the Holocaust*. New York: Conference on Jewish Social Studies.

Friedrich, Ernst. 2014 [1924]. *War against War!* Facsimile of the first edition, with a foreword by Bruce Kent. Nottingham: Russell Press.

Fritzsche, Peter. 2008. *Life and Death in the Third Reich*. Cambridge, MA: Harvard University Press.

Fuchs, Anne. 2012. *After the Dresden Bombing: Pathways of Memory, 1945 to the Present*. Houndmills: Palgrave Macmillan.

Fukuyama, Francis. 1992. *The End of History and the Last Man*. New York: Free Press.

Fulbrook, Mary. 1995. *Anatomy of a Dictatorship: Inside the GDR, 1949–1989*. New York: Oxford University Press.

———. 2005. *The People's State: East German Society from Hitler to Honecker*. New Haven: Yale University Press.

———. 2011. *Dissonant Lives: Generations and Violence through the German Dictatorships*. Oxford: Oxford University Press.

———. 2012. *A Small Town Near Auschwitz: Ordinary Nazis and the Holocaust*. Oxford: Oxford University Press.

Geisel, Christof. 2005. *Auf der Suche nach einem dritten Weg: Das politische Selbstverständnis der DDR-Opposition in den 80er Jahren*. Berlin: Links.

Gellateley, Robert. 2002. *Backing Hitler: Consent and Coercion in Nazi Germany*. Oxford: Oxford University Press.

Gerlach, Christian. 2010. *Extremely Violent Societies: Mass Violence in the Twentieth-Century World*. Cambridge, UK: Cambridge University Press.

Gesellschaft für deutsche Sprache e.V. "Wort des Jahres." Gesellschaft für die deutsche Sprache. http://gfds.de/aktionen/wort-des-jahres (accessed December 2014).

Geyer, Michael. 1992. "Resistance as Ongoing Project: Visions of Order, Obligations to Strangers, Struggles for Civil Society." *Journal of Modern History* 64, supplement: Resistance against the Third Reich (December): 217–41.

Gies, Horst. 1995. "Die Rolle der Gefühle im Geschichtsunterricht des Dritten Reiches und der DDR." *Geschichte in Wissenschaft und Unterricht* 46, no. 3: 127–41.

Gigliotti, Simone. 2009. *The Train Journey: Transit, Captivity, and Witnessing in the Holocaust*. New York: Berghahn.

Ginzburg, Carlo. 1985. "Was ist Mikrogeschichte?" *Geschichtswerkstatt* 6: 48–52.

Ginzburg, Carlo and Carlo Poni. 1991. "The Name and the Game: Unequal Exchange and the Historiographical Marketplace." In *Microhistory and the Lost Peoples* of Europe. Ed. Edward Muir and Guido Ruggiero. Baltimore: Johns Hopkins University Press, 1–10.

Glaeser, Andreas. 2011. *Political Epistemics: The Secret Police, the Opposition, and the End of East German Socialism*. Chicago: University of Chicago Press.

Gleason, Maud. 2001. "Mutilated Messengers: Body Language in Josephus." In *Being Greek under Rome: Cultural Identity, the Second Sophistic and the Development of Empire*. Cambridge, UK: Cambridge University Press, 50–85.

Goffman, Erving. 1956. *The Presentation of Self in Everyday Life*. Edinburgh: University of Edinburgh, Social Sciences Research Centre.

———. 1974. *Frame Analysis: An Essay on the Organization of Experience*. New York: Harper & Row.

Goldhagen, Daniel J. 1996. *Hitler's Willing Executioners: Ordinary Germans and the Holocaust*. New York: Knopf.

Gottwaldt, Alfred B. and Diana Schulle. 2005. *Die Judendeportationen aus dem Deutschen Reich, 1941–1945: Eine kommentierte Chronologie*. Wiesbaden: Marix.

Goyens, Tom. 2007. *Beer and Revolution: The German Anarchist Movement in New York City, 1880–1914*. Urbana: University of Illinois Press.

Grau, Günter. 1999. "Return of the Past: The Policy of the SED and the Laws against Homosexuality in Eastern Germany Between 1946 and 1968." *Journal of Homosexuality* 37, no. 4: 1–21.

———. 2002. "Liberalisierung und Repression: Zur Strafrechtsdiskussion zum §175 in der DDR." *Zeitschrift für Sexualforschung* 15, no. 4: 323–40.

Greenblatt, Stephen. 1980. *Renaissance Self-Fashioning: From More to Shakespeare*. Chicago: University of Chicago Press.

Greiner, Bettina. 2014. *Suppressed Terror: History and Perception of Soviet Special Camps in Germany*. Lanham: Lexington.

Grill, Johnpeter H. and Robert L. Jenkins. 1992. "The Nazis and the American South in the 1930s: A Mirror Image?" *Journal of Southern History* 58, no. 4: 667–94.

Groeben, Otto Friedrich von der. 1694. *Guineische Reise-Beschreibung, nebst einem Anhange der Expedition in Morea*; published with *Orientalische Reise-Beschreibung des Brandenburgischen Adelichen Pilgers O.F. von der G*. Marienwerder: Simon Reinigern.

Gröning, Gert and Joachim Wolschke-Bulmahn. 1987. *Der Drang Nach Osten: Zur Entwicklung der Landespflege im Nationalsozialismus und während des 2. Weltkrieges in den "eingegliederten Ostgebieten."* Munich: Minerva.

Grossman, Wasili S. 1994. "Die Ermordung der Juden in Berditschew." In *Das Schwarzbuch. Der Genozid an den sowjetischen Juden*. Ed. Ilja Ehrenburg, Wasili Grossmann, and Arno Lustiger. Reinbek bei Hamburg: Rowohlt, 59–72.

Grossmann, Atina. 1991. "Feminist Debates about Women and National Socialism." *Gender & History* 3, no. 3: 350–58.

———. 2007. *Jews, Germans, and Allies: Close Encounters in Occupied Germany*. Princeton: Princeton University Press.

———. 2011. "The 'Big Rape': Sex and Sexual Violence, War, and Occupation in Post-World War II Memory and Imagination." In *Sexual Violence in Conflict Zones: From the Ancient World to the Era of Human Rights*. Ed. Elizabeth D. Heineman. Philadelphia: Pennsylvania State University Press, 137–51.

Gruner, Wolf. 1997. *Der Geschlossene Arbeitseinsatz deutscher Juden: Zur Zwangsarbeit als Element der Verfolgung 1938–1943*. Berlin: Metropol.

———. 2002. *Öffentliche Wohlfahrt und Judenverfolgung: Wechselwirkungen lokaler und zentraler Politik im NS-Staat (1933–1942)*. Munich: Oldenbourg.

———. 2005. *Widerstand in der Rosenstrasse: Die Fabrik-Aktion und die Verfolgung der "Mischehen" 1943*. Frankfurt a.M.: Fischer.

Gudehus, Christian. 2006. *Dem Gedächtnis zuhören: Erzählungen über NS-Verbrechen und ihre Repräsentation in deutschen Gedenkstätten*. Essen: Klartext.

Gudehus, Christian and Michaela Christ, eds. 2013. *Gewalt: Ein interdisziplinäres Handbuch*. Stuttgart: J.B. Metzler.

Gürtler, Bernd. 1988. "Hip Hop in Sachsen." *Unterhaltungskunst* 6: 12–13.

Haase-Hindenberg, Gerhard. 2007. *Der Mann der die Mauer öffnete: Warum Oberstleutnant Harald Jäger den Befehl verweigerte und damit Weltgeschichte schrieb*. Munich: Heyne.

Habermas, Jürgen. 1992. "Staatsbürgerschaft und nationale Identität." In *Faktizität und Geltung*. Ed. Jürgen Habermas. Frankfurt a.M.: Suhrkamp, 632–60.

———. 1997. *A Berlin Republic: Writings on Germany*. Trans. Steven Randall. Introduction by Peter Uwe Hohendahl. Lincoln: University of Nebraska Press.

Haeming, Anne. 2014. "Der Grenzer, Der Die Mauer Öffnete: 'Ich Habe Nur Das Menschliche Getan.'" *Die Tageszeitung* (5 November), sec. Alltag. http://www.taz.de/Der-Grenzer-der-die-Mauer-oeffnete/!148937/. (accessed January 2015).

Hagemann, Karen. 1990. *Frauenalltag und Männerpolitik: Alltagsleben und gesellschaftliches Handeln von Arbeiterfrauen in der Weimarer Republik*. Bonn: Dietz.

Haider, Edgar. 2006. "Romanisches Café, Berlin." In *Verlorene Pracht: Geschichten von zerstörten Bauten*. Ed. Edgar Haider. Hildesheim: Gerstenberg, 163–67.

Halder, Winfrid. 2006. *Innenpolitik im Kaiserreich 1871–1914*. Darmstadt: Wissenschaftliche Buchgesellschaft.

Hammer, Espen. 2006. "Cavell and Political Romanticism." In *The Claim to Community: Essays on Stanley Cavell and Political Philosophy*. Ed. Andrew Norris. Stanford: Stanford University Press, 164–85.

Hammerich, Kurt and Michael Klein, eds. 1978. *Materialien zur Soziologie des Alltags*. Opladen: Westdeutscher.

Happe, Barbara. 2001. "Urnengemeinschaftsanlagen: Zur Bestattungs- und Friedhofskultur in der DDR." *Deutschland Archiv* 34, no. 3: 436–46.

Harley, J. Bryan. 1988. "Maps, Knowledge and Power." In *The Iconography of Landscape*. Ed. Denis Cosgrove and Stephen Daniels. Cambridge, UK: Cambridge University Press, 277–312.

Harootunian, Harry. 2000. *History's Disquiet: Modernity, Cultural Practice, and the Question of Everyday Life*. New York: Columbia University Press.

Harris, Marvin. 1988. *Culture, People, Nature: An Introduction to General Anthropology*, 5th ed. New York: Harper & Row, 131–33.
Harsch, Donna. 2007. *Revenge of the Domestic: Women, the Family, and Communism in the German Democratic Republic*. Princeton: Princeton University Press.
Hartwig, Jürgen. 1994. "Einleitung." *Rundbrief*, 3.
Harvey, David. 2003. *Paris: Capital of Modernity*. New York: Routledge.
Harvey, Elizabeth. 2003. *Women and the Nazi East: Agents and Witnesses of Germanization*. New Haven: Yale University Press.
Hauptmann, Gerhart. 1924. *Ausblicke*. Berlin: Fischer.
Hauptmeyer, Carl-Hans, Detlef Schmiechen-Ackermann, and Thomas Schwark, eds. 2011. *Grenzziehung—Grenzerfahrung—Grenzüberschreitung: Die innerdeutsche Grenze 1945–1990*. Darmstadt: Wissenschaftliche Buchgesellschaft.
Haury, Thomas. 2002. *Antisemitismus von Links: Kommunistische Ideologie, Nationalismus und Antizionismus in der frühen DDR*. Hamburg: Hamburger Edition.
Hauss, Friedrich, Rainer Land, and Andreas Willisch. 2006. "Umbruch der Agrarverfassung und der Zerfall der ländlichen Gesellschaft." *Politik und Zeitgeschichte* 37, no. 11: 31–38.
Headland, Thomas N., Kenneth Pike, and Marvin Harris, eds. 1990. *Emics and Etics: The Insider/Outsider Debate*. Newbury Park: Sage.
Heidegger, Martin. 2014. *Überlegungen II–XV (Schwarze Hefte 1931–1938)*. Heidegger Gesamtasusgabe, vols. 94–96. Ed. Peter Trawny. Frankfurt a.M.: Klostermann.
Heinsohn, Kirsten, Barbara Vogel, and Ulrike Weckel. 1997. "Einleitung." In *Zwischen Karriere und Verfolgung: Handlungsräume von Frauen im nationalsozialistischen Deutschland*. Ed. Kirsten Heinsohn, Barbara Vogel, and Ulrike Weckel. Frankfurt a.M.: Campus, 7–23.
Henke, Klaus-Dietmar, ed. 2011. *Die Mauer: Errichtung. Überwindung, Erinnerung*. Munich: Deutscher.
Hensel, Jana. 2009. *Achtung Zone: Warum wir Ostdeutschen anders bleiben sollten*. Leipzig: Piper.
Herbert, Ulrich, Karin Orth, and Christoph Dieckmann, eds. 1998. *Die nationalsozialistischen Konzentrationslager: Entwicklung und Struktur*. Göttingen: Wallstein.
Herod, Andrew. 2010. *Scale*. New York: Routledge.
Herspring, Dale Roy. 1998. *Requiem for an Army: The Demise of the East German Military*. Lanham: Rowman & Littlefield.
Hertle, Hans Hermann and Maria Nooke. 2011. *Die Todesopfer an der Berliner Mauer 1961–1989*. Potsdam: Zentrum für Zeithistorische Forschung.
Herzog, Dagmar. 2005. *Sex after Fascism: Memory and Morality in Twentieth-Century Germany*. Princeton: Princeton University Press.
Heuss, Theodor. 1963. *Erinnerungen 1905–1933*. Tübingen: Rainer Wunderlich.
Hilberg, Raul. 1961. *The Destruction of the European Jews*. New Haven: Yale University Press.

Hobsbawm, Eric J. 1994. *The Age of Extremes: A History of the World, 1914–1991.* New York: Pantheon Books.
Hoffrogge, Ralf. 2011. *Sozialismus und Arbeiterbewegung in Deutschland: Von den Anfängen bis 1914.* Stuttgart: Schmetterling.
Honer, Anne and Roland Hitzler. 2011. *Kleine Leiblichkeiten: Erkundungen in Lebenswelten.* Wiesbaden: VS Verlag für Sozialwissenschaften.
Horwitz, Gordon J. 2008. *Ghettostadt: Łódź and the Making of a Nazi City.* Cambridge: Harvard University Press.
Hübner, Oskar and Johannes Moeglin, eds. 1910. *Im steinernen Meer.* Berlin-Schöneberg: Hilfe.
Hunt, Lynn. 2014. "The Self and Its History." *American Historical Review* 119, no. 5: 1576–86.
Husserl, Edmund. 1970. *Logical Investigations,* vol. 2. Trans. John N. Findlay. London: Routledge & Kegan Paul.
———. 1973. *Experience and Judgment, Investigations in a Genealogy of Logic.* Trans. James S. Churchill and Karl Amerik. Evanston: Northwestern University Press.
Illichmann, Jutta. 2007. *Die DDR und die Juden: Die deutschlandpolitische Instrumentalisierung von Juden und Judentum durch die Partei- und Staatsführung der SBZ/DDR von 1945 bis 1990.* Frankfurt a.M.: Lang.
Institut für Kommunalwirtschaft, ed. 1979. *Weltliche Bestattungsfeiern.* Dresden: Institut für Kommunalwirtschaft.
Jahoda, Marie, Paul Felix Lazarsfeld, and Hans Zeisel. 1960 [1933]. *Die Arbeitslosen von Marienthal: Ein soziographischer Versuch mit einem Anhang zur Geschichte der Soziographie.* Allensbach: Verlag für Demoskopie.
Jarausch, Konrad H. 1999. "Care and Coercion: The GDR as Welfare Dictatorship." In *Dictatorship as Experience: Towards a Socio-Cultural History of the GDR.* Ed. Konrad H. Jarausch. New York: Berghahn, 47–72.
Jarausch, Konrad and Michael Geyer. 2004. *Shattered Past: Reconstructing German Histories.* Princeton: Princeton University Press.
Jarraway, David. 2003. "'Absence of More': The Struggle for Unique Self-Authorization in Gertrude Stein." In *Going the Distance: Dissident Subjectivity in Modernist American Literature.* Baton Rouge: Louisiana State University Press, 18–44.
Jefferies, Matthew. 2003. "Lebensreform: A Middle-Class Antidote to Wilhelminism?" In *Wilhelminism and Its Legacies: German Modernities, Imperialism, and the Meanings of Reform, 1890–1930.* Ed. Geoff Eley and James Retallack. New York: Berghahn, 91–106.
Jeinsen, Gretha von. 1955. *Silhouetten: Eigenwillige Betrachtungen.* Pfullingen: Günther Neske.
Johnson, Jason. 2017. *Divided Village: The Cold War in the German Borderlands.* New York: Routledge.
Johnson, Molly Wilkinson. 2008. *Training Socialist Citizens: Sports and the State in East Germany.* Leiden: Brill Academic Publishers.

Jones, Adam, ed. 1985. *Brandenburg Sources for West African History, 1680–1700.* Studien zur Kulturkunde, vol. 77. Wiesbaden: Franz Steiner.
Jones, Sara. 2011. *Complicity, Censorship, and Criticism: Negotiating Space in the GDR Literary Sphere.* Berlin: De Gruyter.
Joseph, Detlev. 2010. *Die Juden und die DDR: Eine kritische Untersuchung.* Berlin: Das Neue Berlin.
Jünger, Ernst. 1920. *In Stahlgewittern: Aus dem Tagebuch eines Stosstruppenführers.* Leisnig: Robert Meier.
———, ed. 1930. *Krieg und Krieger.* Berlin: Junker und Dünnhaupt.
———. 1978–2003. *Sämtliche Werke.* 22 vols. Stuttgart: Klett-Cotta.
———. 1993. "War and Photography." Trans. Anthony Nassar. *New German Critique* 59 (spring/summer): 24–26.
Jureit, Ulrike, ed. 2002. *Verbrechen der Wehrmacht: Dimensionen des Vernichtungskrieges 1941–1945, Ausstellungskatalog.* Ed. Hamburger Institut für Sozialforschung. Hamburg: Hamburger Edition.
Kakel, Carroll P. 2011. *The American West and the Nazi East: A Comparative and Interpretive Perspective.* New York: Palgrave Macmillan.
Kalela, Jorma. 2012. *Making History: The Historian and the Uses of the Past.* London: Palgrave Macmillan.
Kaplan, Marion A. 1998. *Between Dignity and Despair: Jewish Life in Nazi Germany.* New York: Oxford University Press.
———. 2001. *Der Mut zum Überleben: Jüdische Frauen und ihre Familien in Nazideutschland.* Berlin: Aufbau.
Kaschnitz, Marie Luise. 1986. *Orte und Menschen: Aufzeichnungen.* Frankfurt a.M.: Insel.
Katznelson, Ira and Aristide R. Zolberg. 1986. *Working-Class Formation: Nineteenth-Century Patterns in Western Europe and the United States.* Princeton: Princeton University Press.
Kershaw, Ian. 1993. "'Working Towards the Führer': Reflections on the Nature of the Hitler Dictatorship." *Contemporary European History* 2, no. 2: 103–18.
———. 1998. *Hitler, 1889–1936: Hubris.* London: Allen Lane, Penguin Press.
Kläre-Bloch-Schule. 1992. *Ein Leben ohne Vorurteile, dazu Zivilcourage: Broschüre anlässlich der Namensgebung der Kläre-Bloch-Schule.* Berlin: Eigenverlag.
Kleditzsch, Torsten. 2014. "25 Jahre nach Fall der Mauer sind sich Ost und West nah wie nie." *Berliner Tagesblatt* 70, no. 2/3, 230, 1.
Klee, Ernst. 2010. *"Euthanasie" im Dritten Reich: Die "Vernichtung lebensunwerten Lebens."* Completely revised new edition. Frankfurt a.M.: Fischer.
Klein, Gabriele and Malte Friedrich. 2003. *Is This Real?: Die Geschichte des HipHop.* Frankfurt a.M.: Suhrkamp.
Klein, Kerwin Lee. 1995. "In Search of Narrative Mastery: Postmodernism and the People without History." *History and Theory* 34, no. 4: 275–98.
Klimke, Martin. 2010. *The Other Alliance: Student Protest in West Germany and the United States in the Global Sixties.* Princeton: Princeton University Press.

Klose, Bernhard. 1996. *Ehescheidung und Ehescheidungsrecht in der DDR—ein ostdeutscher Sonderweg?* Baden-Baden: Nomos.

König, Wolfgang. 2000. *Geschichte der Konsumgesellschaft.* Stuttgart: Franz Steiner.

Koonz, Claudia. 1987. *Mothers in the Fatherland: Women, the Family and Nazi Politics.* New York: St. Martin's Press.

Korb, Alexander. 2013. *Im Schatten des Weltkriegs: Massengewalt der Ustasa gegen Serben, Juden und Roma in Kroatien 1941–1945.* Hamburg: Hamburger Edition.

Korff, Gottfried. 1986. "Rote Fahnen und geballte Faust: Zur Symbolik der Arbeiterbewegung in der Weimarer Republik." In *Transformationen der Arbeiterkultur, Beiträge der 3. Arbeitstagung der Kommission "Arbeiterkultur" in der Deutschen Gesellschaft für Volkskunde in Marburg vom 3. bis 6. Juni 1985.* Ed. Peter Assion and Deutsche Gesellschaft für Volkskunde. Marburg: Jonas, 86–107.

———. 2002. *Museumsdinge: Deponieren-exponieren.* Cologne: Böhlau.

Koshar, Rudy. 2000. *German Travel Cultures.* Oxford: Berg.

Kosmala, Beate. 2002. "Missglückte Hilfe und ihre Folgen: Die Ahndung der 'Judenbegünstigung' durch NS-Verfolgungsbehörden." In *Überleben im Untergrund: Hilfe für Juden in Deutschland 1941–1945.* Ed. Beate Kosmala and Claudia Schoppmann. Berlin: Metropol, 205–21.

———. 2004. "Retterinnen und Retter von Juden im, Dritten Reich (1941–45)." In *Zivilcourage Lernen: Analysen, Modelle.* Ed. Gerd Meyer, Ulrich Dovermann, Siegried Frech, and Günther Gugel. Bonn: Bundeszentrale für politische Bildung, 106–15.

———. 2007. "Stille Helden." *Aus Politik und Zeitgeschichte*, no. 1415: 29–34.

Kowalczuk, Ilko-Sascha. 2013. *Stasi konkret: Überwachung und Repression in der DDR.* Munich: Beck.

Kracauer, Siegfried. 1963. *Das Ornament der Masse: Essays.* Frankfurt a.M.: Suhrkamp.

Kramer, Mark. 1974. *Der Friedhof: Gestaltung und Pflege.* Dresden: Institut für Kommunalwirtschaft.

Kranz, Tomasz. 2008. "Lublin-Majdanek—Stammlager." In *Der Ort des Terrors, Geschichte der nationalsozialistischen Konzentrationslager. Vol. 7: Niederhagen/Wewelsburg, Lublin-Majdanek, Arbeitsdorf, Herzogenbusch (Vught), Bergen-Belsen, Mittelbau-Dora.* Ed. Wolfgang Benz, Barbara Distel, and Angelika Königseder. Munich: Beck, 33–84.

Kraus, Marita, ed. 2008. *Sie waren dabei: Mitläuferinnen, Nutzniesserinnen, Täterinnen im Nationalsozialismus.* Göttingen: Wallstein.

Kroll, Hans. 1967. *Lebenserinnerungen eines Botschafters.* Cologne: Kiepenheuer & Witsch.

Krondorfer, Björn. 1995. *Remembrance and Reconciliation: Encounters between Young Jews and Germans.* New Haven: Yale University Press.

Kundrus, Birthe. 2003. "Handlungsräume: Zur Geschlechtergeschichte des Nationalsozialismus." In *Frauen und Widerstand.* Ed. Jana Leichsenring. Münster: LIT, 14–25.

Kundrus, Birthe and Beate Meyer. 2004. *Die Deportation der Juden aus Deutschland: Pläne—Praxis—Reaktionen 1938–1945*. Göttingen: Wallstein.

Kurz, Thomas. 1988. *Blutmai: Sozialdemokraten und Kommunisten im Brennpunkt der Berliner Ereignisse von 1929*. Bonn: Dietz.

Kwiet, Konrad. 1988. "Nach dem Pogrom: Stufen der Ausgrenzung." In *Die Juden in Deutschland 1933–1945: Leben unter nationalsozialistischer Herrschaft*. Ed. Wolfgang Benz. Berlin: Beck, 545–659.

Laabs, Dirk. 2012. *Der Deutsche Goldrausch: Die Wahre Geschichte Der Treuhand*. Munich: Pantheon.

Lacroix, Bernard and Jacques Lagroye. 1992. *Le Président de la République: usages et genèses d'une institution*. Paris: Presses de la fondation nationale des sciences politiques.

Lahusen, Susanne. 2013. *Zukunft am Ende: Autobiographische Sinnstiftungen von DDR-Geisteswissenschaftlern nach 1989*. Bielefeld: Transcript.

Lanwerd, Susanne and Irene Stoehr. 2007. "Frauen- und Geschlechterforschung zum Nationalsozialismus seit den 1970er Jahren: Forschungsstand, Veränderungen, Perspektiven." In *Frauen und Geschlechtergeschichte des Nationalsozialismus*. Ed. Johanna Gemacher and Gabriella Hauch. Vienna: Studienverlag, 22–68.

Le Blanc, Paul. 1993. *Lenin and the Revolutionary Party*. Atlantic Highlands: Humanity.

Le Corbusier. 2007 [1923]. *Toward an Architecture*. Los Angeles: Getty.

Leask, Phil. 2012. "Power, the Party and the People: The Significance of Humiliation in Representations of the German Democratic Republic." Ph.D. diss., University College, London.

Lefebvre, Henri. 1974. *Kritik des Alltagslebens*. Munich: Carl Hanser.

———. 1991. *The Production of Space*. Oxford: Blackwell.

Leis, Heinrich. 1926. "Großstadtstraße." *Die Woche* 28, no. 45: 1139.

Lemke, Michael. 2011. *Vor der Mauer: Berlin in der Ost-West-Konkurrenz 1948 bis 1961*. Cologne: Böhlau.

Lepetit, Bernard. 1993. "Architecture, géographie, histoire: usages de l'échelle." *Genèses* 13: 118–38.

Lepsius, M. Rainer. 2013. *Institutionalisierung politischen Handelns: Analysen zur DDR, Wiedervereinigung und Europäischen Union*. Wiesbaden: Springer.

Levi, Primo. 1986. "Primo Levi's Heartbreaking, Heroic Answers to the Most Common Questions He Was Asked about 'Survival in Auschwitz.'" *New Republic*, 17 February. http://www.newrepublic.com/article/119959/interview-primo-levi-survival-auschwitz (accessed 23 October 2014).

Levinger, Matthew. 2000. *Enlightened Nationalism: The Transformation of Prussian Political Culture, 1806–1848*. Oxford: Oxford University Press.

Ley, Astrid. 2009. "Vom Krankenmord zum Genozid. Die Aktion '14f13' in den Konzentrationslagern." *Dachauer Hefte* 25: 36–49.

Lidtke, Vernon L. 1985. *The Alternative Culture: Socialist Labor in Imperial Germany*. New York: Oxford University Press.

Liebman, Stuart, ed. 1995. *Berlin 1945: War and Rape: "Liberators Take Liberties."* Cambridge, MA: MIT Press.
Lindenberger, Thomas, ed. 1999. "Die Diktatur Der Grenzen." In *Herrschaft und Eigen-Sinn in der Diktatur: Studien zur Gesellschaftsgeschichte der DDR*. Cologne: Böhlau, 13–44.
———. 2007. "SED-Herrschaft als soziale Praxis, Herrschaft und 'Eigen-Sinn': Problemstellung und Begriffe." In *Staatssicherheit und Gesellschaft: Studien zum Herrschaftsalltag in der DDR*. Ed. Jens Giesecke. Göttingen: V&R, 23–47.
———. "Eigen-Sinn, Herrschaft und kein Widerstand." Docupedia-Zeitgeschichte. http://docupedia.de/zg/Docupedia:Thomas_Lindenberger (accessed November 2014).
Lloyd, Christopher. 1991. "The Methodologies of Social History: A Critical Survey and Defense of Structuralism." *History and Theory* 30, no. 2: 180–219.
Lower, Wendy. 2010a. "Living Space." In *Oxford Handbook of Holocaust Studies*. Ed. Peter Hayes and John K. Roth. Oxford: Oxford University Press, 310–25.
———. 2010b. "Male and Female Holocaust Perpetrators and the East German Approach to Justice, 1949–1963." *Holocaust and Genocide Studies* 24, no. 1: 56–84.
———. 2013. *Hitler's Furies: German Women in the Nazi Killing Fields*. Boston: Houghton Mifflin Harcourt.
Luckmann, Thomas. 1979. "Phänomenologie und Soziologie." In *Alfred Schütz und die Idee des Alltags in den Sozialwissenschaften*. Ed. Walter M. Sprondel and Richard Grathoff. Stuttgart: Enke, 196–206.
Lüdtke, Alf. 1982. *"Gemeinwohl," Polizei und "Festungspraxis": Staatliche Gewaltsamkeit und innere Verwaltung in Preussen, 1815–1850*. Göttingen: V&R.
———. 1989. *Alltagsgeschichte: Zur Rekonstruktion historischer Erfahrungen und Lebensweisen*. Frankfurt a.M.: Campus.
———. 1991a. "Alltagsgeschichte: Zur Aneignung der Verhältnisse. Ein Gespräch mit Alf Lüdtke." In *Österreichische Zeitschrift für Geschichtswissenschaften*, vol. 2. Vienna: Verlag für Gesellschaftskritik, 104–13.
———. 1991b. *Herrschaft als soziale Praxis: Historische und sozialanthropologische Studien*. Göttingen: Vandenhoeck und Reprecht.
———. 1991c. "Lebenswelten und Alltagswissen." In *Handbuch der deutschen Bildungsgeschichte. Vol. 4: 1870–1918*. Ed. Christa Berg. Munich: Beck, 57–90.
———. 1993. "'Coming to Terms with the Past': Illusions of Remembering, Ways of Forgetting Nazism in West Germany." *Journal of Modern History* 65, no. 3: 542–72.
———. 1994a. *Alltagskultur, Subjektivität und Geschichte: Zur Theorie und Praxis von Alltagsgeschichte*. Münster: Westfälisches Dampfboot.
———. 1994b. "'Helden der Arbeit'—Mühen beim Arbeiten: Zur missmutigen Loyalität von Industriearbeitern in der DDR." In *Sozialgeschichte der DDR*. Ed. Hartmut Kaelble, Jürgen Kocka, and Hartmut Zwahr. Stuttgart: Klett-Cotta, 188–213.

———. 1995. *The History of Everyday Life: Reconstructing Historical Experiences and Ways of Life*. Princeton: Princeton University Press.
———. 1998. "Die Fiktion der Institution: Herrschaftspraxis und Vernichtung der europäischen Juden im 20. Jahrhundert." In *Institutionen und Ereignis*. Ed. Reinhard Blänkner and Bernhard Jussen. Göttingen: V&R, 355–79.
———. 2002. "'Deutsche Qualitätsarbeit'—ihre Bedeutung für das Mitmachen von Arbeitern und Unternehmern im Nationalsozialismus." In *Firma Topf & Söhne: Hersteller der Öfen für Auschwitz: Ein Fabrikgelände als Erinnerungsort?* Ed. Aleida Assmann, Frank Hiddemann, and Eckhard Schwarzenberger. Frankfurt a.M.: Campus, 123–38.
———. 2003. "Alltagsgeschichte—ein Bericht von unterwegs." *Historische Anthropologie* 11, no. 2: 278–95.
———. 2006. "Alltag: Der blinde Fleck?" In *Deutschland Archiv* 39: 894–901.
Lüdtke, Alf and Reiner Prass. 2008. *Gelehrtenleben: Wissenschaftspraxis in der Neuzeit*. Cologne: Böhlau.
Ludwig, Andreas. 2012. "'Übereinstimmung,' 'Teilhabe' und 'Zufriedenheit'—Die sozialistische Lebensweise." In *Alltag: DDR. Geschichten, Fotos, Objekte*. Ed. Andreas Ludwig. Berlin: Links, 277–81.
Lutz, Burkart and Holle Grunert. 1996. "Der Zerfall der Beschäftigungsstrukturen der DDR 1989–1993." In *Arbeit, Arbeitsmarkt und Betriebe*. Ed. Burkart Lutz, Hildegard M. Nickel, Rudi Schmidt, and Arndt Sorge. Opladen: Leske+Budrich, 69–120.
Luxemburg, Rosa. 1913 [1970]. "Karl Marx." In *Leipziger Volkszeitung* 60. In *Gesammelte Werke*, Vol. 3. Ed. Günter Radczun. Berlin: Dietz, 178–84.
Lyotard, Jean-François, Geoffrey Bennington, and Brian Massumi. 1984. *The Postmodern Condition: A Report on Knowledge*. Minneapolis: University of Minnesota Press.
Madarász, Jeannette Zsusza. 2006. *Working in East Germany. Normality in a Socialist Dictatorship, 1961 to 1979*. Basingstoke: Palgrave.
Magnússon, Sigurður G. and István M. Szijártó. 2013. *What Is Microhistory?: Theory and Practice*. Milton Park: Routledge.
Maier, Charles. 1997. *Dissolution: The Crisis of Communism and the End of East Germany*. Princeton: Princeton University Press.
Mailänder, Elissa. 2010. "Work, Violence and Cruelty: An Everyday Historical Perspective on Perpetrators in Nazi Concentration Camps." *L'Europe en formation* 357 (autumn): 30–51.
———. 2015. *Female SS Guards and Workday Violence: The Majdanek Concentration Camp, 1942–1944*. Lansing: Michigan State University Press.
Mailänder Koslov, Elissa. 2009. *Gewalt im Dienstalltag: Die SS-Aufseherinnen des Konzentrations- und Vernichtungslagers Majdanek 1942–1944*. Hamburg: Hamburger Edition.
Major, Patrick. 2009. *Behind the Berlin Wall: East Germany and the Frontiers of Power*. Oxford: Oxford University Press.

Malitz, Bruno. 1933. *Die Leibesübungen in der nationalsozialistischen Idee*. Munich: Eher.

Mallmann, Klaus-Michael. 1996. *Kommunisten in der Weimarer Republik: Sozialgeschichte einer revolutionären Bewegung*. Darmstadt: Wissenschaftliche Buchgesellschaft.

———. 2002. "'Mensch, ich feiere heute den tausendsten Genickschuß.' Die Sicherheitspolizei und die Shoah in Westgalizien." In *Die Täter der Shoah. Fanatische Nationalsozialisten oder ganz normale Deutsche?* Ed. Gerhard Paul. Göttingen: Wallstein, 109–36.

Mallmann, Klaus-Michael and Gerhard Paul. 2000. "*Resistenz* or Loyal Reluctance?" In *Nazism*. Ed. Neil Gregor. Oxford: Oxford University Press, 248–52.

Marpe, Harald. 2014. *Kläre Bloch: Die Geschichte einer mutigen Frau*. Berlin: Kiezbündnis Klausenerplatz.

Marx, Karl. 1852. "Der 18te Brumaire des Louis Napoleon." *Die Revolution* 1.

Marx, Karl and Friedrich Engels. 1972. "Manifest der Kommunistischen Partei." In *Werke*, vol. 4. Berlin: Dietz.

Mazower, Mark. 2000. *Dark Continent: Europe's Twentieth Century*. New York: Vintage Books.

McElligott, Anthony. 1998. *Contested City: Municipal Politics and the Rise of Nazism in Altona, 1917–1937*. Ann Arbor: University of Michigan Press.

McLellan, Josie. 2011. *Love in the Time of Communism: Intimacy and Sexuality in the GDR*. Cambridge, UK: Cambridge University Press.

———. 2012. "Glad to Be Gay behind the Wall: Gay and Lesbian Activism in 1970s East Germany." *History Workshop Journal* 74, no. 1: 105–30.

McMillan, Dan. 2014. *How Could This Happen: Explaining the Holocaust*. New York: Basic Books.

Medick, Hans. 1994. "Mikro-Histoire." In *Sozialgeschichte, Alltagsgeschcihte, Mikro-Histoire*. Ed. Winfried Schulze. Göttingen: Vandenhoeck & Ruprecht, 40–53.

———. 1996. *Weben und Überleben in Laichingen, 1650–1900: Lokalgeschichte als Allgemeine Geschichte*. Göttingen: Vandenhoeck & Ruprecht.

Megargee, Geoffrey P. 2007. *War of Annihilation: Combat and Genocide on the Eastern Front, 1941*. Lanham: Rowman & Littlefield.

Merkl, Peter. 2012. *Small Town and Village in Bavaria: The Passing of a Way of Life*. New York: Berghahn.

Mertens, Lothar. 1998. *Wider die sozialistische Familiennorm: Ehescheidungen in der DDR 1950–1989*. Opladen: Westdeutscher.

Metz, Johann Baptist. 1972. "The Future in the Memory of Suffering." *Concilium* 76: 9–25.

———. 1981. "Christians and Jews after Auschwitz." In *The Emergent Church: The Future of Christianity in a Postbourgeois World*. Trans. Peter Mann. New York: Crossroad, 17–33.

———. 1987. "Communicating a Dangerous Memory." In *Communicating a Dangerous*

Memory: Soundings in Political Theology: Supplementary Issue of Lonergan Workshop Journal. Ed. Fred Lawrence. Atlanta: Scholar Press, 37–54.

———. 1992. "Anamnestic Reason: A Theologian's Remarks on the Crisis in the Geisteswissenschaften." In *Cultural-Political Interventions in the Unfinished Project of the Enlightenment.* Ed. Axel Honneth, Thomas McCarthy, Claus Offe, and Albrecht Wellmer. Trans. Barbara Fultner. Cambridge, MA: MIT Press, 189–94.

———. 1998. "Theology as Theodicy." In *A Passion for God: The Mystical-Political Dimension of Christianity.* Ed. J. Matthew Ashley. New York: Paulist, 54–71.

———. 2006. *Memoria Passionis: Ein provozierendes Gedächtnis in pluralistischer Gesellschaft.* In Zusammenarbeit mit Johann Reikerstorfer. Freiburg: Herder.

———. 2007. *Faith in History and Society: Toward a Practical Fundamental Theology.* Trans. Matthew Ashley. New York: Crossroad.

Meyer, Beate. 1999. *"Jüdische Mischlinge": Rassenpolitik und Verfolgungserfahrung 1933–1945.* Hamburg: Dölling und Galitz.

———. 2011. *Tödliche Gratwanderung: Die Reichsvereinigung der Juden in Deutschland zwischen Hoffnung, Zwang, Selbstbehauptung und Verstrickung (1939–1945).* Göttingen: Wallstein.

Meyer, Thomas and Pavel Uttitz. 1993. "Nachholende Marginalisierung—oder der Wandel der agrarischen Sozialstruktur in der Ehemaligen DDR: Ergebnisse einer Befragung der Mitglieder einer Produktionsgenossenschaft." In *Sozialer Umbruch in Ostdeutschland.* Ed. Rainer Geißler. Opladen: Leske + Budrich, 221–50.

Miller, Martin A. 1998. *Freud and the Bolsheviks: Psychoanalysis in Imperial Russia and the Soviet Union.* New Haven: Yale University Press.

Mills, C. Wright. 1959. *The Sociological Imagination.* Oxford: Oxford University Press.

Miquel, Marc von. 2001. "Juristen: Richter in eigener Sache." In *Karrieren im Zwielicht. Hitlers Eliten nach 1945.* Ed. Norbert Frei. 2nd ed. Frankfurt a.M.: Campus, 181–240.

Mitchell, W.J. Thomas. 1994. *Picture Theory: Essays on Verbal and Visual Representation.* Chicago: University of Chicago Press.

Moeller, Robert G. 2001. *War Stories: The Search for a Usable Past in the Federal Republic of Germany.* Berkeley: University of California Press.

Moses, Dirk. 2007. *German Intellectuals and the Nazi Past.* New York: Cambridge University Press.

Mütter, Bernd and Uwe Uffelmann, eds. 1992. *Emotionen und historisches Lernen: Forschung, Vermittlung, Rezeption.* Frankfurt a.M.: Diesterweg.

Naimark, Norman M. 1995. *The Russians in Germany: A History of the Soviet Zone of Occupation, 1945–1949.* Cambridge, MA: Belknap Press of Harvard University Press.

Neumann, Klaus. 2000. *Shifting Memories: The Nazi Past in the New Germany.* Ann Arbor: University of Michigan Press.

Niethammer, Lutz. 1982. "Anmerkungen zur Alltagsgeschichte." In *Geschichte im Alltag, Alltag in der Geschichte.* Ed. Klaus Bergmann and Rolf Schörken. Düsseldorf: Pädagogischer Verlag Schwann, 11–29.

———. 1988. "*Die Menschen machen ihre Geschichte nicht aus freien Stücken, aber sie machen sie selbst*": *Einladung zu einer Geschichte des Volkes in NRW*. Berlin: Dietz.

———. 1989. "Annäherung an den Wandel: Auf der Suche nach der volkseigenen Erfahrung in der Industrieprovinz der DDR." In *Alltagsgeschichte: Zur Rekonstruktion historische Erfahrungen und Lebensweisen*. Ed. Alf Lüdtke. Frankfurt a.M.: Campus, 283–345.

Niven, Bill, ed. 2006. *Germans as Victims: Remembering the Past in Contemporary Germany*. Basingstoke: Palgrave Macmillan.

Nora, Pierre. 1984–92. *Les lieux de mémoire*. Paris: Gallimard.

———. 2011. "From Reasons for the Current Upsurge in Memory." In *The Collective Memory Reader*. Ed. Jeffrey K. Olick, Vered Vinitzky-Seroussi, and Daniel Levy. New York: Oxford University Press, 437–41.

Nothnagle, Alan L. 1999. *Building the East German Myth: Historical Mythology and Youth Propaganda in the German Democratic Republic, 1945–1989*. Ann Arbor: University of Michigan Press.

Oeser, Alexandra. 2009. "'1968' als Filter der, NS-Vergangenheit: 'Hamburger Geschichtslehrer und die Erziehung zu "mündigen Bürgern" im Geschichtsunterricht.'" In *Eine Welt zu gewinnen! Formen und Folgen der 68er Bewegung in Ost- und Westeuropa*. Ed. Hanco Jürgens, Jacco Pekelder, and Falk Bretschneider. Leipzig: Leipziger Universitätsverlag, 135–63.

———. 2010. *Enseigner Hitler: Les adolescents face au passé nazi en Allemagne. Interprétations, appropriations et usages de l'histoire*. Paris: Éditions de la Maison des sciences de l'homme.

———. 2016. "Rire du passé nazi en Allemagne: l'Eigensinn des adolescents face à l'histoire scolaire du nazisme." *Sociétés contemporaines* 99, nos. 3–4: 105–125.

Ohse, Marc-Dietrich. 2003. *Jugend nach dem Mauerbau: Anpassung, Protest und Eigensinn*. Berlin: Links.

Olle DDR Dauerausstellung. Museumsbaracke "Olle DDR." n.d. http://www.olle-ddr.de/. 27 November 2010.

Oppel, Stefanie. 2007. "Marianne Eßmann: Von der Kantoristin zur SS-Aufseherin. Dienstverpflichtung als Zwangsmaßnahme?" In *Im Gefolge der SS: Aufseherinnen des Frauen-KZ Ravensbrück. Begleitband zur Ausstellung*. Ed. Simone Erpel, Jeanette Toussaint, Johannes Schwartz, and Lavern Wolfram. Schriftenreihe der Stiftung Brandenburgische Gedenkstätten, no. 17. Berlin: Metropol, 81–88.

Orth, Karin. 2002. *Das System der nationalsozialistischen Konzentrationslager: Eine politische Organisationsgeschichte*. Munich: Pendo.

Ossaria: Essen wie im Osten. http://www.osseria.de/. Accessed November 2016.

Ostovich, Steven T. 2002. "Epilogue: Dangerous Memories." In *The Work of Memory: New Directions in the Study of German Society and Culture*. Ed. Alon Confine and Peter Fritzsche. Urbana: University of Illinois Press, 239–56.

———. 2006. "Melancholy History." In *Missing God? Cultural Amnesia and Political Theology*. Ed. John K. Downey, Jürgen Manemann, and Steven T. Ostovich. Berlin: LIT, 93–101.

---. 2010. "Pauline Eschatology: Thinking and Acting in the Time that Remains." In *Time: Limits and Constraints*. Ed. Jo Alyson Parker, Paul A. Harris, and Christian Steineck. Leiden: Brill, 307–27.

Pabel, Hilmar. 1951. "Wahnsinn—1,358 Kilometer lang!" *Quick: Illustrierte für Deutschland* 4, no. 7: 533–35.

Pätzold, Kurt. 2010. *Die Mär vom Antisemitismus: Mit dem Begleitbuch zur Wanderausstellung "Das hat es bei uns nicht gegeben!—Antisemitismus in der DDR" beginnt ein neues Kapitel der Anti-DDR-Propaganda*. Berlin: Das Neue Berlin.

Paver, Chloe. 2013. "Colour and Time in Museums of East German Everyday Life." In *Remembering and Rethinking the GDR: Multiple Perspectives and Plural Authenticities*. Ed. Anna Saunders and Debbie Pinfold. Basingstoke: Palgrave Macmillan, 132–48.

Pence, Katherine and Paul Betts. 2008. *Socialist Modern: East German Everyday Culture and Politics*. Ann Arbor: University of Michigan Press.

Pfaff, Steven. 2006. *Exit-Voice Dynamics and the Collapse of East Germany: The Crisis of Leninism and the Revolution of 1989*. Durham: Duke University Press.

Phillips, Raymond, ed. 1949. *Trial of Josef Kramer and Forty-Four Others (The Belsen Trial)*. War Crimes Trials Series, vol. 2. London: William Hodge and Company.

Plenzdorf, Ulrich, Rüdiger Dammann, and Klaus Ensikat. 2005. *Ein Land, genannt die DDR*. Frankfurt a.M.: Fischer.

Pohl, Dieter. 2004. "Die Stellung des Distrikts Lublin in der Endlösung der Judenfrage." In *"Aktion Reinhardt:" der Völkermord an den Juden im Generalgouvernement 1941–1944*. Ed. Bogdan Musial. Osnabrück: Fibre, 87–107.

---. 2012. "Massentötungen durch Giftgas im Rahmen der 'Aktion Reinhardt.' Aufgaben der Forschung." In *Neue Studien zu nationalsozialistischen Massentötungen durch Giftgas. Historische Bedeutung, technische Entwicklung, revisionistische Leugnung*. Schriftenreihe der Stiftung Brandenburgische Gedenkstätten, no. 29. 2nd rev. ed. Berlin: Metropol, 185–95.

Port, Andrew. 2007. *Conflict and Stability in the German Democratic Republic*. New York: Cambridge University Press.

Prakash, Gyan. 2002. "The Impossibility of Subaltern History." *Nepantla: Views from South* 1, no. 2: 287–94.

Rader, Olaf B. 2003. *Grab und Herrschaft: Politischer Totenkult von Alexander dem Großen bis Lenin*. Munich: Beck.

Reckwitz, Andreas. 2003. "Grundelemente einer Theorie sozialer Praktiken: Eine sozialthoretische Perspektiv." *Zeitschrift für Soziologie* 32, no. 4: 282–301.

Redlin, Jane. 2009. *Säkulare Totenrituale: Totenehrung, Staatsbegräbnis und private Bestattung in der DDR*. Münster: Waxmann.

Reemtsma, Jan Philipp. 2008. *Vertrauen und Gewalt: Versuch über eine besondere Konstellation der Moderne*. Hamburg: Hamburger Edition.

Reich, Wilhelm. 1971. *Die Sexuelle Revolution*. Frankfurt a.M.: Fischer.

Reichel, Peter. 2001. *Vergangenheitsbewältigung in Deutschland*. Munich: Beck.

Revel, Jaques. 1996. "Micro-analyse et construction du social." In *Jeux d'échelles. La micro-analyse à l'expérience*. Ed. Jaques Revel. Paris: Gallimard Le Seuil, 15–36.

Richter, Sebastian. 2007. *Norm und Eigensinn: Die Selbstlegitimation Politischen Protests in Der DDR 1985–1989*. Berlin: Metropol.

Riemann, Gerhard and Fritz Schütze. 1991. "'Trajectory' as a Basic Theoretical Concept for Analyzing Suffering and Disorderly Social Processes." In *Social Organization and Social Process: Essays in Honor of Anselm Strauss*. Ed. David Maines. New York: de Gruyter, 333–57.

Riffel, Dennis. 2007. *Unbesungene Helden: Die Ehrungsinitiative des Berliner Senats 1958 bis 1966*. Berlin: Metropol.

Rigney, Richard. 2011. "Commie cooking," Experliner, 7. December. http://www.exberliner.com/food/commie-culinary/. Accessed November 2016.

Riley, Kerry Kathleen. 2008. *Everyday Subversion: From Joking to Revolting in the German Democratic Republic*. East Lansing: Michigan State University Press.

Röhr, Werner and Brigette Berlekamp, eds. 1995. *Terror, Herrschaft und Alltag im Nationalsozialismus*. Münster: Westfälisches Dampfboot.

Rorty, Richard, ed. 1967. *The Linguistic Turn: Recent Essays in Philosophical Method*. Chicago/London: University of Chicago Press.

Rosenhaft, Eve. 1983. *Beating the Fascists?: the German Communists and Political Violence 1929–1933*. New York: Cambridge University Press.

Rosenthal, Gabriele. 1995. *Erlebte und erzählte Lebensgeschichte: Gestalt und Struktur biographischer Selbstbeschreibungen*. Frankfurt a.M.: Campus.

Ross, Corey. 2008. *Media and the Making of Modern Germany: Mass Communications, Society and Politics from the Empire to the Third Reich*. Oxford: Oxford University Press.

Roth, Eugen. 1972. *Erinnerungen eines Vergeßlichen: Anekdoten und Geschichte*. Munich: Hanser.

Rousset, David. 1946. *L'Univers concentrationnaire*. Paris: Éditions d' Pavois.

Rubin, Eli. 2008. *Synthetic Socialism: Plastics & Dictatorship in the German Democratic Republic*. Chapel Hill: University of North Carolina Press.

Rudorff, Andrea. 2014. *Frauen in den Außenlagern des Konzentrationslagers Groß-Rosen*. Geschichte der Konzentrationslager 1933–1945, no. 15. Berlin: Metropol.

Rüter, C.F. and Dirk W. de Mildt, eds. 2010. *Justiz- und NS-Verbrechen. Vol. XVIII: Case Numbers 523–546 (1961–1963)*. Amsterdam: Amsterdam University Press.

Sa'ar, Amalia. 2005. "Postcolonial Feminism, the Politics of Identification, and the Liberal Bargain." *Gender and Society* 19, no. 5: 680–700.

Sabrow, Martin, ed. 2007. *Wohin Treibt die DDR Erinnerung?* Göttingen: Vandenhoeck & Ruprecht.

———. 2008. "DDR-Alltag im Museum." In *2 Jahre DDR Museum: Eine Kritische Bilanz*. Ed. DDR Museum. Berlin: DDR Museum, 7–13.

———. 2009. *Errinerungsorte der DDR*. Munich: Beck.

Sälter, Gerhard, ed. 2009. *Grenzpolizisten: Konformität, Verweigerung und Repression in der Grenzpolizei und den Grenztruppen der DDR 1952–1965*. Berlin: Links.

Satjukow, Silke. 2008. *Besatzer: "Die Russen" in Deutschland, 1945–1994*. Göttingen: Vandenhoeck & Ruprecht.
Schabowski, Günter and Frank Sieren. 2009. *Wir haben fast alles falsch gemacht: die letzten Tage der DDR*. Berlin: Econ.
Schaefer, Sagi. 2011a. "Hidden behind the Wall: West German State Building and the Emergence of the Iron Curtain." *Central European History* 44, no. 3: 506–35.
———. 2011b. "Ironing the Curtain: Border and Boundary Formation in Cold War Rural Germany, 1945–1975." Ph.D diss., Columbia University, New York.
———2012. "Re-Creation: Iron Curtain Tourism and the Production of 'East' and 'West' in Cold War Germany." *Tel Aviv Yearbook for German History* 40: 116–31.
———. 2014. *States of Division: Border and Boundary in Cold War Rural Germany*. Oxford: Oxford University Press.
Schalm, Sabine. 2009. *Überleben durch Arbeit?: Außenkommandos und Außenlager des KZ Dachau 1933–1945*. Geschichte der Konzentrationslager 1933–1945, no. 10. Berlin: Metropol.
Scheler, Max. 1963. *Schriften zur Soziologie und Weltanschauungslehre*. Bern: Francke.
———. 1973. *Formalism in Ethics and Non-Formal Ethics of Value*. Trans. Manfred S. Frings and Robert L. Funk. Evanston: Northwestern University Press.
Schiele, Siegfried and Herbert Schneider, eds. 1991. *Rationalität und Emotionalität in der politischen Bildung*. Stuttgart: Metzler.
Schmidt, Ilse. 2002. *Die Mitläuferin: Erinnerungen einer Wehrmachtsangehörigen*. Berlin: Aufbau.
Schmidtmann, Florentine. 2013. "A Bitter Path: Eine Ausstellung über die Bedeutung Bitterfelds in der DDR im Spiegel ausgewählter nonkonformer Kunst." Master's thesis, Freie Universität Berlin.
Schmieding, Leonard. 2008. "Of Windmills, Headspins, and Powermoves. HipHop in the GDR 1983–1989." In *Ambivalent Americanizations: Popular and Consumer Culture in Central and Eastern Europe*. Ed. Sebastian M. Herrmann, Katja Kanzler, Anne Koenen, Zoë A. Kusmierz, and Leonard Schmieding. Heidelberg: Universitätsverlag Winter, 65–85.
———. 2012. "Taking Beat Street to the Streets in Socialist East Germany." In *Participating Audiences and Imagined Communities: The Cultural Work of Contemporary American(ized) Narratives*. Ed. Sebastian M Herrmann, Katja Kanzler, Frank Usbeck, and Alice Hofmann. Leipzig: Leipziger Universitätsverlag, 43–61.
———. 2014. *"Das ist unsere Party:" HipHop in der DDR*. Stuttgart: Steiner.
Schmolling, Rolf. 2006. "Ravensbrück ('Siemenslager')." In *Der Ort des Terrors: Geschichte der nationalsozialistischen Konzentrationslager. Vol. 4: Flossenbürg, Mauthausen, Ravensbrück*. Ed. Wolfgang Benz and Barbara Distel. Munich: Beck, 587–91.
Schnapper, Dominique. 1981. *L'épreuve du chômage*. Paris: Gallimard.
Schneider, Peter. 1982. *Der Mauerspringer*. Darmstadt: Luchterhand.

Schorske, Carl E. 1983. *German Social Democracy, 1905–1917: The Development of the Great Schism*. Cambridge, MA: Harvard University Press.

Schulz, Felix R. 2008. "Disposing of the Dead in East Germany, 1945–1990." In *Between Mass Death and Individual Loss: The Place of the Dead in Twentieth-Century Germany*. Ed. Alon Confino, Paul Betts, and Dirk Schumann. New York: Berghahn, 113–28.

Schumann, Dirk. 2012. *Political Violence in the Weimar Republic, 1918–1933: Fight for the Streets and Fear of Civil War*. New York: Berghahn.

Schütz, Alfred. 1971. "Das Problem der sozialen Wirklichkeit." In *Gesammelte Aufsätze. Vol. 1: Das Problem der sozialen Wirklichkeit*. Den Haag: Nijhoff.

Schütz, Alfred and Thomas Luckmann. 1973. *The Structures of the Life-World*. Evanston: Northwestern University Press.

Schütze, Fritz. 1975. *Sprache soziologisch gesehen. Vol 2: Sprache als Indikator für egalitäre und nicht-egalitäre Sozialbeziehungen*. Munich: Fink.

———. 1976. "Zur Hervorlockung und Analyse von Erzählungen thematisch relevanter Geschichten im Rahmen soziologischer Feldforschung: Dargestellt an einem Projekt zur Erforschung von kommunalen Machtstrukturen." In *Arbeitsgruppe Bielefelder Soziologen: Kommunikative Sozialforschung*. Munich: Fink, 159–260.

———. 1995. "Verlaufskurven des Erleidens als Forschungsgegenstand der interpretativen Soziologie." In *Erziehungswissenschaftliche Biographieforschung*. Ed. Heinz-Hermann Krüger and Winfried Marotzki. Opladen: Leske und Budrich, 116–57.

Schwartz, Johannes. 2007. "Handlungsräume einer KZ-Aufseherin. Dorothea Binz—Leiterin des Zellenbaus und Oberaufseherin." In *Im Gefolge der SS: Aufseherinnen des Frauen-KZ Ravensbrück. Begleitband zur Ausstellung*. Ed. Simone Erpel, Jeanette Toussaint, Johannes Schwartz, and Lavern Wolfram. Schriftenreihe der Stiftung Brandenburgische Gedenkstätten, no. 17. Berlin: Metropol, 59–71.

———. 2013. "La dynamique sociale de la sélection. L'action 14f13 au camp de concentration de Ravensbrück." *La Revue d'Histoire de la Shoah*, no. 199: 271–92.

Schwarz, Gudrun. 1994. "SS-Aufseherinnen in nationalsozialistischen Konzentrationslagern (1933–1945)." *Dachauer Hefte* 10: 32–49.

———. 2001. *Eine Frau an seiner Seite: Ehefrauen in der "SS-Sippengemeinschaft."* 2nd ed. Berlin: Aufbau.

Schücking-Homeyer, Annette. 2010. "'They Really Do Smell Like Blood': Among Hitler's Executioners on the Eastern Front." *Spiegel Online International*. 28 January. http://www.spiegel.de/international/europe/they-really-do-smell-like-blood-among-hitler-s-executioners-on-the-eastern-front-a-674375.html. Downloaded November 2016.

Scott, Joan Wallach. 1988. *Gender and the Politics of History*. New York: Columbia University Press.

Sebestyen, Victor. 2009. *Revolution 1989: The Fall of the Soviet Empire*. New York: Pantheon Books.

Seghers, Anna. 1946. *Das Siebte Kreuz: Roman aus Hitlerdeutschland.* Amsterdam: Querido.

Seidel, Ina. 1935. *Meine Kindheit und Jugend: Ursprung, Erbteil und Weg.* Stuttgart: Deutsche Verlags-Anstalt.

Sewell, Sara A. 2009. "Mourning Comrades: Communist Funerary Rituals in Cologne during the Weimar Republic." *German Studies Review* 32, no. 3: 527–48.

———. 2012. "Bolshevizing Communist Women: The Red Women and Girls' League in Weimar Germany." *Central European History* 45, no. 2: 268–305.

Sewell, William H., Jr. 2005. *Logics of History: Social Theory and Social Transformation.* Chicago: University of Chicago Press.

Sheffer, Edith. 2007. "On Edge: Building the Border in East and West Germany." *Central European History* 40, no. 2: 307–39.

———. 2011. *Burned Bridge: How East and West Germans Made the Iron Curtain.* New York: Oxford University Press.

Shenfeld, Stepan Yakimovich. 2008. "A Forced Labour Camp. Recollections of Stepan Yakimovich Shenfeld, 1943." In *The Unknown Black Book: The Holocaust in the German-Occupied Soviet Territories.* Ed. Joshua Rubenstein and Ilya Altman. Bloomington: Indiana University Press, 89–99.

Sheringham, Michael. 2006. *Everyday Life: Theories and Practices from Surrealism to the Present.* Oxford: Oxford University Press.

Sider, Gerald and Gavin Smith. 1997. *Between History and Histories: The Making of Silences and Commemorations.* Toronto: Toronto University Press.

Smelser, Ronald M. 1988. *Robert Ley: Hitler's Labor Front Leader.* Oxford: Berg.

Snyder, Timothy. 2010. *Bloodlands: Europe between Hitler and Stalin.* New York: Basic Books.

Soeffner, Hans-Georg. 2004. *Auslegung des Alltags—Der Alltag der Auslegung: Zur wissenssoziologischen Konzeption einer sozialwissenschaftlichen Hermeneutik.* 2nd ed. Stuttgart: UTB.

Sofksy, Wolfgang. 1993. *Die Ordnung des Terrors: Das Konzentrationslager.* Frankfurt a.M.: Fischer.

———. 1997. *The Order of Terror: The Concentration Camp.* Princeton: Princeton University Press.

Staude, John Raphael. 1967. *Max Scheler 1874–1928: An Intellectual Portrait.* New York: Free Press.

Steege, Paul. 2007. *Black Market, Cold War: Everyday Life in Berlin, 1946–1949.* Cambridge, UK: Cambridge University Press.

———. 2011. "Ordinary Violence on an Extraordinary Stage: Incidents on the Sector Border in Postwar Berlin." In *Performances of Violence.* Ed. Austin Sarat, Carleen R. Basler, and Thomas L. Dumm. Amherst: University of Massachusetts Press, 140–63.

Steege, Paul, Andrew Stuart Bergerson, Maureen Healy, and Pamela Swett. 2008. "The History of Everyday Life: A Second Chapter." *Journal of Modern History* 80, no. 2: 358–78.

Steinbacher, Sybille. 2007. *Volksgenossinnen: Frauen in der NS-Volksgemeinschaft.* Göttingen: Wallstein.

———. 2011. *Wie der Sex nach Deutschland kam: Der Kampf um Sittlichkeit und Anstand in der frühen Bundesrepublik.* Munich: Siedler.

Steinweis, Alan. 2009. *Kristallnacht 1938.* Cambridge, MA: Belknap Press of Harvard University Press.

Stephenson, Jill. 2001. *Women in Nazi Germany.* New York: Pearson Longman.

Sternberger, Dolf. 1990. *Verfassungspatriotismus.* Frankfurt a.M.: Insel.

Stiegler, Bernard. 1998. *Technics and Time: The Fault of Epimetheus.* Trans. Richard Beardsworth and George Collins. Stanford: Stanford University Press.

Straughn, Jeremy Brooke. 2005. "'Taking the State at Its Word': Consentful Contention in the German Democratic Republic." *American Journal of Sociology* 110: 1598–650.

———. 2007. "Historical Events and the Fragmentation of Memory in the Former East Germany." *Journal of Political and Military Sociology* 35: 103–23.

———. 2016. "Wo 'der Osten' liegt." In *Der Osten—Neue sozial wissenschafliche Perspectiven auf einen komplexen Gegenstand jenseits von Verurteilung und Verklarung.* Ed. Daniel Kubiak and Sandra Matthäus. Wiesbaden: VS Springer, 195–223.

Strauss, Anselm and Juliet Corbin. 1990. *Basics of Qualitative Research: Grounded Theory Procedures and Techniques.* Newbury Park: Sage.

Strauss, Anselm, Shizuko Fagerhaugh, Barbara Suczek, and Carolyn Wiener. 1985. *Social Organization of Medical Work.* Chicago: University of Chicago Press.

Strebel, Bernhard. 2003. *Das KZ Ravensbrück: Geschichte eines Lagerkomplexes.* Paderborn: Schöningh.

Steuwer, Janosch. 2013. "Was meint und nützt das Sprechen von der 'Volksgemeinschaft'? Neuere Literatur zur Gesellschaftsgeschichte des Nationalsozialismus." In: *Archiv für Sozialgeschichte* 53, 487–534.

Strnad, Maximilian. 2011. *Zwischenstation "Judensiedlung": Verfolgung und Deportation der jüdischen Münchner 1941–1945.* Munich: Oldenbourg.

———. 2013. "Manche Spuren menschlicher Existenz verblassen schneller als andere: Die Geschichte einer 'privilegierten Mischehe' in Memmingen." In *Allgäuerinnen: Ein Lesebuch.* Ed. Barbara Lochbihler and Sabine Schalm. Berlin: Edition Ebersbach, 171–89.

Swett, Pamela. 2004. *Neighbors and Enemies: The Culture of Radicalism in Berlin, 1929–1933.* Cambridge, UK: Cambridge University Press.

———. 2013. *Selling under the Swastika: Advertising and Commercial Culture in Nazi Germany.* Stanford: Stanford University Press.

Swibenko, Nadine. 2008. "Because I'm an Ossi." In *Ambivalent Americanizations: Popular and Consumer Culture in Central and Eastern Europe.* American Studies, vol. 165. Ed. Sebastian M. Herrmann, Katja Kanzler, Anne Koenen, Zoë A. Kusmierz, and Leonard Schmieding. Heidelberg: Universitätsverlag Winter, 121–38.

Szepansky, Gerda. 1983. "Versteckt und gerettet: Kläre Bloch." In *Frauen leisten Widerstand 1933–45: Lebensgeschichten nach Interviews und Dokumenten*. Ed. Gerda Szepansky. Frankfurt a.M.: Fischer, 196–205.

Taylor, Frederick. 2006. *The Berlin Wall: A World Divided, 1961–1989*. New York: HarperCollins.

Taylor, Frederick and Anna Raith. 2014. "Die Mauer im Kopf ist immer noch da." Deutschlandfunk, 3 October. http://www.deutschlandfunk.de/25-jahre-mauerfall-die-mauer-im-kopf-ist-immer-noch-da.694.de.html?dram:article_id=299322%20auch (accessed December 2014).

Taylor, Gabriele. 1985. *Pride, Shame and Guilt: Emotions of Self-Assessment*. Oxford: Clarendon.

Taylor, Victor E. and Charles E. Winquist. 2000. *Encyclopedia of Postmodernism*. London: Routledge.

Teichler, Hans Joachim. 1985. "Ende des Arbeitersports 1933?" In *Arbeiterkultur und Arbeitersport*. Ed. Hans Joachim Teichler. Clausthal-Zellerfeld: DVS, 196–234.

———. 1987. "'Wir brauchten einfach den Kontakt zueinander': Arbeitersport und Arbeitersportler im 'Dritten Reich.'" In *Illustrierte Geschichte des Arbeitersports*. Ed. Hans Joachim Teichler and Gerhard Hauck. Bonn: Dietz, 231–41.

Thiessen, Malte. 2007. *Eingebrannt ins Gedächtnis: Hamburgs Gedenken an Luftkrieg und Kriegsende 1943 bis 2005*. Munich: Dölling und Galitz.

Thompson, John B. 1995. *The Media and Modernity: A Social Theory of the Media*. Cambridge: Polity Press.

Thüringer Ministerium für Soziales, Familie und Gesundheit. 2006. *Der totgeschwiegene Terror: Zwangsaussiedlung in der DDR*. Erfurt: Thüringer Landesamt für Vermessung und Geoinformation.

Thurn, Hans Peter. 1980. *Der Mensch im Alltag: Grundrisse einer Anthroplogie des Alltagslebens*. Stuttgart: Enke.

Timpe, Julia. 2016. "'Männer und Frauen bei fröhlichem Spiel': Ziele, Gestaltung und Aneignungsversuche von KdF-Betriebssport." In *Sport und Nationalsozialismus*. Ed. Frank Becker and Ralf Schäfer. Göttingen: Wallstein, 85–103.

———. 2017. *Nazi-Organized Recreation and Entertainment in the Third Reich*. London: Palgrave Macmillan

Tönnies, Ferdinand. 1926. *Gemeinschaft und Gesellschaft, Grundbegriffe der reinen Soziologie*. 6th and 7th eds. Berlin: Curtius.

Trevor-Roper, H.R., ed. 2000. *Hitler's Table Talk, 1941–1944: His Private Conversations*. New York: Enigma Books.

Turner, Victor W. 1969. *The Ritual Process: Structure and Anti-Structure*. Chicago: Aldine.

———. 1986. *The Anthropology of Performance*. New York: PAJ.

Uhse, Bodo. 1955. *Die Patrioten, Erstes Buch: Abschied und Heimkehr*. Berlin: Aufbau.

Urry, John. 2007. *Mobilities*. Malden: Polity.

Vann, Richard T. 1998. "The Reception of Hayden White." *History and Theory* 37, no. 2: 143–61.

Veyne, Paul. 1993. "The Final Foucault and His Ethics." Trans. Catherine Porter and Arnold I. Davidson. *Critical Inquiry* 20, no. 1: 1–9.
Vogel, Berthold. 1999. *Ohne Arbeit in den Kapitalismus: Der Verlust der Erwerbsarbeit im Umbruch der ostdeutschen Gesellschaft*. Hamburg: VSA.
Wachsmann, Nikolaus. 2010. "The Dynamics of Destruction: The Development of the Concentration Camps." In *Concentration Camps in Nazi Germany. The New Histories*. Ed. Nikolaus Wachsmann and Jane Caplan. London: Routledge, 17–43.
———. 2015. *A History of the Nazi Concentration Camps*. New York: Farrar, Straus, and Giroux.
Wagner, Manfred. 2001. *"Beseitigung des Ungeziefers …": Zwangsaussiedlungen in den thüringischen Landkreisen Saalfeld, Schleiz und Lobenstein 1952 und 1961. Analysen und Dokumente*. Erfurt: Landesbeauftragter des Freistaates Thüringen für die Unterlagen des Staatssicherheitsdienstes der Ehemaligen DDR.
Wagner-Kyora, George, ed. 2014. *Rebuilding European Cities: Reconstructions, Modernity and the Local Politics of Identity Construction since 1945*. Stuttgart: Steiner.
Walk, Joseph. 1996. *Das Sonderrecht für die Juden im NS-Staat: eine Sammlung der gesetzlichen Massnahmen und Richtlinien, Inhalt und Bedeutung*. Heidelberg: Müller.
Walser Smith, Helmut. 2004. *Die Geschichte des Schlachters. Mord und Antisemitismus in einer deutschen Kleinstadt*. Trans. Udo Rennert. Frankfurt a.M.: Fischer.
Walter, Franz. 2009. *Die SPD: Biographie einer Partei*. Reinbek bei Hamburg: Rowohlt.
Weber, Hermann. 1969. *Die Wandlung des deutschen Kommunismus: Die Stalinisierung der KPD in der Weimarer Republik*, vol. 1. Frankfurt a.M.: Europäische.
———. 1986. *Dokumente zur Geschichte der Deutschen Demokratischen Republik 1945–1985*. Munich: Deutscher.
Weber, Marianne. 2009. *Max Weber: A Biography*. Trans. and ed. Harry Zohn. New Brunswick: Transaction.
Weber, Max. 1958. *The Protestant Ethic and the Spirit of Capitalism*. Trans. Talcott Parsons. New York: Charles Scribner's Sons.
———. 1968. *Economy and Society: An Outline of Interpretive Sociology*, 3 vols. Ed. Guenther Roth and Claus Wittich. New York: Bedminster Press.
Wehler, Hans-Ulrich. 1988. "Königsweg zu neuen Ufern oder Irrgarten der Illusionen? Die westdeutsche Alltagsgeschichte: Geschichte 'von innen' und 'von unten.'" In *Aus der Geschichte Lernen? Essays*. Ed. Hans-Ulrich Wehler. Munich: Beck, 130–51.
Weisbrod, Bernd. 1998. "Entwicklung und Funktionswandel der Konzentrationslager 1937/38 bis 1945: Kommentierende Bemerkungen." In *Die nationalsozialistischen Konzentrationslager. Entwicklung und Struktur*, vol. 1. Ed. Ulrich Herbert, Karin Orth, and Christoph Dieckmann. Göttingen: Wallstein, 349–60.
Weitz, Eric D. 1997. *Creating German Communism, 1890–1990: From Popular Protests to Socialist State*. Princeton: Princeton University Press.
Welzer, Harald and Michaela Christ. 2005. *Täter: Wie aus ganz normalen Männern Massenmörder warden*. Frankfurt a.M.: Fischer.

Wenzel, Birgit and Dagmar Weber. 1989. "Auschwitz in Geschichtsbüchern der Bundesrepublik Deutschland." In *Erziehung nach Auschwitz*. Ed. Hanns-Fred Rathenow and Norbert H. Weber. Pfaffenweiler: Centaurus, 117–36.
White, Hayden V. 1973. *Metahistory. The Historical Imagination in Nineteenth-Century Europe*. Baltimore: Johns Hopkins University Press.
———. 1987. "The Question of Narrative in Contemporary Historical Theory." In *The Content of the Form, Narrative Discourse and Historical Representation*. Baltimore: Johns Hopkins University Press, 26–57.
Wierling, Dorothee. 2002. *Geboren im Jahr Eins: Der Jahrgang 1949 in der DDR. Versuch einer Kollektivbiographie*. Berlin: Links.
Wildt, Michael. 2012a. *Hitler's Volksgemeinschaft and the Dynamics of Racial Exclusion*. New York: Berghahn.
———. 2012b. "Volksgemeinschaft: Eine Gewaltkonstruktion des Volkes." In *Gesellschaft—Gewalt—Vertrauen: Jan Philipp Reemtsma zm 60. Geburtstag*. Ed. Ulrich Bielefeld, Heinz Bude, and Bernd Greiner. Hamburg: Hamburger Edition, 438–57.
Wildt, Michael, Dietmar von Reeken, and Malte Thießen, eds. 2013. *"Volksgemeinschaft" als soziale Praxis: Neue Forschungen zur NS-Gesellschaft vor Ort*. Nationalsozialistische "Volksgemeinschaft." Studien zu Konstruktion, gesellschaftlicher Wirkungsmacht und Erinnerung, vol. 4. Paderborn: Schöningh.
Willems, Susanne. 2002. *Der entsiedelte Jude: Albert Speers Wohnungsmarktpolitik für den Berliner Hauptstadtbau*. Publikationen der Gedenk- und Bildungsstätte Haus der Wannseekonferenz, 10. Berlin: Edition Hentrich.
Wippermann, Wolfgang. 2009. *Dämonisierung durch Vergleich: DDR und Drittes Reich*. Berlin: Rotbuch.
Wojak, Irmtrud and Peter Hayes. 2000. *Arisierung im Nationalsozialismus: Volksgemeinschaft, Raub und Gedächtnis*. Frankfurt a.M.: Campus.
Wolf, Sascha. 2010. *Ost-West-Wanderung im Wiedervereinten Deutschland: Erfahrungen und Perspektiven*. Göttingen: Optimus.
Wolin, Richard. 1992. *The Heidegger Controversy: A Critical Reader*. Cambridge, MA: MIT Press.
Wollasch, Hans-Josef. 1996. *"Sociale Gerechtigkeit und christliche Charitas:" Leitfiguren und Wegmarkierungen aus 100 Jahren Caritasgeschichte*. Freiburg im Breisgau: Lambertus.
Wolle, Stefan. 1998. *Die heile Welt der Diktatur: Alltag und Herrschaft in der DDR 1971–1989*. Berlin: Links.
Wolter, Manfred. 1998. *Aktion Ungeziefer: Die Zwangsaussiedlung an der Elbe. Erlebnisberichte und Dokumente*. Rostock: Altstadt.
Wowtscherk, Christoph. 2014. *Was wird, wenn die Zeitbombe hochgeht? Eine sozialgeschichtliche Analyse der fremdenfeindlichen Ausschreitungen in Hoyerswerda im September 1991*. Göttingen: V&R unipress.
Wrocklage, Ute (in progess). "'Einmagazinierung' der Konzentrationslager 1933–1939. Fotografien und Bildberichte in der deutschen illustrierten Presse." Ph.D. diss., Carl von Ossietzky Universität Oldenburg.

Yones, Eliyahu. 2004. *Smoke in the Sand: The Jews of Lvov in the War Years, 1939–1944*. Jerusalem: Gefen.

Yurchak, Alexei. 2005. *Everything Was Forever, Until It Was No More: The Last Soviet Generation*. Princeton: Princeton University Press.

Zeitgeschichtliches Forum Leipzig [ZFL]. 2007. "Stiftung Haus der Geschichte der Bundesrepublik Deutschland." Konzept. http://www.hdg.de/leipzig/ausstellungen/dauerausstellung/konzept (accessed 25 February 2015).

Zeitreise, Lebensart DDR 1949–1989. Concept Paper (Entwicklungskonzept). Radebeul: n.d. Print.

Zimmerman, Klaus. 1993. "Labour Responses to Taxes and Benefits in Germany." In *Welfare and Work Incentives: A Northern European Perspective*. Ed. Alexander B. Atkinson and Gunnar V. Mogensen. Oxford: Clarendon, 192–240.

Newspapers

Burda Newsroom. 2014. "SuperIllu bringt Ost-West-Studie heraus." 1 October. http://www.burda-news.de/content/superillu-bringt-ost-west-studie-heraus (accessed December 2014).

Die Zeit. 2011. "Mauerfall: Der Spitzel macht die Mauer auf." *Die Zeit* (8 November 2011). http://www.zeit.de/2011/45/S-Jaeger (accessed January 2015).

Frank, Arno. 2014. "Schwer überbelichtet." *taz* 16/17 August, 20–22.

Für die proletarische Frau [For the Proletarian Woman], supplement to *Sozialistische Republik*, 23 June 1930.

Gesellschaft für Deutsch-sowjetische Freundschaft, 1975.

KPD, Ortsgruppe Mittweida. 1931. *Rote Fahne*, 14 August.

Neues Deutschland, 25 January 1963.

Presse Portal. 2014. "N24-Emnid-Umfrage zum Fall der Mauer: 25 Jahre Mauerfall: Deutsche sehen mehr Gemeinsames als Trennendes/Aber: Jeder Fünfte war noch nie im anderen Teil Deutschlands." *Presse Portal*, 1 October 2014. http://www.presseportal.de/pm/13399/2845144/n24-emnid-umfrage-zum-fall-der-mauer-25-jahre-mauerfall-deutsche-sehen-mehr-gemeinsames-als (accessed November 2014).

Shabecoff, Philip. 1966. "Country Cousin of the Berlin Wall." *The New York Times*, July 10.

Verein zur Dokumentation der DDR-Alltagskultur e.V. 1997. Mitglieder stellen sich vor: Jürgen Friedhoff. *Rundbrief*, 9.

———. 1999. Mitglieder stellen sich vor: Jan Faktor, *Rundbrief*, 7.

"Wie ich zur Roten Front kam" [How I Came to the Red Front]. *Frauenwacht* 4/5, 1928.

[Worker Correspondent. No number.] 1932. "Vorgeschmack vom 3. Reich" [A Foretaste of the Third Reich]. *Sozialistische Republik*, 6–7 August.

Worker Correspondent. [No number]. 1932. "SA-Strolche überfallen Jungarbeiter" [SA Hoodlums Attack Young Worker]. *Sozialistische Republik*, 11 September.

———. 270. 1929. "Das Los einer kinderreichen Familie" [The Lot of Families with Many Children]. *Sozialistische Republik,* 19 April.
———. 531. 1931. "Wir marschieren an der Mieterfront" [We Are Marching on the Renter Front]. *Sozialistische Republik,* 14 August.
———. 946. 1932. "Polizeijagd auf Fahnen und Transparente" [Police Hunt for Flags and Banners]. *Sozialistische Republik,* 10 November.

Unpublished Material

Archiv des Deutschen Caritasverbandes e.V. (ADCV)

ADCV 236.40.025 [From the Diary of a Caritas People's Day Collection Box]. Nr. 223. 16 May 1935

Archiv der Staatlichen Gedenkstätte Majdanek (APMM)

Sygn. XX 26.
Bl. 16. Fernschreiben Nr. 295. Chef der Amtsgruppe D–Konzentrationslager des SS-Wirtschafts-Verwaltungshauptamtes, Richard Glücks, an den SS- und Polizeiführer von Lublin, Odilo Globocnik. Oranienburg, 20 January 1943.
Bl. 258. Der Lagerkommandant Max Koegel an die Amtsgruppe D–Konzentrationslager des SS-Wirtschafts-Verwaltungshauptamtes, betr. Aufseherinnen für das Frauenlager KGl. Lublin. Lublin, 11 December 1942.

Archiv Gedenkstätte Deutscher Widerstand Berlin (ArchGdW)

Dossier Erich Bloch.
Dossier Kläre Bloch.
  Interview Kläre Bloch (geb. Begall). 1986. Geführt von Marion Neiss und Irina Wandrey.
  Tagebuch [Diary] Klära Bloch [here: Kläre Jung] (geb. Begall). March–August 1945.

Bundesarchiv (BArch)

B162 (Zentrale Stelle der Landesjustizverwaltungen in Ludwigsburg).
  AR-Z 77/72, Bd. 1.
  AR-Z 77/72, Bd. 4.
  1682. Testimony Erna Leonhard. 14 December 1960.
  Bayerisches Landeskriminalamt. 76-K 41676. Koe.
    Testimony Florentina Bedner. 29 November 1976.
    Testimony Heinrich Barth. 2 March 1977.

NS 4 (Konzentrationslager).
　Ra Bl. 7. Konzentrationslager Ravensbrück, Kommandantur, Az. 260, Betr. Bewerbung als Aufseherin. Undated, probably Fall 1944.
NS 5 (Deutsche Arbeitsfront).
　IV/39. Ermittlungsbericht über die 'KdF'-Fahrt nach Eschwege 8–15 August 36, Betr. Bund Niederdeutscher Heimatwanderer. 22 August 1936.
　IV/94. Vortrag. Richtlinien und Praxis der kommunistischen Internationale zur Zersetzung der Betriebsgemeinschaft von Gau-I-Referent Pg. [Guidelines and Practice of the Communist International for the Destruction of the Factory Community]. Notter. 24 January 1938.
RS (Rasse- und Siedlungshauptamt).
　B 0125, Heiratsgesuchakte Hans Joachim Ehlert, born 2 April 1893
　Ärztlicher Untersuchungsbogen Hertha Ließ. 1. July 1941
　Handschriftlicher Lebenslauf Hertha Ließ. Ravensbrück, 4 July 1941.
R 58 (Reichssicherheitshauptamt)
　316. Bericht. "Volkstanzkreis 215 Guben." 23 December 1936.
SAPMO (Stiftung Archiv der Parteien und Massenorganisationen der DDR)
　RY1 I 4/3/1.
　"Die Tagung des 1. Reichskongresses der Roten Frauen- und Mädchen-Bundes." Material II. 20–22 November 1926.
　"Richtlinien des Roten Frauen- und Mädchenbundes." Undated, ca. 1926.
　RY1 I 4/3/2.
　"Bericht des Roten Frauen- und Mädchen-Bundes, Deutschland." 7 May 1926.
SgY 30 (SAPMO, Erinnerungen)
　2058. Alfred Nothnagel.

Bayerisches Hauptstaatsarchiv München (BayHStAM)

Herger, Renate. 2004. "Zur Geschichte der Bayerische Grenzpolizei." Introduction to Findbuch *Präsidium der Bayerischen Grenzpolizei*. Munich: Bayerisches Hauptstaatsarchiv München.
Präsidium der Bayerischen Grenzpolizei (PrBayGrePo). Nrs. 1365, 23 April 1946; 1366, 25 May 1948; 1367, 26 March 1951.

Bundesbeauftragte für die Unterlagen des Staatssicherheitsdienstes der ehemaligen Deutschen Demokratischen Republik (BStU)

000050-57. Horst and Erna Petri Trial. 19 September 1961. Also accessible at the US Holocaust Memorial Museum Archives, RG 14.068, fiche 566.
MfS-HA XX/9, Nr. 1680.

Deutsches Literaturarchiv Marbach (DLaM)

Brief [Letter]. 16 August 1918. Bestand: Jünger, Ernst. Von ihm an Jünger, Friedrich Georg. Abschriften 1912–1945, Bl. 16.
Brief [Letter]. 19 April 1929. Bestand: Jünger, Ernst. An ihn von Schultz, Edmund. 1929–1949.

Landesamt für Bürger- und Ordnungsangelegenheiten, Berlin, Einwohnermeldeamt und Entschädigungsbehörde (LaBO)

Entschädigungsakte, Nr. 5379. Erich Bloch.
Liste. Versteckorte von Erich Bloch. Angefertigt 1 February 1952 von Klära Jung (geb. Begall).
Schreiben. Erich Bloch an den Berliner Magistrat. 25 July 1949.
Schreiben. Rechtsbeistand Emanuel Bloch an das Entschädigungsamt Berlin. 18 November 1955.

International Tracing Service Archive, Bad Arolsen (ITS)

Miscellaneous Records. USSR. Schenk-Bericht. "Verhalten der Reichsdeutschen in den besetzten Gebieten" (Galizien). 14 May 1943. Also available with pages missing in the Bundesarchiv Koblenz, R58/1002.

Interviews

Interview. Dieter. 2010. Research Collection Thomas Gurr.
Interview. Gerste. February 2003. Research Collection Alexandra Oeser.
Interview. Stephan Holstein. 2 July 2012. Research Collection Maximillian Strnad.
Interview. Alexander Morawitz. 2008. Dresden. 29 February. Research Collection Leonard Schmieding.
Interview. Inge Müller. October 2003. Research Collection Alexandra Oeser.
Interview. Peter Rausch. 28 June 2010. Research Collection Josie McLellan.
Interview. Annette Schücking-Homeyer. 30 March 2010. Research Collection Wendy Lower.
Interview. M. Schultze. February 2003. Research Collection Alexandra Oeser.
Interview. Hans-Joachim Stephan. 2009. Research Collection Jonathan Bach.
Interview. Michael Unger. 14 April 2011. Research Collection Josie McLellan.

Landesarchiv Berlin (LAB)

Erklärung. Gertrud Bruck und Hildegard Abraham. 20 November 1964.
Senatsverwaltung für Inneres. B Rep. 004, AZ 0253/22, UH-Sache 1343. Kläre Bloch, geb. Begall.

Mahn- und Gedenkstätte Ravensbrück/Stiftung Brandenburgische Gedenkstätten (MGR/StBG)

KL 17/9. Gefangenenstärkemeldungen des gesamten Lagers und der einzelnen Häftlingsblocks des Frauen-Konzentrationslagers Ravensbrück.
KL 18/10–15. Arbeitseinteilungslisten des Frauen-Konzentrationslagers Ravensbrück.

Museum für Sepulkralkultur, Kassel (MfSk)

Thomas, Karl. Unpublished. "Technologische Grundkonzeption zur Grundsatzentscheidung: Neubau Große Feierhalle mit Kremationsanlage in Dresden—Heidefriedhof," Institut für Kommunalwirtschaft, Dresden.

National Archives and Records Administration, United States (NARA)

Record Group 238. Roll 50. M1019. 7 May 1947.

Private Collections

Private Collection Sandro Bartels.
    Figas, Peter. 1989. "1. DDR-offener Rap-Workshop im Jugendklub Nickern."
    TJ Big Blaster Electric Boogie. 1989. "Ich fürchte, das Hin und Her läßt sich nicht sparen."
Private Collection Lutz Schramm.
    Brief [Letter]. 1989. Alexander Morawitz an Lutz Schramm.
    TJ Big Blaster Electric Boogie. 1989. "Time to Fite."

Shoah Foundation Institute for Visual History and Education at the University of Southern California (SFI)

Interview. Mikail Vul. 1996. Code 25159.
Interview. Mikhail Aronowitsch Vanshelboim. 1997b. Code 27225. Shitomir/Ukraine.
Interview. Mariia Jefimowna Beizerman. 1997a. Code 27766. Berditschew/Ukraine.
Interview. Nina Kordash. 1997c. Code 38524. New York.

Stadtarchiv Memmingen (StadtA MM)

Nachlass Gugenheimer (NLG)
    Bericht [Report]. Dr. L. Kraemer. 15 April 1948.
    Bestätigung [Certificate] der Schule. 19 January 1955.
    Bestätigung [Certificate] des Memmingen Stadtrats. 29 January 1949.
    Bestätigung [Certificate] Georg Kolb. 18 February 1949.

Bestätigung [Certificate] Theo Grünfeld. 16 October 1978.
Brief [Letter]. Alfred Guggenheimer an Graf von Schaesberg. 10 January 1944.
Brief [Letter]. Alfred Guggenheimer an Wilhelm. 10 January 1944.
Brief [Letter]. Laura Eisfeld an Annemarie und Ursula Guggenheimer. 19 March 1945.
Brief [Letter]. Ruth Weikersheimer an Frau Pick. 5 December 1946.
Eidesstattliche Erklärung. Ursula Guggenheimer. 25 May 1959.
Entscheidung [Decision] des Beschwerdeausschusses beim Landesamt für Soforthilfe. 10 July 1950.
Erklärung. 1. Pferdeknecht Georg Martin. 15 February 1962.
Gesuch [Application] der Memminger Wohnungsbau e.G. an das Amtsgericht Memmingen. 25 April 1974
Lebenslauf Alfred Guggenheimer.
Postkarten. Alfred Guggenheimer aus Theresienstadt an Annemarie und Ursula.
Schreiben. Bayerisches Landesentschädigungsamt an Annemarie Guggenheimer. 29 December 1971.
Schreiben. Dr. Laube an Annemarie Guggenheimer. 29 June and 18 August 1942.
Schreiben. Ludwig Bach an das Verwaltungsgericht Augsburg. 27 May 1949.
Schreiben. Rechtsanwalt Dr. Hans Raff an Annemarie Guggenheimer. 17 September 1958.
Schreiben. Ursula Guggenheimer an das Bayerische Hilfswerk. 30 July 1949.
Schreiben. Vertrauensmann der Reichsvereinigung der Juden in Deutschland. Geschäftsstelle Augsburg. 11 August 1942.
Schreiben. Viehwirtschaftsverband Bayern an Alfred Guggenheimer. 30 November 1937.
Personalmeldebögen.
Sammelakten zu den Sterberegistern.
Sterbefallanzeige Ursula Elisabeth Guggenheimer, 1981

Staatsarchiv München (StAM)

Oberfinanzdirektion (OFD) 12596. Alfred Guggenheimer. Urteil. Landgericht Memmingen. 11 June 1942.
Polizeidirektion. 13222. Alfred Guggenheimer.
Spruchkammerakten (SpKA) Karton 1734 Wilhelm Schwarz (2.4.1902). Urteil. Landgericht Memmingen gegen Wilhelm Schwarz und andere wegen Hausfriedensbruchs. 23 September 1948.

The National Archives of England and Wales (TNA), Kew/Richmond, Former Public Record Office

War Office 235/15. Hertha Ehlert. Cross-examined by Major Munro. Lüneburg. 15 October 1945. Bl. 74–78.

Thüringisches Staatsarchiv Greiz (ThStAG)

Kreisrat des Landkreises Schleiz (KrLkS). Nr. 44, 7 September 1945; 96, 21 March 1952; 98, July 1949.

Thüringisches Hauptstaatsarchiv Weimar (ThHStAW)

Land Thüringen Ministerium des Innern. Nr. 1129, March 1948; 1131 Tätigkeitsbericht.

Volksbund Deutsche Kriegsgräberfürsorge e.V., Archiv

GN 1.2. Lr. Soldatenfriedhof Berditschew. 1992/93.

Walter Kempowski Biografienarchiv, Akademie der Künste, Berlin (KBio)

6232. Erdmann, Peter. 2001. "Stasi Files and related Procedural Files."
6588. Mandelbaum, Michael. Unpublished. *Wie ein Mensch wird, was er ist, oder Wir sind die Sklaven unseres Verstandes, oder Studie eines Lebens.*

AUTHORS

Jonathan Bach (Ch. 5) is chair of the interdisciplinary global studies undergraduate program and associate professor of international affairs at The New School in New York. His articles have appeared in *Cultural Anthropology, Theory, Culture & Society, Cultural Politics, Public Culture, Studies in Comparative and International Development,* and *Geopolitics*. He is the author of *Between Sovereignty and Integration: German Foreign Policy and National Identity after 1989* (1999) and *What Remains: Everyday Encounters with the Socialist Past in Germany* (forthcoming); and he is co-editor of *Learning from Shenzhen: China's Post-Mao Experiment from Special Zone to Model City* (2017).

Andrew Stuart Bergerson (Chs. 1, 10, throughout as lead author) is the author of *Ordinary Germans in Extraordinary Times: The Nazi Revolution in Hildesheim* (2004, forthcoming in German translation as *Entscheidung im Alltag*); and *The Happy Burden of History: From Sovereign Impunity to Historical Responsibility* (2011) with K. Scott Baker, Clancy Martin, and Steve Ostovich. He is currently one of the project leaders for *Trug und Schein: Ein Briefwechsel* (www.trugundschein.org), an intermedial project in the public humanities.

Susanne Beer (Ch. 7) is research coordinator at Centre Marc Bloch in Berlin, a Franco-German research center for social sciences. She published the book *Immanenz und Utopie: Zur Kulturkritik von Theodor W. Adorno und Guy Debord* (2012) as well as articles in the *Online Encyclopedia of Mass Violence* and *Medaon: Magazin für jüdisches Leben in Forschung und Bildung*. Her scholarship also appeared in the edited collections *Schlüsselwerke der Kulturwissenschaften, Alterität—Erzählen vom Anderssein*, and *Le Lieu du genre*. Her doctoral research concerns practices of solidarity and assistance to Jews during the Holocaust.

Mark E. Blum (Chs. 1, 3, 10) is professor of history at the University of Louisburg in Kentucky. His major publications include *The Austro Marxists, 1890–1918: A Psychobiographical Study* (1985), *Continuity, Quantum, Continuum, and Dialectic: The Foundational Logics of Western Historical Thinking* (Peter Lang, 2006), *Kafka's Social Discourse: An Aesthetic Search for Community* (Lehigh University Press, 2011), and *Austro-Marxism: The Ideology of Unity*, a forthcoming two-volume anthology with William Smaldone.

Michaela Christ (Ch. 8) is head of the research division Long-Term Socioecological Research of the Norbert Elias Center for Transformation Design & Research (NEC) at the Europa-Universität Flensburg as well as editor of the magazine *Medaon: Magazin für jüdisches Leben in Forschung und Bildung*. Her major publications include articles in *Soziologie*, *Emulations*, *L'Europe en formation*, *Soziale Passagen*, and *Zeitschrift für Geschichtswissenschaft*; the book *Die Dynamik des Tötens: Die Ermordung der Juden in Berditschew, Ukraine 1941–1944* (2011), and the edited volumes *Gewalt: Ein interdisziplinäres Handbuch* (2013) with Christian Gudehus and *Soziologie und Nationalsozialismus: Positionen, Debatten, Perspektiven* (2014) with Maja Suderland.

Cristina Cuevas-Wolf (Ch. 5) is the resident historian at the Wende Museum of the Cold War in Culver City, California. Her major works of scholarship include articles in *New German Critique*, *Visual Resources*; chapters in the edited volumes *Elective Affinities: Testing Word and Image Relationships* and *A Hard, Merciless Light: The Worker-Photography Movement, 1926–1938* (2011); and contributions to a range of exhibitions on East German material culture. Current exhibition project focuses on Hungary's Cold War visual culture.

Mary Fulbrook (Ch. 8) is professor of German history at University College London and Dean of the UCL Faculty of Social and Historical Sciences. She currently serves on the Council of the British Academy, the Academic Advisory Board of the foundation for the former Nazi concentration camps at Buchenwald and Mittelbau-Dora, and the International Advisory Board of the Chancellor Willy Brandt Foundation. Her recent major publications include the Fraenkel Prize–winning *A Small Town near Auschwitz: Ordinary Nazis and the Holocaust* (2012) and *Dissonant Lives: Generations and Violence through the German Dictatorships* (2011). Her work on the German Democratic Republic includes *The People's State: East German Society from Hitler to Honecker* (2005) and *Anatomy of a Dictatorship: Inside the GDR, 1949–89* (1995). She has written widely in other areas; her writings include *Historical Theory* (2002) and *German National Identity after the Holocaust* (1999) as well as general overviews of German history.

Eva Giloi (Ch. 3) is associate professor in the history department at Rutgers University, Newark campus. Her dissertation, "Ich Kaufe Mir Den Kaiser": *Royal Relics and the Culture of Display in 19th Century Prussia*, received the Fritz Stern Prize from the German Historical Institute in Washington, D.C. in 2001. Her major publications include articles in *Intellectual History Review* and *Central European History*, her book *Monarchy, Myth, and Material Culture* in Germany 1750–1950 (2011), and the edited volume *Constructing Charisma: Celebrity, Fame, and Power in Nineteenth-Century Europe* (2010) with Edward Berenson.

Thomas Gurr (Chs. 1 and 10) is a Wissenschaftlicher Mitarbeiter at the Institute for Sociology at the Leibniz Universität Hannover as well as a researcher for the project Stigma-Bewusstsein von Arbeitslosen und Vorurteile gegenüber Arbeitslosen. His dissertation research and publications focus on inequality, poverty, and social work. With Joachim Merchel, Yvonne Kaiser, and Laura Kress, he recently published the book *Schwer erreichbare Jugendliche: Eine Herausforderung für die Jugendsozialarbeit* (2015).

Jason Johnson (Ch. 9) is an assistant professor of history at Trinity University in San Antonio, Texas. His dissertation won the Harold Perkin Award for the Best Dissertation in History from Northwestern University. His articles and forthcoming book, *Divided Village: The Cold War in the German Borderlands*, focus on the effects of the inner-German border on those living along it.

Craig Koslofsky (Ch. 9) is a professor of history at the University of Illinois, Urbana-Champaign. His major publications include the books *Evening's Empire: A History of the Night in Early Modern Europe* (2011) and *The Reformation of the Dead: Death and Ritual in Early Modern Germany, 1450–1700* (2000); essay volumes edited with Bernhard Jussen, *Kulturelle Reformation: Sinnformationen im Umbruch 1400–1600* (1999) and with Brian Sandberg, *Campaign Communities: Gender and the State in Early Modern Warfare* (forthcoming); and *The Journal of Ship's Surgeon Johann Peter Oettinger: A German Account of the Atlantic Slave Trade, 1688–94* edited with Roberto Zaugg and translated by him.

Dani Kranz (Ch. 5) is an associate professor of sociology and empirical research methods at the Hochschule Rhein-Waal in Kleve. Her scholarship explores Jewish, Israeli, and German identities, with articles appearing in *Austausch* and *European Review of History* as well as forthcoming chapters in edited volumes on non-Jewish migration from the global north to Israel, German and Israeli concepts of citizenship, and the aftermath of the Shoah for young Jews in Germany.

Phil Leask (Ch. 4, throughout as peer reviewer) is an honorary research associate at University College London. He writes on everyday life in the GDR and on humiliation and its consequences. He has contributed to an edited volume on the GDR, *Becoming East German: Socialist Structures and Sensibilities after Hitler* (Mary Fulbrook and Andrew I. Port, 2013) and has published a number of journal articles, reviews, and essays as well as short stories and novels. He is currently working on a project concerning women's letters and accounts of their lives in the GDR.

Wendy Lower (Ch. 8) is John K. Roth Professor of History and George R. Roberts Fellow at Claremont McKenna College, California. Her recent publications include articles in the *Journal of Genocide Research* and *Holocaust and Genocide Studies*; an essay volume edited with Ray Brandon, *The Shoah in Ukraine: History, Testimony, Memorialization* (2008); and the books *Nazi Empire-Building and the Holocaust in Ukraine* (2007), *The Diary of Samuel Golfard and the Holocaust in Eastern Galicia* (2011), and *Hitler's Furies: German Women in the Nazi Killing Fields* (2013). She received the Baker Burton Award for the best first book in European history from the Southern Historical Association in 2007.

Elissa Mailänder (Ch. 6) is associate professor at the Centre d'histoire de Sciences Po in Paris. Her major publications include articles in *L'Europe en formation, German History, Journal of Genocide Research, Online Encyclopedia of Mass Violence*, and *zeitgeschichte*; an essay collection edited with Ralph Gabriel, Monika Neuhofer, and Else Rieger, *Lagersystem und Repräsentation: Interdisziplinäre Studien zur Geschichte der Konzentrationslager Studien zum Nationalsozialismus* (2004); and the book *Female SS Guards and Workaday Violence: The Majdanek Concentration Camp, 1942–1944* (2015).

Josie McLellan (Ch. 9) is reader in modern European history at the University of Bristol. Her major publications include articles in *English Historical Review, German History, History Workshop Journal, Journal of Modern History, Past & Present*, and *Rundbrief Fotografie* as well as the books *Antifascism and Memory in East Germany: Remembering the International Brigades 1945–1989* (2004) and *Love in the Time of Communism: Intimacy and Sexuality in the GDR* (2011).

Alexandra Oeser (Chs. 1, 6, 10) is maîtresse de conférences in the department of sociology at the Université Paris Ouest Nanterre La Defense as well as the Insitute des Sciences sociales et politique. Her major publications include articles in *Journal of Comparative Family Studies, Revue d'histoire de la Shoah, Revue suisse sur les didactiques de l'histoire, Sociétés contemporaines, Sociétés et Représentations*; a special issue of *Sociétés contemporaines* (2015) titled "Domination au quotidien, traduire les théories de pouvoir"; a collection of essays edited with Solène Billaud, Sibylle Gollac, and Julie Pagis, *Histoires familiales: Les conditions sociales de reproduction* (2015); and the book *Enseigner Hitler: Les adolescents face au passé nazi en Allemagne. Interprétations, appropriations et usages de l'histoire* (2010).

Steve Ostovich (Chs. 1, 3, 10) is a professor of philosophy at the College of St. Scholastica in Duluth, Minnesota. His recent books include *Missing God? Cultural Amnesia and Political Theology*, coedited with John Downey and Juergen Manemann (2006); *The Courage of Faith: Some Philosophical Meditations* (Liturgical Press, 2009); and *The Happy Burden of History: from Sovereign Impunity to Historical Responsibility* (2011) with Andrew Stuart Bergerson, K. Scott Baker, and Clancy Martin.

Will Rall (Ch. 6) is a doctoral student in history at the University of Tennessee–Knoxville. His dissertation focuses on charity work in the Third Reich.

Leonard Schmieding (Chs. 1, 2, 10, throughout as lead author) is an independent history provider working at the intersections of Germany and America, museums and memorial culture, and research and public engagement. He previously worked as a Postdoctoral Fellow in Global and Trans-Regional History at the German Historical Institute in Washington, DC. He received his doctorate in history from the University of Leipzig in 2011 with a dissertation on hip-hop culture in the German Democratic Republic that has since been published as *"Das ist unsere Party": HipHop in der DDR* (2014).

Johannes Schwartz (Ch. 7) received the title of Doctor designatus (Dr. des.) by the University of Erfurt in 2011. Since then, he has worked for various concentration camp memorial sites and documentation and culture centers in Germany and Austria. With Simone Erpel, Jeanette Toussaint, and Lavern Wolfram, he edited the essay collection *Im Gefolge der SS: Aufseherinnen des Frauen-KZ Ravensbrück: Begleitband zur Ausstellung* (2007) and with Wojciech Lenarczyk, Andreas Mix, and Veronika Springmann *KZ-Verbrechen: Beiträge zur Geschichte der nationalsozialistischen Konzentrationslager und ihrer Erinnerung* (2007). His dissertation will be published with Hamburger Edition under the title *Gewalt und Geschlecht: Handlungsräume von KZ-Aufseherinnen in Ravensbrück und Neubrandenburg*.

Sara Ann Sewell (Ch. 4) is a professor of history at Virginia Wesleyan College and the Executive Director of the Lighthouse: Center for Experiential Learning. Her work has appeared in a variety of history journals. Her latest publication is "Spectacles of Everyday Life: The Disciplinary Function of Communist Culture in Weimar Germany," in *German Visual Culture* (2015).

Paul Steege (Ch. 2, throughout as peer reviewer) is an associate professor at Villanova University in Pennsylvania. His articles have appeared in *Deutschland Archiv*, *Central European History*, and *Journal of Modern History* as well as in the edited collections *In Earth Ways: Framing Geographical*

Meanings and *Sterben für Berlin? Die Berliner-Krisen 1948 : 1958*. He published his first book in 2007: *Black Market, Cold War: Everyday Life in Berlin, 1946–1949*.

Maximilian Strnad (Ch. 7) is a doctoral student at the Ludwig-Maximillians-Universität München. His scholarship has appeared in the edited collections *Allgäuerinnen, Judenverfolgung in München*, and *Neuhauser-Werkstattnachrichten, Münchner Beiträge zur Jüdischen Geschichte und Kultur*. He edited a collection of essays with Michael Brenner, *Der Holocaust in der deutschsprachigen Geschichtswissenschaft* (2013), and wrote the books *Flachs für das Reich: Das jüdische Zwangsarbeitslager "Flachsröste Lohhof" bei München* (2013) and *Zwischenstation "Judensiedlung." Verfolgung und Deportation der jüdischen Münchner 1941–1945* (2011).

Julia Timpe (Ch. 6) is a lecturer in contemporary history at Jacobs University Bremen. She recently completed the monograph *Nazi-Organized Recreation and Entertainment in the Third Reich* (2017), which examines the practices and propaganda of the Nazi leisure organization Kraft durch Freude and contributed to the edited volume *Sport und Nationalsozialismus* (2016).

Heléna Tóth (Ch. 4) is Akademische Rätin a.Z. at the Universität Bamberg. She has contributed chapters to *Changing European Death Ways, Vergessene Vielfalt: Territorialisierung und Internationalisierung in Ostmitteleuropa, Migrationserfahrungen und Migrationsstrukturen*, and *Europäische Identität, Identitäten in Europa*. Her articles have appeared in *Hungarian Historical Review, Transnational Subjects, Yearbook of the Consortium on the Revolutionary Era*, and *Harvard Library Bulletin*. Her books include *Cityscapes in History: Creating the Urban Experience* (2014) with Katrina Gulliver and *An Exiled Generation: German and Hungarian Refugees of Revolution, 1848–1871* (2014).

INDEX

action-oriented grounded theory, 18
Adler, Friedrich, 74
aesthetics, 38, 113
affective directness, 74–75
affective relations, 52, 75, 126, 127. *See also* families
agency: memory and, 136–37; self-authorization and, 225; structures *vs.*, 14–15; unruliness and, 128. *See also* autonomy; intentionality/intentions; self-authorization
Aktion 14f13, 181–82, 191–92
Aktion Reinhardt, 154–55, 192
alienation, 6, 18, 60, 71–73, 128
Allensbach Institute, 3
Allgemeinst-Wirkliche, 61
Allinson, Mark, 103
All Quiet on the Western Front (Remarque), 47
Alltag: apprehension of, 59; definition of, 20–22. *See also* consensus; microsocial interactions; plasticity; self-authorization
alltäglich, 57–58, 62, 67
Alltagsgeschichte, 20
Alltagswelt, 57
alterity, 13
Altreich, 162, 169, 184, 189, 194
Ankersmit, Frank R., 270
antifascism, 89
anti-Semitism, 168–200; education about, 150–52; everyday *vs.* eliminationist, 220–21; gender relations and, 189–94; personal *vs.* institutional, 25, 176–77, 181–82, 187–89, 199, 207, 222–24; postwar, 150–51, 194–98, 200. *See also* anti-Semitism, women's responses to; laws/regulations, anti-Semitic; Nazi East; Shoah
anti-Semitism, women's responses to: postwar, 195–98, 200; prewar, 171–80;
during World War II, 155–56, 180–89, 224. *See also* Begall, Kläre; Ehrich, Elisabeth (Else); Guggenheimer, Annemarie; Halata, Luzie; Ließ, Hertha; Schücking-Homeyer, Annette
Anti-Socialist Law of 1878, 84
Apel, Linde, 182
apperception, 58, 72, 77
apprehension, 18–19, 59; communal will and, 76; life world *vs.* larger world and, 228; ordinariness and, 57, 67; plasticity and, 259; of space, 229
Arcades Project (Benjamin), 68
Arendt, Hannah, 267–68, 272
aristocracy, 62
Aristotle, 74
art, 63–64
Aryans, 26, 178–79, 203. *See also* *Volksgemeinschaft*
Ascona, 64
Assmann, Aleida, 140
asyndeton, 65–66, 68
ATG26, 28
aura/auratic, 117
Auschwitz, 25, 193, 197, 213, 219
ausseralltäglich, 57–58, 62, 67
authenticity, 48–53; collaboration and, 48, 50; culture and, 37, 63; freedom and, 52; as illusory, 53; language and, 42, 51–52; of state *vs.* private museums, 123, 141
authority, 227–52; cooperation with, 48–50, 251, 264–65; definition of, 62–63, 227; of insiders *vs.* outsiders, 242–43; legitimacy of, 230, 240, 245–48; symbols of, 208–9, 232–35, 244–46; terror and, 161–62. *See also* Berlin; Berlin Wall; *Eigensinn* (unruliness); institutions; Mödlareuth; self-authorization; West Africa; worlds, local *vs.* global

autonomy: of concentration camp guards, 182–83; of family, 90, 91; of insiders, 229; limits of, 79–80, 258; self-authorization and, 112, 262; space and, 164. See also agency
Axim, 244–46

BAC (Brandenburger African Company), 231–32, 244–46
Bach, Ludwig, 196
Bahnhof Zoo, 248
Bahr, Herman, 75–76
bargains, 264–65, 268
Baudelaire, Charles, 65, 68–69
Baudrillard, Jean, 126
Bavaria. See Mödlareuth
Bayerisches Hilfswerk, 195–96
Beat Street, 41
Bedner, Florentina, 211
Będzin, 205, 213–14, 216, 219–20
Begall, Kläre: gender relations and, 190; postwar, 197–98; pre-1941, 173, 175–77, 180; sheltering of Jews by, 185–90
Beizerman, Mariia, 207, 217
Bekenntniskirche, 242–43
Benjamin, Walter, 27, 65, 68–73
Bensa, Alban, 27
Berdichev, 205–10; anticipation of German occupation of, 205–7; German occupation of, 208–10, 216–17; mass executions in, 217–19
Berditschew. See Berdichev
Bergen-Belsen, 193, 197
Berlin: blockade of, 237, 238; gay and lesbian scene (East Berlin), 241–43; growth of, 59, 61, 64; map of, 10; Wilhelm Pieck, funeral of (East Berlin), 92. See also Berlin Wall
Berlin Childhood around 1900 (Benjamin), 70
Berliner Tagesspiegel, 198
Berlin Wall: border guards at, 116; creation of, 1; fall of, 119, 139, 266–68; imaginary, 4; plasticity of, 258–59. See also Wende
Besser, Martin, 218
Betriebssportgemeinschaften (BSG), 157
Betroffenheitspädagogik, 150
Betts, Paul, 89–90

Biermann, Wolf, 79, 109
Bildungsbürgertum, 64
Bloch, Emanual, 198
Bloch, Erich, 186–90, 197–98
Blockwart, 187
Bolshevik Revolution, 82–85
Bonn, 119–20
Bourdieu, Pierre, 13
Brandenburger African Company (BAC), 231–32, 244–46
Brandenburg-Prussia, 11, 231, 246–47. See also Prussia
Branitz, 154
Breaking through the Silence (Dauenheimer), 249
Bredel, Willi, 89
Brentano, Franz, 59
British, 197
Bronx, 39, 41–42
BSG (Betriebssportgemeinschaften), 157
Bundestag, 115
bureaucracy: birth of, 144; charisma and, 62–63; concentration camps and, 161; documentation of, 229–30; Mödlareuth border and, 235–41. See also institutions; Mödlareuth

California, 118
capitalism, 3, 7–8, 18, 24, 256
Caritas. See DCV (Deutscher Caritasverband)
cassette tapes, 39, 51
Catholicism, 26–27, 153–54, 159–60, 222
celebrity: celebrity sightings, 64–67, 69–70; celebrity tourism, 66; vs. charisma, 63
Certeau, Michel de, 65–66
charisma, 62–64, 67
Chemnitz (Karl-Marx-Stadt), 100
children: government assistance of, 90; politicization of, 86–87; youth organizations, 85, 93, 157–59, 215
Christianity: Catholicism, 26–27, 153–54, 159–60, 222; Protestant Church, 241–43, 251; symbols of, 216–17
cinema, 68–73; alienation and, 71–73; as paratactic, 70–71; shared experience and, 70

cities: authority in, 62; *Lebensreform* and, 64; social norms of, 73; urbanization, 59–60; walking in, 61–62, 65–71. See also Berlin

class: class conflict, 150; cultural charisma and, 68, 70; emotions and, 106; leisure and, 149–50; performance of, 34; privacy and, 80; social conflict and, 104. See also working class

Cold War, 130, 133, 237. See also Mödlareuth

collective person, 76–78

collectors' museums, 122–30; collections in, 125–28; criticism of, 123–25; operations of, 128–29, 140; popularity of, 122; purpose of, 122–23

Cologne, 87–88

colonialism, 205, 214, 235

communal will, 73–75. See also will

Communist Manifesto (Marx, Engels), 82

community: authority in, 62; cinema and, 72; communal will, 73–75; hip-hop and, 50–52; imagined, 2–3, 77; intention and, 76–77; social question, 60–61, 73, 76; *vs.* society, 60, 62, 68, 70; urbanization and, 60, 64; Wende and, 18

concentration camps: evacuation of, 194–95; Janowska, 221–22; liberation of, 194; purpose of, 161–62; Ravensbrück, 177–78, 181–82, 191–92, 197; for women, 193. See also Majdanek; Night of Broken Glass; Shoah

conformity, 213–14, 224

consensus, 6, 254, 268–72; anti-Semitism and, 189, 195; of concentration camp functionaries, 156; as political, 272; on the Wende, 3

constitution, 151

constitutional patriotism, 148

corruption, 182–83

Cottbus, 154

courage, 151–52

Crane, Susan, 123

Cultural Brewery, 121

culture: cultural heritage, 52; as repressive, 63–64; self and, 38

Dannecker, Martin, 249

Dauenheimer, Karin, 249

DCV (Deutscher Caritasverband), 145, 153–54, 159–60, 165

democracy: after World War II, 200; centrality of, in 20th century, 7; democratic socialism, 256; education and, 149, 151, 164; as end of history, 8; Wende and, 130

democratic centralism, 256

Demokratischer Frauenbund Deutschlands (Democratic Women's Union for Germany), 198

denunciations, 160, 187–88, 219, 264–65

deportations: during Aktion 14f13, 181; fear of, 196; mixed marriages and, 183–84, 190–91, 196, 199; overview of, 172; women's roles in, 214

Der Querulant (Behr), 75–76

Derrida, Jacques, 115

Deutscher Caritasverband (DCV), 145, 153–54, 159–60, 165

Deutsches Historisches Museum (DHM), 119–20, 137

deutschmark, 237, 238

DHM (Deutsches Historisches Museum), 119–20, 137

Die Neue Zeit, 74

Dieter, 1–5; historical imagination of, 2; identity of, 23; life world of, 17–18; memories of, 27; plasticity and, 258–59; sociological imagination of, 2–3; unemployment of, 2, 16, 21, 260–61; as Wende-loser, 3–5, 257, 260–61

Dilthey, Wilhelm, 59

dioramas, 128

discontinuities, 13

divorce: in GDR, 103–6; of mixed marriages in Nazi Germany, 183–85, 196, 199; unemployment and, 4

Dix, Otto, 36

Documentation Center for GDR Everyday Culture, 137

Douglas, Mary, 144

Dreier, Hans, 219

Dresden, 38–39, 51

Duchhardt, Heinz, 246

Durkheim, Emile, 143
Dutch, 244–46

Eastern Europe. *See* GDR (German Democratic Republic); Nazi East
East German Material Culture and the Power of Memory, 132–33
East Germany. *See* GDR
economics: capitalism, 3, 7–8, 18, 24, 256; Cold War and, 237; families and, 81–82, 96; trade, 231–32, 245; World War I and, 24, 81–82. *See also* unemployment
education: about inner-German border, 243–44; about Shoah, 148, 150–52, 162–64; function of, 148–49; in GDR, 38–39, 90; museums and, 119–20; as normative, 147; rites of passage and, 91; in socialist values, 92; of women, 189
EEC (European Economic Community), 1–2
Ehlert, Hans-Joachim, 178–79, 192
Ehrich, Elisabeth (Else), 156, 193
Eigensinn (unruliness), 146–47, 152–64, 254–55; as beneficial to institutions, 147–48, 158–64, 166–67; of institutional agents, 152–57, 166, 181–83, 237–38; of institutional objects, 157–59, 166; private space and, 187
Eighteenth Brumaire of Louis Napoleon (Marx), 16
Einsatzgruppen, 169
Eisenhüttenstadt, 137
Eisfeld, Laura, 191
Eisner, Kurt, 63
emic, 22
emotions: bureaucracy and, 144; SED's failure to understand, 94, 104, 106, 110–11; use of, by institutions, 148, 150–51; violence and, 161
empathy, 74
employment. *See* unemployment; work
Endlösung, 204
Endsieg, 193
Engels, Friedrich, 82
English language, 51–52
Enquete Commission, 115
entertainment, 148–50

Epelfeld, Naum, 207
Erdmann, Peter, 79, 108–9
Erfahrung, 58–59, 76
Erlebnis: definition of, 58; intentionality and, 77; as ordinary/extraordinary, 69–70, 76; phenomenology of, 59–60; reintegration of, 78
Erntefest, 192, 197
ethics, 38, 144
ethnicity, 23
etic, 22
European Economic Community (EEC), 1–2
European Union (EU), 2, 130
everyday. *See Alltag*
experience: collective personhood and, 77; communication of, by objects, 137; examination of, 56–57; of fleeting encounters, 69; immediacy of, 69; kinds of, 58; shared, 70. *See also Erlebnis*; life world; ordinary/extraordinary

Fabrikaktion, 186
Faktor, Jan, 125–26
Fallada, Hans, 89
families, 79–112; centrality of, 80, 109–10; communist theories about, 82–83, 110; divorce, 4, 103–6, 183–85, 196, 199; economic pressures on, 81–82, 96; mixed marriages in Nazi Germany, 183–86, 190–91, 196, 199; political discord within, 95–96, 187; politicization of, 84–89, 106–8; privacy of, 80, 87, 89–90; radicalization of, 82, 96–99; state intrusion into, 108–10. *See also* children; divorce; families in the GDR; funerals
families in the GDR, 89–94; antifacism and, 89; centrality of, 90–91; divorce of, 103–6; funerals and, 99–102; rites of passage for, 91–94; as traditional, 89–90
fascism, 7–8, 89. *See also* Nazi Germany
Fassin, Eric, 27
Fechner, Eberhard, 156
Federal Republic of Germany (FRG). *See* FRG
feminism, 249
Fifth Party Congress, 91

Figas, Peter, 51
film. *See* cinema
Final Solution, 204, 213
flaneur, 65, 69
folk practices, 40, 136
Fontane, Theodor, 60
Formalism in Ethics and Non-Formal Ethics of Values (Scheler), 76–77
Foucault, Michel, 38, 143
14f13. *See* Aktion 14f13
frame of reference, 203, 208, 212, 218, 221–22, 224
France, 181
Frauenwacht, 95–96
Freedman, Paul, 133
Freidank, Gustav, 91, 94
Freidenker (Free Thinker movement), 91
FRG (Federal Republic of Germany): alienation in, 128; borders of, 235; constitution of, 151; formation of, 1, 82; former Nazis, punishment of, in, 194–95, 197; founding of, 89, 194, 240; map of, 9; *Ossis vs. Wessis*, 262–63. *See also* Wende
Friedman, Philip, 222
Friedrich, Ernst, 36
"Friedrich Engels und die Naturwissenschaft" (Adler), 74
Fulbrook, Mary, 116
funerals: collective funerals, 100; collectors' museums as, 128; eulogies, 93–94, 101, 111; family/state conflict over, 101–2; in Nazi East, 208–9; politicization of, 91–94
Fürnberg, Louis, 94

Galicia, 223
gay men, 241–43, 248–50
GDR, material culture of, 113–42; in collectors' museums, 122–30, 140; identity and, 133–35; in state-sponsored museums, 119–22, 133, 139–40. *See also* collectors' museums; WM (Wende Museum of the Cold War)
GDR (German Democratic Republic): as dictatorship, 116, 121, 123, 256; economy of, 15–16; education in, 38–39; folk traditions in, 136; formation of, 1, 82, 240–41; gay and lesbian scene in, 241–43;
housing shortages in, 103–6; intrusiveness of, 109; leaders of, 89; map of, 9; official narrative about, 115–17, 122, 128, 139–40; as periphery, 9, 13; regulations of, 41, 48–50; rhetoric of, 100; Soviet influence on, 132, 137; Soviet reform, opposition to, by, 2. *See also* Berlin Wall; families in the GDR; funerals; GDR, material culture of; Ministry for State Security (MfS); Mödlareuth; Morawitz, Alexander; *Ostalgie*; SED; Wende
Geheime Staatspolizei (Gestapo). *See* Gestapo
Gemeinschaft, 60, 62
Gemeinschaft und Gesellschaft (Tönnies), 60
gender. *See* gender roles; masculinity; women
gender roles: in communist theory, 82–83; in families, 37, 81–84; racial hierarchy and, 189–94, 203–4; Shoah and, 221–24
General Government, 154–55
Geoctroyeerde Westindische Compagnie (GWIC), 245
Georg, Friedrich, 36, 47
George, Stefan, 63–64
George-Kreis, 63
German Communist Party (KPD). *See* KPD
German Democratic Republic (GDR). *See* GDR
German Historical Institute, 132
Germanization, 205, 211, 219
German language, 51
German question, 7
German Resistance Memorial Center, 173
German Revolution, 84
Germany: bureaucracy in, 63; centrality of, in 20th century conflicts, 7; definition of, 8–13; as imagined community, 2–3; Imperial Germany, 84; maps of, 9–11, 31n1–3; urbanization of, 59–60; Weimar Republic, 24, 80–83, 87–88, 90. *See also* FRG (Federal Republic of Germany); GDR (German Democratic Republic); Nazi Germany; reunification; Weimar Republic
German Youth Movement, 64
Gesamtperson, 76–78

Gesellschaft, 60, 62
Gesellschaft für Deutsch-Sowjetische Freundschaft, 198
Gestapo (Geheime Staatspolizei), 186, 188–89, 214, 219–20
ghettos: description of, 210, 212; liquidation of, 217–20; psychological/physical consequences of, 216
Ghyczy, Peter, 113–14
glasnost, 2
Gleichschaltung, 149–50
globalization, 24
Goffman, Erving, 147, 203
Gold Coast, 12, 244–46. *See also* Groeben, Otto Friedrich von der
Gorbachev, Mikhail, 1–2
Göttingen, 55–56
Great Depression, 82, 96
Great War. *See* World War I
GrePo (Grenzpolizei), 236–38, 247
Groeben, Otto Friedrich von der: authority, absence of, and, 231–35; local *vs.* global awareness of, 244–47
Grundgesetz, 151
Guggenheimer, Alfred, 172; deportation of, 190–91, 196, 199; divorce of, 183–85; Nuremberg Laws and, 175–76
Guggenheimer, Annemarie: divorce of, 183–85, 199; gender relations and, 190–91; postwar, 195–97; pre-1941, 172–74, 176, 180
Guggenheimer, Ursula Elisabeth, 172–73, 176, 195–97
Guineische Reise-Beschreibung (Groeben), 231, 233–34
Gurs, 181
GWIC (Geoctroyeerde Westindische Compagnie), 245

habitus, 67
Halata, Luzie, 155–56, 224
Hamburg, 162
Handlungsräume, 169
Harsch, Donna, 90
Hartwig, Jürgen, 128
Harvest Festival, 192, 197
Hauptmann, Gerhard, 63

HdG (Stiftung Haus der Geschichte der Bundesrepublik Deutschland), 119–21
Heidegger, Martin, 18, 115
Heinsohn, Kirsten, 169
Herrschaft, 208
Heuss, Theodor, 61, 67
HIB (Homosexual Interest Group Berlin), 248–49, 251
hierarchy: gender *vs.* racial, 189–94; patriarchy, 82–83, 189–90; social, 162–64, 166, 210, 225. *See also Volksgemeinschaft*
Himmler, Heinrich, 182
hip-hop, 38–43, 48–52; audience participation and, 47; community and, 50–52; licensing of, in GDR, 48–50; lyrics of, 51–52
history: end of, 8; of GDR, official, 115–17, 122, 128, 139–40; historical imagination, 2; macro *vs.* micro, 119–20; official, 27; self, location of, in, 33, 40, 43; as storytelling, 4, 16–17; teaching of, 148–52, 162–64; of victors, 27
Hitler, Adolf, 47
Hobsbawm, Eric, 7
Hof County, 235–37, 243–44
Holocaust. *See* Shoah
Holy Roman Empire, 11, 246
Holzhauer, Peter, 133–34
Homosexual Interest Group Berlin (HIB), 248–49, 251
homosexuality, 241–43, 248–52
Honecker, Erich, 49, 103, 259
"How I Came to the Red Front," 95–96
humor, 162–64, 166
Hunt, Lynn, 43
Husserl, Edmund, 59, 269

ICOM (International Council of Museums), 123
identity: assertion of, 128, 140; collective, 125; employment and, 260; material culture and, 133–35; memory and, 26; self-authorization and, 262–63. *See also* self
ideology, 18, 100, 106, 116. *See also Volksgemeinschaft*

imagination: historical, 2; imaginary Berlin Wall, 4; imaginary West, 248, 249; imaginative space, 41–43; imagined community, 2–3, 77; sociological, 2–3
immigration. *See* migration
Imperial Germany, 84
incommon: actions and, 256; cinema and, 71; community and, 74–75, 77; consensus and, 269, 272; definition of, 61; folk practices, 136; institutions and, 144, 164; memory and, 118; plasticity and, 139, 261; self-authorization and, 268; self-fashioning and, 38; social question and, 76; societal will and, 73; Wende and, 116–17
individuality, 77–78, 149
Innere Mission, 159
inner-German border. *See* Berlin Wall; Mödlareuth
insider/outsider, 21, 228–29, 235, 238, 241–43
Inspektion der Konzentrationslager (IKL), 155, 182
In Stahlgewittern. *See Storm of Steel* (Jünger)
Institut für Kommunalwirtschaft, 94
institutional actors/functionaries, 145–46; anticipatory obedience of, 156, 176, 206, 224–26; institutions, shaping of, by, 166, 183; unruliness of, 146–47, 181–83, 229–30, 237–38. *See also* Eigensinn (unruliness)
institutional policy, 145–46; anticipatory obedience to, 156, 176, 206, 224–26; institutional agents, influence of, on, 183; of KdF, 148
institutions, 143–67; agents, kinds of, in, 145–46; collapse of, 23; definition of, 143–44; frame of reference of, 218; goals of, 148–52, 159; micro- vs. macro-analytical study of, 146; plasticity of, 258. *See also* bureaucracy; institutional actors/functionaries; institutional policy
intentionality/intentions: audiences for, 76; celebrity and, 66–67; cinema and, 72; community and, 68; consent and, 269; empathy and, 75; intentional nonnoticing, 65; multiplicity of, 81; toward objects, 135, 139; will and, 73, 74. *See also* agency

International Council of Museums (ICOM), 123
interpersonal relationships, 55–78; charisma and, 61–64; cinema and, 68–73; essence of, 55, 74–77; kinds of, 75; urbanization and, 59–61; urban walking and, 64–67; will and, 73–76. *See also* cinema; families
interpretive frameworks, 23
Interwar Period, 7
Iron Curtain, 9, 248. *See also* Berlin Wall; Mödlareuth
irony, 5, 141–42, 147–48, 157

Jäger, Harald, 266–67
Jampol, Justinian, 131–32
Janowska, 221–22
Jarausch, Konrad, 116
Jatki, 210
Jeinsen, Gretha von, 37
Jewish star, 180–81, 209, 219
Jews: classification of, in Nazi racial theory, 175; cooperation of, with Nazis, 215–16; DCV, service of, towards, 154; emigration of, 171–72, 206–7; reintegration of, postwar, 194–95; social exclusion of, 150; stereotypes of, 190. *See also* anti-Semitism; Shoah
joy production, 150, 165
Judenhäuser, 172, 183
Jugendweihe, 91
Jünger, Ernst, 33–34, 43–48; audience collaboration and, 46–48; journals of, 52–53; self-image of, creation of, by, 34–38

Kafka, Franz, 60
Kampfbund gegen den Faschismus (Fighting League against Fascism), 98
Kapos, 182
KdF (Kraft durch Freude), 145; communist youth groups and, 157–59; goals of, 148–50, 152, 165
Kennzeichnungspflicht, 180–81, 209, 219
Kershaw, Ian, 183
King Peter, 232–35, 245
Kirchner, Ernst Ludwig, 36
kitsch, 141

Klausa, Udo, 205, 213–14, 220–21
Kohl, Helmut, 2, 120
Kollontai, Alexandra, 82–83
Koonz, Claudia, 214
Korff, Gottfried, 119
KPD (German Communist Party), 80–81; families, politicization of, by, 85–88, 90; funerary culture of, 91–92; Nazis and, conflict between, 98–99; persecution of, 89; SPD and, merging of, 82; tenets of, 84–85; use of, by families, 95–97; women, recruitment of, by, 107–8
Kraff, Erna, 181–82, 197
Kulturbrauerei, 121
Kundrus, Birthe, 170
Kürwille, 73. See also will

labor camps, 154, 172, 180–81, 205, 216, 219. See also concentration camps
Labor Exchange, 177
LaKw (Landesamt für Kommunalwesen), 239
Landau, Felix, 222–23
Landau, Gertrude, 222–23
Länder, 2
Landesamt für Soforthilfe, 196
language, 39, 42–43, 51–52, 270
Law for the Protection of Mother and Child and the Rights of Women, 102–3
laws/regulations: about families, 83, 85, 102–3, 175, 185–86, 191; dissent and, 116; education and, 151; of GDR, 41, 48–50; as impersonal, 60; sheltering of Jews and, 189; as societal will, 74; welfare law, 96–97. See also institutional policy; laws/regulations, anti-Semitic
laws/regulations, anti-Semitic: about marriage, 175, 185–86, 191; emigration and, 171–72, 177; ghettoization, 210, 212, 216–20; influence of, on behavior, 176, 199; Nuremberg Laws, 175, 185, 195; yellow star, 180–81, 209. See also deportations; ghettos; Shoah
Lebensreform, 63–64
Le Figaro, 68
Leipzig, 119, 162
leisure, 148–50
lesbians, 241–43, 249–50

Levi, Primo, 202
Ley, Robert, 150
Ließ, Hertha: postwar, 195, 197–98; pre-1941, 172–73, 177–80; at Ravensbrück, 181–83, 191–92, 199
life experiments, 64
life world, 17–22; cinema and, 71; institutions and, 165–66; violence and, 211, 217. See also worlds, local *vs.* global
living space, 24, 213
Łódź, 216
Los Angeles, 118, 137–38
Los Angeles Times, 139
loyal reluctance (Mallmann and Paul), 160
Lublin-Majdanek. See Majdanek
Lüdtke, Alf, 50, 118, 123, 144, 208, 254

magnetism, 69
Majdanek, 145; extermination of inmates at, 192–93, 197; guards, anticipatory obedience of, at, 154–56; guards, unruliness of, at, 160–61
Mandelbaum, Michael, 104–6
Mann, Thomas, 60
marriage. See divorce; families
Marshall Plan, 1
Marx, Karl, 16, 82
Marxism, 20
masculinity, 34, 36, 55. See also Jünger, Ernst; Morawitz, Alexander; Scheler, Max
material culture. See GDR, material culture of
May Day (1929), 87–88
McLellan, Josie, 99–100
Mecklenburg-Vorpommern (MV). See MV
Memmingen, 175–76, 183, 196
memory: agency and, 18, 136–37; auratic quality of, 117; collective, 125, 131, 135; communicative, 140; dangerous memories, 24–27; funerals and, 128; of GDR, official narrative about, 115–17, 122, 128, 139–40; of mass shootings, 219; objects, centrality of, in, 128–29; self and, 43, 113; unreliability of, 115–16. See also GDR, material culture of
men, 34, 36
mercantilism, 231, 245
Metz, Johann Baptist, 25–27

MfS (Ministry for State Security). *See* Ministry for State Security
microsocial interactions, 6, 254–57; of family, 112; of institutional agents, 156; within institutions, 146–47; in museums, 118; as source of meaning, 58
migration/immigrants: across inner-German border, 240; of Jews, 171–72, 177, 206–7; post-Wende, 17; Wende Museum and, 118, 137–38
Ministry for State Security (MfS): collaboration with, 79, 109, 264–65; dictatorship and, 116; families, surveillance of, by, 79, 108–9; gays and lesbians, surveillance of, by, 241–43, 251–52
Minsk, 211, 214
modernism, 113
modernity: definition of, 6–7, 68; as fragmented, 263–64; outliers and, 13; Shoah and, 25
Mödlareuth, 235–41; eastern documentation on, 239–41; establishment of, 235; local *vs.* global worlds at, 243–44, 247–48; western documentation on, 236–38
Monnickendam, 137
Monte Verità, 64
morality/ethics, 38, 144
Morawitz, Alexander, 33–34; on authenticity, 249; collaborations of, 48–52; education of, 38–39; imaginary West and, 248; performances of, 47–48; self-fashioning of, 39–43
Mülheim, 88
Müller, Inge, 151
museums, 117–18; collectors' museums, 122–30, 140; state-sponsored, 119–22, 139–40; Wende Museum of the Cold War, 131–39. *See also* collectors' museums; WM (Wende Museum of the Cold War)
music: folk music, 40; hip-hop, 38–43, 47, 48–52; rock music, 40. *See also* hip-hop
MV (Mecklenburg-Vorpommern): as periphery, 9, 13, 17–18; social/economic decline of, 14–15, 259
mysticism, 63–64

Nadel, Marjan, 223
nationalism, 36, 203–4, 238
National People's Army (NVA), 39
National Socialism. *See* Nazi Germany
National Socialist German Workers' Party (NSDAP), 176, 183, 196. *See also* Nazi Germany
Nationalsozialistische Volkswohlfahrt (NSV). *See* NSV
NATO (North Atlantic Treaty Organization), 1–2
nature, 63–64, 74, 75
Naturheilstätte, 64
Naumann, Hertha. *See* Ließ, Hertha
Nazi East, 25, 201–26; German emigration to, 204–5, 211; Jewish responses to occupation in, 215–17; Jews, rescuers of, in, 189; mass murder in, 172, 217–24; women's roles in, 211–15. *See also* Berdichev
Nazi Germany: collectivism of, 149; communists and, 88, 98–99; fall of, 89, 194, 235; GDR opposition to, 116; gender relations in, 189–94; Heidegger and, 18; institutions, competition between, in, 152–54; memory of, 24–27; normalization of, 123; rise of, 53, 82; rites of passage in, 91; surveillance in, 187; symbols of, 154, 159–60. *See also* anti-Semitism; KdF; Majdanek; Nazi East; SS (Schutzstaffel); *Volksgemeinschaft*
neo-Nazis, 150–51
Netherlands, 137
Neues Deutschland, 266
New York Times, 243
Nicht der Homosexuelle ist pervers (Praunheim), 249
Night of Broken Glass, 172, 175–76
Nora, Pierre, 116
normalcy, 5, 20–21, 75–76, 141. *See also* ordinary/extraordinary
norms, 73, 75–76, 146, 156
North Atlantic Treaty Organization (NATO), 1–2
nostalgia. *See* Ostalgie
Nothnagel, Alfred, 157–58
Novhorod Volynsk, 214–15

NSDAP (National Socialist German Workers' Party), 176, 183, 196. *See also* Nazi Germany
NSV (Nationalsozialistische Volkswohlfahrt), 153–54, 160, 214–15
Nuremberg Laws, 175, 185, 195
NVA (National People's Army), 39

Oberböhmsdorf, 241
Oelhafen, Otto von, 212
Öffentlichkeit, 251
Ohse, Marc-Dietrich, 135
Oranienburg, 182, 192
ordinary/extraordinary, 21, 57–59; celebrity sightings and, 65–67, 69–70; fleeting encounters and, 69; incommon and, 61; local *vs.* global awareness and, 244; noticing of, 69–70; violence as, 202
Ossis, 262–63
Ostalgie: definition of, 3; family life and, 111; identity and, 128; *vs.* official history, 116, 123; reasons for, 23, 123; reunification celebrations and, 16

Pabel, Hilmar, 238, 247
"Painter of Modern Life" (Baudelaire), 68
parataxis, 70–71
Paris, 68–69
participatory dictatorship, 256
Partywohnungen, 250
patriarchy, 82–83, 189–90
Peace of Westphalia, 246
People's Police, 79, 238, 247
perestroika, 2
performance: of anti-Semitism, 188–89; authority and, 50; community and, 52; of self, 47; self-authorization as, 268
Petri, Erna, 223–24
phatic function, 66–67
phenomenology, 18–19, 57, 59–60, 68, 229
Pieck, Wilhelm, 92
Pisski, 210
place, 64–65, 227. *See also* space
plastic, 129
plasticity, 5–6, 58, 258–61; of authority, 265, 268; material objects and, 129–30, 135, 139

Płaszów, 193
Plenzdorf, Ulrich, 122
Pohl, Dieter, 192
Poland, 154, 181, 205. *See also* Nazi East
police: border police, 236–38, 247, 265–67; Gestapo, 186, 188–89, 214, 219–20; KPD and, 87–88; mass shootings and, 217–18
policy. *See* institutional policy
policy makers, 145
politburo, 2, 259, 265, 266
politics: education and, 150–52; fascism, 7–8, 89; *vs.* lived experience, 123–24; participation in, 240–41; plasticity and, 261. *See also* democracy; families; socialism/communism
poststructuralism, 15, 17, 259
power: *Alltag* and, 21; authority and, 227; *Eigensinn* and, 254–55; families and, 80; *vs.* force, 267–68; humor and, 162–64; institutions, competition between, and, 152–53; institutions, definition of, and, 143–44, 147; official *vs.* unofficial, 147; race and, 177; technology of, 229, 242. *See also* authority
practices of self. *See* self
Praunheim, Rosa von, 249
PrBayGrePo (Präsidium der Bayerischen Grenzpolizei), 236
prison, 109
privacy: of family, 80, 83, 87, 89–90; housing shortage and, 105–6; state intrusion upon, 109–10, 185–89, 199
propaganda, 81, 86, 88, 91, 96, 138
Protestant Church, 241–43, 251
Protestant Ethic and the Spirit of Capitalism (Weber), 75
Prussia, 11, 144, 161. *See also* Brandenburg-Prussia

Quick: Illustrierte für Deutschland, 238, 247

race/racism: hierarchy of, *vs.* gender, 189–94; Jews as, 175; racial stereotypes, 190; SS and, 170–71, 192–93. *See also Volksgemeinschaft*
radio, 125, 127, 176, 187
Raila, 241

Rajsko, 193
rape, 237
Rassenschande, 185
Rausch, Peter, 248–49
Ravensbrück, 177–78, 181–82, 191–92, 197
Red Aid, 85–86
Red Army, 206–7
Red Cross, 211, 214–15
refugees, 206–7
Reich, Wilhelm, 249
Reich Labor Service, 211
religion, 92, 136, 150, 261. *See also*
  Christianity; Jews
Remarque, Erich Maria, 47
reparations, 196–98
representation, 262
reunification, 2; anniversary celebrations
  of, 16; criticism of, 3, 140; garbage
  and, 119; German borders and, 8;
  narratives about, 27, 116–17, 119–20,
  140, 257; obsolescence following, 115;
  unemployment and, 15. *See also* Wende
RFB (Roter Frontkämpferbund), 87
RFMB (Roter Frauen- und Mädchenbund),
  107–8
rhetoric, 100
rights, 151–52, 200
ritual: *Alltag* and, 20, 57; as interstitial, 48;
  lifecycle rituals, 91–94. *See also* funerals
Rivne. *See* Rowno
rock music, 40
Romanies, 169
Romanisches Café, 173, 177, 180, 186
Romaniv, 211
room for maneuver, 144, 169–70, 180, 203
Rosenhaft, Eve, 98
Rote Fahne, 99
Rote Hilfe, 85–86
Roter Frauen- und Mädchenbund (RFMB),
  107–8
Roter Frontkämpferbund (Red Front
  Fighters League), 87
Rowno, 212–13
RSHA (Reichssicherheitshauptamt), 191
Rubin, Eli, 129
ruptures (term), 5–6, 22–24. *See also Alltag*
rural areas, 59, 60, 62, 66

RuSHA (SS Main Office for Race and
  Settlement), 178–79, 192, 193
Russia. *See* Soviet Union

Sabrow, Martin, 115, 12–24
Sabrow Commission, 115–16
Säuberung, 183
SBZ (Soviet Zone of Occupation). *See*
  Soviet Zone of Occupation (SBZ)
Schabowski, Günter, 266
Scheler, Maria, 56
Scheler, Max, 55–56, 73, 76–78
Schleiz County, 239–41, 248
Schmidt, Ilse, 212–13
Schramm, Lutz, 39
Schücking-Homeyer, Annette, 214–15
Schultz, Edmund, 47
Schulz, Felix Robin, 102
Schutzhaft, 175
Schutzstaffel (SS). *See* SS
Schwartz, Wilhelm, 176, 185, 196
Schwulenbewegung, 248
SED (Socialist Unity Party of Germany):
  creation of, 82; as dictatorship, 121, 256;
  on divorce, 103; on emotions, 104, 111;
  on families, 83, 90–91, 95, 108–10; gay/
  lesbian activists and, 251–52; leadership
  of, 265; protests against, 2; publications
  by, 89, 240; rites of passage developed
  by, 91–94, 102, 111; social conservatism
  of, 89–90. *See also* GDR (German
  Democratic Republic)
Seghers, Anna, 89
Selbstbildnis als Soldat (Kirchner), 36
self, 32–54; authenticity of, 37; boundary
  crossing and, 8; as collaborative, 46–51;
  collectors and, 126; as cultural artifact,
  38; as determined, 261–62; frame of
  reference and, 212; historicity of, 40, 43;
  ideology and, 108; instability/fragility of,
  33, 40, 53–54, 78, 106, 262; memory and,
  43; naming and, 38–40; performance of,
  47, 52, 55; political identity and, 88, 96;
  ruptures and, 23; self-deception, 40, 109;
  self-fashioning, 33–38, 187, 224; welfare
  and, 21. *See also* Jünger, Ernst; Morawitz,
  Alexander; self-authorization

self-authorization, 6; bargains and, 264–65, 268; as collaborative, 48; during fall of Berlin Wall, 266–67; of families, 111–12; identity and, 262–63; institutions, functioning of, and, 227; overview of, 261–68; as performance, 50, 268; photography and, 36; to question authority, 244; as self-determination, 262; Shoah and, 225; subjectivity and, 269. *See also Eigensinn* (unruliness)
self-control, 48
Self-Portrait as Soldier (Kirchner), 36
self-portraits/selfies, 32–3336, 54, 135–36
Serbia, 213
sex/sexuality: divorce and, 104–6; homosexuality, 241–43, 248–52
Shabecoff, Philip, 243–44
Shenfeld, Stepan Yakimovich, 221
Shoah: causes of, 202; distancing from, 212–13; education about, 148, 150–51, 162–64; ghettos, 210, 212, 216–20; Jewish goods, plundering of, during, 207, 214–15; Jewish resistance movements during, 219–20; mass shootings during, 25, 211, 217–19, 224–25; memory of, 24–27; overview of, 171–72, 180–81; sheltering of Jews during, 185–89; women, complicity of, during, 211–15. *See also* anti-Semitism; concentration camps; deportations; ghettos; Majdanek; Ravensbrück
Shoah Foundation Institute for Visual History and Education, 206
short twentieth century, 7
Siemens, 192
Sierra Leone, 232–35
Silesia, 205, 216
Simmel, Georg, 73
Sinti, 169
Sixth Party Congress, 90
Smith, Joseph, 63
Social Darwinism, 151
Social Democratic Party of Germany (SPD), 82, 84–85
socialism/communism, 7, 8; clothing aesthetic of, 107–8; collective, primacy of, in, 100, 103, 135; families, theories about, within, 82–83; in FRG, 198; in Nazi Germany, 157–59; role of family in, 90, 110; secularism of, 92–93; stereotypes about, 131; symbols of, 87–88. *See also* families; GDR (German Democratic Republic); KPD; SED
Socialist Unity Party (SED). *See* SED
social mobility, 180
social organizations, 85
social question, 60–61, 73, 76
societal will, 73. *See also* will
Society for German–Soviet Friendship, 198
Soeffner, Hans-Georg, 56–57
solidarity, 183, 199, 238
Sombart, Werner, 73
Soviet Occupation, 24
Soviet Union, 1–2; Bolshevik Revolution, 82–85; border guards of, 236–37; colonization of Central Europe by, 235; fall of, 130; family law in, 85; Nazi Germany, fall of, and, 89, 194; Red Army, 206–7. *See also* Mödlareuth; Nazi East
Soviet Zone of Occupation (SBZ), 82
space: asyndetic, 65–67; autonomy and, 163–64; definition of, 205; embodiment and, 251; emotional, 104; experience and, 58; imaginative, 41–43; living space, 24, 213; parallel, 164, 167, 185, 187–88, 217, 250; politicization of, 86–88; representations of, 229; ritual, 48; semipublic, 55–56, 250; urban *vs.* rural, 59–60. *See also* life world; privacy; worlds, local *vs.* global
SPD (Social Democratic Party of Germany), 82, 84–85
Spiegel Online International, 214–15
SR *(Sozialistische Republik)*, 87–88, 97, 98
SS-Aufseherinnen, 155
SS Main Office for Race and Settlement (RuSHA), 178–79, 192–93
SS (Schutzstaffel): corruption of, 181–83; family of, 221–24; mass shootings by, 169, 217–18, 223; religion and, 222; women in, 155, 178, 191–94. *See also* Ließ, Hertha
SS-Sippengemeinschaft, 170, 178–80
Stalingrad, 193
Stasi. *See* Ministry for State Security (MfS)

State Archive of Thuringia (ThStAG), 239
Staude, John Raphael, 56
Steege, Paul, 144, 167
Stephan, Hans-Joachim, 128
Stiftung Haus der Geschichte der Bundesrepublik Deutschland (HdG), 119
Storm of Steel (Jünger), 33, 37, 46–47
storytelling/narratives, 2–3, 37–38; bargains and, 264–65; funerals and, 100; genres of, 3–5; modernity and, 263–64; purpose of, 263; as self-focused, 223; subjectivity and, 170; as validation, 268
structures, 14–15, 117, 259–60. *See also* agency; institutions
Struwe, Ilse. *See* Schmidt, Ilse
Super Illu, 3
Switzerland, 64, 189
symbols: of authority, 208–9, 232–35, 244–46; of Christianity, 216–17; of Nazi Germany, 154, 159–60; of socialism/communism, 87–88; symbolic degradation, 13

Taylor, Frederick, 4
Taylor, Gabriele, 109
technology: cassette tapes, 39, 51; cinema, 68–73; photography, 34–37, 135–36; of power, 229, 242; television, 248–49; urbanization and, 59; vinyl records, 51
Teichler, Hans Joachim, 158
television, 248–49
temporality, 58, 142
"Ten Commandments of Socialist Morality" (Ulbricht), 90
terror, 161–62
Theresienstadt, 191
Third Reich. *See* Nazi Germany
ThStAW (Thüringisches Hauptstaatsarchiv Weimar), 240
Thüringer Volk, 240
Thuringia. *See* Mödlareuth
Thüringisches Hauptstaatsarchiv Weimar (ThStAW), 240
"Time to Fite" (TJ Big Blaster Electric Boogie), 32, 52
TJ Big Blaster Electric Boogie. *See* Morawitz, Alexander

"To a Passerby" (Baudelaire), 69
Tönnies, Ferdinand, 60–61, 73–75
topography, 23, 27
Tractirung der Blancen, 232–33
trade, 231–32, 245
Tränenpalast, 121
transnationalism, 8
trash, 119
trust, 109, 123
Two-Plus-Four Treaty, 7–8

Uhse, Bodo, 89
Ukraine, 211–15, 221–22. *See also* Berdichev
Ulbricht, Walter, 90
"under erasure" (Derrida), 115
unemployment: responses to, 19; Wende and, 2–4, 15–16, 21, 260; of women, 97, 177
Unger, Michael, 251
United Nations Declaration of Human Rights, 151
United States: colonization of Central Europe by, 235; FRG, formation of, and, 1; Mödlareuth and, 237; musical culture of, 39, 41–42, 51, 249. *See also* WM (Wende Museum of the Cold War)
University of Southern California, 206
unruliness. *See Eigensinn* (unruliness)
urbanity. *See* cities
USSR. *See* Soviet Union

Vanshelboim, Mikhail Aronowitsch, 209–10
vegetarianism, 64–65
Vergangenheitsbewältigung, 148
Versailles Treaty, 81–82
Veyne, Paul, 38
violence: at Berlin Wall, 265; coping with, 162; institutional *vs.* individual, 160–61; insulation from, 212–13; normalization of, 214, 222, 224–25; as ordinary/extraordinary, 202; ruptures as, 22. *See also* Nazi East; Shoah
Vogel, Barbara, 169
Völkerprinzip, 151
Volksdeutsche, 211

Volksgemeinschaft, 25–26, 145, 168–69, 225; divorce and, 184; education about, 151–52; leisure and, 148, 150, 152, 158; as personal, 176; private space and, 187; unruliness and, 154, 160. *See also* anti-Semitism
Volksgenossin, 170
Volkspolizei, 79, 238, 247
Voss, Mattheus de, 232
voyeurism, 67
Vul, Mikhail, 206

Wagner, Richard, 64
"Walking in the City" (Certeau), 65
Walter, Franz, 84
War against War (Friedrich), 36
War Cripples (Dix), 36
Warsaw, 216, 219
Warsaw Pact, 2
Weber, Max, 57, 62–64, 67, 73, 75
Weckel, Ulrike, 169
Weimar Republic, 24; communists in, 80–81, 87–88; family in, 83, 90; formation of, 81–82. *See also* KPD
Weisbrod, Bernd, 193–94
welfare, 21, 96–97, 116
welfare dictatorship, 116
Wende, 1–5, 256–57; cultural obsolescence and, 115; families and, 111; historical narratives about, 8, 116–17, 120–21; life worlds and, 17–19; as outside event, 21; ruptures, kinds of, following, 22–23; self-authorization and, 262–63; social/economic decline following, 4, 14–17, 259–60; winners *vs.* losers, 3–5, 21. *See also* Berlin Wall; GDR, material culture of; MV; reunification
Wende Museum of the Cold War (WM). *See* WM
Wessis, 262–63
West Africa, 12, 31n4. *See also* Groeben, Otto Friedrich von der
Wie ein Mensch wird, was er ist (Mandelbaum), 104–6
Wildt, Michael, 161
Wilhelm II, 81

Wilhelmine Empire, 24
will, 73–76, 228; communal will, 73–75; *Kürwille*, 73; societal will, 73
Willhaus, Elisabeth, 221–22
Willhaus, Gustav, 221–22
Wirtschaftsverwaltungshauptamt (WVHA), 155
WM (Wende Museum of the Cold War): collections/programs of, 132–36, 138–39; founding of, 131–32; German museums and, comparison between, 131, 137; local context of, 137–39; use/influence of, 132–33, 138–39
women: childbearing, state incentivization of, for, 102–3; clothing of, 107–8; employment of, 90, 97, 103; feminism, 249; lesbians, 241–43, 249–50; organizations for, 85; rape of, 237; recruitment of, by KPD, 107–8; women's suffrage, 81. *See also* anti-Semitism, women's responses to; gender roles
work: beautification of, 149; cities and, 65; in concentration camps, 160–61, 178, 191–92, 199; interpersonal relationships at, 75; murder as, 215; as source of identity, 106
working class: idealization of, 84; mobilization of, by KPD, 85–87; Nazi movement and, 222; radicalization of, 95–99
"Work of Art in the Age of Mechanical Reproduction" (Benjamin), 68
worlds, local *vs.* global, 228, 230, 243–52; in East Berlin gay culture, 248–52; at inner-German border, 238, 243–44; for West African traders, 244–47. *See also* life world
World War I, 7, 47, 81–82. *See also* Jünger, Ernst
World War II, 1, 7–8. *See also* Nazi Germany

youth organizations, 85, 93, 157–59, 215
Yurchak, Alexei, 248

Zentralhaus für Kulturarbeit, 91
Ziegenhorn, Rudi, 266
Zwickau, 100

www.ingramcontent.com/pod-product-compliance
Lightning Source LLC
Chambersburg PA
CBHW070906030426
42336CB00014BA/2317